GEOMETRY AND ATMOSPHERE

Research funded by

Arts & Humanities
Research Council

Geometry and Atmosphere
Theatre Buildings from Vision to Reality

C. Alan Short
Peter Barrett
Alistair Fair

with
Monty Sutrisna
Giorgos Artopoulos

ASHGATE

Published by
Ashgate Publishing Limited
Wey Court East
Union Road
Farnham
Surrey, GU9 7PT
England

Ashgate Publishing Company
Suite 420
101 Cherry Street
Burlington
VT 05401-4405
USA

www.ashgate.com

British Library Cataloguing in Publication Data
Short, C. A.
  Geometry and atmosphere : theatre buildings from vision to reality.
  1. Theaters--England--Design and construction. 2. Theaters--England--Design and construction--Management. 3. Theaters--England--Design and construction--Costs. 4. Theaters--England--Design and construction--Case studies. 5. Theaters--England--Design and construction--Management--Case studies. 6. Theaters--England--Design and construction--Costs--Case studies.
  I. Title II. Barrett, Peter, professor. III. Fair, Alistair. IV. Sutrisna, Monty. V. Artopoulos, Giorgos.
  725.8'22'0942-dc22

Library of Congress Cataloging-in-Publication Data
Short, C. Alan (Charles Alan), 1955- author.
  Geometry and Atmosphere : Theatre Buildings from Vision to Reality / by C. Alan Short, Peter Barrett and Alistair Fair.
      pages cm
  Includes bibliographical references and index.
  ISBN 978-0-7546-7404-7 (hardback : alk. paper) 1. Theater architecture.
  I. Barrett, Peter (Peter Stephen), 1957- author. II. Fair, Alistair, author. III. Title. IV. Title: Theatre Buildings from Vision to Reality.
  NA6821.S54 2011
  725'.8220941--dc22

ISBN 9780754674047 (hbk)

2010046820

MIX
Paper from
responsible sources
FSC® C018575
www.fsc.org

Printed and bound in Great Britain by the
MPG Books Group, UK

Contents

List of Figures and Plates

FIGURES

Foreword: The Olivier Theatre, within the National Theatre, London (*Mike Smallcombe; courtesy of the National Theatre*)

PLATES (CHAPTER 9)

List of Tables

Notes on Contributors

C. Alan Short is The Professor of Architecture at the University of Cambridge, a Professorial Fellow of Clare Hall, Cambridge, and Chairman of Short and Associates Ltd, architects.

Peter Barrett is Professor of Management in Property and Construction in the School of the Built Environment at the University of Salford. He was formerly Pro-Vice-Chancellor, Research.

Dr Alistair Fair is a Research Associate in the Department of Architecture at the University of Cambridge, and a Junior Research Fellow at Wolfson College, Cambridge.

Dr Monty Sutrisna is Director of Postgraduate Training and Outreach in the School of the Built Environment at the University of Salford.

Dr Giorgos Artopoulos recently completed a Ph.D. exploring computational techniques that enhance the way architects speculate in design, in the Digital Studio of the Department of Architecture at the University of Cambridge.

The Foreword was written by **Sir Richard Eyre**, the theatre, film and television director, and for ten years Director of the National Theatre (1987-1997).

This book was written as part of the 'Designing Dynamic Environments for the Performing Arts' project, funded by the UK Arts and Humanities Research Council. The other team members, whose work fundamentally informed the material presented here, were:

Patricia Sterry, formerly Professor of Heritage, Design and Culture at the University of Salford.

Anne Dye, Research Associate, University of Cambridge (2005-2007); Commission for Architecture and the Built Environment, London (2007-2010); now Director of Technical Research, Royal Institute of British Architects, London.

Dr Zeynep Toker, formerly Research Associate, University of Cambridge, now at California State University, Northridge.

The film which accompanies this book was made by **Brian Ashbee** and **Peter Cook**, both freelance directors, with **Dr François Penz**, Reader in Architecture and the Moving Image, University of Cambridge.

Foreword

Sir Richard Eyre

The Olivier Theatre, within the National Theatre, London

The history of the creation of the National Theatre, like that of most public buildings, is one of utopianism, pragmatism, wilful ego and confusion, but, out of its foggy origins, the architect, Denys Lasdun, built something which now has classical status. It endures; it isn't subject to the whims of fashion; it is loved. The front of house is superb: it has a sense of grandeur and occasion combined with a demotic accessibility. Worn and warmed by time and use, the public spaces have become indisputably one of the most welcoming places in London.

But two of the National Theatre's three auditoria – the Olivier and the Lyttelton – are not easy spaces, at least if they are measured against the criteria that actors, designers, directors and audiences instinctively understand.

If you sit in the centre of the centre stalls block of the Olivier theatre you think, 'This is thrilling, I'm at the centre of this marvellous space, there's a real feeling of event.' But if you sit at the side of the stalls you feel marginal to the action, and if you sit at the back of the circle you feel disenfranchised – remote, detached and unable to hear properly. The volume of the auditorium is much larger than it needs to be to accommodate a comparatively small number of people. There are 1160 seats in a space that feels larger than the Theatre Royal, Drury Lane, which seats over a thousand more people. The consequence is that a disproportionate volume of space needs to be animated by the actors' voices in order to make themselves audible – to be exact, nine times the ideal volume. To compound the difficulty, there are large areas of wall and balcony made of concrete, a material which is acoustically unfriendly. So, until the installation of a sound enhancement system in 1997, it was very hard for even the most technically accomplished actors to make themselves heard in all parts of the auditorium.

The Lyttelton theatre was built as it was because of Laurence Olivier, who said, 'I must have a conventional proscenium theatre which can accommodate visiting companies from all over the world'. For a playhouse, the proscenium is extraordinarily wide. It was supposed to be a 600-seat theatre, but, quite late in the process, Jennie Lee, then Arts Minister, insisted on the addition of a balcony to make the theatre more cost-effective. Denys Lasdun was compromised by having to insert one into a finished design, and it was too late in the day to create something with a satisfactory relationship to the stalls. The result is that actors on the Lyttelton stage have to make a decision as to where they're going to look. It's what you might call 'the nodding dog syndrome', their heads bending from floor to ceiling to embrace the whole audience.

In the National Theatre, the only performance space that all actors, directors, writers and audiences unequivocally love is the Cottesloe. In the planning of the National, it was ignored by the artistic committee, a blank hole that was referred to as a 'studio space'. People love it because you can more or less do what you like in it: it's the artists' territory.

The problems with the National's two large auditoria are very far from unique. From 1973 to 1978 I ran Nottingham Playhouse. Designed by Peter Moro and opened in 1963, its public spaces are wholly successful but the auditorium has problems with audibility and sightlines. It's circular, which has the effect of distancing the stage from the audience. Unless actors come far downstage, instead of being drawn towards the audience, they are pushed outside the perimeter of the auditorium. And the clashing reflections of sound bouncing off the unsympathetic curved concrete walls make for intractable acoustic properties.

But in spite of the problems, you couldn't say that Nottingham Playhouse and the National Theatre don't 'work'. You can't say that they're not successful theatres. They're both distinguished buildings by distinguished architects, with a great flair for the design for public spaces. However, the auditoria have succeeded because of the will of stubborn and gifted people who have taken the view that if we can't change it, we'll find ways of making it work.

What makes a good theatre? The proportions have to seem right – the slope of the stalls, the rake of the stage, the elevation of the circle, the width and height of the proscenium. The actors have to be seen and heard, the audience have to feel comfortable with them, the attention has to be focused, and everyone has to share more or less the same viewpoint of the action. I have never understood why architects, or at least those who design theatres, seem so reluctant to draw on the lessons of the past. A theatre, more than any other building, save perhaps a public lavatory, must be defined by its function: it's there in order for a few hundred human beings to sit in the dark and watch and listen to a few other human beings on a lit platform. Yet almost without exception, theatres built in the last thirty or forty years provide bad sightlines, poor acoustics, stage proportions that don't relate to the human figure, and self-advertising architectural features which intrude on the audience's attention. Most of the successful working theatres in Britain are Victorian and Edwardian buildings. They are largely horseshoe-shaped and lined with plaster and lath – specifically designed instruments for putting on plays and for staging musical theatre. I was once talking to Albert Finney about theatre design and I told him that Peter Brook had said that a theatre should be like a violin, its tone coming from its period and age, tone being its most important quality. 'Yes', said Albert, 'But who'd build a violin out of fucking concrete?'

Perhaps architects and builders will always be frustrated in dealing with people who work in the theatre. Our art is so ephemeral, theirs is so permanent. Theatre involves conscripting an audience into believing in illusion; architecture involves real people confronting real space. We work to non-negotiable deadlines; architects – and more particularly builders – operate on a fluctuating and pliable calendar.

An example: during my last year at the NT, I presided over a £30 million renovation project which, among other things, removed the road that divided the theatre from the river, created a new exterior public space and placed the bookshop within the old *porte cochère*. At the first team meeting – architects, contractors and theatre managers sitting round a large table – I said, 'I can tell you now which play is going to be opening in the Olivier theatre in a year's time. The play will open at 7pm on the 12th November. If it's not there on the night there'll be a public scandal. Are you prepared to commit yourselves to similar targets?' There was a very long silence, a lot of looking covertly round the room, each daring the other to speak first. Oh, and the answer was 'no'.

An ideal situation for designing and building new theatres – or at least new auditoria – would be for architects to take advice from directors and designers, but always with the caveat that they may be motivated by aesthetic ideologies that will change over the years. Acoustic advice is essential and, most importantly, the opinions of actors and audiences. They will be honest, pragmatic and their advice will be entirely empirical. In the end, architects have to remember the inviolable rule of the art form: theatre will *always* depend on the scale of the human figure, the sound of the human voice, and our desire to tell each other stories.

Acknowledgements

This book results from a research project funded by the UK Arts and Humanities Research Council, entitled 'Designing Dynamic Environments for the Performing Arts'. The work was undertaken by a team of researchers from the University of Cambridge and the University of Salford.

The project was vigorously supported by a Sounding Panel of key figures, who gave generously of their time to attend advisory meetings. The members included: David Adamson, Office of Government Commerce; Fran Birch, The Theatres Trust; Clare Booth, Arts Council England; Professor Rachel Cooper, University of Lancaster; Sir Richard Eyre CBE, Theatre Director; Paul Iles, then at Blackpool Grand Theatre; Sebastian Macmillan, University of Cambridge; Jim Meikle, Davis Langdon; Alison Minto, Arts Council England; Paul Morrell OBE, now Government Chief Construction Advisor, then at Davis Langdon; Mark Price, The Theatres Trust; Kate Trant, CABE; Elanor Warwick, CABE; Timothy West CBE, Actor; Professor John Worthington, DEGW Architects.

As a project which relied substantially on access to archives and to the recollections of key players, we are grateful to all the theatres examined by the study and to their staff: Belgrade Theatre, Coventry; Contact Theatre, Manchester; Curve, Leicester; Hackney Empire Theatre; Lighthouse, Poole; and The Lowry, Salford. Clients, funders, and members of the design and construction teams for each case study were extraordinarily candid and gave most generously of their time to be closely interviewed.

The project was welcomed by many in the sector more generally. We are grateful to The Theatres Trust, and its Directors, first Peter Longman and then Mhora Samuel, for hosting meetings, for much advice and information, and for providing a platform for dissemination via their magazine, *Theatres*, and at their annual conference. CABE and Arts Council England provided a valuable opportunity for impact through the invitation to the team to write their 'Client Guide for Arts Capital Projects'. The document, embodying the research findings, was published online in early 2009 as 'Building Excellence in the Arts', a successor to Dr Alexi Marmot's pioneering 2002 guide.

The project team was successful in winning funding from the Centre for Research in the Arts, Social Sciences and Humanities (CRASSH) at the University of Cambridge in its annual competition for a Symposium in September 2006, which brought together fifty invited participants, including representatives from the case studies, for a stimulating discussion of the issues. The discussions were continued over an excellent dinner at Clare Hall.

The book is supported by a broadcast-quality film, made as part of the research project by François Penz, Brian Ashbee and Pete Cook of the Cambridge University Moving Image Studio. The actor Timothy West CBE kindly agreed to narrate the film, which can be viewed online at <http://sms.cam.ac.uk/media/1095045>.

We are grateful to Dr Giorgos Artopoulos, whose specially commissioned photographs are found throughout this book, to all those who allowed us to reproduce images, and to Dr Stamatina Rassia for digitizing our initial ink drawing of a new model process. We are extremely grateful to David Staples and Theatre Projects Consultants for contributing to the cost of the colour plates in Chapter 9. Sarah Charters, Val Rose and the team at Ashgate have devoted much time to this project and their efforts are hugely appreciated.

Last, but by no means least, we would like to express our particular gratitude to Sir Richard Eyre CBE for writing the Foreword to this book. His text builds on the impassioned and (for the architects present) somewhat intimidating declaration he delivered to the first Sounding Panel meeting. Borne of much experience of theatre architecture it poses a considerable challenge to the design and construction communities.

The inclusion of colour plates in this book was made possible by a donation from Theatre Projects Consultants

THEATRE
PROJECTS
Consultants

List of Abbreviations

ACE	Arts Council of England (often written as 'Arts Council England' in its publications)
ACP	Arts Capital Programme
CABE	Commission for Architecture and the Built Environment
CAC	'Conditions', 'Actions/Interactions', 'Consequences'
CEMA	Council for the Encouragement of Music and the Arts
ERDF	European Regional Development Fund
NAO	National Audit Office
OJEC/OJEU	*Official Journal of the European Communities/Union*, the official record of the EC (since 2003, the EU), which includes invitations to tender.
QS	Quantity Surveyor
RIBA	Royal Institute of British Architects
VE	Value Engineering

Introduction

Alan Short and Alistair Fair

'You intuitively know, when you walk into an auditorium, if it is yielding, if it is a sacred space – in which something extraordinary can happen – or if it is a dead space … you know it instantly. A dead auditorium takes that much more work.'[1]

'For many clients the process of creating a building is both an inspiring and a draining process. Some are overwhelmed by the results of their endeavours – fantastic buildings, and some – despite all their best efforts – are left underwhelmed by the results.'[2]

Fig. 0.1 The Quays theatre, The Lowry, Salford

More than £1 billion has been spent by the Arts Council of England (ACE) Lottery Fund, much of it on buildings (fig. 0.1). But for a significant proportion of recipients, the envisioning, procurement and delivery of their projects were problematic. After being involved in a major refurbishment project, one experienced theatre administrator vowed that she would *'never, never, never do a building again, because it is just too stressful'*.[3] Peter Longman, Director between 1996 and 2006 of The Theatres Trust, the National Public Advisory Body for the sector, has commented that *'Arts buildings are seriously bad for your artistic health'*.[4] Periodic newspaper headlines attest to the difficulties.[5] The National Audit Office (NAO) reported in 1999 that, of fifteen ACE Lottery funded projects which it reviewed, twelve were over budget and seven were also damagingly late in completion.[6] A further NAO review in 2006-2007 revealed that a quarter of all the 24,000 projects funded through the various Lottery schemes since 1995 were completed late.[7] The design of buildings for the arts is never going to be straightforward or quick. It requires complex technical and practical matters to be reconciled with more intangible factors – the 'geometry and atmosphere' of our title, suggested by the criteria which the Actor Timothy West CBE told us are present in successful performance spaces. However, Sir John Bourn, head of the NAO, has also suggested that some Lottery-funded clients were guilty of 'poor planning and a lack of project management skills'.[8]

Is the NAO's dismissive diagnosis adequate? Will it help future clients to do better in shepherding their creative 'vision' safely through the design process? This book presents the findings of a three-year research project which was funded by the Arts and Humanities Research Council (AHRC). Six relatively recent Capital Arts Projects were investigated, ranging in project cost from £4.5 million to more than £68 million. Though focussed on buildings for theatre, the issues are not necessarily unique to the arts, as is evident from, the increasing cost estimates of the 2012 London Olympics, from an initial £2.4 billion to a sum in excess of £9 billion at the time of writing.[9] We ask: have significant numbers of existing Capital Project Clients really been negligent? Would yet more strictures really deliver more successful projects, or simply compound the problem? In practice, do the funding and approval processes enable or stifle design creativity? Are arts buildings just 'different'? Do they warrant a different process? Might the process (which is closely tied to the Royal Institute of British Architects sequential 'Plan of Work' (fig. 0.2)) merit reform?

In considering our key questions, the histories of the six case study projects were examined in detail. The events and circumstances behind every appreciable design change, cost increase and delay were analysed, much as construction lawyers and auditors might work but with a much broader arsenal of techniques honed in Arts and Humanities research. Project archives were systematically examined. Virtually all the key project stakeholders were interviewed. The deliberate use of 'semi-structured' interviews allowed the interviewees to tell us much more than might be the case

had a more prescriptive format been used. The interview transcripts were analysed, phrase by phrase, using software particular to the Humanities and Social Sciences, to help us establish the relative significance of interviewees' responses across the projects. This is an aggrieved community with a lot to say. The complex financial and contractual histories of each case were dramatically brought to life by each set of participants' accounts. Very revealingly, they did not wholly align. The different constituencies speak different languages.

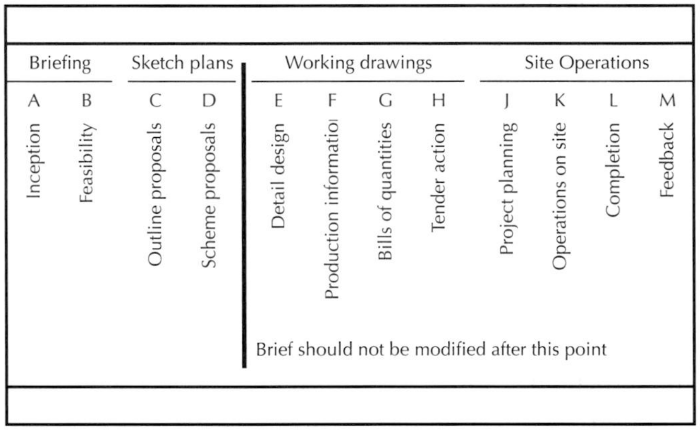

Briefing		Sketch plans		Working drawings				Site Operations			
A	B	C	D	E	F	G	H	J	K	L	M
Inception	Feasibility	Outline proposals	Scheme proposals	Detail design	Production information	Bills of quantities	Tender action	Project planning	Operations on site	Completion	Feedback

Brief should not be modified after this point

Fig. 0.2 *The RIBA Plan of Work, 1964 version, a sequential, unfolding scheme for design which was originally invented for the delivery of schools but which has become the industry-standard way of understanding how projects should be structured and managed. It assumes that a design can be quickly fixed, with minimal subsequent variation, but does this way of working allow for the changes which may become necessary as specialist consultants assist in the delivery of detailed designs?*

Our findings were constantly challenged by a very distinguished, disparate and pro-active Sounding Panel, including the former Director of the National Theatre, Sir Richard Eyre (still bruised from his encounters with several prominent architects, as he recounts in his Foreword to this book), the Actor Timothy West CBE, leading Cost and Theatre Consultants, senior Design Management academics, senior Capital Projects officers at Arts Council England, the Head of Research at the Commission for Architecture and the Built Environment (CABE), the Director of The Theatres Trust, and a senior figure from the Office of Government Commerce. The consensus amongst them, including the management specialists, was that it was even more important to know 'what actually happened' in the realization of Capital Projects, and not just Arts Capital Projects, to be able to interrogate current policies and to propose meaningful change.

Such was the strength of feeling encountered that virtually every project participant was extraordinarily candid. Many testimonies were captured on film.[10] What emerges in the research is a labyrinthine and often corrosive Capital Project process which can engender problems and has even, in a limited number of well publicized cases, led to complete failure.

THE LITERATURE

Many of those working in theatre to whom we spoke complained that their community had to 'reinvent the wheel' every time an Arts Capital Project was attempted, and asked in exasperation, 'where is the guidance?' One former theatre administrative director commented:

> I was looking for a book: "How to buy a £3 million building". Couldn't find it. Went to the RIBA, went to bookshops, libraries. How to be a client ... beyond ... the booklets that the Arts Council had provided. I think we could have benefited from either some training or some ... book. I think we would have avoided some mistakes early on.[11]

Theatre organizations are unlikely to have much experience of the design and construction process, at least at this scale, though, as we shall see (and as Sir Richard Eyre's Foreword has noted), they will be well-versed in conceiving, designing and realizing theatre productions according to rigid timescales and budgets (figs 0.3 and 0.4). In addition, designers and other consultants may be new to the type owing to its relative rarity.

Fig. 0.3 The workshops, Contact Theatre, Manchester

Fig. 0.4 Stage right, Lighthouse, Poole

There is, in fact, an extensive and useful literature on theatre design. Numerous discursive texts have engaged with the philosophical and conceptual aspects of the subject; particularly rooted in the experience of design and compelling in its analysis is Iain Mackintosh's *Architecture, Actor and Audience*.[12] In addition, those involved in the design process can turn to many sources of practical and technical advice. Since the 1970s, the classic text has been Roderick Ham's *Theatre planning*, later revised as *Theatres: Planning Guidance for Design and Adaptation*.[13] Ham's book, borne of his experience as an architect of several theatres and his membership of the Association of British Theatre Technicians' Theatre Planning Committee (which has reviewed schemes since the 1960s), offers a practical discussion of the design issues inherent in the type and has become established as the standard introduction to the subject. The work has recently been almost entirely rewritten and significantly expanded by a group of experts under the editorship of Judith Strong.[14] Ian Appleton's *Buildings for the Performing Arts* is similar in intent, while George Izenour has tackled the subject from a North American perspective with a particular focus on the design of multi-purpose spaces.[15] These studies all offer a broad-ranging framework, setting out the roles and processes involved in commissioning and realizing a building, and offering calculations and other strategies by means of which a viable design might be generated. They are, however, essentially targeted at designers rather than clients, who may appreciate the value of understanding how, for example, sightlines are calculated, but who are unlikely to have to apply this knowledge in practice. 'Step-by-step' guides for clients engaging with the Arts Capital Programme have been produced by the Commission for Architecture and the Built Environment and Arts Council England. The 2002 *Client Guide for Arts Capital Projects* was critiqued by the present authors in 2007.[16] Though undeniably helpful for its readership, it was of necessity somewhat generic in its approach and, like CABE's *Creating Excellent Buildings*, focussed on the pre-design stages. A substantially revised and expanded version of the guide by the present authors, drawing on the findings of the research presented in this book, was published online by CABE in early 2009 as *Building Excellence in the Arts*.[17]

Strong and Appleton both include brief case studies to illuminate specific points. In this respect, they recall a broader type of writing on architecture, the case study anthology.[18] Such anthologies helpfully present a variety of solutions to the question 'what is a theatre' and offer a valuable overview, but there is limited scope for the detailed investigation of individual cases. For a closer treatment, it is necessary to turn to the accounts that accompany the opening of major Arts venues,[19] or which, occasionally, chart the course of an unsuccessful project.[20] But the analysis in such works, whilst often drawing productively on the recollections of project participants, is rarely entirely dispassionate and lacks the depth that would be added by comparative analysis. The investigations of the National Audit Office, meanwhile, are more detached and rooted in analysis of project records, but we are increasingly sceptical that financial autopsy exposes the real causes of difficulty; such a field of enquiry is much too narrow. Post-occupancy evaluation (POE), meanwhile, has evolved into a substantial science in its own right, pioneered by Bill Bordass and others, and popularized in the clinical and sometimes brutal 'Probe' studies of innovative built work.[21]

There is an extensive literature on briefing and subsequent construction management; key recent studies have been undertaken by Blyth, Worthington, and Barrett.[22] Previous investigations have shown that British construction professionals do not always listen to their clients, even blaming them at times. The means by which designs are 'value engineered' to reduce their likely out-turn cost during design (and construction) has also been considered extensively.[23] But how accessible are such studies to clients (and design teams) working in the Arts?

This book, therefore, is not a technical design guide, nor a conventional anthology, a stylistic critique, a philosophical analysis of performance space, or an academic text about briefing and construction. It is intended to be read alongside such works. Though recognizing the value, as Sir Richard Eyre's Foreword discusses, of the human scale, of an intimate actor/audience relationship, and of sympathetic materials ('geometry and atmosphere'), it does not offer a single solution to the design of the 'ideal' theatre. The case studies confirm that different philosophies and spatial configurations can all be valid. The aim of the book is to consider how an initial spark of creativity – a 'vision' – is given built form, and the effect of the process of achieving that built form on the 'vision'. The book presents the design of buildings in a much broader context than much contemporary architectural criticism, which is preoccupied with form and stylistic nuance. The research group included a forensic Quantity Surveyor, a prominent Construction Management academic and an observer of audience behaviour from Salford University, who all contributed much to the understanding of the Principal Investigator (an architect) and the rest of the team at the University of Cambridge: a classically trained architectural historian, a researcher with a background in the physical sciences and environmental engineering, and a former arts administrator. This breadth represents a continuation of the stress on a rounded, 'humanistic' understanding of architecture for which Cambridge has long been known.[24] Our literature search suggests the resulting case 'histories' are amongst the most detailed accounts of contemporary building projects currently available. They owe something in spirit to William Curtis' minute-by-minute reconstruction of Le Corbusier's design journey for the Carpenter Center for the Visual Arts, assembled through the interrogation of Julian de la Fuente's drawings.[25]

The first part of the book comprises six case studies, bookended by chapters offering a historical perspective. The second part of the book offers cross-case analysis and conclusions. The case studies are bodies of experience on which others may wish to draw for good practice, reassurance or forewarning. They are an attempt to counter the 'one-off' nature of the type; often the knowledge gained in conceiving

and overseeing a project is essentially lost, as client teams may well never have the opportunity (or the wish) to undertake the process again. By capturing and reporting that experience, with extensive quotations from those involved, denoted by italics, the book is intended to provide the arts community with insights and guidance in achieving best value, in its widest sense, when commissioning capital projects. Although public funding streams are now flowing more slowly than they did in the late 1990s and early 2000s, schemes are still being devised and developed. We hope that the analysis will also be useful to those in other sectors where public money is spent on major building projects.

THE CASE STUDY PROJECTS

Theatres are a diverse type, ranging from purpose-built civic landmarks to *ad hoc* converted spaces. They offer an almost infinite capacity for refinement and nuance deriving from the dramatic intent and style of their promoters; they will also be informed by the ideas of their designers as well as the practical realities of the context within which they are realized. Theatre design is neither straightforward nor standardized, as one Artistic Director confirmed:

I think it's important that a space has character and that it is specific. ... I think there are pluses and minuses with the design of Contact but it has character and personality, and young people respond to it. You don't want a generic, multi-use thing that has an institutional arts centre feel.[26]

Theatres are, in fact, particularly bespoke:

I think the problem is that really the client should [drive the] design [of] the theatre. And I think that a client that can't design its own theatre space is probably not going to be a very good client.[27]

Thus this book considers different understandings of theatre architecture at a variety of scales, some all-new and others including a degree of refurbishment. Inevitably, however, the breadth of the type means that some approaches are not considered. There are none conceived as 'found spaces', that is, performance venues in converted buildings, though some of the case studies discussed here metamorphosed into something of this kind as new personnel inherited the buildings conceived by their predecessors. The completed buildings in those cases were, in effect, souvenirs of former visions.

The narrative commences with a design and construction history of The Lowry in Salford, which recently celebrated its first decade in operation (figs 0.5 and 0.6). This was a project conceived in the abstract as an iconic centrepiece around which to regenerate Salford Quays. The original proposition for a contemporary Albert Hall morphed into an opera house and ultimately became a lyric theatre, set within a highly characterized external envelope, 'an exercise in taxidermy' according to the prominent theatre consultant who delivered the mechanics of the new venue. The budget timeline shows the project cost to have always been in excess of the budget, constantly prey to the anxieties of the multiple funding agencies underwriting the scheme.

Fig. 0.6 Lyric Theatre, The Lowry, the larger of the centre's two auditoria

Fig. 0.5 Exterior, The Lowry, Salford (2000), from Imperial War Museum North

Fig. 0.7 Contact Theatre, Manchester (1999), a green theatre for young people

Fig. 0.8 Contact Theatre: Space 1, the main auditorium

cut the Centre's allocation twice without warning, leaving its carefully configured and weighted wish-list stranded. The refurbished centre opened in 2003.

Fig. 0.9 Lighthouse, Poole (2003), detail of the luminous exterior by the artist Peter Freeman

Fig. 0.10 Lighthouse, Poole: the Towngate Theatre after refurbishment

The highly entrepreneurial administrative and artistic directors of the Contact Theatre in Manchester, originally built in the 1960s as the University Drama Department's private theatre, decided attack was the best form of defence as they discovered by accident its very existence was threatened by redevelopment (figs 0.7 and 0.8). They became the first recipients in the North West of a capital grant from the National Lottery (launched in 1994) and were pioneers in the making of a new generation of very low-energy public buildings, easy enough to promise but very difficult to achieve within the customs and practice of the construction industry. The refurbished and extended theatre opened in 1999. In contrast, the management of the Poole Arts Centre arrived at the first round of Lottery capital funding rather later in its life in the late 1990s, when it was under siege by the Audit Commission (figs 0.9 and 0.10). They cut their cloth to suit their operating needs in maintaining a successful venue, the largest arts centre outside London at the time. But even their abstemiousness fell foul of the Lottery administrators who

The Belgrade in Coventry was the first all-new civic theatre built in Britain after the Second World War, opening in 1958. Since the 1960s, its management had wanted to build a second flexible studio theatre alongside the original 'Festival of Britain'-style proscenium theatre, but a Lottery application in the late 1990s failed. The theatre eventually secured a grant from the second ACE Capital Programme, in which all awards were capped at £5 million, necessitating multiple matched funding – a complex undertaking. The budget never quite matched the architect's aspirations and the project was completed in 2007 on a 'design and build' basis (figs 0.11 and 0.12).

is provided, drawing on our earlier account of the project,[28] and insights from Hackney inform the final analysis. Notably, the architect's view of himself as lead consultant appears to have clashed with ACE's insistence on external project management. However, the account is truncated by virtue of its particular sensitivities. The contractor went into liquidation close to the project's completion,[29] while financial and other troubles forced the temporary closure of the theatre entirely in early 2010.[30] We hope, once the sensitivities have receded, to be able to publish a fuller account.

Fig. 0.11 Belgrade Theatre, Coventry (2007): the new theatre building rising behind the original 1958 theatre

Fig. 0.12 Belgrade Theatre, Coventry: the second auditorium, 'B2'

The restoration and extension of the Hackney Empire in 2001-2004 revitalized a building that had originally been designed by the pre-eminent theatre architect of the late nineteenth and early twentieth centuries, Frank Matcham, and which opened in 1901 (fig. 0.13). A summary narrative

Fig. 0.13 Hackney Empire, as extended in 2004

The most fantastical story uncovered by the research comes from the engagement with the city of Leicester of the internationally prominent, New York-based architect, Rafael Viñoly. He delivered the new Haymarket theatre, named 'Curve' on its opening in 2008 (figs 0.14 and 0.15). Viñoly's spatial vision captured exactly the artistic intent of the Haymarket team, 'theatre inside-out'. However, Viñoly's sketches contained within them sufficient latent technical challenges ultimately to quadruple the budget. Two city councils fell in part because of the public fury at the rising cost of the project. Nonetheless, the building was delivered almost exactly as the interview-winning sketch. Is this a triumph of the artistic 'will to form' over dull mediocrity or the diversion of resource from other needs in the community? You may find it amusing to confirm your position on this not infrequent experience as you start to read through this book and to review your opinion as you turn the last page. It is one of the ancient and perennial conundra in the history of architecture.

Fig. 0.14 Curve, Leicester (2008): the exterior of the theatre to Rutland Street

Fig. 0.15 Curve, Leicester: the main auditorium viewed from the stage

THE PROJECT

The AHRC-funded research project 'Designing Dynamic Environments for the Performing Arts' ('DeDEPA') was a collaboration between the universities of Cambridge and Salford. The Principal Investigator was C. Alan Short, The Professor of Architecture at Cambridge; the Co-Investigators at Salford were Professor Peter Barrett (Pro-Vice-Chancellor for Research) and Professor Pat Sterry. The Research Associates were Dr Zeynep Toker and Anne Dye at Cambridge, and Dr Monty Sutrisna at Salford. Alistair Fair held the Ph.D. studentship accompanying the project. The research team was supported by a vigorous and energetic Sounding Panel which constantly challenged the researchers' assumptions and preconceptions. Its membership included: David Adamson, Office of Government Commerce; Fran Birch, The Theatres Trust; Clare Booth, Arts Council England; Professor Rachel Cooper, University of Lancaster; Sir Richard Eyre, Theatre Director; Paul Iles, then at Blackpool Grand Theatre; Sebastian Macmillan, University of Cambridge; Jim Meikle, Davis Langdon; Alison Minto, Arts Council England; Paul Morrell OBE, then at Davis Langdon and now the Government's Chief Construction Adviser; Mark Price, The Theatres Trust; Kate Trant, CABE; Elanor Warwick, CABE; Timothy West CBE, Actor; Professor John Worthington, DEGW Architects.

DeDEPA was completed in November 2007. A 38 minute film 'Geometry and Atmosphere', made by Cambridge University's Moving Image Studio is available at http://sms.cam.ac.uk/media/1095045>, where one should look for 'Geometry and Atmosphere'. As a consequence of the project outcomes, presented at conferences and in refereed publications, Alan Short was commissioned in late 2007 by the Commission for Architecture and the Built Environment (CABE) and Arts Council England (ACE) to rewrite their Client Guidance for Capital Arts Projects (2002) as 'Building Excellence in the Arts' with Peter Barrett, Alistair Fair, Sebastian Macmillan, Pat Sterry, Adrian Cave and Adam Whiteley. The new document was launched online in 2009. The research team subsequently conducted a further thirteen case study reports of Capital Arts Projects at various stages for CABE/ACE.

METHODOLOGY

This research project draws inspiration from a rigorous methodology, familiar to the social sciences but less commonly applied to the world of architecture: grounded theory. The methodology, presented by Barney Glaser and Anselm Strauss in their 1967 book, *The Discovery of Grounded Theory*, begins with systematic data collection. The findings are then analysed carefully at an ever-increasing distance, resulting, in short, in the development of a theory that is 'grounded' in the material. In this case, the aim was to develop a new theory for the briefing and procurement of buildings for the arts by identifying patterns across the case studies, which may match, replicate or contradict. Case studies were matched to a theoretical proposition, the industry standard model of ideal cost management and sequences of working.

As discussed in the Introduction, cases were selected deliberately ('purposive selection'). The criteria for selection included projects' currency, the client type, seating capacity, complexity (multiple performance spaces, for example), the nature of the project (all new-build and/or major refurbishment), source(s) of funding, size of budget, audience type, and style of programming, receiving and/or producing. Accessibility to archives and interviewees was an important consideration. Much of the archive material sought could be considered commercially sensitive, although ultimately in the public realm if public finances were involved.

Two data collection techniques were used, namely semi-structured interviews across the broad constituency of stakeholders with a pre-figured list of questions, and archival research, concentrating on meeting records, cost reports and budget statements recovered from client, consultant, local authority and ACE records. The questions evolved gradually through the fieldwork. Interviewees were drawn from the following categories:

- Design team members, including theatre consultants and acousticians;
- Artistic and administrative directors, executive producers, company staff, Board and Building Committee members;
- ACE officers, and their independent project monitors;
- The construction industry, including project managers and cost consultants;
- Local Authority officers and politicians;
- Users and participants, producers and directors.

The semi-structured nature of the interview technique enabled researchers to allow the interviewees to elaborate on any topic but required all predetermined topics to be covered. Specific topics emerging from the particular contexts of the case studies were also introduced. The interviews were recorded and transcribed, and the transcripts were 'coded' with the key emerging themes according to the principles of grounded theory. The coding frames were merged and edited through an iterative process. NVivo software was used to organize the transcripts by code and assist with the analysis. The abstracted material organized by code was re-analysed and the more profound observations raised to a higher coding level.

Interview data was also used to augment the preliminary archival analysis during incremental cross-case analysis. Budget/cost/design histories for each case study were assembled from archive data. The timelines were annotated with relevant events, key gateways, the involvement of stakeholders and the funding awarded to date. Data were sorted as overall project cost and budget, construction cost and budget, and the budget and available funds for the 'other needs' of the clients which tended to become defined by the residual funds available as construction costs rose. A further analysis was conducted defining variance of perceived out-turn cost from the given budget, and the resulting curves compared to the idealized model.

Notes

1   Stephen Daldry quoted in Hugh Pearman, 'Building the perfect rapport,' *Sunday Times*, 3 November 1998.

2   Joanna Averley, in Commission for Architecture and the Built Environment (CABE), 'Creating Excellent Buildings: a Foundation Guide for Clients' (2003).

3   Ruth Eastwood, formerly of Lighthouse, Poole, in the film 'Geometry and Atmosphere: the conundrum of building for the arts' (2006), accessed on 17 June 2010 at <http://sms.cam.ac.uk>.

4   Peter Longman, in the film 'Geometry and Atmosphere: the conundrum of building for the arts' (2006), accessed on 17 June 2010 at <http://sms.cam.ac.uk>.

5   E.g. 'Top architect in row over theatre's "serious faults"', *Scotsman*, 5 October 2004.

6   National Audit Office, 'Arts Council of England: monitoring major capital projects funded by the National Lottery' (1999), and also its 2003 report, 'Progress on fifteen major capital projects funded by Arts Council England'.

7   'Thousands of lottery works are late and over budget', *Times*, 16 March 2007.

8   'Thousands of lottery works are late and over budget', *Times*, 16 March 2007.

9   See e.g. BBC News, 'Olympics budget rises to £9.3 billion', 15 March 2007, accessed on 17 June 2010 at < http://news.bbc.co.uk/1/hi/uk_politics/6453575.stm>. The impact of the rising costs on other funding streams, including the arts, is evidenced by e.g. the closure of the Arts Council of Wales' Capital Programme, discussed in a press release of January 2008: < http://www.ccc-acw.org.uk/viewnews.asp?id=766>, accessed on 17 June 2010.

10 The film can be viewed at <http://sms.cam.ac.uk>, titled 'Geometry and Atmosphere: the conundrum of building for the arts'.

11 Patrick Martin to Anne Dye, 26 September 2006.

12 Iain Mackintosh, *Architecture, actor and audience* (London, 1993).

13 Roderick Ham, *Theatre planning* (London, 1972); *Theatres: planning guidance for design and adaptation* (London, 1987).

14 Judith Strong (ed.), *Theatre buildings: a design guide* (London, 2010).

15 Ian Appleton, *Buildings for the performing arts: a design and development guide* (Oxford, 1996); George Izenour, *Theater design* (London, 1977).

16 Commission for Architecture and the Built Environment, *Client Guide for Arts Capital Projects* (2002, formerly available from CABE); C.A. Short, P.S. Barrett, A. Dye and M. Sutrisna, 'Impacts of value engineering on five capital arts projects', *Building Research and Information* 35/3 (2007), pp.287-315. See especially pp.308-312.

17 Commission for Architecture and the Built Environment, 'Building excellence in the Arts: a guide for clients', accessed on 27 December 2009 at <http://www.cabe.org.uk/publications/building-excellence-in-the-arts>.

18 See e.g. Michael Forsyth, *Auditoria: a design and development guide* (London, 1987); Judith Strong, *Encore: strategies for theatre renewal* (London, 1998).

19 E.g. Jeremy Myerson, *Making The Lowry* (Salford, 2000); Marcus Binney and Rosy Runciman, *Glyndebourne: building a vision* (London, 1994).

20 E.g. Nicholas Crickhowell, *Opera house lottery: Zaha Hadid and the Cardiff Bay project* (Cardiff, 1997).

21 The work of Bordass and others has been extensively published in *Building Research and Information*. See e.g. B. Bordass and A. Leaman, 'Making feedback and post-occupancy evaluation routine. 1: A portfolio of techniques', *Building Research and Information* 33/4 (2005), pp.347-352.

22 Useful introductions are provided by A. Blyth and J. Worthington, *Managing the brief for better design* (London, 2001); P. Barrett and C. Stanley, *Better construction briefing* (Oxford, 1999).

23 E.g. L.W. Crum, *Value engineering: the organised search for value* (London, 1971), p.6; S.D. Green, 'Beyond value engineering: SMART value management for building projects', *International Journal of Project Management* 12/1 (1994), pp.49-56.

24 Roger Stonehouse, *Colin St John Wilson: buildings and projects* (London, 2007), pp.12-13.

25 William Curtis, 'History of the design', pp.37-227 in Eduard F. Sekler and William Curtis, *Le Corbusier at work: the genesis of the Carpenter Center for the Visual Arts* (Cambridge, Massachusetts, 1978).

26 John McGrath to Alan Short and Zeynep Toker, April 2005.

27 Vikki Heywood to Alan Short and Zeynep Toker, April 2005.

28 Short et al., 'Impacts of value engineering', pp.305-306.

29 'Local firm set to take centre stage at Hackney Empire', *Building* 2003/30, p.13.

30 'Hackney Empire to close in January', *Stage*, 24 September 2009.

1. 'Almost as important as jobs, housing and education': the Context of the Publicly Funded Arts in Britain

Alistair Fair

The theatres featured in this study received contributions towards their capital costs and to their ongoing running costs from central government sources and from local authorities. This brief chapter summarizes the history of public subsidy for the arts in Britain as an introduction to the case studies.[1]

In essence, the practice of public support for the arts was established in Britain during the Second World War, when the potential of cultural activities to engender solidarity in the face of adversity was recognized by the creation of the Council for the Encouragement of Music and the Arts (CEMA) in 1940.[2] CEMA's remit was varied;[3] in the case of the theatre it included the provision of financial support for professional touring productions.[4] Such productions received a wide audience, if only because other forms of entertainment were lacking,[5] and prompted thinking as to how the idea might be extended into peace-time. On this subject, some, including the economist J.M. Keynes, had already advocated a role for the state in supporting the arts.[6] The eventual result was the establishment of the Arts Council of Great Britain, granted its Royal Charter in 1946. The Arts Council operated on the basis of an 'arm's length' process, in which it acted as an independent distributor of the money provided by the government. Its initial remit in the case of theatre was largely limited to subsidy for companies and productions, rather than contributions towards new buildings or the refurbishment of existing ones, not least as the sums available were relatively small.

One consequence of the establishment and gradual expansion of public subsidy for the arts was that the dominance of the commercial touring theatre circuits was challenged. Arts Council policy in the 1950s and 1960s favoured non-profit-making theatres with resident Repertory companies for whom even limited revenue grants could provide a useful degree of stability.[7] Such Repertory theatres usually comprised a group of actors who originated and presented their own productions. They had developed before the First World War in cities including Manchester, Liverpool, Birmingham, and Glasgow, and some had experienced considerable success between the wars.[8] Subsidy was often perceived as a 'rubber stamp' of approval. For example, at Sheffield, the receipt of Arts Council subsidy from 1960, together with the granting of formal association in 1963, prompted the Repertory Company to increase their operations and ultimately led them to commission the new Crucible Theatre, which opened in 1971.[9]

In 1956, the Arts Council supported some thirty companies, by 1970 around fifty, and the amount of money available increased seven-fold between 1952 and 1963, facilitating longer rehearsal periods and a better standard of production (fig. 1.1).[10] The director at Sheffield, Colin George, noted that no longer would the term 'Repertory' be associated with theatres whose stage sets fell apart during productions,[11] while at Leatherhead, Hazel Vincent Wallace commented that 'the old regime of "tatty rep" has gone for ever, killed by the competition of television and the higher standards ... demanded by a far more discriminating public'.[12]

operation under Jack Phipps that supported travelling groups such as Ian McKellen's Actor's Company and the Prospect

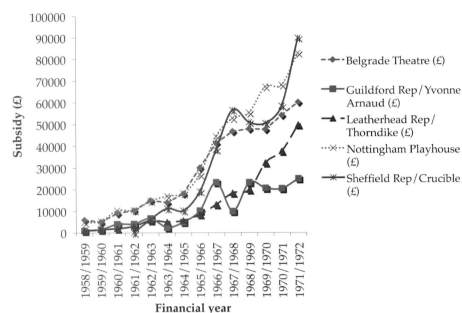

Fig. 1.1 Arts Council revenue grants for selected regional theatres, 1958-72 (based on figures given in the annual reports of the Arts Council)

A belief in the improving nature of the arts was sincerely held by some in government, notably Jennie Lee, who, shortly after taking up Ministerial responsibility in 1965 noted that

> we have accomplished only half a social revolution.
> ... Too many people are culturally semi-literate,
> through no fault of their own ... The opportunity
> to enjoy art has been mostly restricted to people
> with money and leisure. I believe it is one of the
> duties of a Socialist government to change that.[13]

Between 1963 and 1971, the size of the Arts Council's annual grant was trebled, from £2.73m to £9.3m.[14] One beneficiary of this funding increase was the increasingly battered touring sector. In 1970, the Arts Council took over the Dramatic and Lyric Theatres Association, reforming it as an in-house

Theatre Company (which had been co-founded by Iain Mackintosh).[15] The results of this particular development were mixed. The number of major touring venues had already declined from 255 in 1920 to some 24 in 1964,[16] and the advent of support for a limited range of touring groups in some ways actually harmed those operating on a commercial basis in that overall guarantee and fee levels were lowered across the sector.[17] It was only during the late 1970s and 1980s that commercial touring enjoyed a real renaissance, with such productions as the 'blockbuster' musicals of Tim Rice and Andrew Lloyd Webber contributing greatly to the success of groups such as Apollo Leisure, which expanded from a single Oxford theatre to become a major force.[18]

More significant in terms of this particular study was the Arts Council's growing interest during the 1960s in the buildings in which the arts were housed. CEMA's wartime tours had already highlighted the paucity of adequate venues for drama around the country,[19] and Arts Council reports on the subject in 1959 and 1961 showed that matters had not improved.[20] Partly this state of affairs was the result of post-war austerity, in which building for the arts was unlikely to be a major priority when houses and businesses needed to be reconstructed after wartime damage, and partly because, with television in the ascendancy, the mood was very much one of 'theatre in crisis'.[21] The Local Government Act of 1948 had, it is true, permitted local authorities to impose a sixpenny levy on the rates for the support of the arts,[22] with it being possible to spend the money not only on what were termed 'entertainments', but also buildings, including concert halls and theatres. Yet while these provisions could produce impressive results, such as in Coventry (where the left-wing city council's concern with the cultural well-being of the local population anticipated Jennie Lee's later views and led to the establishment of the Belgrade Theatre as the first all-new professional theatre to be built since 1939),[23] in practice few authorities ever availed themselves of anything like the full sixpenny rate,[24] not least because funding the arts was often contentious. Sustained debates in the Coventry press in the 1950s reveal the opposition of some councillors to the principle of the subsidized arts,[25] while in Nottingham, the then part-built Playhouse (fig. 1.2) was almost sold by the city authorities to a commercial theatre group in the early 1960s.[26] The 1959 and 1961 reports recommended that the Arts Council adopt a greater role in offering support for building projects as one way to improve conditions. The result was the 'Housing the Arts' programme, initiated in 1965.

Like Arts Council subsidy generally, 'Housing the Arts' was a responsive programme. Grants were awarded to a wide range of projects, from small improvements to existing buildings to whole new theatres. Schemes hoping for awards were assessed on the basis of various factors, including the applicant's proposed artistic policy, the functional suitability of the projected building or alterations, the applicant's

Fig. 1.2 Nottingham Playhouse, workshop in 1963

ability to raise capital funds from other sources, the revenue subsidy implications of the scheme, and the need for the Arts Council to ensure an approximate balance of provision around the country.[27] By 1972, some £2.5m had been spent on theatres.[28] The sums available to any project were capped at a maximum of a third of the total cost and clients had to look elsewhere for the balance of their funding – to local authorities, charitable foundations, business, or the local community.[29] In the case of the Crucible Theatre, for example, 'Housing the Arts' contributed some £300,000 towards the total, which was then one of the largest grants it had made.[30] As with revenue grants, capital funding through the programme was again effectively limited to the non-profit sector, though commercial organizations could receive money for improvements that would allow them to host Arts Council-supported companies.

By the 1970s, a wide variety of theatre groups received regular revenue funding from the Arts Council. Indeed, the so-called 'fringe' scene owed much to the existence of subsidy from the late 1960s onwards.[31] An early beneficiary was the Traverse Theatre, Edinburgh, 40% of whose income came in the form of Arts Council subsidy in 1966.[32] For some, this kind of funding was the key to lever further money out of local authorities: this was the case for the Wakefield Tricycle Company, which was helped in 1980 to locate and fit out a permanent home in Kilburn by the London Borough of Brent. Brent's arts committee under Councillor Terry Hanafin was no less concerned with issues of bringing theatre to a wider audience than Jennie Lee had been more than ten years before.[33]

'Housing the Arts' itself was wound up in the mid 1980s as part of a more general shift in arts policy instigated by Margaret Thatcher's Conservative government, which increasingly encouraged the arts to seek partnerships with private sponsors and placed particular emphasis on issues of economic sustainability.[34] Nonetheless, by that time the programme's impact had been considerable. As was noted in 1981 by Roderick Ham (the architect of a number of theatres in the 1970s and author of the standard text on theatre design), the majority of the main Repertory companies had been rehoused, and many other theatres had also benefited from the sums available.[35] However, in the decade that followed, even without central support for building projects, new theatres such as the West Yorkshire Playhouse (which opened in 1991) were still built.[36] And a particular theme of the 1980s was the substantial remodelling and restoration of Victorian and Edwardian theatres as venues for the resurgent touring sector. Some of these projects, such as the Lyceum, Sheffield, which re-opened in 1991, were able to benefit not only from local authority and private support, but also money from Europe.

The existence of revenue and capital subsidies had architectural implications. Director Hazel Vincent Wallace later recalled that her briefing decisions at Leatherhead were based on the fact that the Thorndike Theatre would be a subsidized Repertory venue, originating its own productions,[37] and so the design combined extensive workshops and rehearsal space with a relatively compact auditorium; it was not necessary to provide the vast seating capacity that a commercial theatre working in this way might have needed to turn in a profit. In addition, subsidy facilitated pluralism in theatre architecture. Of course, theatre has never been entirely homogenous. Even before the foundation of the Arts Council, there had been much experimental work taking place away from the mainstream in such venues as the Festival Theatre, Cambridge. That theatre, which flowered briefly between 1926 and 1933, lacked the usual proscenium arch between its auditorium and stage, and became known for its use of innovative abstract sets.[38] Nonetheless, post-war subsidies made a difference by supporting the distinctive ideas of individuals and groups, allowing them to attempt work which would not necessarily generate a viable profit. They also allowed these groups to create spaces which embodied their ideas; the Crucible's thrust stage, for example, responded to Director Colin George's particular desire for a 'participatory', non-scenic auditorium.[39]

After a decade in which central government had seemingly pulled back from supporting building for the arts, the 1990s were characterized by the introduction of a substantial stream of new funding for capital projects. The National Lottery was created by the National Lottery etc. Act 1993, with the first draw taking place in November 1994.[40] The arts were designated one of the 'good causes' which would be granted a share (initially 16.67%) of the lottery's proceeds. The Arts Council of England, created in April 1994 as a successor organization to the Arts Council of Great Britain, was charged with delivering the proceeds of the Lottery to the arts in England. Its first Capital Programme was announced in March 1995. Though it was later joined by other schemes (one, for example, providing grants to support organizational stabilization), the Capital Programme took the lion's share of the Arts Lottery money – some 80%. It was envisaged that grants would be in excess of £5000, and that the Arts Council would offer up to 75% of the total costs of a project, with the rest being found from what was known as 'partnership funding', i.e., money from local authorities, charities, businesses, regeneration agencies, and the community. Amassing a viable funding package could, therefore, be almost as complex an affair as designing and realizing a piece of architecture.

By the time that the programme ended in 1999, 2238 grants totalling £1.15 billion had been made. Half of this money went to twenty-eight major projects, each of which received more than £5 million. The Royal Opera House was awarded one of the largest sums, around £78.5 million. Applicants initially made a single submission to the Arts Council, but a review of the process by Adrian Ellis Associates in July 1996 led to a new three-stage process (feasibility/design development/full award), partly because it was felt that clients were getting too involved in questions of detail at too early a stage, and partly to minimize risks for the Arts Council by reducing the funding approved at each stage to the minimum level needed.[41] From 1997, projects with a total value of more than £500,000 were required to provide a detailed feasibility study and business plan. They were asked to demonstrate how the impact of the project on their organization would be managed, and to show that they had the organizational capability to manage the development. As the programme bore fruit, there was a corresponding uplift in revenue funding, which increased further after the General Election in 1997 (fig. 1.3).[42]

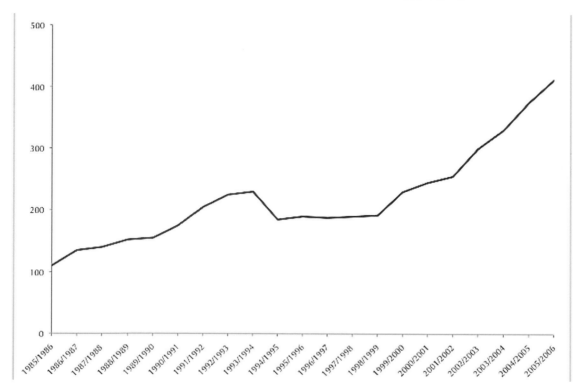

Fig. 1.3 Arts Council grant-in-aid, 1985/6-2005/6

A second programme of Arts Capital Projects was launched in 2000. The budget was substantially smaller at £176 million. It was anticipated that fewer projects would be supported, and the amount of money available to individual applicants was reduced to a maximum of £5 million. The process by which grants were made and managed was informed by the experience of the first wave of funding, not least by a review of fifteen projects that had been funded by the programme which was undertaken by the National Audit Office (NAO) in 1999. The NAO's report noted that twelve of the fifteen projects were over budget, six of these by more than 10%, while seven were delayed, with five delayed by more than three months. (When these projects were re-visited by the NAO in 2003, thirteen were described as having gone over budget, with cost over-runs from 1.7% to 58%, while the delay on four of the fifteen had become more than a year). The NAO therefore proposed more rigorous assessment of projects at the initial stage in order to minimize risks. Accordingly, the changes introduced for the second programme included an increase in the monitoring of projects, with formal reviews, and the requirement for clients to work with the newly-created Commission for Architecture and the Built Environment (CABE), which provided them with expert 'enablers', specialists intended to develop client expertise and ensure continuity of knowledge. In addition, contract forms which provided greater cost and design certainty were encouraged.

The National Audit Office's 2003 report noted that, of the fifteen projects which it investigated, 'the majority ... had not gone according to plan, and when things went wrong it was members of the public who lost out'. In what follows, we apply our own forensic lens to a series of projects from both waves of Arts Lottery funding, to see how the debates and dilemmas were played out, before we return to the historical context in order to see how novel these projects really were in their challenges.

Notes

1   This discussion is based on sections of Alistair Fair, 'British theatres, 1926-1991: an architectural history', Ph.D. thesis, University of Cambridge, 2008.

2   Robert Hewison, *Culture and consensus: England, art and politics since 1940* (London, 1997), pp.30-32; Andrew Sinclair, *Arts and cultures: the history of the fifty years of the Arts Council of Great Britain* (London, 1995), pp.27-32.

3   Hewison, *Culture and consensus*, pp.33-37; Nick Hayes, '"An English War?" Wartime culture and "Millions like us" ', pp.1-32 in Nick Hayes and Jeff Hill (eds.), *'Millions like us?' British culture in the Second World War* (Liverpool, 1999).

4   Sinclair, *Arts and cultures*, p.31; Roy Shaw, *The arts and the people* (London, 1987), p.129.

5   Nick Hayes, 'More than "music while you eat"? Factory and hostel concerts, good culture, and the workers', pp.209-235 in Nick Hayes and Jeff Hill (eds.), *'Millions like us?' British culture in the Second World War* (Liverpool, 1999).

6   J.M. Keynes, 'Art and the state', pp.1-7 in C. Williams-Ellis, *Beauty and the beast* (London, 1937).

7   Peter Longman, interviewed by the author on 9 August 2006.

8   G. Rowell and A. Jackson, *The Repertory Movement: a history of regional theatre in Britain* (Cambridge, 1984), pp.35-54.

9   Sheffield City Archives, LD2317: Kevan Scholes, 'The Crucible Theatre, Sheffield', unpublished typescript of 1976.

10 Rowell and Jackson, *The Repertory Movement*, pp.81-82, and see also the Arts Council's annual report for 1962-1963, p.13.

11 *Daily Mirror*, 17 September 1969.

12 *Leatherhead Advertiser*, 14 October 1966.

13 *Times*, 24 November 1966.

14 Janet (Jennie) Lee entry by Patricia Hollis in the *Oxford New Dictionary of National Biography*, accessed on 27 October 2007 at <http://www.oxforddnb.com/view/article/39853>, and see *Times* 17 January 1970 and 6 February 1970.

15 Jack Phipps, interviewed by the author on 14 August 2006; Paul Iles, 'Issues in theatrical management: Howard and Wyndham and the evolution of the British touring circuit', M.Phil thesis, University of Glasgow, 1997, p.94.

16 Iles, 'Issues', p.89.

17 Iles, 'Issues', p.94.

18 Paul Iles, pers. comm.

19 Sinclair, *Arts and cultures*, p.59

20 Arts Council of Great Britain, *Housing the Arts in Great Britain* v.1 (London, 1959) and v.2 (London, 1961).

21 E.g. Richard Findlater, *The future of the theatre* (London, 1959), pp.1-9; *Financial Times*, 28 March 1958.

22 William L. Roots et al., *The Local Government Act, 1948* (London, 1948), pp.87-91.

23 Fair, 'British theatres', pp. 67-68; Alistair Fair, '"A new image of the living theatre": the genesis and design of the Belgrade Theatre, Coventry, 1948-58', *Architectural History* 54 (2011), pp.347-382.

24 Arts Council, 'Housing the Arts', v.2., p.40; Findlater, *Future of the theatre*, p.10; *Times*, 6 February 1970.

25 *Forward*, 21 March 1958.

26 Nick Hayes, *Consensus and controversy: party politics in Nottingham, 1945-1966* (Liverpool, 1996), pp.162-186.

27 Peter Longman, pers. comm.

28 Victoria and Albert Museum, Theatre Collection, ACGB/120/43: 'Fifteen years of achievements', pp.19-20.

29 Victoria and Albert Museum, Theatre Collection, ACGB/120/47: 'Capital programme committee' documents, minute of 24 March 1964.

30 Sheffield Local Studies Library, MP4788M: 'The new Sheffield Theatre takes shape'.

31 Arthur Marwick, *The Sixties* (Oxford, 1998), p.350; Joyce McMillan, *The Traverse Theatre story* (London, 1988), p.10. For the expansion of subsidy in this sector, see Sinclair, *Arts and cultures*, p.133.

32 McMillan, *Traverse Theatre*, pp.37-38.

33 Hanafin's speech at the launch of the theatre appeal in 1979 referred to art as 'one of a small number of things which make a difference between mere existence and human civilization'. Copy of the speech kindly supplied to the author by Terry Hanafin.

34 Longman, interviewed on 6 August 2006; Michael Holden, interviewed by the author on 27 October 2006. For the general context, see Sinclair, *Arts and cultures*, pp.247-277.

35 Roderick Ham, 'Buildings update: theatres and performance spaces', *Architects' Journal* 174 (1981), pp.309-323 and 355-369. For this, see p.356.

36 Jude Kelly, 'The West Yorkshire Playhouse', pp.74-79 in Ronnie Mulryne and Margaret Shewring (eds.), *Making space for theatre* (Stratford, 1995).

37 Hazel Vincent Wallace, interviewed by the author on 26 October 2006.

38 Paul Cornwell, *Only by failure: the many faces of the impossible life of Terence Gray* (Cambridge, 2004) offers a useful account, though it requires caution, as Richard Cave's review in *Theatres* 3 (2005), p.19 confirms. See also Richard Cave, *Terence Gray and the Cambridge Festival Theatre* (Cambridge, 1980).

39 Colin George, 'Suicide or salvation' *Yorkshire Architect* 17 (1971), pp.386-390. For this, see p.388.

40 The following outline history of the Lottery and the Arts funding process draws upon that given in the National Audit Office's 1999 report, 'Arts Council of England: monitoring major capital projects funded by the National Lottery', especially pp.11-18, and its 2003 report, 'Progress on fifteen major capital projects funded by Arts Council England', pp.12-15.

41 National Audit Office, 'Arts Council of England' (report, 1999), pp.75-77.

42 *Guardian*, 19 January 2008 for the graph reproduced as fig. 1.3.

2. 'A means of unlocking future opportunity': The Lowry, Salford

Alan Short

We got so passionate about this ... You see, there was a huge credibility thing from our point of view ... because [people were surprised by the idea of having] an international Performing Arts Centre [in] Salford.[1]

One of the most important things, I think, is [that] they wanted somebody who actually believed in the vision. To the people who sat on [the selection panel], the vision was everything.[2]

Fig. 2.1 The principal elevation of The Lowry, viewed from the more recent shopping centre opposite, which took the place of the buildings proposed by Stirling and Wilford and suppressed their intended axial approach

Table 2.1 Lowry, case study characteristics

The Lowry, characteristics	
Receiving/Producing	Intended producing house became receiving theatre; also gallery for fixed and rotating exhibitions
Project driver(s)	To contribute to regeneration of derelict inner-city dockland; conceived as part of original Masterplanning exercise
Vision	A major new Arts venue serving immediate city and wider hinterland; a building of national and international significance
Refurbishment/new build	New build on brownfield site
Feasibility study - in house or external consultant?	Initial concept generated as part of Masterplanning exercise. In-house feasibility/business planning with input from specialists to develop design
Part of bigger arts initiative?	No, but located in metropolitan region with multiple theatres
Business plan - scope	Yes Comprehensive
Construction budget set?	£58 million
Final account/current estimated out-turn	£106 million (including associated infrastructure and 'Digital World Centre', a suite of spaces for the creative business sector)
Funding source(s)	Arts Council of England Lottery Fund, Heritage Lottery Fund, Millennium Commission, private benefactors, fundraising
Lead consultant	Architect
Design innovation	Not explicitly
Specialist inputs	Theatre consultants, gallery specialist, acoustician, access consultants, lighting designer
Value Engineering employed?	At Stage D, in response to cost estimates arising from detailed design
Vision creep?	No, but omission of accommodation for resident theatre company removed part of vision
Political climate	Stable, supportive local Labour authority provided commited leadership.
Contract type - contractor involvement in design? - quality/time/money priority?	Management contract No Quality/time/money to time/money/quality
Organizational change?	All-new organization defined and created while building designed and constructed

'The Lowry', Salford, opened its doors in April 2000 (fig. 2.1; Table 2.1). Although the centre, providing auditoria and art galleries, was realized as one of Britain's flagship Millennium projects, The Lowry had in fact been conceived around a decade previously, long before the advent of Lottery funding. It was in the late 1980s that local councillors and leaders had first speculated on the prospect of creating a centre for the arts which might catalyse the regeneration of the Salford Docks. The process by which their 'vision' was realized is the subject of this first case study chapter, which presents a detailed history based on archival research and interviews with participants. It shows how the vision for a centre of national (and international) significance was translated into built reality, both in terms of content (that is, the facilities that were to be provided and the identification of their possible users) and architectural design. The chain of decision-making was long, complex, and at times traumatic for some of its participants; commercial sensitivities still remain. The story highlights the challenges – and the rewards – of delivering a building which might be labelled 'iconic', and of reconciling this agenda with the functional needs and funding mechanisms of the arts. In its origins, The Lowry forms an instructive contrast with some of the other examples to which we shall come, where capital projects were driven by artistic need and intent, but many of the issues which will be highlighted are common to all the case studies.

THE 'VISION'

'The Lowry', as it eventually came to be known, was originally conceived by the City of Salford as a regenerative vehicle, the most visible instrument of their Development Plan (1985) to re-invigorate over ninety hectares of the former Salford Docks at the business end of the Manchester Ship Canal. The Docks had finally closed in 1982 and were acquired by the City Council in late 1983 in the absence of any commercial interest. The architect Peter Hunter, of Shepherd Epstein and

Hunter, could see in this area a potential which others had not. For a nominal fee from the City (these were lean years for UK architects), he worked up a series of evocative sketch plans and aerial views re-imagining the vast piers and basins, one sketch placing the Royal Albert Hall on Pier 8. The Hall seemed to fit comfortably, indicating clearly the scale of the dock infrastructure. Hunter called it, provocatively, 'the Salford Quays Centre for the Performing Arts'.

The Leader of the Council and its senior officers were bewitched by Hunter's idea. Jeremy Myerson has documented this early project-forming period in a book about The Lowry that was published to coincide with its opening,[3] but it is useful to reprise the basic chronology here. A competition was staged to find an architect of substance, with the winning architects James Stirling and Michael Wilford subsequently producing a series of designs for a centre combining performance venues with space for the visual arts, as we will shortly examine in some detail. In October 1994, a Project Steering Group was recruited and convened. It was chaired by the BBC journalist Felicity Goodey, a familiar face on the region's televisions, known for her reports on the decline of local industries. Goodey was rapidly nominated to be the official 'Project Champion' and later chaired the Board of the independent Lowry Trust that was established by the City Council.

Goodey confirmed that by the time she became involved, the broad purpose of the building was agreed, recalling that *'there was a brief that it should be an international arts centre'.*[4] This choice of function was driven, in part, by the prospect of Urban Programme capital grant aid and, when that prospect receded, by the new possibility of Lottery funding for Capital Arts Projects. The 'vision' was sharpened by highly encouraging visits to apparently successful waterfront regeneration projects in Baltimore and Bilbao, demonstrating, in Goodey's own words, a faith, largely blind in the case of Salford (that is, seemingly unsupported by any real data), in *'the power of art space projects as a catalyst'.*[5] This, then, was the 'vision' for the Lowry, a place which was to stimulate radical infrastructural, social and economic change. Goodey regularly reminded the participants of what she perceived as London-centric funding policy, of Salford's unblemished pedigree of poverty, of Engels' vivid accounts of what he witnessed in Salford, a special case beyond even the miserable industrial landscapes he had seen across the rest of the north of England. In the early 1990s, Salford was yielding appallingly low scores for all contemporary quality of life indicators. But for Goodey and her colleagues, it was its population's lack of aspiration that seemed intractable. The building was intended to transform a whole generation's sense of self worth. Thus *'The Lowry would be a means of unlocking future opportunity'*.[6]

Who was to perform at the proposed venue? There was little appreciable foundation of existing arts activity to develop organically. There was no local theatre company to be re-homed, or who might provoke and harass the brief-takers and policymakers. Consultation within the community was wholly speculative. It was often argued that Salford needed housing, schools and hospitals first; there was little local experience of the arts. Salford's University was brand new, its Art and Design operation still gathering strength. And so, although Stirling and Wilford's early designs provided performance venues and galleries, stipulations relating to the exact size, nature and users of these spaces were initially somewhat vague. The Theatre Consultant, appointed in late 1993, subsequently recalled:

There was virtually no brief. The [main] auditorium was varying wildly in size, between 1200 & 2000 seats. Local arts groups were anxious to reduce its size, but others were pointing to the commercial theatre operator, Apollo Leisure, who had acquired the larger Apollo Theatre and the Opera House in Manchester.[7]

The project manager was even more candid, but in contrast, the absence of an 'end-user' made life, in his view, much more straightforward:

There weren't any users for the building, which actually ... makes it slightly unusual and probably made it easier ... because in normal circumstances you'd have a theatre company, an opera company, and there would be a lot of stakeholders with a lot of interests in the different parts of the building. Here we were starting with a clean sheet of paper. Or, I guess, Sir James Stirling was.[8]

If, as we shall see in a later chapter, Curve at Leicester was designed from 'the inside out', putting form around a radical idea for staging performance, The Lowry appears by contrast to have been designed initially on the nose of a man-made peninsula, as a silhouette within which an arts centre was created. Who would come to this silhouette? Central to the rationale for making this major new attraction at the end of Pier 8 work was the provision of parking spaces at a truly prodigious scale. Its future visitors would not all be walking from Salford. Many would be driving for up to an hour or more, pleased to avoid central Manchester:

There was a perception that this was a poor area, but it is very close to motorways. Affluent Penrith, Lancaster and Cheshire all lie within a reasonable journey time ... and Downtown Manchester felt "dodgy", you couldn't park near the Opera House or Apollo.[9]

STEERING THE 'VISION'

You make your plan, formed out of calculation and analysis. If something is to change that plan, it has to be an alternative argument of tremendous force. It can't be, "the press says this," ... or "the Chairman wants [that]".[10]

Despite a certain vagueness during the early stages in terms of exact content, the Theatre Consultant, David Staples, recalled a simple, solid, over-arching 'vision' emanating from Salford City Hall:

The project had good leadership from day one. The local authority was an old-fashioned, patrician, Northern Labour local authority. Not loony left, not New Labour, [but an] old fashioned Northern Labour local authority.[11]

The Leader had a particularly robust attitude to the prospect of Lottery money for Salford:

They were determined to regenerate the city using Lottery money and Councillor Bill Hines was brilliant. His pitch to the Lottery was: "It's our money. It's the people of Salford who are playing the Lottery. We want our money back!"[12]

The idea of building an arts venue gathered momentum:

People started talking about "the Opera House on the Quays". But it was never intended to be just an opera house on the quays; it was always intended to be a performing and visual arts complex offering opera, ballet, drama and light entertainment. Remember, we are a receiving house. We did, in the very early days look at the idea of having a resident company ... and we [talked] to a number of companies: Ballet Rambert, Northern Ballet, even, very casually, Opera North. But we very rapidly dismissed the idea [of having a resident company] for two reasons. When we set our stall out ..., we said that this should become a venue of international significance. There are not [many] international quality opera or ballet companies looking for a home. There are very few; in fact I don't know of any who are looking for a home.[13]

Goodey recalled from her involvement in the Steering Group that, by mid 1994, The Lowry was already being envisaged as a receiving house. But there is no doubt that the scheme

was clearly invented as an opera house; certainly this use is implied by the feasibility studies of 1991 & 1992, in which the form – complete with the classic opera house horseshoe-shaped auditorium – was developed first by Stirling and then by Wilford. These sketches survive in the archive of the Canadian Centre for Architecture and we will examine a key sequence of drawings later in the chapter.

The Council and the new Steering Group realized that, to enable a successful bid in the face of deep scepticism, a credible business plan was essential. On the advice of the impresario Raymond Gubbay, they engaged Stephen Hetherington, an experienced theatre manager and performer. He took delivery of a 'ragbag' of ideas and propositions.

I had to drop a lot of the concepts that were talked about, and, instead, instigate others. I tried to [develop] a solid proposition. That proposition was the basis of the business plan, the Lottery application and subsequently the building design brief.[14]

Hetherington inherited the concept of the 'Lowry Centre Salford', already enshrined on a letterhead. However, his market research consultant's feedback was that 'Centre' evoked a shopping mall, whilst the words 'Lowry' and 'Salford' attracted little interest. He recalled:

The collection [of Lowry paintings] was deemed to be well loved but of no great artistic value, [something] that is [now] changing. We commissioned [a] biography as part of the [development] work, and other material which has instigated a lot of interest in Lowry. However, the [galleries] weren't [only] the Lowry Galleries, they would [also] present ... changing exhibitions. Then the combination, of course, looked very strong.[15]

A further issue was the robustness of the assumption of an opera house, or a producing theatre with its own company:

Notions of "The Salford Opera House" were easy to pick out and drop in the bin very early on because they clearly couldn't be sustained. Others ... had talked about production facilities and I had to drop those as well, as they would have been completely insupportable within the financial parameters. Instead [they] were replaced with a receiving house proposition, or "presenting house", as they are sometimes now called.[16]

I replaced production with receiving house facilities before the Trust was even formed, before the application to the Lottery was ever made. [There] were [still] rehearsal [spaces] for visiting companies, for communities and local organizations. [However, The Lowry] was never [going to be] producing its own works in the way that repertory theatre does.[17]

Hetherington conceived a resilient landscape of complementary revenue-earning activities, conjuring up the paradigm of a 'village', a helpful analogy though one which sits oddly with contemporary place-making preoccupations which typically resort to 'urban' imagery:

I tried to make it into a village economy ... a mixture of theatres, galleries, restaurants, bars and other things. I suggested quite a mixture of businesses, some of which came to fruition, some of which were never acted upon. The idea was to make this a self-supporting economy.[18]

However, Manchester appeared to be awash with performing arts venues, both publicly subsidized and private. In these circumstances, the 'artistic vision' could be interpreted quite differently: as passive, content-less and opportunistic. Indeed, one Arts Council officer recalled his scepticism on first hearing the proposition, which, he thought, sounded aggressive in the regional context:

The Lowry didn't have an audience. The Lowry was set up where there were existing theatres with an existing audience base. It was setting itself up to compete with them, by poaching everybody else's audiences. The catchment area would take in Arts Council regularly funded organizations and some of the commercial sector. Therefore where The Lowry was to be placed became quite controversial with regards to the commercial sector.

He predicted a simple and inevitable consequence:

The Lowry would want to buy in some of the commercial shows, so effectively the commercial sector would say, "Oh, OK, if you go the Lowry, then the likelihood is that you're not going to be able to play in any of our theatres within this region."[19]

The theatre consultants similarly recalled that the already rich theatrical landscape in Greater Manchester meant that it was difficult to get any purchase on a credible proposition:

It was completely put down by everybody in the performing arts community. It was put down by everybody in the Arts Council. In fact, we had to fight their case for them. And one of the ... most difficult things was to get rid of the name "Salford Opera House", because people went "Whoa! Salford building an opera house?!"[20]

There was a grim tour of Arts Council England Departmental Officers:

We were pretty certain there was a market, simply because there were seven million people living in the catchment area. We had thorough talks with the Arts Council, sitting with the heads of each of the departments (performing arts, touring arts, music, all of them), and then we had meetings also with officers of North West Arts. They were convinced that they should have a study of existing facilities before supporting this, so they opposed the idea. And Arts Council England took an awful lot of warming up to it.[21]

Despite the compelling outcome of Hetherington's risk analysis, the Theatre Consultant, Staples, regretted the absence of a resident company, a real user client:

I've always felt, quite strongly, that touring theatres are missing something. An arts building should be much more vibrant, much more alive. At the time, Opera North and Northern Ballet were looking to their futures and what we really wanted to do was to try and capture both of those.[22]

The Arts Council maintained its bafflement about the content of the actual proposition:

You could see that with a "spec" design it didn't have a client. The Artistic Director who eventually came on board was no more than a buyer. When we questioned the rationale behind the way in which we saw the programming, it was sold to us that "The Lowry will produce its programme like a shopping list, it will take its trolley around the supermarket and pick." Which, I suppose, to the Arts Council, didn't give it much credibility on the basis of what its direction was and how it ... would engage with the community on certain different levels.[23]

Goodey later argued that the team had no alternative but to be aggressive in their early revenue-earning plans. As Project Champion, she remained bitter about the conundrum set her by the funders as the project evolved. The Millennium Fund capped its grant at 50% but disallowed as matching funding any commercial element. *"'We cannot be seen to be funding anything which has a direct commercial development,'"* she was told, responding, *"'that is ridiculous. How can you expect*

the private sector to put in millions of pounds if they don't get any commercial benefit back?" They said, "Yes, we know, it's difficult, isn't it?"[24]

DRAWING THE 'VISION'[25]

Peter Hunter urged the City to hold an international competition for the masterplanning of the peninsula. It was won by the practice of James Stirling Michael Wilford and Partners, then one of the most prominent architectural offices in the world. Much of their archive has been deposited at the Canadian Centre for Architecture (CCA) in Montreal. From these papers and Michael Wilford's 1992 diary, it is possible to construct a close chronology of the project and a possible sequence in which the drawings were developed.

After an initial site visit to Salford on 7 January 1992, a team headed by the architect Laurence Bain generated fourteen 'architectural' masterplans, offering various configurations for the Arts Centre, a hotel, residential developments and commercial space.[26] These fascinating sketches show virtually every then-fashionable post-modern or neo-rationalist gambit. They include two rather overly literal ship-shaped schemes. These are clearly exercises in form, relatively unencumbered by concerns of actual use as befitted the vagueness with which the functional purpose was initially stated. Neither partner was seemingly involved in these sketches, the work being, one might say, that of the sorcerers' apprentices. Nonetheless, discussions with Stirling and Wilford are noted on 16 and 17 January and 4, 11 and 12 February, preparing for a first 'Presentation of Masterplan Options' to the Salford clients, seemingly on 13 February.

It seems that, in February, perhaps during or after the presentation to the client on the 13th, Stirling and Wilford realized they now had to settle down themselves decisively to invent the building and its context. There are a number of outline sketches in Wilford's possession marked 'MW'

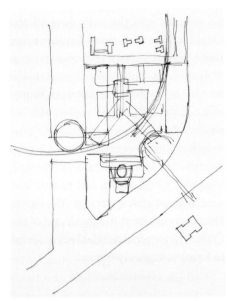

Fig. 2.6 Wilford moves The Lowry to the south, aligning it orthogonally with the western side of the pier

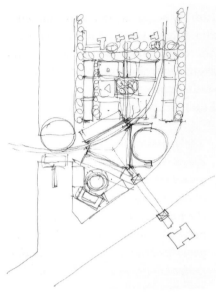

Fig. 2.8 The footbridge across the canal gains a pair of lifts

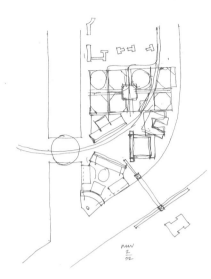

Fig. 2.10 The form of The Lowry is stabilized; to the north, a grid of urban blocks is developing, while to the east, Wilford proposes what seems to be a courtyard building

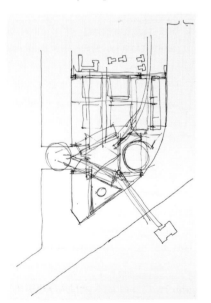

Fig. 2.7 The Lowry is codified as a triangle in this developed Wilford sketch, which tightens the structure of the Plaza and the other buildings around it

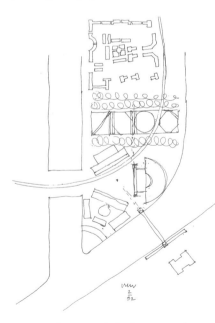

Fig. 2.9 The Lowry is broken apart into its constituent elements in this Wilford sketch; to the east, the Pantheon has been replaced by Epidauros

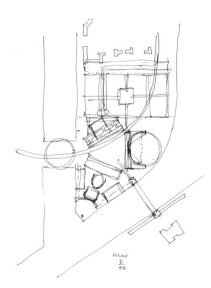

Fig. 2.11 Another Wilford sketch experimenting with options for the Plaza and the urban block to the north

It is figs. 2.7 to 2.11 which deliver the final Masterplan. An Opera House is assembled in the point out of jostling triangles, rectangles, and a drum. It fronts a triangular Plaza, which is now able to address the three 'pulls' of arrival and departure: roads in two directions, and the new bridge to the office building in the third. Figs. 2.10 and 2.11 tighten the corners of the Plaza and increase the size and prominence of the Lowry.

Stirling clearly approved of the theme that was developing, as, on one of two further drawings that elaborate it, we see his characteristic tick.[31] The drawings may relate to an internal design review involving Wilford, Stirling and Bain on 24 March; a date stamped on one of them shows that it, at least, had certainly been created by 1 April, when a second presentation was made in Salford. The two drawings show broadly the same scheme, though the unstamped version (fig. 2.12), featuring the affirmative tick in Stirling's hand, is slightly more developed than the other. The Lowry retains the essence of what had been proposed, but the area to the north of the plaza, whose corners were now truncated and whose sides now gained canopies, was taken up with a series of large buildings more closely related to the line of the dock edge and road.

A second series of drawings records the development of the internal arrangement of the building. Although Wilford's early sketches suggested the position of the main auditorium and galleries within The Lowry, this and other aspects of the design were carefully interrogated, perhaps at around the same time as the basic Masterplan concept was mapped out, or else shortly after, in April 1992. In arranging the building, Stirling and Wilford's direct experience of the quays and the desire to maintain this experience for users of the building came to the fore:

One of the reasons why we chose the tip of the promontory [for The Lowry], was the fact that you had water views out to the docks and the ship canal on two sides. We wanted to put [functions on] those faces that could actually enjoy the daylight and the views out. Unlike the Galleries, the Opera House, of course, is a space that doesn't need daylight, so it seemed sensible to put that in the middle of the plan. The buildings would "moor up" around it, and would also clad the neutral [blind] backstage areas. Rather than present that as the invisible, it could be flanked by the Galleries. That's really what generated the plan.[32]

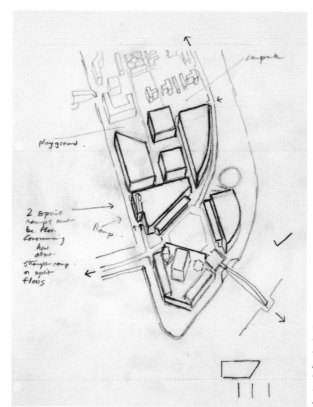

Fig. 2.12 *Axonometric Masterplan sketch featuring Stirling's tick. A simpler, photocopy record version of this drawing also exists in the CCA archive, dated 1 April 1992*

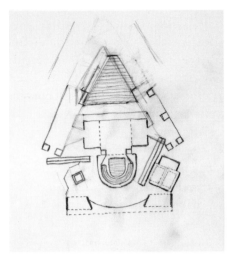

Fig. 2.13 Sketch plan, possibly by Stirling, spring 1992. The focus of the Arts Centre is the main auditorium, still very much an Opera House with radiused rows of seating at the rear of the stalls and, presumably, a gallery above, with vestiges of the horseshoe arrangement (North at foot)

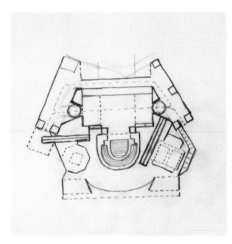

Fig. 2.14 Another sketch plan, with what seems like a route around the building indicated by a broken red line, and long, carefully placed ramps connecting the various foyer levels and energizing the plan (North at foot)

Fig. 2.13 is a soft pencil sketch, possibly in Stirling's hand, arranging the main auditorium north-south, with what are clearly important ramps (a typical Stirling device which is found in many of these early drawings) carefully placed within the plan.[33] Here we see perhaps the noble Salford dockworker, arms flailing, recalling Le Corbusier's depiction of his Stakhanovite counterpart in the plan of the Centrosoyus building, Moscow, in 1929. Stirling shows a stepped surface leading out into the nose of the Quay. The scale is truly heroic. Fig. 2.14 seems to flesh out this plan, although it is perhaps simply taken at a higher level. Galleries are developing and a complete circumferential promenade is apparently indicated by broken red lines. The Chief Executive of the City Council emphasized the potential of this route:

> The other big development I was passionate about in The Lowry, whatever design re-engineering we had, was that I wanted the audience or visitor to be able to walk all the way round the building, inside, to get spectacular views. And so throughout, I fought really hard so that people can [take that] walk.[34]

This demanded that the spaces be linked and traversed 'en-serie', a thoroughly un-modern arrangement.

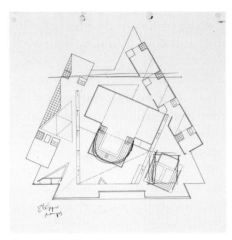

Fig. 2.15 Hardline layout, spring 1992, with pencil amendment by Stirling changing the squared-off auditorium into one with a radiused rear wall and testing the location of the smaller performance space (North at foot)

A series of 'hardline' drawings also explores the internal layout. In what must be the first of this sequence, a square main auditorium and a square studio theatre/rehearsal room are both oriented on the diagonal axis. There are car parking spaces within the eastern side of the building. Wilford was surprised to see this proposal fifteen years later; he may not have seen it at the time. A second drawing shows the upper, gallery level of this proposal (fig. 2.15). Here, however, it appears that Stirling has overdrawn a horseshoe-shaped auditorium in pencil and reoriented the smaller performance space north-south, aligning its rear wall parallel with the main front. The next drawing in the sequence works up the curved auditorium but retains the diagonal orientation of the second theatre; indeed, in a further proposal, it is turned to the opposite diagonal, while some indication of dressing rooms and workshops is also now given. A further trio of drawings show three levels of a scheme that places the main auditorium on axis with the main front. They keep the second performance space on the diagonal. The way that these drawings show Stirling rejecting a square-edged auditorium in favour of the curved arrangement shown in figs. 2.13 and 2.14 suggests that they may predate those two sketches. Perhaps, after one of the internal reviews which took place in March 1992 or the 1 April presentation in Salford (for which a formal hardline drawing would have been entirely appropriate), Stirling sought to move away from the square scheme. Did he add the curve during a meeting or review? Equally, however, the absence of dates on the hardline drawings means that the scheme shown in fig. 2.15 may in fact be a development of the sketched figs. 2.13 and 2.14, demonstrating a move to a square auditorium which was ultimately rejected in favour of the curved scheme.

Wilford's diary shows that the pace now quickened, with meetings on consecutive days in April and May. A third presentation in Salford took place on 19 May. There was a major in-house review on 24 May and further discussions on 2, 3, 19 and 22 June. Fig. 2.16 shows a scheme of June 1992

which was subsequently published in the second volume of the practice's complete works, covering 1975-1992.[35] It is clearly related to both Stirling and Wilford's sketches. The opera house is on axis with the main front. Its auditorium is semicircular with a broad gallery; the stage has two wings. There are two rehearsal rooms, a square studio theatre, a hexagonal tower, two stepped wings, somewhat less emphatic and engaged with the main auditorium form, flanked by prodigious 'technical' space, undoubtedly destined for a major resident company. Beyond the end of the building, set on the tip of the pier, is an external amphitheatre, a real attempt to celebrate the sense of place by allowing the quays to form the backdrop for productions. It is difficult to imagine how such a sprawling plan could be elevated into a coherent silhouette but fig. 2.17, showing elevations, indicates a rather literal nautical theme, with funnels and 'porthole' windows combined with banded stone-faced walls – all familiar Stirling/Wilford tropes. An axonometric of a slightly later version of the same proposal reveals more of the scheme, and further typical Stirling devices including a zig-zag screen wall between the main Lowry and the external amphitheatre. Some elements of the design proposed at this stage survive in the built structure: the canted bays of the east elevation which faces the present Imperial War Museum North, for example.

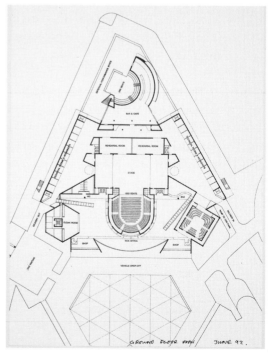

Fig. 2.16 The Lowry, layout as at June 1992, with 1200-seat main performance space, square studio theatre, and external amphitheatre in the nose of the pier (North at foot)

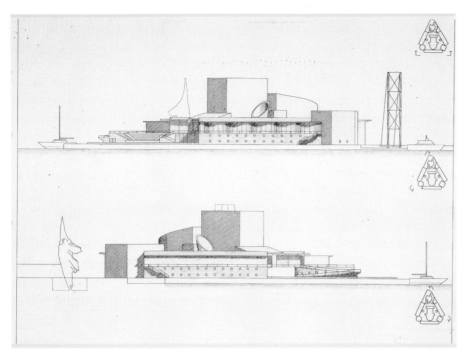

Fig. 2.17 External elevations, June 1992, with familiar Stirling/Wilford elements including banded stonework and porthole windows

the triangle, has received a great deal of attention. Very interestingly, on 9 June 1994, the architects inserted a drawing of Frank Matcham's London Coliseum into a cross section of the Lowry (fig. 2.19), as if to confirm the concept, or perhaps thoroughly to debunk it. The drawing may have been an attempt to demonstrate the scale of the proposed new theatre to English National Opera, based at the Coliseum. It is not clear why it was produced and Wilford believes that he never saw this drawing at the time. Interestingly the relative scales of the old and new are not dissimilar.

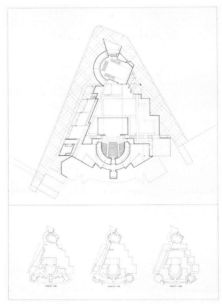

Fig. 2.18 June 1994, and the external performance space has moved indoors

On 26 June 1992, Stirling died suddenly, having suffered complications during a routine hospital procedure. Despite this catastrophe, the fourth and final 'Presentation of the Masterplan and Preliminary Design' went ahead on 14 July. Wilford records that the scheme then lay dormant for a year as its proposed content was tested and proved, or improved, by specialist consultants and as the opera house idea finally slid through the clients' fingers. By 1994, design work had resumed in earnest, as the outcome of the various discussions with practitioners and funders began to inform the developing proposition. Fig. 2.18 shows a plan of 25 May 1994, credited to a practice now called Michael Wilford and Partners. The main auditorium has become semicircular, and the square studio originally located on the diagonal adjacent to the main auditorium has now disappeared. The external amphitheatre has moved indoors to become a small theatre, within a curved envelope that retains clear overtones of the external amphitheatre had been proposed in 1992. Exhibition areas for the visual arts are developed as long thin saloons and the form of the Lowry's huge public frontage, the wide end of

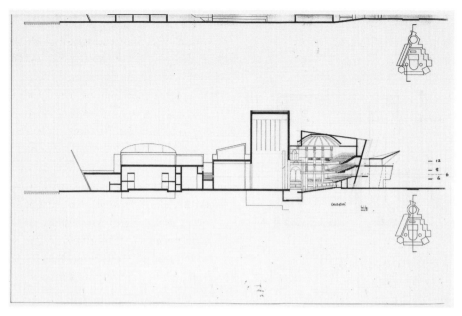

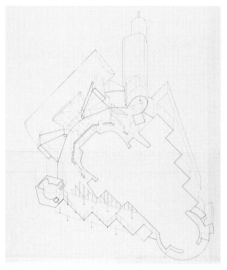

Fig. 2.19 *Frank Matcham's London Coliseum inserted within The Lowry, 1994 – an attempt to show its scale to possible clients?*

Fig. 2.21 *A 'worm's-eye view', characteristic of the Stirling/Wilford practice, showing the huge canopy and the administration tower*

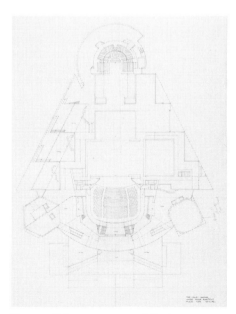

Fig. 2.20 *February 1995, and the two auditoria are lined up*

By 20 February 1995, it is clear from fig. 2.20 that the essential plan of the built version of the Lowry had been established. Both auditoria are arranged in line, like a great engine, and the design of the huge canopy has been evolved, it would appear, in homage to that of Le Corbusier's Capitol building at Chandigarh (see fig. 2.1). One of the practice's characteristic Choisy-derived worm's-eye views dwells on the promenade around the auditoria and backstage, which are both shown completely blank (fig 2.21). The galleries are not described in detail, but we know they were the particular object of much external audit and intervention.

Thus far, then, we have seen that Stirling and Wilford began with consideration of place: how The Lowry would generate and contribute to an urban experience, a key question given the *tabula rasa* presented by the site, its industrial history, and the concern with regeneration. The design development was strongly geometric, with public spaces, the building as a whole, and its constituent elements all being conceived as related three-dimensional volumes that would come together to create a composed whole with a strongly nautical flavour. One sketch (fig. 2.22) is particularly interesting, as it compiles in deconstructed fashion the constituent pieces that might make the plan: curved segments, hexagonal towers, and triangular elements. This geometrical approach was of course never entirely divorced from questions of function. But it did present certain challenges, not least as the detailed brief for The Lowry was gradually developed after the arrival of Stephen Hetherington.

Fig. 2.22 A deconstructed Lowry: the 'shapes' used in the design

During 1993 and 1994, specialist consultants were appointed to work alongside the architects to develop the functionality of the emerging brief. The theatres were developed as performance spaces after the appointment of theatre consultants in the late autumn of 1993. The consultants recall they were presented with a semi-circular main auditorium. David Staples of Theatre Projects later reflected:

> *They didn't have a lot of auditorium experience ... Jim and Michael both believed in very pure form, and they wanted it to be circular, or part of a circle. Not a good scheme, you can't apply that sort of purity to theatre building and get it to work.*[36]

Staples went on:

> *The team in Michael Wilford's office subsequently referred to themselves as the "taxidermy department" – they were trying to stuff an arts centre into a great Jim Stirling exterior.*[37]

Both the theatres and the galleries were revisited on a number of occasions in this period. In part, this process formed a response to specialist input:

> *The galleries were redesigned three or four times, a difficult process. At certain times I had to go back to Michael and say, "we are not doing this." Each time he drew breath, he got his rubber out, and we started again. He was just wonderful ... There was one occasion before the design concept [was finalized.] I had spent a day with the Tate and National Gallery for their views on the design. Their words were, "not good enough", so I had to go to Michael again and [ask him to take another look at the design], but he*

Fig. 2.23 The Lyric Theatre, 2010

did … Of course that is all before the design was costed. That's where the effort has to be directed, before you get back to the point of saying "that's it now, we are going to build this." Once you have done that, it really is it.[38]

But it was not simply a question of refining the design. The brief, too, was volatile. Staples and his colleagues, Louis Fleming and Iain Mackintosh, set about reviewing the main performance space (fig. 2.23). Then, once the principle of a new lyric theatre had been established as a working proposition there was enormous debate about its size. The proposition was for 1200 seats. However, the Theatre Projects team was developing a more directed strategy:

[1200 seats] we felt to be too small, because Manchester has the Opera House and the Palace, which are over 2000 seats and Salford is only a mile and a half from those theatres. How would a new centre in Salford compete with those theatres? … How would a smaller theatre compete and be able to get shows? … [However] the Palace and Opera House were old Victorian theatres, [with] lots of seats which weren't very good. And we could design in Salford a theatre with fewer seats which would achieve a higher box office capacity. So a group like Opera North, who had previously gone to the Palace and Opera House, could go to a smaller theatre in Salford and take away more money after a week's run than they could by going to the Opera House.[39]

The second auditorium was transformed, as we have seen, from the outdoor amphitheatre of the first designs (a somewhat optimistic proposition in the wet Salford climate) so that it became a full-scale indoor theatre (fig. 2.24). In parallel, the North American arts consultants Lord Cultural Resources were appointed to cut through the confusing messages and programme the visual arts content (fig. 2.25).

Fig. 2.24 The Quays Theatre: the external amphitheatre concept transformed into a galleried indoor theatre

Fig. 2.25 The art galleries, a promenade around the theatre auditoria

With all this specialist input, The Lowry might easily seem like an example of 'design by committee'. Indeed, the influence of Theatre Projects on the auditoria is especially evident, with similarities to certain other venues on which the consultancy has worked. However, the results are on the whole convincing and coherent. And, for Wilford, the collaboration was generally productive and balanced:

The front of the first tier is the closest to the main stage of any theatre in the UK with a capacity of this size, 1750 seats. This [was achieved by] working with [Theatre Projects] to really pull the balcony as far forward as possible [without] compromising sightlines from the rear of the stalls. This was a vigorous, partnership, ... constructive conflict. We were at each other's throats a lot of the time, but out of that process came something very rich. The dialogue was equal because we would always challenge them to explain and justify their prejudice before taking [anything] on board.[40]

THE CAST I: THE AUDIENCES

There was no existing audience to interrogate, which, as we have discovered, some of the project participants, 'the Cast', thought was a clear advantage. There was, however, a voluble local electorate with strong views on the prioritizing of public funds. The Architect introduced himself to this constituency, but with a clear preconception of exactly what they might contribute. In an exchange with Professor Pat Sterry, a specialist in audience and visitor representation, Wilford discussed the process; the text in square brackets was added later by Wilford when reading the interview transcript:

Wilford: The one [consultation event was in a Banqueting suite] opposite City Hall, ... where they [provided dinner] ... it was open ... it was quite amazing. There was real, true public participation. But I'm a strong believer [that] you participate with the public after everyone [on the project team] has crystallized their ides and you present that crystallized concept to the public. You don't invite the public to contribute to the development of the concept ... I am a strong believer that [the latter] is a recipe for disaster.
Sterry: So you drive the vision?

Wilford: Yes, sell the vision.
Sterry: And they don't impact on the vision?
Wilford, Yes, [they do, through their comments,] but not fundamentally.[41]

Stephen Hetherington also thought that a wholly democratized envisioning process would ultimately be unworkable. Commenting on what might usefully be done with the outputs of a consultation exercise, he explained:

You take all this stuff, share it, and there is a lot of dialogue... I then have to go back to my desk and say, "does anything that we are intending to develop alter this base plan? Because [if it does,] I have to alter my arithmetic." If that [financial plan] gets worse, I [have to] find some other way to make it better. [All the changes have] to channel back ... At that point you have to make a decision in a closed room with a very small number of people ... you can't make that decision by consultation; you have to make that decision on your own.[42]

Hetherington was insistent on maintaining the integrity of the Business Plan and fearful of exposing it to contamination by a well-intentioned wish-list of propositions conjured up in a meeting hall. He continued:

You can consult as much as you like about all kinds of things that may happen, but the truth is that it's mostly a public relations proposition. It is not intended to [fundamentally] change what you are actually doing if you've got it right in the first place [and if the business proposition has been agreed] ... I fully understand why there is need for consultation, but just a blanket "we will consult!" is bonkers.[43]

He captured the great conundrum facing all those trying to manage and deliver a viable, coherent capital arts project:

If you give in and say, "yes, we will do it," and you know you are knowingly weakening the proposition you are about to fulfil ... why would you do that?[44]

THE CAST II: THE FUNDERS

The Lowry was one of the first major projects to make a big Lottery bid. Felicity Goodey later suspected the Lottery leaders were *'making up the rules as they went along'*.[45] Indeed, a recurring theme in the chapters of this book will be the way that external pressures, not least from the National Audit Office, ultimately obliged the Arts Council Lottery to adjust its practices for later capital projects. Goodey recalled the anxious speculation as to which Lottery body the project should approach. Eventually three Lottery bodies decided to break their rules and co-fund the project.[46] The Leader of the City Council, John Willis, explained:

One of the things we learnt was that the Arts Council didn't fund dead artists. That was Heritage. So we [split] the site up and [said], "the two theatres will go for Arts Council Support, the Galleries will go for Heritage, because that's painting and it's a dead painter, the commercial areas [will go to the] Millennium [Fund]." So there was a constant tension, "does that fit there, or does that fit here?"[47]

It was a tenuous proposition and one which was unprecedented. The Arts Council Capital Project Officer recalls that the Millennium Fund initially refused to fund more than 50% of the project, but that in an extraordinary and not wholly predictable development, Lord Gowrie, the then Chair of Arts Council England, intervened and expressed an interest in the two proposed theatres. This sparked Millennium Fund interest in the proposition, and the Heritage Lottery Fund then also volunteered itself as a co-funder for the appropriate parts of the project.

The funding award was announced on 22 February 1996, but the euphoria was relatively short lived as the extreme complexity of satisfying the three principal funders unfolded. Soon there were additional funding issues to consider. Goodey remembered sinister exchanges:

Before the building had been designed in any detail, we naturally had to put a package together. There were two problems that arose fairly rapidly thereafter. One was that we had a set budget, and the public funding bodies are quite rigid in sticking to that. There is no room for you to go back and say, "well actually, now that we have started to design in details we find x, y and z, we need to flex the budget." [They would reply,] "No, that's your budget, that's it."

The principal funders then took a somewhat brutal stance with respect to their on-going involvement in the project. There wasn't to be any:

Worse than that, when we bid for that original budget, we had assumed that that was purely the capital budget. We assumed wrongly that we would then go back and talk about the revenue budget, because there has to be a revenue budget in the start-up phase. Here we were, a private charitable trust with no resource, and to build a building like this and get it up and operational while you're building the business, you clearly have to have funding. You can't do that on nothing. To our horror, the lottery fund just turned round and said, "oh no, that's it. Not a penny more. Oh, by the way, you do everything at your own risk." And that was a serious challenge.[48]

Setting the budget for perpetuity on a concept design has been a recurring phenomenon in Arts Capital Projects, and will be a recurring theme in this book. We have discussed the practical consequences of the problem in a paper published in 2007,[49] and in our guidance for capital arts clients,

'Building Excellence in the Arts' (2009), commissioned by Arts Council England and the Commission for Architecture and the Built Environment.[50] This is a fundamental issue deriving, we believe, in part from the archaic but ubiquitous Royal Institute of British Architects 'Plan of Work' and its accompanying risk management model. The 'Plan of Work' implies that projects should develop to an ever-greater degree of design (and thus cost) certainty. However, as we will see in this and subsequent chapters, the issue with projects in the arts tends to be that early studies (in some cases produced by a different architect from the eventual scheme) generate a financial trajectory which then becomes inviolate, even as the design evolves, for example on the appointment of specialist consultants and the operational implications of the initial concept become clear. Indeed, Goodey revealed that the Business Plan which had been produced as the Bid was being assembled was effectively dismantled by the denial of revenue support.

Stephen Hetherington recalled that the continuous scrutiny of the funding bodies was wearing:

Monitoring is hugely expensive. It costs millions just to be able to comply with the contracts. Then you get, for example, the Arts Council choosing not to attend monitoring committees, [meaning that a whole set of] information ... has to be produced by the professional team. You run into thousands of pounds every meeting, tens of thousands sometimes. To get a series of financial reports into a different format [for the funder] may take a consultant firm a day and a half, they may be charging £1500 a day ... one item on an agenda could easily be £10,000. The way in which the funders behave [affects] the budgets. [The funder] is sometimes incredibly supportive and sometimes very destructive.[51]

Goodey observed that the public sector process managed the £100 million plus, *'as if it was their own money'*.[52] She echoed Hetherington's view that the process was simply too

onerous. Not only that, it was periodically counterproductive, exhausting resources rather than contributing to them. The Leader of the Council was regularly challenged to match funders' contributions. Salford is not a rich authority, and the resources it was committing were already under debate locally. But the pressure didn't stop. John Willis recalls several months of challenges from the funding bodies to deliver more cash. The allocation of monies to the different elements of the building became controversial particularly in areas which could be deemed to have multiple uses. Willis recalls constant anxiety that there would be a shortfall in funds, for which the City Council would be directly liable.

The Trust's own Project Director, Steve Thorncroft, recalled another crippling development. There were no allowances for finance charges in the application and none in the award, nor any indication that they would have been funded if they had in fact been included. Quite simply, the grant funding didn't arrive in time to pay the bills arising from £110 million of project expenditure. Interest charges alone were reported as being of the order of an unanticipated £2.5 million. Funds were also inadequate, Thorncroft believed, for setting up the organization to run the project in the early stages, the so-called 'common costs' in the project budget. We have seen that the Architects conceived the scheme with little or no specialist input from acousticians or theatre consultants, technical or otherwise or any other design professionals. The relentless slow dance of the RIBA's 'Plan of Work' is the unintended template for the cash starving of projects in the critical early stages.

THE CAST III: THE PROLIFERATING PROFESSIONAL TEAM

Whilst the architect generated the concept plan largely unaided, waves of new consultants and sub-consultants were required as soon as each tranche of funding was in place, a development which was bewildering to the City Council and the new Lowry Trust. The client invited external peer review of consultants' proposals:

We didn't rely in any instance wholly on consultants. We tested everything from the theatre design through to the gallery design through to the bars and cafés. We tested it on professional operators and we were very rigorous in that. We brought in professionals at every stage too, and often informally we simply invited people to come in and talk to us, to have a look round and look at the plans, before it was built or while it was being built. We visited a number of theatres ourselves, we talked to theatres around this country. Michael Wilford visited theatres all over the world.[53]

However, whilst the size of the two theatres was the subject of much debate, there is little evidence of significant adjustments to the plan as a result of this process.

The consulting specialists appeared to the client to be the cause of yet more bills:

There was a core team ... but then there were consultants here, there were consultants there. You know, if you ever wanted to do an exercise as to how much consultants cost on these projects and how many times you were required to ask the consultants to re-check that something had been done, that would be quite an eye-opener.[54]

Within this hugely extended family, tensions inevitably developed. Goodey described the employer's predicament:

Now, if things start to go wrong in a big project like this, everybody starts blaming each other. And the client's problem is, who do I believe?[55]

To manage the process, Steve Thorncroft was appointed as client representative in late 1997. Upon his arrival, Thorncroft found that the contractor had been chosen and that a 'management contracting' model for managing the delivery of the building had been formally adopted, the implications of which we will examine shortly. His appointment was inspired and very necessary, on top of the appointment of a major national project management practice. Thorncroft recalled that he joined:

... a very small client team at that time, which was principally arts based and did not have anyone [with] a property or construction background. There were a couple of people who had been seconded from Salford City Council, one was an engineer, one was a quantity surveyor and one was a planner. So we had some professional expertise within the client team, but they would be the first to admit themselves that they were from a local authority background. This was all completely new to them. They had never been involved in a project of this scale and magnitude, complexity and use.[56]

He found many of the principal consultant appointments also in place:

When I joined, the professional consultants were all on board and so the expertise was there. The management contractor was also on board. I think [that one] of the reasons that the need was identified for someone of my background to join was that the client was increasingly being faced with issues that it didn't have the expertise to deal with, and the construction team and the consultants were equally finding it a bit frustrating that they didn't have anyone to talk to who ... understood the questions that they were asking them and perhaps what needed to be done.[57]

Goodey later recalled the value which she felt Thorncroft was able to bring to the project:

You've got a huge number of different practices [and] professions that you're dealing with. Having our own in-house project director, a senior person, highly experienced, enabled us to deal with all of those different practices and weld them together to lead them as a team.[58]

ENGINEERING VALUE AT STAGE D, DESIGNING THE LOWRY IN EARNEST

The Architect summarized the actual status of the scheme at the conclusion of the Lottery Bid exercise, regardless of the generic content of Workstage D:

The building was visually designed, [although] I don't think it was structurally designed. I don't think the systems were done. I think the QS made allowances for these aspects of the project and I guess Theatre Projects made allowances for all the theatre equipment [and] the fitting out of the theatres, but it was done on a budget basis and not as a result of any detailed design, because ... Salford couldn't afford to take the project to [that stage] ... [without assurances that funding would be guaranteed]. It's the same old dilemma, they couldn't afford to take the project to the stage where it could be sufficiently developed to be sure about the budget, but what the funding bodies want is a [firm] budget and so the QS produced a budget, based on area calculations, rates per square metre, [and allowances for special aspects].[59]

Wilford's comment simply exposes the enduring conundrum in the history of Arts Capital Projects in the UK, the drive to declare a fixed budget prematurely as a requirement to secure the public funding needed to continue work, yet on the basis of a design for which there has been little opportunity to secure and fund expert input. This issue is then coupled to the funders' aversion to contingencies, i.e., unassigned sums of money to cover the unexpected.

The timeline (fig. 2.26) summarizes the attempts to hold costs close to £50 million, then £60 million, through the second half of 1995 and the early part of 1996. The Client's Construction Project Director, Thorncroft, later rehearsed a familiar turn of events in capital projects:

During the design process for a hugely complicated building, the QS produces the cost plan, to a design and a specification. [As the] design develops three months along the line, six months along the line, he re-costs the scheme against his cost plan. [In the case of The Lowry,] I think the very first time that happened, the budget was something like five, six, seven million pounds over budget. Why was it six million pounds over budget? Well, I don't think anything had particularly changed; the design had developed and there were more details there. The QS was more able to cost more accurately what it was in this massively complicated building that needed to be done. So, quite early in the process, there was a value engineering exercise to find six million pounds.[60]

Even for a project of this size, £6 million is a very significant sum to have to excise, equivalent to between two and three thousand square metres of floor area. There are anecdotal reports that a whole floor was removed from the scheme. Goodey was exasperated by the subsequent 'Value Engineering' process:

Because, again, of the inflexibility of the public sector funding bodies or their inability to be flexible, we ended up taking out of the building at that stage things which we [were] forced to put back into the building later on. Which is a silly waste of time and money. For example, in order to get back down to that original budget, we were forced to take out the lift in the pit. Which meant that from an operational point of view ... we

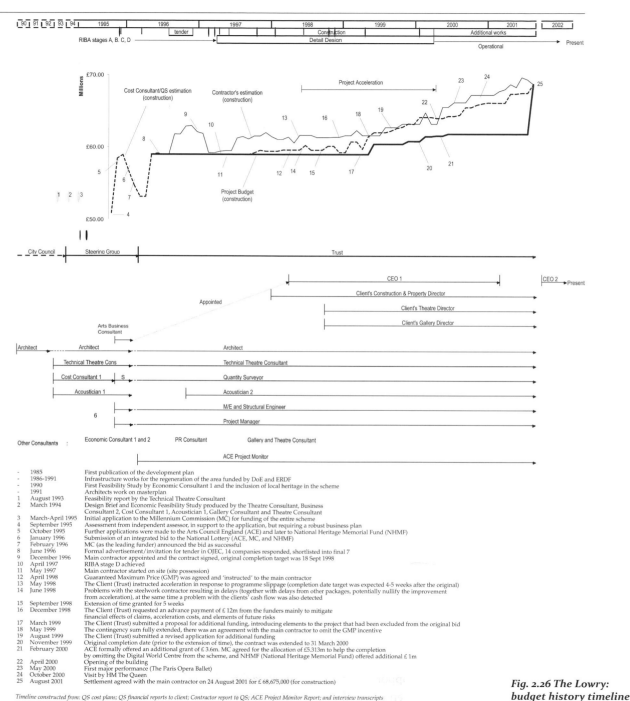

Fig. 2.26 The Lowry:
budget history timeline

-	1985	First publication of the development plan
-	1986-1991	Infrastructure works for the regeneration of the area funded by DoE and ERDF
-	1990	First Feasibility Study by Economic Consultant 1 and the inclusion of local heritage in the scheme
-	1991	Architects work on masterplan
1	August 1993	Feasibility report by the Technical Theatre Consultant
2	March 1994	Design Brief and Economic Feasibility Study produced by the Theatre Consultant, Business Consultant 2, Cost Consultant 1, Acoustician 1, Gallery Consultant and Theatre Consultant
3	March-April 1995	Initial application to the Millennium Commission (MC) for funding of the entire scheme
4	September 1995	Assessment from independent assessor, in support to the application, but requiring a robust business plan
5	October 1995	Further applications were made to the Arts Council England (ACE) and later to National Heritage Memorial Fund (NHMF)
6	January 1996	Submission of an integrated bid to the National Lottery (ACE, MC, and NHMF)
7	February 1996	MC (as the leading funder) announced the bid as successful
8	June 1996	Formal advertisement/invitation for tender in OJEC, 14 companies responded, shortlisted into final 7
9	December 1996	Main contractor appointed and the contract signed, original completion target was 18 Sept 1998
10	April 1997	RIBA stage D achieved
11	May 1997	Main contractor started on site (site possession)
12	April 1998	Guaranteed Maximum Price (GMP) was agreed and 'instructed' to the main contractor
13	May 1998	The Client (Trust) instructed acceleration in response to programme slippage (completion date target was expected 4-5 weeks after the original)
14	June 1998	Problems with the steelwork contractor resulting in delays (together with delays from other packages, potentially nullify the improvement from acceleration), at the same time a problem with the clients' cash flow was also detected
15	September 1998	Extension of time granted for 5 weeks
16	December 1998	The Client (Trust) requested an advance payment of £12m from the funders mainly to mitigate financial effects of claims, acceleration costs, and elements of future risks
17	March 1999	The Client (Trust) submitted a proposal for additional funding, introducing elements to the project that had been excluded from the original bid
18	May 1999	The contingency sum fully extended, there was an agreement with the main contractor to omit the GMP incentive
19	August 1999	The Client (Trust) submitted a revised application for additional funding
20	November 1999	Original completion date (prior to the extension of time), the contract was extended to 31 March 2000
21	February 2000	ACE formally offered an additional grant of £3.6m. MC agreed for the allocation of £5.313m to help the completion by omitting the Digital World Centre from the scheme, and NHMF (National Heritage Memorial Fund) offered additional £1m
22	April 2000	Opening of the building
23	May 2000	First major performance (The Paris Opera Ballet)
24	October 2000	Visit by HM The Queen
25	August 2001	Settlement agreed with the main contractor on 24 August 2001 for £68,675,000 (for construction)

Timeline constructed from: QS cost plans; QS financial reports to client; Contractor report to QS; ACE Project Monitor Report; and interview transcripts

*have a three stage pit ... every time we needed to alter
[the stage setting], instead of doing it mechanically as
we'd intended, we'd have to do it manually. That has
a cost, a major, major cost. Now that has since been
rectified but it's a foolish way of ... building a building.
[You're forced] into a situation where you have to
knowingly take out elements which at a later date
impact on the commercial viability of that building.*[61]

Goodey praised the architect warmly for his ingenuity in
re-engineering the design, but not without cost:

*The interesting thing about the value engineering
exercise is that it was Michael Wilford, as often as
not, who solved much of our problems by designing
solutions. For example, we removed our second rehearsal
room. We didn't want to, but we removed our second
rehearsal room because that enabled us to take a
huge amount of steelwork out of the building, which
was very expensive and made a huge contribution to
getting back down to budget. That was a shame ... we
could have done with that second rehearsal room, and
again, you see that had a long-term impact on our
operations. And again, we've actually now moved to
create ourselves a second rehearsal space. We knew
at the time we didn't want to do it, but because of
the inflexibility of the budget we were forced to.*[62]

The Funders, certainly the Arts Council Officers, were not
pleased at this omission:

*The Lowry was conceived on the basis that it would have
a resident company and the resident company would
have assisted and been part of that sort of process. But
that was never going to happen, it was too early on in the
design process and, once we lost the rehearsal space as
part of the value engineering, we lost the ability to have*

*a resident organization. We didn't have an organization
that was familiar with theatre to assist the design brief.*[63]

The leader of the City Council recalled the time delay in the
project before 'costs started to worry ... and then it never goes
away for the rest of the project. And it was tough'.[64] This was
not a happy experience. The City was wholly implicated in the
cost over-runs. Goodey explained that the City bankrolled
the Trust and the project. She commended the client's bank
for their solid support, and the constant availability of a line
of credit.

Hetherington, later to become the CEO, is wary of the
industry-standard value engineering process:

*If you appear to be going over budget, the funders will
say, "take something out, cut something back." But at
a certain point in the project, in order to do that, you
have to engage the professional team in two exercises:
one is cutting and the other is remaking the building
with that bit missing. Those two exercises can cost more
than the saving in bricks and mortar you have taken out,
so the net saving is a net cost. The commercial sector
is well accustomed [to this and so] will make as few
as possible variations. It is a curse of all these [public]
projects and one that the Lowry Trust was brilliant and
consistently solid about not making variations ... But
[the loss of the rehearsal room] was forced on us by the
[funders] and ... cost us more than the saving. And it
took out a valuable part of the building in the process.*[65]

For all the sophisticated construction management theory
supporting the concept of managing value, engineering
value or re-engineering it, Hetherington remained wholly
sceptical about his own particular experience of this science:

*You use the expression "Value Engineering." It's a
euphemism for cutting costs. It is the actual process
of [reducing] cost without reducing function. You*

can call it what you like, [but] you sit down in a room to cut costs. I object to the expression "VE" because it [implies] that you can increase value. You can't. There are examples where you can cut and it can improve things, but these are very rare.[66]

The imposition of construction management methodology onto this process, which started very 'traditionally', as we have seen, with a master architect at work entirely on his own, introduced an additional dimension, the delayed revelation of actual cost.

CONSTRUCTING THE LOWRY

That's what construction management's all about ... you're designing and developing your scheme whilst it's being built.[67]

What I'm sure of is that [having to] let a contract by a certain date [simply] to meet a grant funding requirement is not the way you should take decisions on procurement of a £60 million construction contract. But that was decided, so we got on with it.[68]

A relatively small but critical European Regional Development Fund grant required a rapid start to construction. The cost consultants prescribed a contract management path for the construction, a process requiring the disentangling of the work into coherent 'packages' relating to specific trades. Bovis won the tender, specializing in delivering through this contractual mechanism. Theoretically, this approach enables the design stage to be embedded within the construction, saving time. However, the first package, comprising the concrete substructure, was returned significantly above budget. Delays in receiving Lottery funds stage by stage incurred finance charges. The clock was ticking. The process was clearly extremely stressful. The competing funders seemed to be jealous over which pieces of construction their grants appeared to be funding.

Value Engineering was constant. The facilities for a potential resident company were, as we have seen, finally excised in their entirety. The Lowry became a receiving house by default. In effect, the project was £6-7 million underfunded on a £59 million construction budget. The timeline (fig. 2.26) shows intense efforts through the end of 1996 to staunch five to six million pounds of anticipated over spend. The contract with Bovis was signed in December of that year, the contractor clearly assisting in the cost cutting process so that, by early February 1997, the cost was reported as hitting the budget of £59 million for the first and only time. Stage D was signed off in April 1997, the site being 'possessed' by Bovis the following month.

Management contracting is common enough elsewhere in the world, particularly in the United States, but commencement of construction at this early design stage is probably less common. To compound the situation, the opening date was fixed and announced. After all, The Lowry had become a Millennium Project. The whole of the construction cost allowance was premised on 'Provisional Sums', cost allowances for packages of work, to be expended as the construction proceeded. In effect, every issue of design information became a 'Variation Order', because there was little or no detailed design at the time of signing the Contract. The first stages, the piling and the retaining structures, came in over-budget. The timeline shows project out-turn costs rising within the first four months of construction through mid 1997 back to the original figure which prompted the first Value Engineering exercises.

The timeline indicates the commencement of 'Acceleration' payments made to expedite completion. More funds were found in early 1999 but the cost consequences of accelerating the works took some time to trickle through. The Capital Projects Officer at the Arts Council explains this Faustian deal, struck to save Millennial face:

They weren't going to defer or move that opening night: the show must go on. This is The Lowry. And that's where the problem started ... The Trust decided to accelerate the works and, if you accelerate the works ... you can't judge how much that's going to cost you until you actually finish. Salford City Council was paying the bills. So they never knew exactly how much they were paying or what they were paying for, other than their monitoring processes. So you can see what happened. You can deliver to practical completion, right, which was in budget and not actually know how much it cost you.[69]

The timeline shows cost escalating relentlessly. Detailed Design continued until completion. The acceleration strategy was decided upon against the contractor's claims for an Extension of Time, thought to be of the order of a calendar year. There is general agreement that, as one might predict, the final work packages absorbed part of the deficit. The finishes were a disappointment. There was an extensive snagging list. The timeline shows continuing post-completion investment to reinstitute the omitted works and re-engineer parts of the building to recover lost functionality. The Project Champion remains wholly exasperated by this process.

RUNNING THE LOWRY

Making buildings that are cheap to run is expensive in the early stages. The way in which ... you are forced to set budgets because of the funding process ... inevitably means that you end up taking much of that out. To my mind that's wrong and it's false economy. So that would be a major criticism I have. I would have liked us ... to have been able to install more which would have long term minimized running costs and maintenance costs. Big missed opportunity there.[70]

The Arts Council reported that, even operating at full capacity, on opening The Lowry was set to cost £1.2 million a year. An Arts Capital Project should be setting money aside to grow, change and develop as the ACE project officer observed:

That's how it works and you've got to keep on developing the project, you know. The Lowry can't stay the same, because as your audience changes, or as your audience develops, their needs become different, your clientele become different. You have to upgrade things, you've got to change things, your collection must change. All of this, the whole thing must keep on moving.[71]

Fig. 2.27 Looking towards the Lyric stage, with technical areas beyond

Fig. 2.28 Stage and auditorium in the Lyric Theatre

Ten years on, the auditoria (figs. 2.27 and 2.28) and galleries present a range of shows and exhibitions; the foyers are a busy meeting place (figs. 2.29-2.31). Although the design of the building has not been universally praised,[72] when measured against its original objectives, the project must be deemed a success. The Lowry has made a significant contribution to the regeneration of the Quays. Although the rest of the Stirling/Wilford masterplan was ultimately abandoned, with the site opposite The Lowry being principally used for a commercial shopping centre, the mall and the nearby Imperial War Museum North have both added to the centre of gravity that had been established by The Lowry, generating a steady stream of visitors throughout the day. No doubt the recent arrival of the BBC on the opposite quayside will only add to The Lowry's 'regulars' (fig. 2.32).

Fig. 2.29 The café bar in the foyer

Fig. 2.30 Staircases thread their way through the foyers

Fig. 2.31 The eastern foyer, with the promenade leading through the restaurant

Fig. 2.32 The western side of The Lowry: the theatre 'get-in'

which 'owns' the project) towards the invention of a memorable exterior form, design from the outside in. Theatre design is difficult. The blank volumes of auditorium and stage require soft, peripheral activity to make a vibrant and porous carapace. The Lowry arrived through the making of a vast public matrix of future development and infrastructure. The key sketches show the 'cells' of the auditoria and their backstage rooms floating in the stiff architectural jelly, such that the essential nature of the auditoria could change profoundly once an apparent need could be 'cooked up'.

The need to start construction rapidly to secure a relatively small grant, the adoption of an open-ended contractual form to deliver a design still in its very early stages and the fixing of a date for a grand public opening constitute the ingredients of a particularly toxic cocktail imposed by others. Relaxing any one of the constraints would probably have eased a very fraught process beyond measure. In such circumstances, the finished building (fig. 2.33) must be seen as a remarkable achievement.

Fig. 2.33 The canopy: a reference to Le Corbusier's Capitol at Chandigarh in Salford?

CONCLUSIONS

Implicit in the idea of using iconic capital projects to drive economic and social regeneration is the inversion of the 'normal' process a design from the inside out (by which the design for a new arts building is developed out of the needs, aspiration and working practices of an arts organization

Notes

1   John Willis to Monty Sutrisna and Pat Sterry, 15 March 2005.
2   Dennis Bate to Monty Sutrisna, April 2006.
3   Jeremy Myerson, *Making the Lowry* (Salford, 2000).
4   Felicity Goodey to Zeynep Toker, 14 April 2005.
5   Felicity Goodey to Zeynep Toker, 14 April 2005.
6   Felicity Goodey to Zeynep Toker, 14 April 2005.
7   David Staples to Alan Short and Alistair Fair, December 2007.
8   David Staples to Alan Short and Alistair Fair, December 2007.
9   David Staples to Alan Short and Alistair Fair, December 2007.
10 Stephen Hetherington to Pat Sterry and Monty Sutrisna, 25 April 2005.
11 David Staples to Alan Short and Alistair Fair, December 2007.
12 David Staples & Louis Fleming to Anne Dye, February 2006.
13 Felicity Goodey to Zeynep Toker, 14 April 2005.
14 Stephen Hetherington to Pat Sterry and Monty Sutrisna, 25 April 2005.
15 Stephen Hetherington to Pat Sterry and Monty Sutrisna, 25 April 2005.

16 Stephen Hetherington to Pat Sterry and Monty Sutrisna, 25 April 2005.

17 Stephen Hetherington to Pat Sterry and Monty Sutrisna, 25 April 2005.

18 Stephen Hetherington to Pat Sterry and Monty Sutrisna, 25 April 2005.

19 Desmond Patrick to Anne Dye and Monty Sutrisna, 12 September 2005.

20 David Staples and Louis Fleming to Anne Dye, February 2006.

21 David Staples and Louis Fleming to Anne Dye, February 2006.

22 David Staples to Alan Short and Alistair Fair, December 2007.

23 Desmond Patrick to Anne Dye and Monty Sutrisna, 12 September 2005.

24 Felicity Goodey to Zeynep Toker, 14 April 2005.

25 This section of the chapter summarizes Alistair Fair and C. Alan Short, 'Collage architecture? Stirling and Wilford's Lowry', [forthcoming article].

26 Canadian Centre for Architecture, Montreal, AP140.S2.SS1.D99. P10, masterplan drawings.

27 Canadian Centre for Architecture, Montreal, AP140.S2.SS1.D99.P11, for the CCA drawings.

28 Michael Wilford to Alan Short and Alistair Fair, November 2007.

29 Michael Wilford to Alan Short and Alistair Fair, November 2007.

30 Michael Wilford to Alan Short and Alistair Fair, November 2007, edited by Wilford.

31 Canadian Centre for Architecture, Montreal, AP140.S2.SS1.D99.P9, for the two Stirling drawings.

32 Michael Wilford to Alan Short and Alistair Fair, November 2007, edited by Wilford.

33 Canadian Centre for Architecture, Montreal, AP140.S2.SS1.D99.P9, early design drawings folder.

34 John Willis to Monty Sutrisna and Pat Sterry, 15 November 2005.

35 M. Wilford and R. Muirhead, James Stirling Michael Wilford and Associates: Buildings and Projects 1975-1992 (London, 1994).

36 David Staples & Louis Fleming to Anne Dye, February 2006.

37 David Staples & Louis Fleming to Anne Dye, February 2006.

38 Stephen Hetherington to Pat Sterry and Monty Sutrisna, 25 April 2005.

39 David Staples to Alan Short and Alistair Fair, November 2007.

40 Michael Wilford to Alan Short, Pat Sterry and Anne Dye, 11 May 2006.

41 Michael Wilford to Alan Short, Pat Sterry and Anne Dye, 11 May 2006, edited by Wilford.

42 Stephen Hetherington to Pat Sterry and Monty Sutrisna, 25 April 2005.

43 Stephen Hetherington to Pat Sterry and Monty Sutrisna, 25 April 2005, edited by Hetherington.

44 Stephen Hetherington to Pat Sterry and Monty Sutrisna, 25 April 2005.

45 Felicity Goodey to Zeynep Toker, 14 April 2005.

46 The Millennium Commission's previous unwillingness to co-fund projects was, according to Lord Crickhowell, one of the causes for the failure of the contemporaneous Cardiff Opera House scheme. See Nicholas Crickhowell, Opera House Lottery: Zaha Hadid and the Cardiff Bay Project (Cardiff, 1997), p.73.

47 John Willis to Monty Sutrisna and Pat Sterry, 15 November 2005.

48 Felicity Goodey to Zeynep Toker, 14 April 2005.

49 C.A. Short, P.S. Barrett, M. Sutrisna, and A. Dye, 'Impacts of value engineering on five capital arts projects', Building Research and Information 35/3 (2007), pp.287-315.

50 Short and Associates, 'Building excellence in the Arts: a guide for clients', accessed on 27 December 2009 at <http://www.cabe.org. uk/publications/building-excellence-in-the-arts>.

51 Stephen Hetherington to Pat Sterry and Monty Sutrisna, 25 April 2005.

52 Felicity Goodey to Zeynep Toker, 14 April 2005.

53 Felicity Goodey to Zeynep Toker, 14 April 2005.

54 John Willis to Monty Sutrisna and Pat Sterry, 15 November 2005.

55 Felicity Goodey to Zeynep Toker, 14 April 2005.

56 Steve Thorncroft to Zeynep Toker, 15 April 2005.

57 Steve Thorncroft to Zeynep Toker, 15 April 2005.

58 Felicity Goodey to Zeynep Toker, 14 April 2005.

59 Michael Wilford to Alan Short, Pat Sterry and Anne Dye, 11 May 2006.

60 Steve Thorncroft to Zeynep Toker, 15 April 2005.

61 Felicity Goodey to Zeynep Toker, 14 April 2005.

62 Felicity Goodey to Zeynep Toker, 14 April 2005.

63 Desmond Patrick to Anne Dye and Monty Sutrisna, 12 September 2005.

64 John Willis to Pat Sterry and Monty Sutrisna, 15 November 2005.

65 Stephen Hetherington to Pat Sterry and Monty Sutrisna, 25 April 2005.

66 Stephen Hetherington to Pat Sterry and Monty Sutrisna, 25 April 2005.

67 Desmond Patrick to Anne Dye and Monty Sutrisna, 12 September 2005

68 Stephen Hetherington to Pat Sterry and Monty Sutrisna, 25 April 2005.

69 Desmond Patrick to Anne Dye and Monty Sutrisna, 12 September 2005.

70 Felicity Goodey to Zeynep Toker, 14 April 2005.

71 Desmond Patrick to Anne Dye and Monty Sutrisna, 12 September 2005.

72 For a selection of responses, see Steve Rose, 'But does it work?', Guardian, 21 July 2007, accessed on 16 June 2010 at <http://www. guardian.co.uk/artanddesign/2007/jul/21/architecture>.

3.   'Defining the essence of the organization through architecture': Contact Theatre, Manchester

Alan Short

I think it's important that a space has character and that it is specific. ... I think there are pluses and minuses with the design of Contact but it has character and personality, and young people respond to it. You don't want a generic, multi-use thing that has an institutional arts centre feel.[1]

In 1965, Manchester University completed a 300-seat theatre to reinforce its highly regarded Drama Department. The theatre was designed by Grenfell Baines' then recently founded interdisciplinary practice, the Building Design Partnership (BDP), whose name recognized their de-individualized, collective ethos in the manner of Walter Gropius' famous American office, The Architects' Collaborative. The theatre historian and academic Richard Southern is credited as a 'consultant', an early reference to the meaningful involvement of a theatre consultant.[2] Three decades later, the theatre was radically rebuilt and extended in a single project which took six years to realize, between 1993 and late 1999 (Table 3.1). This re-imagining of the theatre, known as 'Contact' since the 1970s, forms the subject of this chapter, which explores how and why the 'vision' for the theatre changed considerably over the course of the project, with the eventual building becoming almost a 'found space' for the group which inherited it.

CONTEXT: THE CONTACT THEATRE'S HISTORY

A notional theatre building was included in the University's early 1960s master plan, preserved in the form of a large model in the Estates Office. The theatre was signified by a grey box in the south-east corner of the Arts & Humanities quadrangle, broadly where BDP's eventual University Theatre ended up. However, by 1972 the University was relieved to hand responsibility for the upkeep of the building and its programming as a theatre to the newly formed Contact Theatre Company, the 'Young Vic of the North', which focused on producing drama for and with young people.

Baines' design (figs. 3.1-3.4) delivered a compact, rectangular, brick box with disproportionately thick walls concealing a steel frame, but with an inconsistently acoustically transparent woodwool and copper roof. The sound of rain was clearly audible during performances. The auditorium was bookended by a stylish, two-storey foyer with a bar and a café to the south and a compact bank of dressing rooms to the north, the whole being contained within a simple shoebox form. An asymmetric roof climbed northwards just fast enough to capture one layer of limited flying apparatus within its depth above the fixed stage. A vertiginous deck of widely spaced boards hanging off the underside of the roof trusses gave iron-stomached technicians

Table 3.1 Contact Theatre, case study characteristics

Contact Theatre, characteristics	
Receiving/Producing	A resident repertory company occupied theatre in the 1960s. Contact Theatre company formed 1972
Project driver(s)	Perceived threat of eviction/unworkable 1960s configuration
Vision	'The Young Vic of the North'
Refurbishment/new build	Refurbished existing building /substantial new build
Feasibility study – in house or external consultant?	Yes In house
Part of bigger arts initiative?	No, one of eight competing theatres in Manchester
Business plan – scope **Construction budget set?**	Yes 'business as usual', enhanced Original study proposed £1 million refurbishment, revised to £3.2m out of a total of £4.8m for lottery bid
Final account/current estimated out-turn	£3.3 million, 2000
Funding source(s)	Arts Council of England Lottery Fund/long lease from University of Manchester/minimal fund raising
Lead consultant	Architect
Design innovation	Natural ventilation and passive cooling of all spaces requiring input from university researchers funded by the Department of Trade and Industry (DTI)
Specialist inputs	Technical theatre systems consultants, acoustician, airflow modelling, University of Wales (Cardiff)
Value Engineering employed? – which stage?	Yes, through Workstages E, F, G (as design requirements for acoustically viable natural ventilation received from research team), after tender, and throughout construction Workstage K (see project timeline Figure 3.2)
Vision creep?	'Young persons producing' model transformed into platform for new work, some produced in-house, less age limited
Political climate	Stable, ACE adoption of the Boyden Report and the Theatre Review favoured Contact's change to a mixed economy model
Contract type - contractor involvement in design? - quality/time/money priority	JCT '92 with Quantities (Traditional) No Pre contract: quality/money/time; morphed into money/time/quality post contract
Organizational change?	Company restructured and reduced significantly through course of construction

Fig. 3.1 The Contact Theatre as originally built, photographed on the day of the Lottery award, 1995

access to lighting positions above the audience. The stage was unusually wide at sixteen metres, fifty-two feet six inches in imperial, and was rumoured to have acquired a considerable provenance by the early 1990s. Peter Brook reportedly chose Contact for the UK premiere of *The Man Who*.[3]

However, the theatre's reputation was not matched by what had become of its building by the early 1990s. Audiences (and performers) were thought to be disenchanted by the 'broken-back' rake of seating, which was flat at the front and steep at the back (a leitmotif of 1960s multi-purpose halls), and by its unaltered and then-unfashionable 1960s interiors. One Artistic Director later recalled:

Contact's auditorium had straight rows and then slightly angled bits at the side, very straight, very like a lecture theatre. All the seats were blue. It had a horrible rake and then flat seats on the floor. It was ugly as sin.[4]

Also problematic was its noisy and dysfunctional mechanical ventilation. By the early 1990s, the noise problem was habitually dealt with by simply not switching on the machine. The resulting absence of any ventilation engendered a relentless build-up of heat throughout even midwinter performances. Temperatures in excess of 40° C were recorded by the winning architects during the 1993 pantomime

season. The engineer for the rebuilding project, Max Fordham, watched a production in late 1993 in amazement as theatrical smoke, introduced briefly on stage early on in the performance, simply failed to move and dissipate. Eventually it hung as a cloud at shoulder level amongst the first seven or eight rows. Even more unsustainable perhaps was the location of all of the back-of-house activities, management, design, set-building, rehearsal, wardrobe, props and studio, in an inter-war school building 100 metres to the east, which came to be known, without much affection, as the Brickhouse. Actors in costume, directors, pieces of set, props, assistant stage managers, and technicians all processed back and forth across a windswept and frequently wet car park every afternoon and evening.

The theatre's then Administrative Director, Vikki Heywood, made a routine visit to the University Estates Department one morning in 1992. Such meetings usually involved the theatre being admonished once more for late night disturbances. However, on this occasion, Heywood caught sight of a drawing inadvertently left on a meeting room table. It showed an ambitious Masterplan for the south western part of the campus which clearly required the eradication of the Brickhouse and much else. But without the facilities provided in that building, the entire theatre operation would be unsustainable.

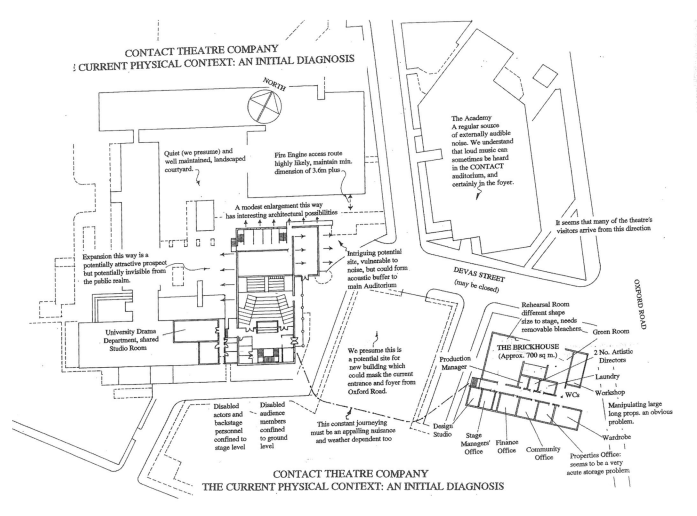

CONTACT THEATRE COMPANY
CURRENT PHYSICAL CONTEXT: AN INITIAL DIAGNOSIS

NORTH

Quiet (we presume) and well maintained, landscaped courtyard.

Fire Engine access route highly likely, maintain min. dimension of 3.6m plus

The Academy
A regular source of externally audible noise. We understand that loud music can sometimes be heard in the CONTACT auditorium, and certainly in the foyer.

It seems that many of the theatre's visitors arrive from this direction

A modest enlargement this way has interesting architectural possibilities

Expansion this way is a potentially attractive prospect but potentially invisible from the public realm.

Intriguing potential site, vulnerable to noise, but could form acoustic buffer to main Auditorium

DEVAS STREET (may be closed)

OXFORD ROAD

Rehearsal Room different shape size to stage, needs removable bleachers.

Green Room

University Drama Department, shared Studio Room

We presume this is a potential site for new building which could mask the current entrance and foyer from Oxford Road.

Production Manager

THE BRICKHOUSE (Approx. 700 sq m.)

2 No. Artistic Directors

Laundry

Workshop

Manipulating large long props. an obvious problem.

Disabled actors and backstage personnel confined to stage level

Disabled audience members confined to ground level

This constant journeying must be an appalling nuisance and weather dependent too

Design Studio

Stage Managers' Office

Finance Office

Community Office

WCs

Wardrobe

Properties Office: seems to be a very acute storage problem

CONTACT THEATRE COMPANY
THE CURRENT PHYSICAL CONTEXT: AN INITIAL DIAGNOSIS

Fig. 3.2 *The theatre in context, 1993: 'an initial diagnosis' for the design competition*

PROJECT DRIVERS

It was Vikki who started the process at Contact. The Brickhouse was a terrible sort of brick built shed, on a bit of land which fronted the Oxford Road. It was our face to the public and what a shoddy face it was. ... There was ... an architect's drawing, for desired future development of the University which included our space, the Brickhouse – which was where all our offices were.[5]

Vikki Heywood's accidental discovery of the university's redevelopment plans became the driver, after many years of problematic operation, to finally and urgently create an integrated producing house on a single site. Brigid Larmour, the Artistic Director who was in post in 1993, recalled:

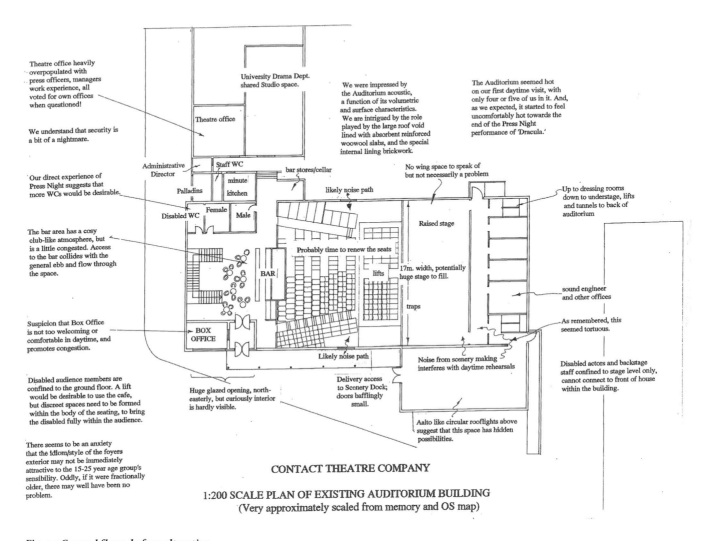

Theatre office heavily overpopulated with press officers, managers work experience, all voted for own offices when questioned!

We understand that security is a bit of a nightmare.

Our direct experience of Press Night suggests that more WCs would be desirable.

The bar area has a cosy club-like atmosphere, but is a little congested. Access to the bar collides with the general ebb and flow through the space.

Suspicion that Box Office is not too welcoming or comfortable in daytime, and promotes congestion.

Disabled audience members are confined to the ground floor. A lift would be desirable to use the cafe, but discreet spaces need to be formed within the body of the seating, to bring the disabled fully within the audience.

There seems to be an anxiety that the idiom/style of the foyers exterior may not be immediately attractive to the 15-25 year age group's sensibility. Oddly, if it were fractionally older, there may well have been no problem.

University Drama Dept. shared Studio space.

Theatre office

Administrative Director

Staff WC

minute kitchen

Palladins

Female

Disabled WC

Male

bar stores/cellar

We were impressed by the Auditorium acoustic, a function of its volumetric and surface characteristics. We are intrigued by the role played by the large roof void lined with absorbent reinforced woowool slabs, and the special internal lining brickwork.

The Auditorium seemed hot on our first daytime visit, with only four or five of us in it. And, as we expected, it started to feel uncomfortably hot towards the end of the Press Night performance of 'Dracula.'

No wing space to speak of but not necessarily a problem

likely noise path

Raised stage

Probably time to renew the seats

BAR

lifts

17m. width, potentially huge stage to fill.

traps

Up to dressing rooms down to understage, lifts and tunnels to back of auditorium

sound engineer and other offices

BOX OFFICE

Likely noise path

Delivery access to Scenery Dock; doors bafflingly small.

Noise from scenery making interferes with daytime rehearsals

As remembered, this seemed tortuous.

Disabled actors and backstage staff confined to stage level only, cannot connect to front of house within the building.

Huge glazed opening, north-easterly, but curiously interior is hardly visible.

Aalto like circular rooflights above suggest that this space has hidden possibilities.

CONTACT THEATRE COMPANY

1:200 SCALE PLAN OF EXISTING AUDITORIUM BUILDING
(Very approximately scaled from memory and OS map)

Fig. 3.3 Ground floor, before alteration

We had a sixties relic in the main theatre building which [had] a wonderful but very problematic stage. And so Vikki and I talked about it ... and thought we'd better get ahead of this particular game or they will be evicting us. .. Because we didn't really imagine that they would understand that we couldn't function without a rehearsal room or a workshop or offices.[6]

Once the panic started to subside, the need to re-group physically triggered broader self-examination within the Company:

The building affects the profile and the perception of the Company ... [it is] locked into a complex relationship with the programming.[7]

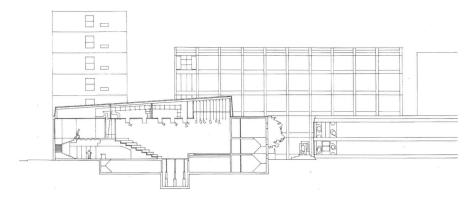

Fig. 3.4 Section through the theatre before alteration, with Manchester University's Humanities buildings behind and adjacent. Drawn for the competition entry

Contact's management extracted a mandate from the Board to bid to ACE for a one-off fixed grant to fund a feasibility study. At the time, such grants were set at £10,000, whatever the intended size of the project. In Contact's case, the money was used to investigate how the operation might be unified on one site. There was the inkling of £1 million from a much larger combined University-City bid to the European Regional Development Fund (ERDF). Contact's plan was to first find an architect to mastermind the study and lead other consultants as necessary to broker a scheme with the Company. Roger Stonehouse, the University's Professor of Architecture, assembled a shortlist of thirty-two architects through the spring of 1993. Six spent the autumn worrying the problem, namely the challenge of fitting so much volume onto a tight site, and were subsequently interviewed in sequence, in some discomfort, in a classroom set out for the re-examination of summer failures.

The panel chose the only architects who had never designed a theatre, Alan Short and Brian Ford. Short recalls elaborating on the latent theatrical content of an engineering school in Leicester, a brewery in Malta, and extensions to a Hertfordshire boarding school, unconvincingly he thought at

Heywood considered that:

We had to change the building to underpin the artistic policy. The trick was to find the way of defining the essence of the organization through architecture.[8]

THE CAST

Governance of the Company and its building was already complicated. The University maintained a keen but not wholly benign interest. The Estates Department seems to have perceived the theatre simply as the source of frequent late-night call-outs and unpaid repair bills. The Vice-Chancellor and the senior executives were troubled by this then thirty-year-old drain on their resources.

On the other side, the theatre's Board was populated by City Councillors, noted Mancunian actors, and active and Emeritus Professors; the chair was the charming and persuasive Emeritus Professor of American Studies, Dennis Welland.

Arts Council England (ACE) delivered an annual revenue grant through its regional entity Northwest Arts. There was in addition some corporate sponsorship. The youth theatre component of the company seemed to have developed a semi-independent existence and was particularly threatened by the likely demolitions. By 1993, Contact comprised a full sixty-eight member producing company. Fig. 3.5 reveals, probably incompletely, the proliferation of interests and constituencies circling around and within Contact.

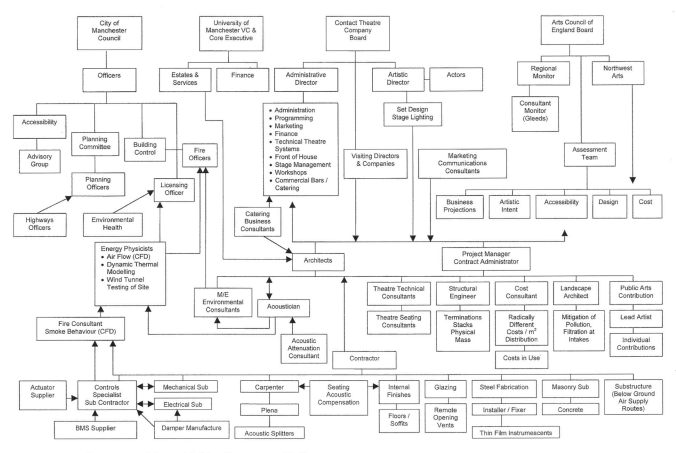

Fig. 3.5 Contact Theatre, participants' fields of interest and influence

the time, and the opportunities waiting to be imagined in the idea of a sustainable theatre for young people. In their embarrassed haste to leave, Ford forgot his umbrella. They decided against returning for it, fearing they would overhear the Panel members' amusement at their tortuous attempts to develop some spontaneous theatrical credibility, an unwelcome additional sadness to add to the expensive train fares from London. However, the original Artistic Director later recalled:

We went with these particular architects because we liked their ideas about environmentally sustainable heating and cooling. We liked their ideas about how to work with the client and they proved to be tremendously good at that in the stages that we [Brigid Larmour & Vikki Heywood] actually went through.[9]

Nonetheless, looking back somewhat ruefully, her successor speculated:

It was clear, or it became clear, that our initial decision to go with a design team [managed] by the architect was not the best decision.[10]

Figs. 3.6, 3.7, 3.8 and 3.9 are from the architects' competition entry. Options A and C proposed brand new studios and rehearsal rooms, built around the north end of the theatre. The more abstemious Option B, figs. 3.8 and 3.9, was the winning competition scheme of small accretions, developed

in full recognition of the notional £1 million budget. Within the opened-up shell is packed at least some of the residue from the Brickhouse. A galleried studio is formed out of the two-storey foyers, while a new foyer colonizes the void between the east flank of the 1965 box and the residual nineteenth century cross street. A very small workshop is prised into the north end, accessible shower boxes are threaded into the dressing rooms, a tiny office block inhabits the Humanities courtyard, a rehearsal room sits on top of the dressing

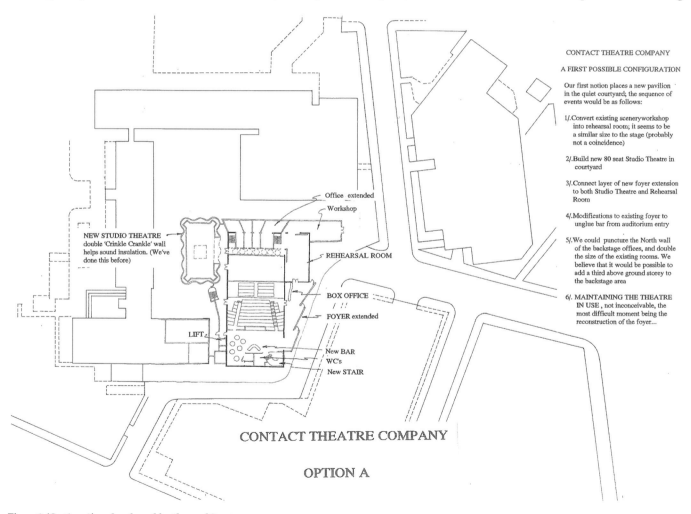

CONTACT THEATRE COMPANY

A FIRST POSSIBLE CONFIGURATION

Our first notion places a new pavilion in the quiet courtyard; the sequence of events would be as follows:

1/. Convert existing scenery workshop into rehearsal room; it seems to be a similar size to the stage (probably not a coincidence)

2/. Build new 80 seat Studio Theatre in courtyard

3/. Connect layer of new foyer extension to both Studio Theatre and Rehearsal Room

4/. Modifications to existing foyer to unglue bar from auditorium entry

5/. We could puncture the North wall of the backstage offices, and double the size of the existing rooms. We believe that it would be possible to add a third above ground storey to the backstage area

6/. MAINTAINING THE THEATRE IN USE, not inconceivable, the most difficult moment being the reconstruction of the foyer...

NEW STUDIO THEATRE double 'Crinkle Crankle' wall helps sound insulation. (We've done this before)

Office extended

Workshop

REHEARSAL ROOM

BOX OFFICE

FOYER extended

LIFT

New BAR
WC's
New STAIR

CONTACT THEATRE COMPANY

OPTION A

Fig. 3.6 'Option A' as developed by the architects, 1993

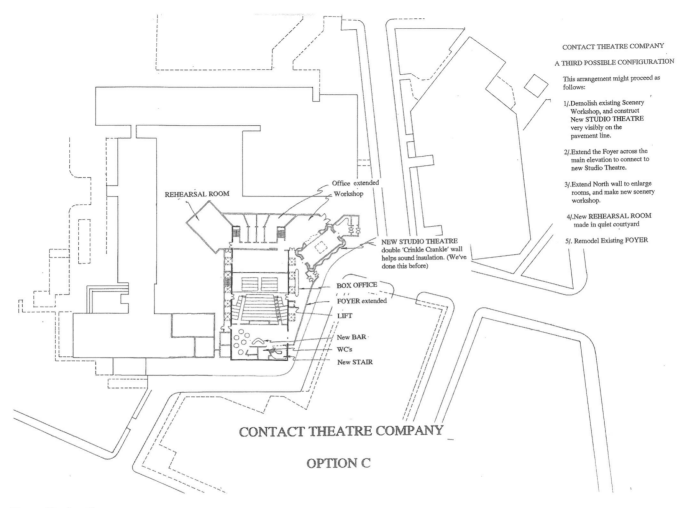

CONTACT THEATRE COMPANY

A THIRD POSSIBLE CONFIGURATION

This arrangement might proceed as follows:

1/. Demolish existing Scenery Workshop, and construct New STUDIO THEATRE very visibly on the pavement line.

2/. Extend the Foyer across the main elevation to connect to new Studio Theatre.

3/. Extend North wall to enlarge rooms, and make new scenery workshop.

4/. New REHEARSAL ROOM made in quiet courtyard

5/. Remodel Existing FOYER

REHEARSAL ROOM

Office extended
Workshop

NEW STUDIO THEATRE
double 'Crinkle Crankle' wall
helps sound insulation. (We've
done this before)

BOX OFFICE
FOYER extended
LIFT
New BAR
WC's
New STAIR

CONTACT THEATRE COMPANY

OPTION C

Fig. 3.7 'Option C', 1993

rooms. Paraphernalia is inserted to naturally ventilate the auditorium, incorporating stacks and air intakes. The auditorium itself is re-seated 'continentally', without aisles, accessed across bridges enabling wheelchair users to choose any row. The stage is untouched: it was sacred space, as far as the designers could tell, with two broad forestage lifts and an undercroft. However a vague notion of a flexible proscenium is indicated, a telescopic 'prosc' which could shutter down to circumscribe small productions but also open up to release the full sixteen metre width. At the time, perhaps, there was a suspension of disbelief: the stage was thought to be Contact's unique attribute. In retrospect, however, the initial Artistic Director rued this pre-occupation:

All over the country, people are pulling back from those big stages, because they speak to a time when there was less alternative entertainment to theatre. We thought [in the 1960s that] cinema [was] going ... [to be] dead.

Therefore you would guarantee a certain scale of audience and ... every kind of play would happen on stage. Whereas now the only kind of play that happens on stage is the kind of play which uniquely will bring people out to see it, which either means it's got to have staggeringly good actors or it's ... very, very strong.[11]

The scheme provides visitors in the foyers with views into the workshops (fig. 3.8, which bears the annotation 'may not be popular with your crew') – an interesting proposition which anticipates the later Curve, Leicester.

THE SEARCH FOR FUNDING

Within three months of the feasibility study commencing, the hoped-for European Regional Development Fund (ERDF) grant arrived in Manchester. However, it was diverted immediately into the Business School, a huge blow for Contact. Yet ironically, having been released from this notional £1 million cap, the content of the project swelled to embrace needs and aspirations collected from an exhaustive consultation exercise. Every constituency, almost every member of the Company, was interrogated.

I would be very surprised if at that stage we would have done

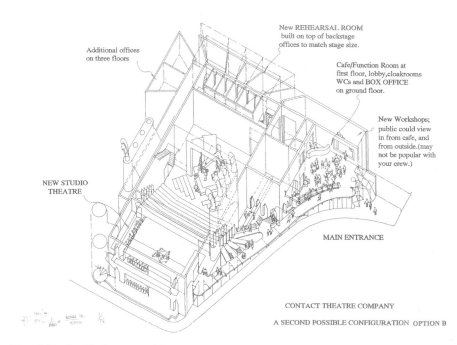

Fig. 3.8 'Option B', the competition-winning scheme, 1993: axonometric

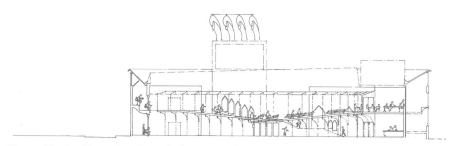

Fig. 3.9 'Option B', section through the proposed new foyers

much more than enshrine the big aspiration onto a piece of paper, which was to build a building that young people would come to an identify with and feel a sense of ownership. I wouldn't have imagined we did any [precise room data sheets] ... I don't think we would have known that it was necessary. And ... it grew like Topsy.[12]

As the study progressed, the architect addressed the whole Company, including visiting troupes, every

Wednesday in the auditorium, between the matinee and the evening performance. The discussion was led from the stage, accommodated by whichever set was in place. Much of the debate happened across Robinson Crusoe's island. After the loss of the European funding stream, hopes were revived by the announcement of the new National Lottery fund dedicated to the arts. Intelligence from the Regional Arts Board and arts apparatchiks urged Contact to make bold, expansive proposals with real impact and chutzpah to attract the attention of the London-centric panel.

But just as the project was beginning to develop, both the Artistic and Administrative Directors, its original envisioners, moved on to bigger posts: Vikki to run the Royal Court and Brigid to become a London-based producer in the commercial sector. A new Administrative Director, Patrick Martin, and a new Artistic Director, Ben Twist, inherited the emerging scheme and the idea of a lottery bid. Martin, in particular, felt a little at sea:

> I was looking for a book: "How to buy a £3 million building". Couldn't find it. Went to the RIBA, went to bookshops, libraries. How to be a client ... beyond ... the booklets that the Arts Council had provided. I think we could have benefited from either some training or some ... book. I think we would have avoided some mistakes early on.[13]

Under its new directors, the Company spent 1994 reflecting on its style and position as a producing entity. At the same time, the design grew in ambition in the light of the scale of project which, it was thought, would be most likely to secure some rumoured, pre-assigned share of the Lottery funding for the north-west, around four to five million pounds total project cost. Indeed, the region was behind in the regional recipient league table, and so Contact was warned against excessive modesty, thought to be wholly counter-productive. All this intelligence was communicated in turn to the architects. The 'vision' now fully embraced the idea of a truly

'green' building for young people, a low energy, passively ventilated and cooled collection of performance spaces. This was a recipe not attempted in a city centre in modern times. The technical challenges were considerable; indeed, the developing design was bringing them into clearer focus, but vital insights from engineers, acousticians and energy physicists were unavailable. The funding regime simply did not allow for any meaningful involvement from them, the investment that had been made so far being speculative until the final decision to build had been made.

The Contact timeline (fig. 3.10) maps the budgetary movement from the loss of the fixed ERDF funds through the aspirational period anticipating a forthcoming Lottery 'gamble'. During 1994 (figs. 3.11, 3.12, and 3.13), a significant new building was conceived alongside the existing. The Board struggled to interpret the evolving designs and to understand the consequences.

> I remember when we first had the plans [...] how complicated it all seemed and how difficult it was to comprehend. Because none of us were used to reading plans in that way. Once [it was] explained ... it made perfect sense, but how we then kept abreast of that so when things went or when things were cut or we lost this or we went it becomes extremely complex ... I think we [could] have ... [had] some kind of induction into that.[14]

The new studio theatre had become a discrete object lifted two floors up above a substantial scene assembly area and workshop. The format of the main auditorium at this stage, not unlike the Cottesloe auditorium in the National Theatre, was developed during the one-month-long involvement of a prominent theatre consultant. Although it was never a literal copy, the application of the Cottesloe model to Contact represents what was then something of an industry 'standard' approach for a theatre of this size and scale. During a Company-wide consultation evening in mid-January in the upper foyer, the theatre consultant, appointed after

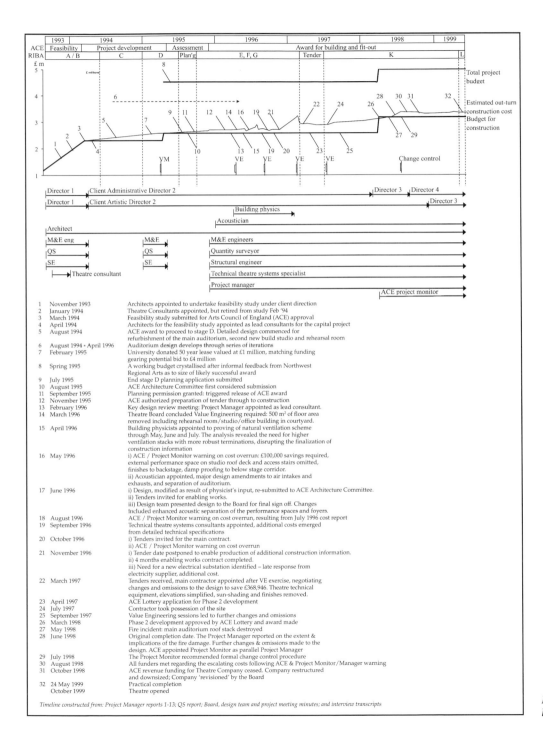

	1993	1994	1995	1996	1997	1998	1999
ACE	Feasibility	Project development	Assessment		Award for building and fit-out		
RIBA	A / B	C	D	Plan'g	E, F, G	Tender	K	L

The following numbered key and timeline annotations appear:

1 November 1993 — Architects appointed to undertake feasibility study under client direction
2 January 1994 — Theatre Consultants appointed, but retired from study Feb '94
3 March 1994 — Feasibility study submitted for Arts Council of England (ACE) approval
4 April 1994 — Architects for the feasibility study appointed as lead consultants for the capital project
5 August 1994 — ACE award to proceed to stage D. Detailed design commenced for refurbishment of the main auditorium, second new build studio and rehearsal room
6 August 1994 - April 1996 — Auditorium design develops through series of iterations
7 February 1995 — University donated 50 year lease valued at £1 million, matching funding gearing potential bid to £4 million
8 Spring 1995 — A working budget crystallised after informal feedback from Northwest Regional Arts as to size of likely successful award
9 July 1995 — End stage D planning application submitted
10 August 1995 — ACE Architecture Committee first considered submission
11 September 1995 — Planning permission granted: triggered release of ACE award
12 November 1995 — ACE authorized preparation of tender through to construction
13 February 1996 — Key design review meeting: Project Manager appointed as lead consultant.
14 March 1996 — Theatre Board concluded Value Engineering required: 500 m² of floor area removed including rehearsal room/studio/office building in courtyard.
15 April 1996 — Building physicists appointed to proving of natural ventilation scheme through May, June and July. The analysis revealed the need for higher ventilation stacks with more robust terminations, disrupting the finalization of construction information
16 May 1996 — i) ACE / Project Monitor warning on cost overrun: £100,000 savings required, external performance space on studio roof deck and access stairs omitted, finishes to backstage, damp proofing to below stage corridor.
ii) Acoustician appointed, major design amendments to air intakes and exhausts, and separation of auditorium.
17 June 1996 — i) Design, modified as result of physicist's input, re-submitted to ACE Architecture Committee.
ii) Tenders invited for enabling works.
iii) Design team presented design to the Board for final sign off. Changes included enhanced acoustic separation of the performance spaces and foyers.
18 August 1996 — ACE / Project Monitor warning on cost overrun, resulting from July 1996 cost report
19 September 1996 — Technical theatre systems consultants appointed, additional costs emerged from detailed technical specifications
20 October 1996 — i) Tenders invited for the main contract.
ii) ACE / Project Monitor warning on cost overrun
21 November 1996 — i) Tender date postponed to enable production of additional construction information.
ii) 4 months enabling works contract completed.
iii) Need for a new electrical substation identified – late response from electricity supplier, additional cost.
22 March 1997 — Tenders received, main contractor appointed after VE exercise, negotiating changes and omissions to the design to save £368,946. Theatre technical equipment, elevations simplified, sun-shading and finishes removed.
23 April 1997 — ACE Lottery application for Phase 2 development
24 July 1997 — Contractor took possession of the site
25 September 1997 — Value Engineering sessions led to further changes and omissions
26 March 1998 — Phase 2 development approved by ACE Lottery and award made
27 May 1998 — Fire incident: main auditorium roof stack destroyed
28 June 1998 — Original completion date. The Project Manager reported on the extent & implications of the fire damage. Further changes & omissions made to the design. ACE appointed Project Monitor as parallel Project Manager
29 July 1998 — The Project Monitor recommended formal change control procedure
30 August 1998 — All funders met regarding the escalating costs following ACE & Project Monitor/Manager warning
31 October 1998 — ACE revenue funding for Theatre Company ceased. Company restructured and downsized; Company 'revisioned' by the Board
32 24 May 1999 — Practical completion
October 1999 — Theatre opened

Timeline constructed from: Project Manager reports 1-13; QS report; Board, design team and project meeting minutes; and interview transcripts

Fig. 3.10 Contact Theatre: budget history timeline

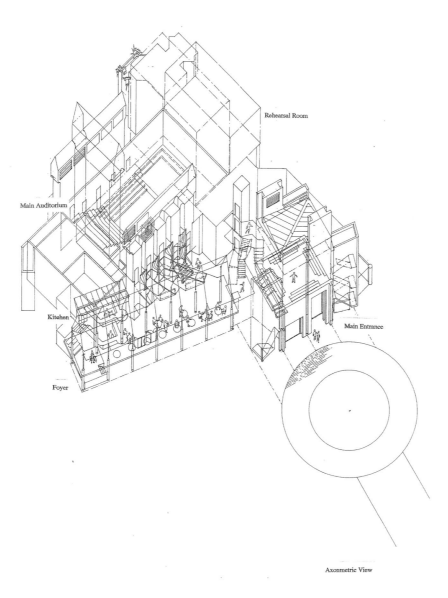

Rehearsal Room

Main Auditorium

Kitchen

Main Entrance

Foyer

Axonmetric View

Fig. 3.11 The scheme develops in scale and ambition

the architect and in part by the architect, presented the idea of a flexible, flat-floored, galleried black box. The

Company said nothing on the night. This puzzled the architects, who knew it was not what the Company then wanted.

After a frantic day of telephoning and an emergency trip to London produced no alternative options, the consultant promptly resigned by refusing to return to Manchester.

The Architect became, by default, the keeper of the auditorium plan, the scribe for the second Artistic Director's surprisingly reactionary wish for a more architecturally formed space, without the flexibility of the consultant's scheme which in turn had reflected the wishes of the original client team, as we shall discuss shortly. Interestingly, the Artistic Director had come from the hyper-flexible Traverse in Edinburgh. The new team presided over the completion of an increasingly ambitious study, submitting it in March 1994. A dead period loomed. As a morale-booster the design team was appointed for the duration of the project, much appreciated but meaningless in reality. The architects continued to develop the scheme through Workspace C to develop momentum. The envisioning was clearly still in progress.

The feasibility study was well received. ACE released an award to proceed to a Workstage D submission in August 1994 for a capital award to develop, tender for and build the design to be approved at this still relatively early stage. Later in the Lottery process an additional approval stage was introduced at tender return. By 1995 (figs. 3.14 and 3.15), the design had developed further. The workshops

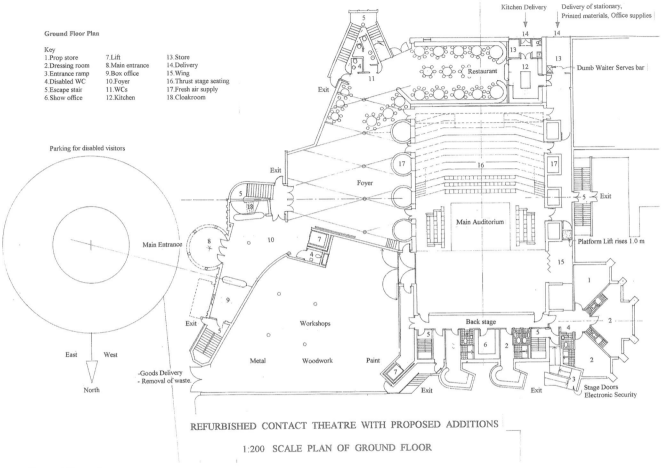

Ground Floor Plan

Key
1.Prop store   7.Lift   13.Store
2.Dressing room   8.Main entrance 14.Delivery
3.Entrance ramp   9.Box office   15.Wing
4.Disabled WC   10.Foyer   16.Thrust stage seating
5.Escape stair   11.WCs   17.Fresh air supply
6.Show office   12.Kitchen   18.Cloakroom

Parking for disabled visitors

Kitchen Delivery   Delivery of stationary,
                     Printed materials, Office supplies

Restaurant   Dumb Waiter Serves bar

Exit

Exit

Foyer

Main Auditorium

Exit

Platform Lift rises 1.0 m

Main Entrance

East   West

North

-Goods Delivery
- Removal of waste.

Workshops

Metal   Woodwork   Paint

Back stage

Stage Doors
Electronic Security

Exit   Exit

REFURBISHED CONTACT THEATRE WITH PROPOSED ADDITIONS

1:200 SCALE PLAN OF GROUND FLOOR

Fig. 3.12 Ground floor plan, 1994

had swelled to enable full sets to be assembled off stage, supported by metal and woodworking shops and a paint booth. The plan places the entrance on axis with the main southerly artery, Oxford Road, and slides the arriving audience sideways across foyers and into the southerly end of the auditorium. The auditorium is not yet much transformed but the backstage building is liberally extended, with plumbing 'inside the walls' and new spaces beyond. Air intake and exhaust towers march along each long side of the auditorium. There is some vague verification of their likely size. Elevations were developed in brick and zinc, expressing rather than suppressing the infrastructure needed to avoid artificial environmental control. Sustainability was certainly built into the Lottery pre-qualification requirements but had not yet acquired the urgency subsequently given to it by the Government Chief Scientist and the Intergovernmental Panel for Climate Change ten years later. The ACE Architecture Committee approved the increasingly idiosyncratic design. Manchester's Planning Committee granted planning approval in the nick

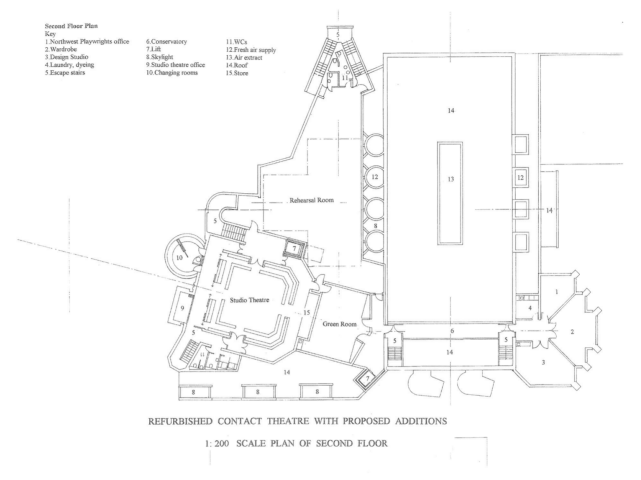

Second Floor Plan
Key
1. Northwest Playwrights office
2. Wardrobe
3. Design Studio
4. Laundry, dyeing
5. Escape stairs
6. Conservatory
7. Lift
8. Skylight
9. Studio theatre office
10. Changing rooms
11. WCs
12. Fresh air supply
13. Air extract
14. Roof
15. Store

REFURBISHED CONTACT THEATRE WITH PROPOSED ADDITIONS

1: 200 SCALE PLAN OF SECOND FLOOR

Fig. 3.13 Second floor plan, 1994

of time to secure the first major Lottery Award to the North West in November 1995.

The July 1995 Stage D version of the design contained little considered input from structural and mechanical & electrical engineers: what input there was had been squeezed out through goodwill in response to moral pressure from the architects. There

had been one cost review. This was all entirely as envisaged in the Workstage descriptions offered by the RIBA and its sister Engineering and Surveying Institutes. The timeline (fig. 3.10) shows an uplift at this point as an overall project budget was defined for the first time for the bid, with the construction consuming a larger slice of the overall figure than had been anticipated. The

bid, like many others at this time, was geared to the prospects for raising the mandatory 25% matching funding, a million pounds out of four million plus – a seemingly insurmountable hurdle. The University was persuaded to surrender a fifty-year lease which the City Treasurer happily valued at £1 million and which the Arts Council accepted as cash in kind.

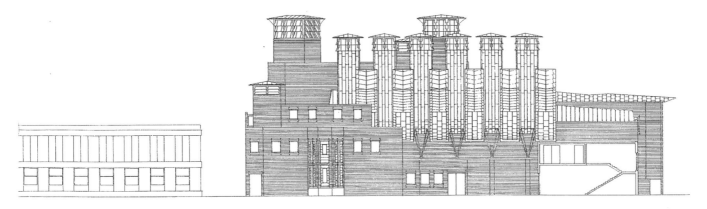

Fig. 3.14 Elevation as proposed to the Humanities Courtyard, 1995

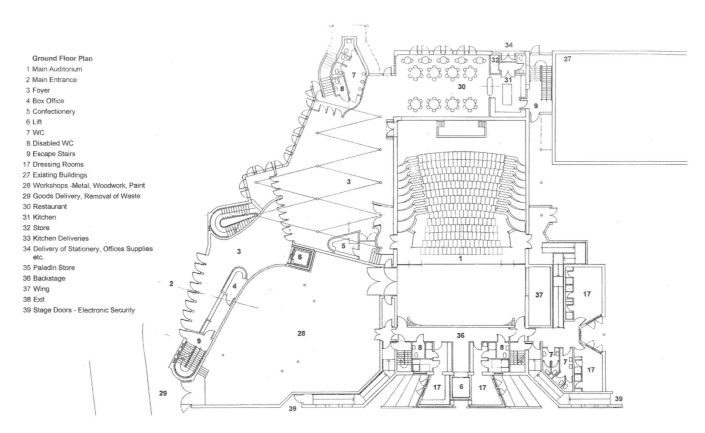

Ground Floor Plan

1 Main Auditorium
2 Main Entrance
3 Foyer
4 Box Office
5 Confectionery
6 Lift
7 WC
8 Disabled WC
9 Escape Stairs
17 Dressing Rooms
27 Existing Buildings
28 Workshops -Metal, Woodwork, Paint
29 Goods Delivery, Removal of Waste
30 Restaurant
31 Kitchen
32 Store
33 Kitchen Deliveries
34 Delivery of Stationery, Offices Supplies
    etc.
35 Paladin Store
36 Backstage
37 Wing
38 Exit
39 Stage Doors - Electronic Security

Fig. 3.15 Plan, 1995: the Lottery scheme

Workstage E commenced with the re-engagement of the co-consultants. Following the departure of the theatre consultant, a development which we have already noted, the co-consultants found the mid-1995 version considerably evolved from the spring 1994 scheme. The auditorium design continued to be refined and re-formed for two and a half years at 1:20 scale by the architects and Artistic Director. Ben Twist later recalled the departure of the theatre consultant and the subsequent development of the design according to his own ideas:

> *I had different views on what the auditorium*
> *should be to the previous artistic director. It was*
> *going to be a black box and I didn't want that.*[15]

Twist was sceptical about the extent to which flexibility would ever be needed for 95% of what they might stage. He thought that the black box was 'boring' and 'very eighties', arguing that the theatre *'should be a glorious place to be in ... you should want to have your dinner in there'*. Twist believed that it can take an inordinate amount of effort for a flexible space to become energized compared to a 'formed space', in which the physical environment can provide an initial level of energy to which a performance can add.

> *[The black box] starts at zero, or possibly even minus*
> *twenty, so you've got to do an awful lot more work to*
> *get it to a hundred per cent. I also argued that [Contact]*
> *was never going to be a [good] flexible space because the*
> *shape wasn't right. It was rectangular, and if you want*
> *to do things in the round you need a square space – a*
> *bit more like the Young Vic, or the Royal Exchange.*[16]

The design evolved accordingly, developing a waisted single parabolic rake. Every row was now accessed from within the envelope. Plush bench-seated boxes lined the outer walls:

> *We thought they might be quite fun for a young*
> *audience. You could squeeze in lots of people and they*
> *would feel a little less regulated than [in] the seats.*[17]

The boxes curve towards the centre of the stage (fig. 3.16). The illusion of rotation is intended to re-centre optically the periphery of the seating rake as the stage is either widened or choked down, so that there is some sense of the audience positively oriented to the stage, a species of virtual flexibility with no moving parts. The four front rows can still be removed and raised and lowered on two 1965 screw jack lifts. This arrangement, formed but with a little flexibility, was perfectly adequate for Twist:

> *I think it's better to have a really good space*
> *that works well in the way that it's set out,*
> *with a degree of flexibility built in.*[18]

Twist suggested that the box benches might be covered in ocelot fabric as a further useful contribution to the baseline energy level of the space, though this suggestion ultimately failed to find support.

Fig. 3.16 The auditorium boxes, an illusion intended to 'narrow' the space whilst also generating a sense of concentrated energy

Twist's 'vision' was very personal, though representative of a broader school of thought which sought a recovery of pre-modern 'positive space', that is, space which avoids notions of universality or unlimited adaptability and which provides a defined architectural framework. In contrast, the eventual recipient of the re-built auditorium, John E. McGrath, appointed as Artistic Director in 1999, remembered his immediate thoughts on entering the auditorium for the first time: *'The fixed seating ... just seemed completely insane given the goal of the organization'*.[19] But on reflection, and after treating Contact as a 'found space', McGrath reflected that he had *'come to be very fond'* of the theatre.

The mid 1995 scheme site plan reflected the University's decision to permit the slight displacement of an adjoining road, a decision which made a huge difference to the potential achievable new space but also added cost. The new additions were now at least equivalent in area to the existing building and probably larger in volume. Implicit in this piling-up of performance spaces above and adjacent to foyers and workshops, all punctured by fresh air intakes and exhausts, was the need for absolute acoustic isolation of all the principal spaces to the point of complete structural discontinuity between them. As specialist consultants were finally appointed sequentially through the early part of 1996, technical responses to the problems of separation implicit in the design started to emerge at a cost, in design time as well as money.

A tiny grant from the then Department of Trade and Industry (DTI)-sponsored Energy Design Advice Scheme (EDAS) funded the making of a series of computational and wind tunnel models at the University of Wales in Cardiff (fig. 3.17). The timeline (fig. 3.10) shows a series of 'perturbations' through stages E, F and G as the innovatory content of the design was unravelled and reassembled under the guidance of specialists. The sizes of the air intakes and exhausts swelled as it was realized that the necessary acoustic attenuators would be 2.4 metres long to counter the ambient noise recorded during a twenty-four hour acoustic survey of

Fig. 3.17 Testing a revised theatre model in the Cardiff University wind tunnel, 1995

the site. Central Manchester proceeds at a relentless 84 dBA. In addition, rock bands played next door in the Academy, whose ventilation was, like that of pre-refurbishment Contact, so inadequate that stricken crews simply opened all the doors during performances in order to ensure a flow of air.

Further costs accrued from the detail of floating concrete structures on resilient neoprene pads to eliminate noise transmission. The doubling of concrete slabs and the transfer structures required to bridge over the workshops also added cost over and above the early assumptions. By June 1996, work in the wind tunnel in Cardiff clearly showed the urgent need for the various ventilation stacks to be at least as high as the surrounding eleven-storey buildings. If they were lower, the whole system would stall or even reverse. A new design for chimney tops was needed which would be wholly robust to wind turbulence (fig. 3.18). In fact subsequent monitoring by the BP Institute for Multi-Phase Fluid Flow shows that even the built stacks do reverse periodically and accommodate up and down flows simultaneously, without detriment to the internal conditions, but in 1996 this science was very much still emerging. The client sensed another agenda revolving around environmental design research and innovation:

Fig. 3.18 The terminations to the ventilation stacks, engineered by Stephen Morley, as built

They managed to sneak the [natural ventilation] in and I'm sure as an architect or as an engineer you have to kind of look around trying to find the opportunity to do that and it may not come along very often. But there are some times you have to hide your enthusiasm from the client or else the client is going to rumble what you're actually doing![20]

Martin later added to his comment:

The brief was to produce an exciting working theatre, not to break new ground in air handling. The fact that we broke new ground in air handling was great, but that was a bonus for me as the client.[21]

In the meantime, costs were reported as rising at every monthly project meeting. A project manager was appointed in fulfilment of an ACE award condition. By mid-March 1996 the Board reluctantly directed the project team to 'value engineer' the scheme. Five hundred square meters of floor area were excised, including the tower in the Humanities courtyard that would have housed the rehearsal room, studio and offices. By mid-May, the ACE Monitor was warning of cost overrun but the timeline shows the input from specialists was not yet complete. In fact the acoustician was only formally appointed in May. The architects continued to develop the design (fig. 3.19). The scheme, now much modified, went back to David Rock's ACE Architecture Committee in June. The committee panicked because the building was materially different to that which they had previously seen, but Rock ushered the resubmission through.

Fig. 3.19 Architect's study model, made as the consultants offered specialist input

The Board signed the scheme off in July 1996 (fig. 3.20) against a cost report which the ACE Monitor decided was unsound later that August. The Chairman of the Board explained how they summoned up their own theatre world's endemic optimism:

There was so much information to take in, and also too because none of us had ever been involved in anything like this before. The people who were designing the building, ... Ballast Wiltshire, the university, all of those people were inputting into this. Day by day, we were just hoping that everything was going to be possible.[22]

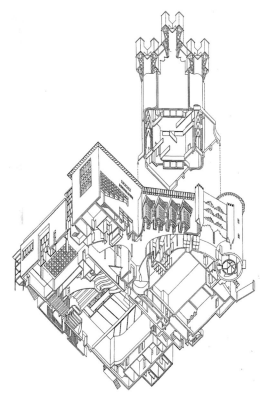

Fig. 3.20 The executed scheme, 'worm's-eye' view to illustrate the means of distributing air through the building

Tenders were issued for an 'enabling works' package, that is a preparatory contract to clear the site and make the necessary demolitions. The technical theatre systems consultants were appointed after competitive interview. Their assessment of the actual cost of the Company's technical aspirations exceeded the budget allowance significantly. The prospective tender date for the main works was set back to develop more construction information as the electricity supplier finally responded, over a year after inquiry, that a new sub-station would be required, adding yet more cost.

VALUE ENGINEERING

The timeline (fig. 3.10) shows a gathering spike in projected costs through the 1996/97 winter and the consequence of a ferocious 'Value Engineering' session at the point of tender. Value Engineering as a concept was introduced in the late 1940s, 'a disciplined procedure directed towards the achievement of necessary function for minimum cost without detriment to quality, reliability, performance or delivery'.[23] Editing out provision for drama whilst gauging the likely effect of these omissions on the client's operational 'vision' was a not wholly understood exercise on either side of the table. The clients felt they were faced with baffling decisions to make:

What would be unique about the arts? Well, probably that requirements are likely to be individual and so even harder to specify or price, so when it comes down to ... "Do you want the fly-tower or do you want the air-conditioning or do you want the nice bar?", it's going to be even harder for them to prioritize and make those judgements.[24]

The relationship with the Arts Council became ambivalent. Successive Administrative Directors recall an alternate bad-cop/good-cop flavour to the meetings:

We trusted our architects implicitly and that was absolutely the right decision. But as far as the project management of a major scheme went, we were very inexperienced. And at that point ... the Arts Council were so concerned about not coaching that they weren't giving advice.[25]

I found [the project monitor's] role confusing. These [monitors] were brought in as supplementary project managers [to] work for us on the board of management [by] the Arts Council, to make sure that all the information that was needed to make decisions was available ... Gleeds helped us work with the project managers and with the

Quantity Surveyors to unearth what those additional costs might be, which enabled us to know what the financial situation was ... There was a whole period of time where the exact ... [cost] was not known ... I suppose you ... [are] a naïve client.[26]

But how much of the extra cost deriving from the detailed design of the construction, traditional in itself but in an innovative configuration, could have been anticipated at Workstage D? This had been the moment at which the budget was set, immovably for all time, for many projects under the funder's protocols. The ACE Lottery administrators derided contingency sums, refusing, at the time, to fund against unknowns. Patrick Martin remembers peremptory treatment from ACE:

They weren't keen on contingencies. I can remember exactly that.... we had a 10-15% general project contingency in and we were told to take it out. You know, "Describe what it is you're spending all the money on and if you can't describe it, leave it out. There's no slack." And then, lo and behold, everyone has to go back and ask for more.[27]

CONSTRUCTING CONTACT

The commencement of the enabling works signalled the end of the

Company's occupation of the original building, marked, characteristically, with a huge party. On 24 July 1997 the contractor commenced in earnest. By September more Value Engineering was necessary. Finishes were removed from the contract, remedial damp-proofing to the cellars eliminated, even bird mesh to the stacks was deleted. The timeline (fig. 3.10) shows that by mid-1998 all the notional Value Engineering savings had reappeared in the projected out-turn cost. Some of the projected savings were an illusion, attached to work items impossible to disentangle from the main works, whilst others released disproportionately little actual reduction in cost.

While construction was underway (fig. 3.21), the Company endeavoured to busy itself with a national tour, organized from a line of 'relocatables' with bright red doors that were set up alongside the site. The tour slowly failed. The Chairman recalled an extremely difficult period:

We tried to tour for a while and we lost an inordinate amount of money [...], and then we decided [...] we'd close. Because we were not producing work the Arts Council took the grant away. We continued to exist with only the education department working, and only the grants coming in for that work. We ceased operations, in other words, and then because we'd lost our grant, we had

Fig. 3.21 Under construction and nearing completion, c.1998

to make a number of redundancies and practically the whole company went. I think five staff remained.[28]

In March 1998, Contact's follow-up second bid to ACE was successful. The timeline shows the consequent uplift in budget to meet the gently climbing cost line. But one day in May of that year, at 9.30am after a hearty site breakfast, a roofing subcontractor set fire to the timber structure of a roof stack, while working a bitumen seal to the edge of the felt. The fire spread along the roof; the subcontractor was in shock. Contact appeared on the national television news. The opening was delayed for eleven months, too long to retain the full Company. The then Artistic Director rued the strategy ten years on:

One of the big things I regret really is ... saying that we would keep on all the staff and not close down the activities of the organization during the building [project]. I would never recommend that to anybody now. I think there is a feeling that you're going to lose your audience and [that they] won't come back. My view is that the audience you're going to want it's not necessarily the same one that you've got at the moment anyway. It's often worse to put on not very good shows in not very good venues while your own theatre is closed, getting not very good audiences and losing lots of money. In a way I'd rather have a bit less money and go into hibernation for a period and really plan well to open the new building.[29]

The Artistic and Administrative Directors changed once more, two further post-holders completed the building before the posts were merged into a single role in 1999, to which John E. McGrath was appointed. He inherited a 'vision' and an infrastructure that had been conceived five years earlier. The original Contact building had been subsumed by a substantial brick structure, dominated by the ventilation towers and alluding in its detailing to an eclectic range of sources, from periodic

appearances by the spirit of Frank Furness to traditional Mediterranean festival banners (figs. 3.22, 3.23, and 3.24). Internally, it contained extensive facilities for a resident company to rehearse and build its own productions. However, these facilities were not to be used as planned. McGrath later explained how the context for the funding and practice of drama had changed with the new millennium approaching:

There was just beginning to be a rethink of funding in the theatre ... So the [Peter Boyden] report came ... and the Theatre Review, which

completely transformed funding of theatre ... The Arts Council began to look at where theatre was going and what it was doing. I think it started off by thinking of Contact and its particular focus on young people and its change from a Repertory model to ... what they were calling then "mixed-economy model" ... At first they thought we were on the left field, but I think that, by the end of the whole review, we had very much become a model for them of where theatre could be going. We were pulling in audiences whose average age was probably about forty years younger than most

Fig. 3.22 Contact, complete in 1999

Fig. 3.23 *Festival of Our Lady of Victory, 8 September, Naxxar, Malta*

theatres, [and who] were by and large new theatregoers that came from a really wide range of communities. The whole audience pattern and artist pattern of the building had really turned around in quite a short time after opening...[30]

McGrath inherited a building, in a sense, from another era (figs. 3.25 and 3.26), a collection of 'found spaces' which could be colonized by the building's users in sometimes unanticipated ways. By 2004 the Repertory model had completely evaporated.

Take a company like Nitro, formerly Black Theatre Co-op, which has done a lot of work here. They're a national touring company but they've developed a bunch of different projects with us. ... Those kinds of viewpoints wouldn't have had a conversation with the old model of building, but they are crucial to a theatre that can speak to a city as diverse as Manchester. [The new building has allowed us to] focus on people who hadn't worked here before, finding ways that they can have a relationship with the building and a creative stake in the organization.[31]

Fig. 3.24 *The detailing of the air inlets, revealing some intervention by the late Frank Furness*

Fig. 3.25 *The main theatre, 'Space 1', in 2010*

Fig. 3.26 The studio theatre

Fig. 3.27 Looking down into the foyer, a meeting place for Manchester's young people

REFLECTIONS

Contact was conceived at the beginning of the Lottery. As was the case with The Lowry, procedures were still being formulated, but far too much credence was given to the apparent resolution of the feasibility stage design and its estimated cost. And, also recalling The Lowry, the implications of this 'sense' of completion at a very early stage reverberated much later in the process. The essential specialist inputs each carried a cost for which there was already no provision. Innovative design is of necessity iterative but the standard plans of work adopted by this and many other funders heavily penalize the revisiting of each successive design stage. This was compounded by the near absence of design contingency funds, a consequence of the then prevailing Arts Council of England policy. Managing this creeping overspend during the later stages of design and construction was very harrowing for those involved. The client team hung on to their 'vision', which was delivered almost in its entirety: no spaces were lost. However, the quality of finishes was heavily diluted and in some cases finishes were omitted in their entirety. The 'vision' which propelled the project, of a fully-fledged sixty-eight person strong company producing its own work, failed during the delivery of the building. Contact was violently restructured, becoming a platform for emerging artists. The new 'vision' creatively inhabits a shell from an earlier time (figs. 3.27 and 3.28), 'hermit crab-like' as the first administrative director/custodian for the project later described it. But this strategy clearly works for the organization, whose recent publicity celebrates its distinctive, dramatic architecture, making much of the silhouettes of the ventilation towers.

Fig. 3.28 Treated as 'found space', the foyers have become a venue in their own right, hosting performances and music nights

Notes

1   John E. McGrath to Alan Short and Zeynep Toker, April 2005.
2   Frederick Bentham, *New theatres in Britain* (London, 1970), p.100. For more on the history of this profession, see Chapter 8 of this book.
3   As recounted to Alan Short by Vikki Heywood and Brigid Larmour, c.1994.
4   Ben Twist to Alan Short and Zeynep Toker, April 2005.
5   Brigid Larmour to Zeynep Toker, April 2005.
6   Brigid Larmour to Zeynep Toker, April 2005.
7   David Martin to Zeynep Toker, April 2005.
8   Vikki Heywood to Alan Short and Zeynep Toker, April 2005.
9   Brigid Larmour to Zeynep Toker, April 2005.
10 Patrick Martin to Anne Dye, 26 September 2006.
11 Brigid Larmour to Alan Short and Zeynep Toker, April 2005.
12 Vikki Heywood to Alan Short and Zeynep Toker, April 2005.
13 Patrick Martin to Anne Dye, 26 September 2006.
14 Wyllie Longmore to Alan Short and Zeynep Toker, April 2005.
15 Ben Twist to Alan Short and Zeynep Toker, April 2005.
16 Ben Twist to Alan Short and Zeynep Toker, April 2005.
17 Ben Twist to Alan Short and Zeynep Toker, April 2005.
18 Ben Twist to Alan Short and Zeynep Toker, April 2005.
19 John E. McGrath to Zeynep Toker and Alan Short, April 2005.
20 Patrick Martin to Anne Dye, 26 September 2006.
21 Patrick Martin, e-mail to Alistair Fair, 7 January 2010.
22 Wyllie Longmore to Alan Short and Zeynep Toker, April 2005.
23 L.W. Crum, *Value engineering: the organized search for value* (London, 1971).
24 Patrick Martin to Anne Dye, 26 September 2006.
25 Patrick Martin to Anne Dye, 26 September 2006
26 Fiona Gasper to Zeynep Toker, April 2005.
27 Patrick Martin to Anne Dye, 26 September 2006.
28 Wyllie Longmore to Alan Short and Zeynep Toker, April 2005.
29 Ben Twist to Zeynep Toker, April 2005.
30 John E. McGrath to Alan Short and Zeynep Toker, April 2005.
31 John E. McGrath to Alan Short and Zeynep Toker, April 2005.

4. 'An exercise in knowing abstemiousness': Poole Arts Centre – 'The Lighthouse'

Alan Short and Peter Barrett

Well into their capital project, the Poole Arts Centre Trust (PACT) and its Senior Managers made a calculated withdrawal from their original aspirations for a piece of iconic design in order to ensure key operational improvements were not lost. Their 1978 arts centre was the size of the Festival Hall,[1] but, as this chapter shows, was transformed by the end of 2003 for a mere £5.7 million, considerably less than £200 per square metre (figs. 4.1 and 4.2; table 4.1).[2] To have undertaken a full replacement, it was calculated in 2002, would have cost £45 million or more. One can only speculate as to how many similarly serviceable buildings were lost to the Lottery because they defied perceptions of what a new arts building should look like.

Fig. 4.1 Poole Arts Centre, before refurbishment

Table 4.1 Lighthouse, Poole, case study characteristics

	Lighthouse, Poole, characteristics
Receiving/Producing	Receiving
Project driver(s)	Dilapidations commitment, poor image[a]
	Additional flexible performance space
Vision	Enhance existing building to attract younger audiences
Refurbishment/new build	Refurbishment[b]
Feasibility study	Yes
– in house or external consultant?	External consultants: Bonar Keenleyside[f], plus in-house skills: CEO experienced in arts business planning
Part of bigger arts initiative?	No
Business plan	Yes
– scope	Comprehensive
Construction budget set?	Construction budget set by non-construction professionals and then reduced by funder twice before design work commenced[c,d]
Final account/current estimated out-turn	£5.7m
Funding source(s)	Arts Council of England Lottery Fund, Poole Borough Council, fundraising
Lead consultant	Architect
Design innovation	Yes, natural ventilation of foyers and new flexible performance space, but design principles established by same design team through Contact Theatre design
Specialist inputs	Acoustician, technical theatre systems specialist, access. No theatre consultant as deliberate client choice
Value Engineering employed?	Yes
– which stage?	Stage D, F, throughout construction
Vision creep?	No
Political climate	Stable, but funder ACE experiencing financial problems
Contract type	New engineering contact
– contractor involvement in design?	Yes, 2 stage[e]
– quality/time/money priority?	Money/time/quality
Organizational change?	Programmed restructuring through ACE stabilization grant[f]

a 'The brief identifies that Poole Arts Centre needs to change; it must "regenerate", "re-invent" or "revitalize". Comment on how you would address this change to create a coherent building ambience in a multi-function centre serving educational, community and artistic needs?'.
Taken from the 'Project Specific Questionnaire' issued to the competing design teams with the Architect's Brief.
b 'We found that our average audience member was well into their seventies', Robin Cave interview.
'The (arts business consultants) were brought in by the freeholder to sort out the business'. Robin Cave interview.
c 'People in that stage had to use historical cost data but all bets are off with respect to a large existing building. A relatively small amount of money spent at the initial stage would save a great deal'. Project Quantity Surveyor.
d 'Before feasibility went in, you could talk to the Arts Council and get an expectation of the maximum figure you could get'. Robin Cave interview.
e 'We came in at the end of stage D. Our first influence was to recommend a two-stage process. It brought the contractor in at an early stage so they had a full understanding of the building before the design was completed and understood the full risk profile of the project, and they fully bought into it'. Client's Project Manager for construction, 2006, transcript.
f Robin Cave interview.

events but became known principally as the home of the Bournemouth Symphony Orchestra.

This traumatic progress was clearly not forgotten twenty years later when Poole Arts Centre Trust (PACT), the centre's operating company, challenged the Borough Council (the freeholder) to intervene to repair and revitalize the building. The building envelope was failing faster than PACT could cope with financially. The saline seaside environment was corroding the brick ties in the cavity walls, a serious concern. In addition, the felt roof covering was failing, with the resulting leaks damaging the integrity of the woodwool slabs that formed the roof deck, a popular construction at the time, whilst winter gales lashed the thin aluminium window frames and doors. The exterior was stained and the building looked curiously abandoned to the passer-by (fig. 4.4), while the internal spaces presented a 'tired' appearance (fig. 4.5).

Fig. 4.4 The Arts Centre in 1999, with the tired and stained elevations of the original silver service dining room

RECOURSE TO THE LOTTERY

PACT's challenge to the local authority misfired. PACT had a full-repairing 99-year lease from the Borough Council and a revenue grant of £100,000 a year adjusted periodically for inflation. The council's priority was simply to safeguard its capital investment. By the early 1990's enthusiasm for the original 'vision' had all but evaporated; Margaret Thatcher's government was taking a particular interest in local government finance. The Technical Director recalled:

Fig. 4.5 The ground floor foyer, 1999, much obstructed by years of accretions

In 1991, [the Council] came round to assess the value of their asset and, at the time, the then Director of the building instructed those of us who were showing them round to show the building in its worst light, in the hopes of getting some money out of the Borough Council to "tart it up a bit". Consequently we went round [saying things like] "oh, look, the roof's falling off and the wall's falling down and this needs doing and we'll have to close

in a year unless you do it." And the report came back from the Borough saying that unless the Arts Trust spent – I think it was a million and a half pounds – in the next eighteen months, the centre would close.[6]

The million and a half was attached to the dilapidations report alone; it included nothing for re-visioning or for changing anything more fundamentally. Furthermore, the money and the necessary repairs were not forthcoming. Quite the reverse, in fact: the Centre was now *in extremis*. A stand off ensued. The Director retired, and Ruth Eastwood was appointed as the new Administrative Director. At just this time, 1994, the National Lottery was announced. PACT turned to the Arts Council Lottery Fund, whose officers were not unreceptive.[7]

RE-VISIONING TO A VOLATILE BUDGET

Poole Arts Centre, as opened in 1978, comprised:[8]

– The Wessex Hall (fig. 4.6), a major concert venue incorporating the aforementioned moveable floor, and kitted out for part-time cinema use.
– Kitchens for extensive 'Silver Service' dining rooms and self-service restaurant facilities on the first floor, and also serving the Wessex Hall when used in flat floor mode for large civic banquets and private events. (In raked seating mode the connecting doors were stranded, a storey height above the Wessex Hall floor.)
– A 650-seat proscenium arch theatre, the Towngate Theatre (fig. 4.7), also equipped as a cinema, with a ten metre

deep stage and a bowed leading edge, an orchestra pit for twenty musicians, which could become a bow shaped forestage, but no supporting workshops or scene assembly for mounting home grown productions.
– A visual arts gallery, the Seldown Gallery, half a stair flight below entry level.
– A dance studio.
– A meeting room deep in the plan with no windows.
– A craft workshop similarly deep in the plan below the flat-floored entry level to the Wessex Hall.
– Foyer at two levels, with ice cream kiosks and licensed bars.
– Administrative offices for staff and for the Bournemouth orchestras.
– A small cinema, a late addition by the first Director during construction, carved out of administrative space, the loss of which had been a recurrent problem for the organization.

The Chairman, who had been Chief Executive of the National Lifeboat Institution, and three senior officers set to work re-visioning the Centre. Ruth Eastwood engineered a very comprehensive consultation exercise, engaging with her staff at all levels and also, most importantly, with the customers. Eastwood summarized the 1997 audience figures in the context of the idealized audience composition for the second Joint Council and Poole Arts Trust Working Party

Fig. 4.6 The Wessex Hall, as refurbished

Fig. 4.7 The Towngate Theatre auditorium: the actor's view

meeting of 9 December 1999,[9] a group set up to foster, in words of the Chairman, Brian Miles, 'a relaxed, beneficial working relationship ... which would help Poole Arts Centre become accessible, beneficial and integral to the lives of Poole residents, whilst becoming a local resource of national significance'. Eastwood revealed that 63.5% of the real audience was female as against an 'aspired-to' 55%. Only jazz events attracted a male majority. Audience research showed 'an even balance of patrons across each social group'. She used this statistic to debunk the perception that the privileged derived most use and enjoyment from the Centre. But were they all attending the same events? The Borough's Policy Director suggested that operatic performances were increasingly patronized by aspirant workers in the new software and telecommunications industries. Eastwood reported that opera and rock concerts had been programmed on the same nights in 1997. Figures for young audiences were very low: 1.5% aged 16-18, 5.5% between 25 and 34, but 27.4% aged 65 or over. The Centre had staged Irvine Welsh's *Trainspotting*, attracting young audiences – and a string of complaints.

The task was clear, as the Centre's Technical Director, Robin Cave, later explained in conversation with Peter Barrett and Alan Short:

Cave: The first information we got together [related to] our audience cross-section. We found that our average audience member was well into their seventies. We [demonstrated] that we were [also] one of the main rock and roll bases on the South Coast. And it became pretty obvious that we needed to lower [our age profile]. We needed to get into the education field and young people's theatre, and [a] small performance space was important to us to allow us to do that. There's another side to this business, which is community use and we needed to [consult with] the people who would be using it, [to ask] what they wanted to be different from what they had before. And we included [in the consultation], because we're a receiving house,

all those people who come in and present concerts of whatever kind. We wanted to have the chance to see what alterations they would [suggest].

Barrett: How did you physically do that – meetings?

Cave: Yes.

Barrett: An open event or one-to-one discussions?

Cave: [With] people who regularly came and used the place professionally, there were one-to-one discussions, over a matter of a year probably, and they came in saying, "we're looking to do this." As [far as] I'm aware in the community there were open meetings, well publicized [and] held here.

Barrett: Did [the results of these meetings] get rolled into the brief for the designs, or did they become a document in their own right?

Cave: It all rolled into the design brief.[10]

The first priority emerging amongst any number of remedial works to the existing building was for a new, intermediate size auditorium:

The one thing that we were lacking was not a "black box studio", but a place to put all those smaller events that we did in spurious places. We used to do jazz in the function rooms, lunchtime recitals in the Art Gallery, and literature in the café. [We wanted] to give those things a home of their own and to make a base for the education work which we wanted to increase.[11]

In March 1996, Hilary Keenlyside of Bonar Keenlyside was appointed as arts business consultant to facilitate this re-visioning and put costs to it of a sort which would chime

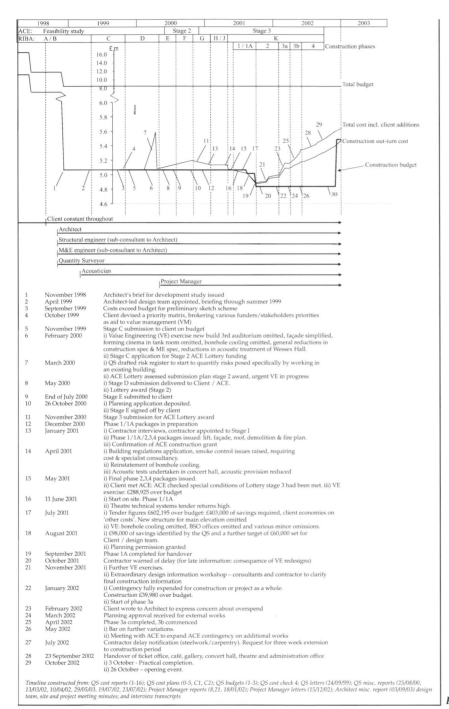

1998	1999	2000	2001	2002	2003

ACE: Feasibility study | Stage 2 | Stage 3

RIBA: A/B | C | D | E | F | G | H/J | K

1/1A | 2 | 3a | 3b | 4 — Construction phases

£m
16.0
14.0
12.0
10.0
8.0
6.0
5.8
5.6 — Total cost incl. client additions
5.4 — Construction out-turn cost
5.2 — Construction budget
5.0
4.8
4.6

— Total budget

Client constant throughout

Architect

Structural engineer (sub-consultant to Architect)

M&E engineer (sub-consultant to Architect)

Quantity Surveyor

Acoustician

Project Manager

1	November 1998	Architect's brief for development study issued
2	April 1999	Architect-led design team appointed, briefing through summer 1999
3	September 1999	Costs exceed budget for preliminary sketch scheme
4	October 1999	Client devised a priority matrix, brokering various funders/stakeholders priorities as aid to value management (VM)
5	November 1999	Stage C submission to client on budget
6	February 2000	i) Value Engineering (VE) exercise new build 3rd auditorium omitted, façade simplified, forming cinema in tank room omitted, borehole cooling omitted, general reductions in construction spec & ME spec, reductions in acoustic treatment of Wessex Hall. ii) Stage C application for Stage 2 ACE Lottery funding
7	March 2000	i) QS drafted risk register to start to quantify risks posed specifically by working in an existing building. ii) ACE Lottery assessed submission plan stage 2 award, urgent VE in progress
8	May 2000	i) Stage D submission delivered to Client / ACE. ii) Lottery award (Stage 2)
9	End of July 2000	Stage E submitted to client
10	26 October 2000	i) Planning application deposited. ii) Stage E signed off by client
11	November 2000	Stage 3 submission for ACE Lottery award
12	December 2000	Phase 1/1A packages in preparation
13	January 2001	i) Contractor interviews, contractor appointed to Stage I ii) Phase 1/1A/2,3,4 packages issued: lift, façade, roof, demolition & fire plan. iii) Confirmation of ACE construction grant
14	April 2001	i) Building regulations application, smoke control issues raised, requiring cost & specialist consultancy. ii) Reinstatement of borehole cooling. iii) Acoustic tests undertaken in concert hall, acoustic provision reduced
15	May 2001	i) Final phase 2,3,4 packages issued. ii) Client met ACE: ACE checked special conditions of Lottery stage 3 had been met. iii) VE exercise: £288,925 over budget
16	11 June 2001	i) Start on site. Phase 1/1A ii) Theatre technical systems tender returns high.
17	July 2001	i) Tender figures £602,195 over budget: £403,000 of savings required, client economies on 'other costs'. New structure for main elevation omitted ii) VE: borehole cooling omitted, BSO offices omitted and various minor omissions.
18	August 2001	i) £98,000 of savings identified by the QS and a further target of £60,000 set for Client / design team. ii) Planning permission granted
19	September 2001	Phase 1A completed for handover
20	October 2001	Contractor warned of delay (for late information: consequence of VE redesigns)
21	November 2001	i) Further VE exercises. ii) Extraordinary design information workshop – consultants and contractor to clarify final construction information
22	January 2002	i) Contingency fully expended for construction or project as a whole. Construction £39,980 over budget. ii) Start of phase 3a
23	February 2002	Client wrote to Architect to express concern about overspend
24	March 2002	Planning approval received for external works
25	April 2002	Phase 3a completed, 3b commenced
26	May 2002	i) Bar on further variations. ii) Meeting with ACE to expand ACE contingency on additional works
27	July 2002	Contractor delay notification (steelwork/carpentry). Request for three week extension to construction period
28	23 September 2002	Handover of ticket office, café, gallery, concert hall, theatre and administration office
29	October 2002	i) 3 October - Practical completion. ii) 26 October – opening event.

Timeline constructed from: QS cost reports (1-16); QS cost plans (0-5, C1, C2); QS budgets (1-3); QS cost check 4; QS letters (24/09/99); QS misc. reports (25/08/00, 13/03/02, 10/04/02, 29/05/03, 19/07/02, 23/07/02); Project Manager reports (8,21, 18/01/02); Project Manager letters (15/12/02); Architect misc. report (03/09/03) design team, site and project meeting minutes; and interview transcripts

with what Poole might reasonably expect to win from the Lottery. The Capital bid was submitted in November 1996, assessed through August 1997, and an award was made in April 1998, capped at £10 million.

The timeline (fig. 4.8) reveals, however, that, by early 1998, a £16 million Capital project was being configured with the Arts Council's officers, comprising £12 million of Lottery money matched by £4 million from other sources, the gearing being established as 75% grant to 25% matching funding. PACT's transformational 'vision' for the centre was based on this figure, which, it emerged during the research, was established entirely by working back from an assessment of the potential for raising matching funds that could be deduced from the arts business consultant's informal intelligence-gathering and from Eastwood's involvements with Arts Council England. No construction professionals were involved, as the Technical Director recalled to Short and Barrett: *'The original costs for the project were put together when none of the project team had yet been appointed. We inherited all of this ...'*.[12] However, the budget was cut twice in rapid succession in 1998. A design competition through the winter of 1997-1998 proceeded on the basis of an £8.5 million construction budget, but with the brief for a £12.5 million

Fig. 4.8 Lighthouse, Poole: budget history diagram

construction project. However, even this reduced sum was cut by ACE once more, to £6.5 million. The budget had, therefore, detached itself from the scope of the work that had been envisaged and bid for. We argue that, to interpret the outcome of this project and probably many others, one has to know this back history. The result in this case was, as the Quantity Surveyor, John Howell, observed mournfully, 'we were always on the back foot'.[13]

The client confirmed the rapid and bewildering nature of the downsizing:

When we started, we were looking at the initial budget being something like £16 or £17 million, because we were encouraged by the Arts Council to anticipate a Lottery grant of between £10 and £12 million. I think the day after we interviewed [the architect] they chopped that to something like £9 million ... and then, very shortly after we started looking at it, it was cut down to £6.5 million.[14]

Cave pointed out that this collapse in prospective resource came after PACT's intense consultation and brokering across its competing constituencies:

There were some really serious bits of trimming back done early on, after ... we'd already spoken to all our partners and had brainstorming sessions with all our user groups. We ended up with a situation where they were all expecting one thing and we knew that we didn't have the money to do [things at] the scale that they were expecting. But we had to manage their expectations and give everybody part of what ... they were hoping for.[15]

By 1998, the National Audit Office had thoroughly infiltrated Arts Council England's Lottery accounts. They were shortly to publish a pretty damning report which altered the scale and nature of funding.[16] PACT wished it had been earlier in the queue:

I think it was a matter of timing when you were going into the Lottery. We came just at the tail end of the "honey-pot" time. If you were ready with your feasibility when the Lottery first came out, all you had to do was slap it in and the money arrived the next day. And it did: you got the money upfront. It's only as things went along, and as the Audit Commission [became involved that there were more] checks and [balances].[17]

Before the brokering of Lottery funding, in October 1998 an advertisement was placed in the European Union Journal (OJEU) for Lead Consultants to drive the design team. The necessarily elaborate full European procurement process was entered into, led by Bonar Keenlyside. Candidates were interviewed in early December 1998. Forty-four completed Questionnaires and Expressions of Interest were received. By November an Architect's Brief had been broadly agreed and signed off by the Board. Nine practices were shortlisted and subsequently invited to complete and submit a Pre-Qualification Questionnaire.

On 26 February 1999, four practices were selected to comment and expand upon a Project Specific Questionnaire.[18] It set challenging but exciting questions, drafted with a discernible sense of urgency, such as 'what, in your understanding, is the unique "flavour" of the cultural environment at Poole ... as compared with other UK towns or cities?' (Bournemouth perhaps?) and, 'Poole Arts Centre needs to change: it must "regenerate", "re-invent" or "revitalize". Comment on how you would address this change to create a coherent building ambience [sic] in a multi-function centre ...' and then 'In a hypothetical scenario, how at this early stage would the design team approach conflicts between various performers' and audience requirements for the large auditorium if serious compromise is to be avoided?' This latter question was probably about the quality of the Wessex Hall acoustic, potential improvements to which had the potential to absorb the entire budget.

The Questionnaire continued to probe bidders' views on the opportunities for enhancing the sustainability of the building, and their views on the reasonable design life of key items. Provocatively, it asked for comments on the statement, 'A thermally comfortable and highly stimulating environment would tend to militate against the interest of energy efficient buildings and the use of long life fittings'. There were also knowing questions about quality control of information and co-ordination and with great prescience, 'What quality checking systems are employed to ensure that ... contingency sums need only be spent on genuine unforeseen items?' It questioned what cost monitoring and control would be provided up to tender stage and, turning to the construction phase, asked simply, 'What safeguards will be in place to ensure that the budget is not exceeded by variations during the construction period?'

The fourteen page, November 1998 Architect's Brief was issued with large scale drawings of the Centre.[19] It was divided into 'Background', a summary of the situation with the Lottery; 'Artistic Development' summarizing the mission '... the home of artistic excellence ... presenting a well balanced programme covering *all* art forms and entertainments' (author's emphasis), concluding 'the opportunity for development and renewal is real and thrilling'. It bemoaned the undeveloped opportunities to 'address participatory needs of its community', and pledged to correct this void with intensive outreach programmes and 'no risk schemes' for first time attendees. 'Refurbishment and remodelling objectives' asserted that 'the activity should define the space not the space define the activity' an important phrase in the 'charrettes' during which the competition entry was invented,[20] and that 'the design should ... *communicate the "wow" factor* internally and externally' (author's emphasis) and facilitate 'installation of a Wurlitzer organ'. 'Internal issues and External issues' summarized the nitty-gritty of required repairs and access problems.

The four competing practices were interrogated in their responses during marathon two-hour interviews in April 1999, responding off the cuff to such additional questions as, 'what is the single worst thing about your practice?' An appointment was made in late April, immediately on hearing the first tranche of funding had been released by the Lottery fund. The winning team had produced a diagnostic study of the building in use on a mid-winter night in early 1999, presented as a 'ghosted' aerial view. The building had looked deserted on that evening, but probably contained 2500 people as every venue was full. The Centre's administrative functions, displaced from their original location to enable the provision of a cinema, had migrated into the foyers and onto its glazed walls, masking the intense crush in the foyers behind when the building was viewed from the street. The foyers seemed large enough during the day but could not begin to absorb 1700 people anxiously seeking refreshment and/or relief in twenty minutes. Many concertgoers stayed glumly in their seats. Those in the know crept quickly up to a much quieter upper circle foyer where one might get to a sofa and a drink. Only the able-bodied could climb in and out of the Seldown Gallery. The Towngate Theatre had a very disconcerting flutter echo across the front of the stage, due to the later concave walls that had been built flanking the stage. Its fly tower was too low to be fully flexible, while the backstage areas, not least the star dressing rooms, showed the legacy of the mid 1970s financial crises. They were almost insanitary.

The summer of 1999 was spent auditing every space in the building, incorporating its occupants' own critique. A long, diverse shopping list of small items emerged, plus a new performance space. Connecting every space was the network of mechanical and electrical services, pipes, cables and ducts. Arup Acoustics made forty-five recommendations, many about enhancing the Wessex Hall acoustic but nothing radical enough to fundamentally change it. Larry Kirkegaard, the Chicago acoustician suggested by the Orchestras, memorably triggered a standing wave on his walk down the rake by clapping his hands at the correct interval. The Hall is too wide to yield a perfect acoustic and his interest was in making fundamental adjustments to the space. However, his bid was unsuccessful.

The architect's Stage C Report appeared in November 1999. It catalogued the investigations and critiqued the fourteen point plan of the competition entry which had included stripping off the main elevation and extending the foyers out by two metres, clearing out the foyers and adding an administration penthouse, demolishing the Seldown Gallery and building a new Flexible Performance Place, dealing with the Towngate Theatre and the Wessex Hall, plus re-landscaping the frontage and gardens beyond (fig. 4.9). It presented two further iterations, Scheme 2 of 9 August and Scheme 3 of 31 August (figs. 4.10 and 4.11). Scheme 2 proposed to extend to the west towards the town, adding new grand stairs, a new box office, a new Flexible Performance Space (FPS), making considerable interventions into the backstage world of dressing rooms, and creating a roof-top café. The client was broadly receptive, with their interest developing in sectioning off whole venues for quiet nights when just the Towngate or the FPS were functioning.

Scheme 3 retracted back into the envelope of the 1978 building, except for the addition of the FPS and a second main stair placed on the elevation. It rapidly evolved into Scheme 4 (figs. 4.12 and 4.13) in which one can see an environmental strategy emerging, to stack ventilate the foyers naturally through six towers propped up along the frontage, white rendered and 'streamlined' in the nautical manner, with mesh sunshading strung between them. This proposal then retracted a little further into a Scheme 5 (figs. 4.14 and 4.15). The Stage C Report opened with computer generated images of the new working façade. Compared with its original appearance, the building would have become unrecognizable (fig. 4.16). The saving from omitting the air-conditioning installations was to fund this physical infrastructure at least in part. The Report summarized the weekly meetings held through this period to try to contain and organize the disparate shopping lists, drowning in the minutiae of operational observations. The life of the building was extremely complicated. Even the cash taken at the various counters went on a convoluted journey through the building. A synthesis was forced at the meeting of 26 October to decide what to submit in progress to the Lottery administrators.

The Report concluded with a distillation of the previous six months of soul searching, generating and critiquing designs into seventeen broad interventions, each notionally costed by the QS and categorized 'Imperative', 'Very Important', 'Important', 'Dropped from List'. The 'Imperative' list dealt with the two main auditoria, the public foyers and delivers a new accessible visual arts gallery. The 'Very Important' list included the new Flexible Performance Space, improvements to the accessibility of backstage areas and technical provision to the auditoria. Last in this section was the transformation of the exterior of the building, including its immediate landscape. The designers were surprised at this ranking; the poor image of the building had seemed during the competition to have been considered the principal problem. 'Important' items included the refurbishment of all the dressing rooms, the making of new art/craft workshops, and the remodelling of the function rooms and kitchen. Edited out of the list altogether were the extension to the Orchestras' accommodation, a new office penthouse, and a simpler entrance into the Towngate Theatre. The clients were decisive and quick in making these judgements, using a device unbeknown to the design team which shall emerge later in the chapter.

THE PROGRESS OF THE LOTTERY BID

In December 1999, the Poole Arts Centre management and representatives of Poole Borough Council met the Arts Council Lottery team in London to discuss the capital bid and the award of a Stabilization Grant. This grant would help to restructure the organization into the form required to survive prolonged phased closures of different

POOLE ARTS CENTRE
SHORT & ASSOCIATES - **Shopping List**

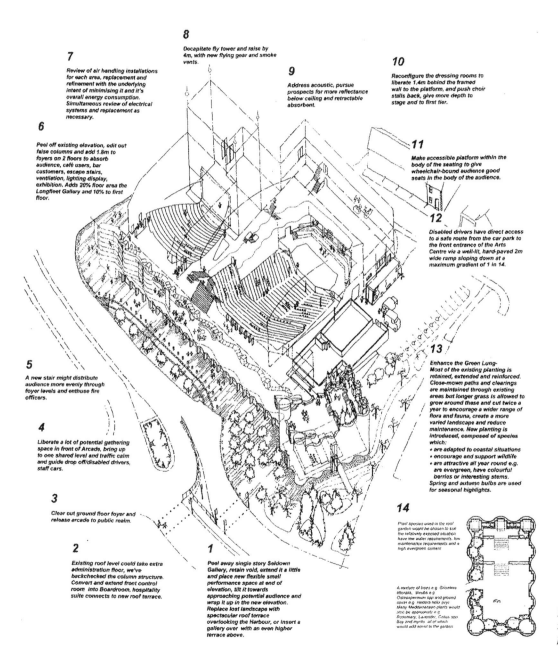

7

Review of air handling installations for each area, replacement and refinement with the underlying intent of minimising it and it's overall energy consumption. Simultaneous review of electrical systems and replacement as necessary.

8

Decapitate fly tower and raise by 4m, with new flying gear and smoke vents.

9

Address acoustic, pursue prospects for more reflectance below ceiling and retractable absorbent.

10

Reconfigure the dressing rooms to liberate 1.4m behind the framed wall to the platform, and push choir stalls back, give more depth to stage and to first tier.

6

Peel off existing elevation, edit out false columns and add 1.8m to foyers on 2 floors to absorb audience, café users, bar customers, escape stairs, ventilation, lighting display, exhibition. Adds 20% floor area the Longfleet Gallery and 10% to first floor.

11

Make accessible platform within the body of the seating to give wheelchair-bound audience good seats in the body of the audience.

12

Disabled drivers have direct access to a safe route from the car park to the front entrance of the Arts Centre via a well-lit, hard-paved 2m wide ramp sloping down at a maximum gradient of 1 in 14.

5

A new stair might distribute audience more evenly through foyer levels and enthuse fire officers.

4

Liberate a lot of potential gathering space in front of Arcade, bring up to one shared level and traffic calm and guide drop off/disabled drivers, staff cars.

13

Enhance the Green Lung-
Most of the existing planting is retained, extended and reinforced. Close-mown paths and clearings are maintained through existing areas but longer grass is allowed to grow around these and cut twice a year to encourage a wider range of flora and fauna, create a more varied landscape and reduce maintenance. New planting is introduced, composed of species which:
• are adapted to coastal situations
• encourage and support wildlife
• are attractive all year round e.g. are evergreen, have colourful berries or interesting stems.
Spring and autumn bulbs are used for seasonal highlights.

3

Clear out ground floor foyer and release arcade to public realm.

14

Plant species used in the roof garden would be chosen to suit the relatively exposed situation have low water requirements, low maintenance requirements and a high evergreen content.

A mixture of trees e.g. Griselinia littoralis, shrubs e.g. Osteospermum spp and ground cover e.g. Hedera helix ivy. Many Mediterranean plants would also be appropriate e.g. Rosemary, Lavender, Cistus spp Bay and myrtle, all of which would add scent to the garden.

2

Existing roof level could take extra administration floor, we've backchecked the column structure. Convert and extend front control room into Boardroom, hospitality suite connects to new roof terrace.

1

Peel away single story Seldown Gallery, retain void, extend it a little and place new flexible small performance space at end of elevation, tilt it towards approaching potential audience and wrap it up in the new elevation. Replace lost landscape with spectacular roof terrace overlooking the Harbour, or insert a gallery over with an even higher terrace above.

Fig. 4.9 Stage C, November 1999: the 'shopping list' of possible interventions

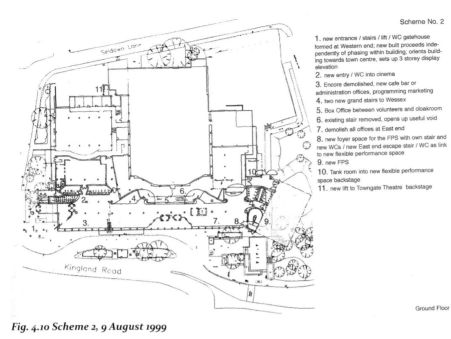

Scheme No. 2

1. new entrance / stairs / lift / WC gatehouse formed at Western end; new built proceeds independently of phasing within building; orients building towards town centre, sets up 3 storey display elevation

2. new entry / WC into cinema

3. Encore demolished, new cafe bar or administration offices, programming marketing

4. two new grand stairs to Wessex

5. Box Office between volunteers and cloakroom

6. existing stair removed, opens up useful void

7. demolish all offices at East end

8. new foyer space for the FPS with own stair and new WCs / new East end escape stair / WC as link to new flexible performance space

9. new FPS

10. Tank room into new flexible performance space backstage

11. new lift to Towngate Theatre backstage

Ground Floor

Fig. 4.10 Scheme 2, 9 August 1999

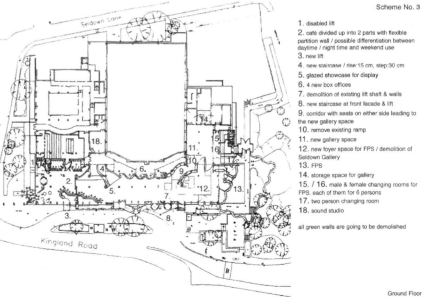

Scheme No. 3

1. disabled lift

2. café divided up into 2 parts with flexible partition wall / possible differentiation between daytime / night time and weekend use

3. new lift

4. new staircase / rise:15 cm, step:30 cm

5. glazed showcase for display

6. 4 new box offices

7. demolition of existing lift shaft & walls

8. new staircase at front facade & lift

9. corridor with seats on either side leading to the new gallery space

10. remove existing ramp

11. new gallery space

12. new foyer space for FPS / demolition of Seldown Gallery

13. FPS

14. storage space for gallery

15. / 16. male & female changing rooms for FPS, each of them for 6 persons

17. two person changing room

18. sound studio

all green walls are going to be demolished

Ground Floor

Fig. 4.11 Scheme 3, 31 August 1999

4. Poole Arts Centre – 'The Lighthouse'

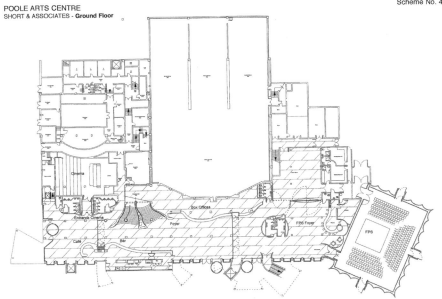

Fig. 4.12 Scheme 4, ground floor plan

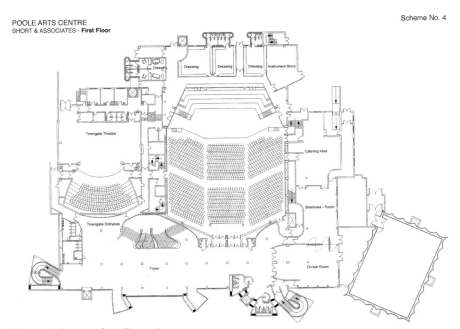

Fig. 4.13 Scheme 4, first floor plan

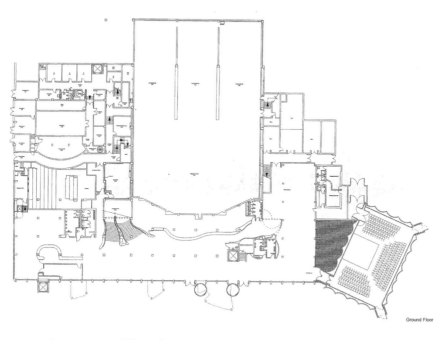

Ground Floor

Fig. 4.14 Scheme 5, ground floor plan

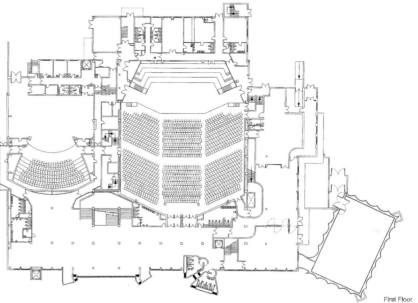

First Floor

Fig. 4.15 Scheme 5, first floor plan

Fig. 4.16 Initial perspective images of a reworked front elevation

revenue-earning parts of the building and ultimately to transform it into the form required to move into and run the refurbished building. The Stage C evaluation arrived in Poole on 10 April 2000, but Malcolm Allen, the Acting Head of Capital Applications, had already written to the Director on 26 January with a commentary on the Stage Evaluation C Visit.[21] He rehearsed the various timetables for consideration by the Capital Advisory Panel and ultimately the Council itself. He encouraged the applicant, without prejudice, saying that if tenders within the budget were returned in January 2001, this 'useful convergence' could

offer 'a potentially very high level of cost and programme certainty around the date when ACE is making a decision on the Stage 3 application'. Turning to the Capital Scheme, he observed that the Trust had been coy about explaining how the physical development proposals would deliver their artistic and corporate vision, 'therefore that potential may not yet therefore [sic] be regarded as proven'. The letter noted that, amongst the various pieces of information required (cost plans, cost benefit analysis, transitional planning, risk analysis, VAT prognosis ...), 'there is concern and potential risk that the figures presented in the

Stage C documentation may prove insufficient to deliver the current scheme, and that the current 5% contingency allowance may prove low for a building of this nature and a project at this stage'. It concluded with 'Information Requirements', a list of fifteen additional reports and strategy documents to be supplied, with an implied deadline of 4 April.

The letter galvanized the Trust's senior officers, who distributed it amongst the design team. The client's new project Steering Group summoned the design team on 11 February to reiterate the Arts Council Lottery's rules of engagement insofar as they meshed with their priorities and those of the Borough, who had offered to match all additional funds raised by the centre. The design team was instructed unambiguously that:

– The project must fall within budget including the provision of sufficient contingency and risk reserves.
– The fabric of the shell to the building was to be made good.
– The building must be suitable to fulfil the programming requirements and aspirations of Poole Arts Centre as outlined in their business plan.
– The front of the building must have a 'wow' factor and enhance the area.
– Greater investment was required in catering provision.

- Any works carried out must have minimum expected life of twenty years.
- The project must create a more comfortable environment for patrons, artistes and staff.

On the basis that these requirements were to be fulfilled, the Board agreed to submission of the next Second Stage application for an interim award, with advance notice that there was a positive intention to submit the Third Stage application. On 9 March, two of the Arts Council's evaluators, Geoff Horley and Arthur Stafford, re-visited Poole to school the Trust in preparing for the Arts Council's Panel. There were some misunderstandings in terms of cost certainty and risk, some inter-contamination of capital and revenue funding. Something had to go. The QS referred to the tidemark on the list of the sixty-seven sub-projects which constituted the scheme at that stage. Where was the essential integrity of the design? The Borough Council reviewed the scheme at this time and asked similar questions. Their senior officer, Jim Bright, reported back that Committee members had observed that the scheme was very different to that which had clinched the competition.[22] Bright offered the personal view that the project had 'changed so much that it had taken away the very reasons you chose the architect'.

Cave sent an e-mail to the architect on 30th March, subject 'Tide marking', which observed unhappily that 'the whole of the project is so inter-dependent that it is hard to find any ways of pruning without revisiting the whole scheme'.[23] However Second Stage funding was awarded on schedule in May, allowing Stage D, Detailed Design, to formally commence. The Stage D Report was delivered in April 2000. The list of consultants had grown considerably including specialists in access, catering, public arts, and landscaping. A project management consultancy was shortly to be appointed.[24] The project proceeded towards the construction phase. This period was planned defensively by the project managers, using a New Engineering Contract form that incorporated a two-stage tender to bring a contractor onto the team early,

and a management contracting-type process which dissolved the project into discrete packages, each of which was aligned to the way in which the industry is de-constructed into subcontractor types and realms. One might reflect that this was an odd way to proceed, the client having previously spotted that the project was highly interconnected. We shall learn how this turned out shortly, but it is worth pausing to consider the Lottery application process and its unintended consequences.

REFLECTIONS ON THE LOTTERY PROCESS

The interim award had been made nearly four years after the initial appointment of the arts business consultant to expedite the application process. Part of this period had been spent waiting for feedback, but much of it was spent assembling the various stage bids. The client recalled:

> I must say I was gobsmacked when you rang the other day and I started looking through the amount of work that I'd got through. The archive of that work is quite immense. Just putting together the applications to the Lottery Trust is monumental ... And each one, you repeat almost all the work you've done but have to re-edit it and re-go through it. When the application left here for the construction works, ... a hired van [was needed] to take it to the Arts Council because you can fill the back of a Luton van with the amount of paper. It's ten copies of everything.[25]

We have encountered similar resentment in other case studies, at the apparent lack of trust, the strain on resources caused by an almost obsessive insistence on due diligence, compounded by its apparent ineffectualness. Here, however, there is a sense of work being displaced back onto the applicant, who, as we have already seen, was thought to be behind in the delivery of reports and justifications during the crucial second stage of submission:

> When we [began, the process was], "that's a good idea, here's a cheque, go and do it, we're not going to check." When the Audit Commission said, "you've got to be more stringent," instead of taking that on board and becoming more stringent themselves, all they've ever done is pass it onto the client. Every time something new comes in, they pass it onto the client ... and without any guidance [as] to what they actually want ... And so they almost act as the middle man and let somebody else to do the work ... and so they're asking people who have got no knowledge of the industry to do the work. You only do it once or perhaps twice in your life but you're being expected to do the work which the supervising body is doing and that's where the anger comes from ... You do it to the best of your ability, then they say, "that's not what we wanted." ... They can't tell you what they do want but they send it back and so it becomes a protracted operation.[26]

Cave later argued that the funders should commit on the basis of the successful application:

> And then say "that's it" and "[this is] now the officer who is going to look after that and you work hand in hand with him." If they were on your side and it was worth doing, why do you have to keep going back again and again? Why can't they have the officer there at a sufficient level to be able to guard their money?

Peter Barrett observed during this conversation that the entire Arts Council Lottery exercise appeared to be about 'risk management', but that well-established protocols for managing risk had become obscured by other agendas. In the earlier period perhaps this was the imperative, to be seen to be awarding funds at the rate expected by their political masters. He suggested to Cave:

> they could actually mitigate their risk by knowing better what was happening. Is that fair?

There is a suggestion here, made in parallel case studies, for example the refusal to countenance contingency sums for the Contact Theatre project, that the Arts Council Lottery team could have been better versed in the functioning of the construction industry. How well prepared was the applicant?

THE APPLICANT'S SECRET TOOL: VALUE ENGINEERING IN PLEASANT SURROUNDINGS

Unbeknown to the design team, the clients empowered themselves in the face of shrinking resources by inventing a sophisticated 'do-it-yourself' Value Engineering model, brokering a weighted matrix of competing stakeholders' needs and aspirations (Table 4.2), including a heading for the complete transformation of the building's dreary and unloved exterior. The Quantity Surveyor (QS) was included up to a point in this confidential strategy, if only because construction costs, as traditionally expressed in the 'elements' of the Victorian 'Standard Method of Measurement' (concrete, bricks, plastering, glazing and so on) tend to be unintelligible to a lay person struggling to decide between the items on an unaffordable shopping list. The QS reconfigured the out-turn cost estimates into 186 identifiable sub-projects, eventually boiled down to 106, which were then organized under the seventeen broad headings conjured up by the Steering Committee in order to make manifest the various constituency's interests.[27]

> We couldn't look at the project in the round. You've got to go into detail. For example, the brick ties which were missing in the external walls and the windows [that were] falling out. You can't just take a chainsaw to the design.[28]

Table 4.2 Lighthouse, Poole, extract from the 'priority matrix' used by the client team to ensure effective Value Engineering

	Cost £	Economical	Political	Practical	Weighting
1. Flexible performance space	99,000-1,140,000				
Shell	600,000	6	9	8	1
Link	50,000	5	3	8	1
Dressing rooms	100,000	3	1	4	3
Timber infill to stairs	5,000	0	0	4	1
M&E	inc. in shell	1	2	8	1
Seating, stage lighting, fitting out	50,000-200,000	6	3	9	5+
Landscaping	25,000	0	0	0	7
Theatre technical systems	160,000	7	2	9	1
2. Wessex Hall	893,000				
Staging	25,000	6	4	6	5
Seating	250,000	10	10	10	1+
Acoustic enhancement	58,000	3	10	8	1
Disabled access/Balcony works	25,000	0	5	0	5
Theatre technical systems	485,000	3	0	9	1
General redecoration	50,000	9	9	9	1
3. Wessex backstage	252,000-353,000				
Instrument store relocation	60,000-85,000	0	0	6	5
Toilets	12,000-18,000	6	10	10	2
Dressing rooms and general refurbishment	180,000-250,000	2	4	8	1

	Cost £	Economical	Political	Practical	Weighting
4. Towngate Theatre	650,000				
Acoustic enhancement	35,000	6	7	3	1
Disabled access	20,000	10	10	10	1
Theatre technical systems	570,000	3	0	9	1
Seating					
General redecoration	25,000	9	9	9	1
5. Towngate backstage	180,000-350,000				
New Lift (to plant room level)	100,000	0	3	8	1
Disabled access and facilities	30,000-50,000	1	8	8	1
Upgrade showers and dressing rooms	50,000-200,000	5	2	6	2
General redecoration		9	9	9	1
6. Façade	530,000-715,000				
New lifts	200,000	4	5	5	1
Staircases	125,000	2	8	5	3
Toilets	110,000	2	8	5	3
Brise-soleil	10,000-30,000	2	8	5	3
New cladding inc. structural frame	Not an option	-	-	-	-
Masonry cladding	15,000-20,000	2	8	5	3
Window repairs/replacement	20,000-120,000	2	8	5	3
New entrance doors	40,000-100,000	2	8	5	3
New signage	10,000 up	2	8	5	3

Key

1+ Vital to our continued business

1 Of great imporatance to PACT

2 Important that these areas are refurbished but not necessarily requiring a rebuild

3 Whilst acknowledging the importance of the façade as a whole these items are dependent on other parts of the scheme

4 Of vital importance but there may be a more economical way of providing them

5+ Could manage without if absolutely necessary

5 Would be nice but we could manage without unless other parts of the scheme demand their inclusion

6 Would be important, if dividing screens happen

>7 Come bottom of our list of requirements

Value Engineering discussions were held off-site in a Theatre Managers' club in Covent Garden, the most significant being in February 2000. The sessions were startlingly quick and unambiguous. The QS, Howell, recalled how carefully briefed he had to be on the distribution of predicted costs:

We had to be able to fire answers off the cuff and say, "if we take this out or change this, what's the result?" fairly rapidly. The problem with a building like this is [that] nothing's in isolation. You make one change and it immediately affects three or four other issues ... associated with it.[29]

Time in the form of accelerating inflation was eating away at the budget.

One of the concerns we were having at that stage was programme: because the original programme had already slipped, and was continuing to slip. All the time it was slipping was during a period of what I would call relatively high inflation, so we were losing money to inflation all the time because the end budget was not getting increased to take account of that. Any cost advice we gave had to be conditional on achieving a certain programme otherwise every year that went by another 5% of the budget would disappear.[30]

Cave later reminded the QS of his tactics for the Value Engineering meeting:

You'd divided the project into tiled compartments. There were about forty or fifty pieces of work which had been issued to the design team and to us before hand so we'd gone away and decided if there were any of these that we now thought we could do without. If not, were there any of these that we thought we could simplify or lessen. It was at that meeting where we took the decision that, instead of having a purpose built separate

building linked to this one with a small scale performance space, we would use part of the building that existed.

The day before, the idea of moving the cinema into what was the tank room had also been raised. The QS insisted:

That was the only way we could treat the building. We couldn't look at it in the round because ... there were considerable areas where we had to do very little, if anything at all. You've got to look at which bits you must do something to, how big are they, how much can we afford to do? And, in some places, however much you have got to do, [when you go in] you're exposing potential problems which you're going to have to solve one way or another. There were brick ties missing, rotted away, in the external walls. The windows were falling out and had to be replaced. There was an argument at one stage to say, "should our Lottery money go against this?" This is really a long-term maintenance issue; it shouldn't be included in that budget at all. That went round the houses several times.[31]

At the crucial February 2000 meeting, which we now know was convened on hearing the Arts Council's views on the Second Stage submission, 'money was drained out of the façade' and put into the backstage provision (figs. 4.17 and 4.18).[32] The architects were dismayed and confused at this news. The old elevations would still 'grin through' the new, metal-clad cooling towers added at the front and above the new studio to the side (fig. 4.19). Six years later, Cave explained to the architect:

In the end, as an Arts Trust, we get our money for what we do inside the building, not what it looks like outside ... If you're going to take Arts Lottery money, there are criteria set down and you have to fulfil [those criteria] with that money. You have to fulfil ... your purpose. Which is nothing to do with the outside of the building

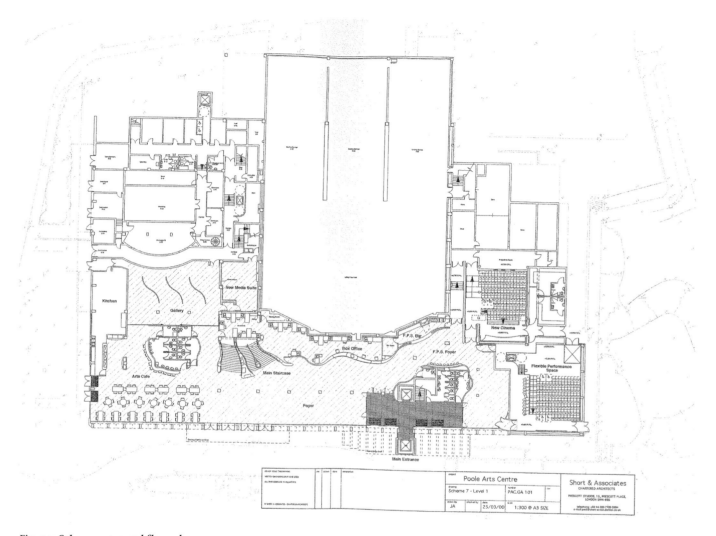

Fig. 4.17 Scheme 7, ground floor plan

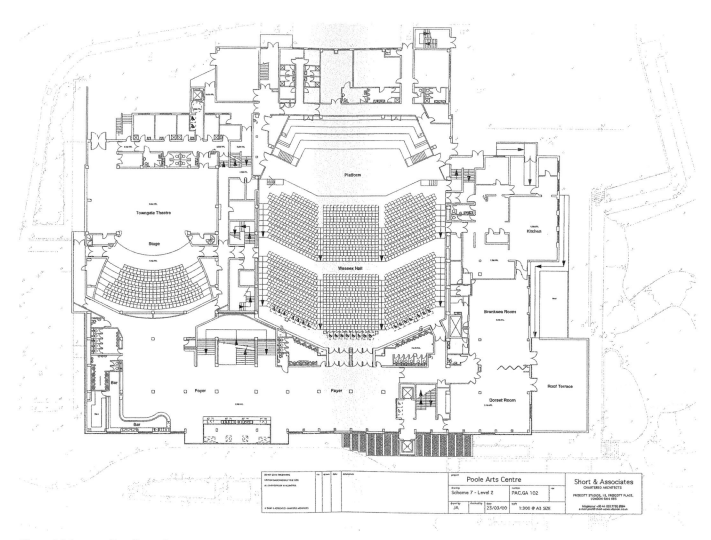

Fig. 4.18 Scheme 7, first floor plan

... The outside of the building was dependant on putting public art in ... and the fact that [the designers] used Peter [Freeman] as a public artist for the outside, for lighting, meant we could change the front of the building. The Lottery ... are [sic] always looking at whether you're fulfilling those criteria and to the right sort of proportion. The longest meetings that I had with our [Arts Council] monitor were about making sure that those criteria were always top of the agenda. They were willing to withdraw the whole grant if you started diverging from what it was they were after.[33]

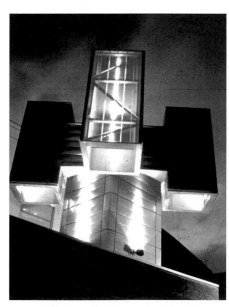

Fig. 4.19 The ventilation stack above the new Flexible Performance Space

THE COST CONSULTANT: MANAGING VALUE

The Northcroft team realized by the autumn of 1999 that the Lottery's arbitrary cuts in the likely award had derailed the 'vision'. No amount of saving and pairing back could save it in its entirety. Northcroft's Quantity Surveyor, John Howell, later recalled:

This [project] was between £12 million and £15 million. It was at that point that we said, "well, hang on, we've got... from the QS point of view, ... challenges, let's not call them difficulties." The whole time through the process, we had an ultimate end user who had an anticipation originally based on a bigger budget. [If] there's a lesson to be learned, that's where it lies. That very first estimate, that very first exercise you do right from day one, long before you've got any real knowledge or detail of the scheme at all, needs to be generous enough ...[34]

We return to one of the central questions of this study: are Arts Projects actually 'different', or are all projects essentially the same in management terms be they to build buildings, aircraft or submarines? Howell continued:

I think the trouble is that people in that sort of situation tend to use historical cost data which is okay if you're building normal buildings. But arts buildings are obviously unique. You can [look at] a certain amount of historic data, but it doesn't work well with buildings of this sort, particularly not when you're dealing with [an] existing building which has got to [be] alter[ed]. You've got to start from scratch and the only way is to get somebody in at that very early stage and start putting some prices to those initial concepts, a very, very crude early statement. But at least you get an order of cost which is more likely to be realistic.[35]

Chris Timlin, the Project Manager, added that the constantly evolving mismatching of budget to project content burnt resources:

Even if the budget was right at first, ... there's still then the issue of the Arts Council saying, "Yes, you have £10 million." The brief then was developed on that basis, but then three months or six months later them [ACE] turning around and saying, "oh, you've only actually got half that amount." Effectively, with that amount of money you're writing off £20,000 of consultant fees ... your time.[36]

The budget set in the context of the whole existing building was relatively very small. As Cave observed, for this reason alone cost per metre rates were meaningless, as they may be for most, if not all, refurbishment projects:

> If you took the whole of the ... building and you gave it two coats of emulsion and a new carpet you would know where to put it. But you are saying you're going to carpet the front room ...[37]

WORKSTAGES E, F, G: RE-CONSTRUCTING POOLE ARTS CENTRE

By June 2000, the scheme had progressed beyond Stage D and the Trust started to present it to the public on notification of the next stage award. The *Daily Echo*, June 15 issue, carried the story 'Mixed views over Arts Centre vision'.[38] Interviewees commented, 'the building looks like a Third World industrial unit, with no charm at all. It will be like flared jeans – flavour of the month now but out-of-date in five years' time'. Others bemoaned the loss of the Bournemouth Sinfonietta for lack of funds; one confessed, 'the Arts Council always baffled me'. One female respondent objected, 'the items that go on at the Arts Centre are too highly priced for the average person. It is a lot of money for a building like that'.

The newly appointed project managers' first task was to renegotiate all the consultants' fees downwards. By October 2000, a full set of General Arrangement drawings had been signed off by the Board. An advertisement was placed in the European Journal for the contractor with a view to appointment in January 2001 with a Stage One tender figure established, all unfolding as the Acting Head of Capital Applications had suggested to coincide with the cycle of Arts Council meetings. The National Lottery offer letter for a grant up to £5,175,000 is dated 16 February 2001, signed by Moss Cooper, Director of Capital Services.[39] It contained nine Special Conditions. These dwelt largely on financial management, residual questions from the evaluation. Special Condition Six: Risk Mitigation required 'an updated risk analysis factoring in the impact of your capital works upon your operations during the transitional project period,' and a payment schedule pegged to the delivery of voluminous documentation discharging the Special Conditions.

The Trust went about interviewing contractors with the same diligence as it had the designers. The client explained:

> We made the assumption, before we interviewed anybody, that there was no point in looking at their professional qualifications because [if] they've answered the advert we assume that they're capable of doing the job. What we said was that "these are the people we're going to work with ... we didn't want to see the Managing Director, we wanted to see the guy that did the job." So we were choosing people ... we thought we would get on with.[40]

In January 2001, Stansells were appointed to Stage One, as constructability consultants in effect. The project manager explained the concept of the two-stage process:

> Essentially ... their appointment is competitively tendered on the basis of a budget cost plan, which is a detailed cost plan. They price their preliminary costs and they declare their own overheads and profit from their costs. And they also price their pre-construction fee; which was £30-40,000 I think. They then work with the team to put together the work packages and tender the work packages in the normal way in the sequential manner over the course of the stage E process, and then feed that back into ... an actual contract value.[41]

The design team settled down to produce the 'work packages'. These packages disentangled the design into demolitions, stripping out, toilets, reflected ceilings, roof, external envelope, windows, glazing, staircases, internal partitions, suspended ceilings, floor finishes, signage, and so on. Their release schedule was fearsome, at least a full package per week. The project by now was intricately phased. Phase One refurbished the Wessex Hall, commencing in May 2001 and completing on time in October. But costs were gently escalating across the myriad items.

The 'bible', as it came to be known within the design team, was the QS's Cost Book 5. The client relied heavily on this account of the base cost of the contract design:

> Following that meeting, or shortly afterwards, what sticks in my memory was cost plan 5, the 5th version of the cost plan. That was the one which was to be "the bible." Everyone, every consultant, signed up for it ... So all the time we keep going back and saying that's what we said it's going to be.[42]

The QS explained how he expected this document to be used:

> A designer drawing something could look at it and see what cost [was] allowed [for] a specific thing. Carpet, for example: if you were carpeting a particular area, you knew you had to obtain a carpet within £X per square metre or it wouldn't fly. Wall finishes, too: in many cases we didn't know what was going on the wall, but as long as it was less than £10 per square metre [it was fine].[43]

The logic of the packaging strategy eluded the design team, particularly the architects, because the unpicking proliferated work. The QS explained the drivers from the industry side in a particularly transparent way:

> Where the difficulty arises is that architects, quantity surveyors and contractors think of the project in different ways. [Architects] think in terms of plans and elevations and section, [quantity surveyors] think in terms of elements, and contractors think in terms of the work packages. The difficulty always comes where those three visions of the project don't actually line up.

> There was a very brief period to go from your concept and outline design through to working drawings that could actually be built. That was probably the most fraught part of the project, as far as we were concerned, [when we were] packaging the work up ... because we had [telescoped the process]. Normally for two stage [procurement], ... the contractor gets in early but we don't give him the project to get started until the Stage Two figure has been agreed. In this case we couldn't do that because we didn't have time. We had to let an individual part of the project in advance to get it going, which is not ideal. As it happened, with this contactor it worked very well but in different circumstances we could have been taken for a ride. It's a real risk. But I think by the time we took the risk we had a good enough idea of what this contractor was made of and to think it was a risk that was worth taking.[44]

Howell and Timlin expanded on this theme:

> Howell: I guess you could say, with a project of this sort, probably it's the only way you could deliver it. We do it umpteen times but, generally speaking, where you're dealing with alterations in a complex building and the building remains in use all these are issues that make it more complex. If it were a new-build theatre I would say, "let's think about it." If we want to go that way we have to have a special reason for doing it.

> Timlin: You have the general risk of working in an existing building and not knowing [everything].

> Howell: Absolutely. The foundations that we found in that old tank room, for example. If you want curtain walls, how do you do that without making it clear exactly which curtain wall you're going to use before you start? So it's maintaining those competition issues. It's very difficult. These are issues that I don't think have been addressed

by the profession as a whole, by the industry as a whole, and it's happening increasingly all the time. You're being driven down a particular route by the product security and I think it's another subject for study really.[45]

However, the inexorable rise in costs through the spring of 2001 alarmed the client, to the extent that the Chairman was urged to write in dismayingly formal terms to the architect, who was appalled.[46] His response dwelled on the package process, the lodging of delivered work to the QS where it seemed to him it stuck whilst desperate cost analysis and negotiations were transacted. The contractor lodged a formal claim against steelwork information on 15 October 2001, observing drily:

we would be pleased to receive your drawing programme for all *the works* [his emphasis] *and we will then advise you of our completion date.*[47]

Nonetheless, the work proceeded pretty much to schedule, but to the consultants' astonishment the client team started to instruct new work and re-introduce omitted items. There was an end game in progress with the Arts Council, concealed from the designers for three years.

END GAME

The timeline (fig. 4.8) shows costs rising through the final stages of the project. PACT started to instruct more work; the design team was baffled. The Trust's Project Director explained:

It became obvious to me ... that I wasn't playing the game like you should do. I should be carrying on spending because I found out that the Lottery actually put a contingency sum in for you ... if you overspend. So I needed to spend to get it.[48]

Indeed, there seemed to be little love lost between the Arts Council and PACT, which was still confused some years later by their shifting relationship with the principal funder of the capital project:

There should be a way whereby the deliverer of the public money becomes part of the team at the very beginning ... writing that brief is done with the agent ... they are going to be a partner .. they can help put together a professional team right at the beginning and there is not this "stuttering progress" [that means that] until I know I've got more money I can't go any further.[49]

Similar feelings were expressed across the case studies. The Trust was more able to negotiate at the other end of the exercise, with the contractor using the provisions of the New Engineering Contract to settle the claim for more time and pay a little extra to maintain a reciprocal atmosphere of co-operation.

End of the project, we had a debt of £150,000 which we've now paid off. And we spent ... in the end the total project spend was £9.3 million.[50]

VISION CREEP?

Peter Barrett probed the client on the outcome after a twelve-year journey. He asked:

In terms of the 'vision', then: going right back to the start of this project, lots of aspirations raised and then some of them not able to be fulfilled ... you set off on the project process which you described and steered. What about when it's finished, now that it's being used? Is it anything like the original vision?

The client maintained the 'vision' had survived (figs. 4.20-4.25):

> *Yes, it's very much like the original. There are still things which would have been nice to do. It would have been nice to have completely changed the look of the outside of the building. It would have been nice to have a bigger small performance stage, bigger in the sense [of having] more room around it. But everything we set out to be able to do [in] the building, we are able to do. And with one or two minor criticisms ... what we've done has been well received by the people who use it. Certainly the [number of] people who use it has increased and I don't just mean in [terms of] bums on seats, but as a cross section of the community who come in and use this [centre] now, it's far more than would have come before because they didn't' like the building. The average age now has dropped to thirty-five. And ... we've cracked that awkward age group, the twenty to thirty-five year olds. Which is hard to get into with this kind of building.[51]*

As with other examples in this book, the project also saw changes in the client organization:

Fig. 4.20 The Towngate Theatre, 2010

Fig. 4.21 The ground foyer café, 2010

Fig. 4.22 Translucent panels allow passers-by to gain some sense of the activity within the building at night

Fig. 4.23 The cinema, created within the former plant area

At the same we were doing this we had to completely change the structure of the company, the organization, the way we worked. The whole business has changed completely; you wouldn't recognize it.[52]

PROJECT LEARNINGS

When asked about the general learnings from their capital project which might be applied elsewhere, Cave commented:

I think there's a problem with arts projects and it will always be the same. We are such a poor profession ... you have to cut your cloth according to the width. You'll always going to have to make what you do fit the budget. And ninety-nine times out of one hundred that money is going to [be] public money.

Does intense risk avoidance actually engender risk?

There's really an argument about risk, whether you manage risk by embracing it or if you manage it by building a big wall between yourself and it. People have gone for the latter, and it's a dodgy way of doing it really because it means you don't have the information and you don't' have the control.[53]

The dynamic nature of design for the arts comes through very strongly in this project. People were readjusting and accommodating changes all the way through and effectively took control of the chaotic. Cave certainly saw matters thus, suggesting that it was *'only the timescale that made it chaotic really'.*[54]

Perhaps the last word belongs to the wise Quantity Surveyor, an observation on the notion that quantification destroys creativity:

There is the assumption that as soon as you impose a financial discipline on something you're

Fig. 4.24 The first floor foyer

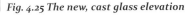

Fig. 4.25 The new, cast glass elevation

immediately going to narrow down options, you're going to remove the flair side of it. And that's not true at all. The most important thing is that if there are to be areas where flair's got to be exhibited, let's find out where they are and make sure, right from the beginning that there's money in there to do it. I think a lot of clients in this field are looking for an iconic building. And then that immediately sends out those kind of messages to say "yes, but ...". As a practice we had to do an investigation into the overrunning cost of the parliament building [Portcullis House, Westminster, the offices used by Members of Parliament]. The conclusion we came to was that the Members of Parliament wanted an expensive building and they got one.[55]

Notes

1   J. Hillier and M. Blyth, *Poole's Pride Regained 1964-1974* (Poole, 1996).
2   Figure calculated for the author by John Howell of Northcroft, the Project Quantity Surveyors.
3   Hillier and Blyth, *Poole's Pride Regained*, passim, for the summary which follows.
4   Thom Gorst, 'Civic life cycles: Short and Associates in Lichfield', *Architecture Today* 143 (Nov. 2003), pp.34-46.
5   Victoria and Albert Museum, Theatre Collection archives, ACGB/120/16: Arts Council papers, ABTT reports 1970-1977.
6   Robin Cave to Alan Short and Peter Barrett, 27 April 2006.
7   Robin Cave to Alan Short and Peter Barrett, 27 April 2006.
8   Short and Associates, November 1999 Design Team Report Workstage C, National Lottery No. 96/1789.
9   Chairman's welcome address opening the Minutes of the Joint Council and Poole Arts Trust Working Party, 9 December 1999, 5pm, copy in Short and Associates archive.
10 Robin Cave to Peter Barrett and Alan Short, 27 April 2006.
11 Robin Cave to Peter Barrett and Alan Short, 27 April 2006.
12 Robin Cave to Alan Short and Peter Barrett, 27 April 2006.
13 John Howell to Alan Short and Peter Barrett, 27 April 2006.
14 Robin Cave to Alan Short and Peter Barrett, 27 April 2006.
15 Robin Cave to Alan Short and Peter Barrett, 27 April 2006.
16 National Audit Office, 'Arts Council of England: monitoring major capital projects funded by the National Lottery', report, 1999.
17 Robin Cave to Alan Short and Peter Barrett, 27 April 2006.
18 'Project Specific Questionnaire' January 1999, Poole Arts Centre Ltd, completed version in the possession of Short and Associates Architects.
19 Poole Arts Trust Ltd, 'Architect's Brief – Development Study', November 1998.
20 Alan Short to Pat Sterry, July 2006.
21 Arts Council England, letter dated 26 January 2000, addressed to Ruth Eastwood, Director Poole Arts Centre from Malcolm Allen, copied to Peter Taylor, Southern Arts Board, no reference.
22 Robin Cave to Alan Short, telephone conversation March 2000, Cave quoting Bright verbatim. Notes in Short's archive.
23 Robin Cave to Short and Associates, e-mail of 30/3/2000, subject 'Tide marking', hard copy in Short and Associates archive.
24 James Nisbet and Partners, Poole office. Interestingly the founding partner James Nisbet became the historian of the costing of building work from the mediaeval period onwards, privately publishing a sequence of booklets.
25 Robin Cave to Alan Short and Peter Barrett, 27 April 2006.
26 Robin Cave to Alan Short and Peter Barrett, 27 April 2006.
27 C.A. Short, P.S. Barrett, A. Dye, M. Sutrisna, 'Impacts of Value Engineering on five Capital Arts Projects', *Building Research and Information* 35/3 (2007), pp.287-315.
28 John Howell to Alan Short and Peter Barrett, 27 April 2006.
29 John Howell to Alan Short and Peter Barrett, 27 April 2006.
30 John Howell to Alan Short and Peter Barrett, 27 April 2006.
31 John Howell to Alan Short and Peter Barrett, 27 April 2006.
32 Alan Short to Pat Sterry, January 2007.
33 Robin Cave to Alan Short and Peter Barrett, 27 April 2006.
34 John Howell to Alan Short and Peter Barrett, 27 April 2006.
35 John Howell to Alan Short and Peter Barrett, 27 April 2006.
36 Chris Timlin to Alan Short and Peter Barrett, 27 April 2006.
37 Robin Cave to Alan Short and Peter Barrett, 27 April 2006.
38 Katherine Hunter, 'Mixed views over Arts Centre vision', *Daily Echo*, 15 June 2000.
39 Letter from Moss Cooper (Arts Council England) to Robin Cave, 16 February 2001, 'Grant reference 00-179, Poole Arts Centre Ltd: Major refurbishment of Poole Arts Centre'.
40 Robin Cave to Alan Short and Peter Barrett, 27 April 2006.
41 Robin Cave to Alan Short and Peter Barrett, 27 April 2006.
42 Robin Cave to Alan Short and Peter Barrett, 27 April 2006.
43 John Howell to Alan Short and Peter Barrett, 27 April 2006.
44 John Howell to Alan Short and Peter Barrett, 27 April 2006.
45 John Howell to Alan Short and Peter Barrett, 27 April 2006.
46 Alan Short to Pat Sterry, July 2006.
47 Letter from Chris Holloway (Project Manager, Stansells) to Short and Associates, ref CTH/510155, in architect's archive.
48 Robin Cave to Alan Short and Peter Barrett, 27 April 2006.
49 Robin Cave to Alan Short and Peter Barrett, 27 April 2006.

50   Robin Cave to Alan Short and Peter Barrett, 27 April 2006.
51   Robin Cave to Alan Short and Peter Barrett, 27 April 2006.
52   Robin Cave to Alan Short and Peter Barrett, 27 April 2006.
53   Robin Cave to Alan Short and Peter Barrett, 27 April 2006.
54   John Howell to Alan Short and Peter Barrett, 27 April 2006.
55   John Howell to Alan Short and Peter Barrett, 27 April 2006.

5.   'Making something extraordinary': Belgrade II, Coventry

Alistair Fair

The re-opening in September 2007 of Coventry's Belgrade Theatre represented the culmination of four years of building work, and many more of planning.[1] Marked by a Gala Night which was hosted by the late Humphrey Lyttelton, the re-opening came just six months before the theatre's fiftieth birthday. It was presented as signalling a return to the values that had characterized the original Belgrade in its early years.[2] This chapter explores the theatre's early twenty-first century capital project, which provided the Belgrade with a second auditorium ('B2'), a rehearsal room, improved backstage accommodation, and expanded front-of-house facilities (Table 5.1). The original 1958 building was also refreshed (fig. 5.1). The chapter highlights not only the challenges of extending a post-war building that is now listed at Grade II, but also issues of funding, multiple and changing ambitions, and 'Value Engineering', as well as the potential tension between making functional space for theatre and making landmark architecture.

Fig. 5.1 Belgrade Theatre: the main entrance in 2008, after restoration

Table 5.1 Belgrade Theatre, case study characteristics

Belgrade Theatre, characteristics	
Receiving/Producing	Receiving and producing
Project driver(s)	Need for a second auditorium to extend performance range plus general refurbishment and upgraded image
Vision	Expansion to England's first post-war purpose-built Civic Theatre, serving the city and its hinterland
Refurbishment/new build	New build second auditorium and refurbishment of existing theatre
Feasibility study	Yes
- in house	Yes
- external consultant	Yes: Levitt Bernstein Architects
Part of bigger arts initiative?	Conceived in present form following abandonment of 1996 plan for Coventry Arts and Media Centre which had established the need for cultural / entertainment facilities in that area
Business plan	Yes
- scope	Comprehensive
Construction budget set?	Yes, derived from pre-feasibility exercise. Initially a £15m refurbishment, reduced to £9.2m of which ca £5.5 was for construction (see timeline)
Final account	£14 million
Funding source(s)	Advantage West Midlands, Arts Council of England, Coventry City Council, ERDF, Charitable plus fundraising
Lead consultant	Project manager
Design innovation	No
Specialist inputs	Acoustician, theatre consultant and technical theatre systems consultants, access consultants, arts business consultants
Value Engineering employed?	Yes
- which stage?	Stage C, largely fit out omissions, continued through stage D and post-tender
Vision creep?	Yes, auditorium form migrated from fixed horseshoe plan through end on configuration to fixed with some flexibility
Political climate	Stable
Contract type	Enabling works under JCT, Phase A and Main contract under GC works, auditorium fit-out as Design and Build
- contractor involvement in design?	No, though auditorium fit-out completed as Design and Build
- quality/time/money priority	money/time/quality
Organizational change?	Restructured before detailed design work commenced

EARLY HISTORY AND AMBITIONS

When it first opened in March 1958, the Belgrade was celebrated as the herald of a new age.[3] Writing in the *Observer*, the critic Kenneth Tynan commented:

Enter most theatres, and you enter the gilded, cupidacious [sic] past. Enter this one, and you are surrounded by the future.[4]

The Belgrade's novelty was two-fold. On the one hand, it was the first all-new professional theatre to be built in Britain for almost twenty years. The only performing arts venue of any real significance to have been constructed since the end of hostilities in 1945 was the Royal Festival Hall, London (1951), a showpiece example of the same Scandinavian-infused Modernism which was to inform the design of the Belgrade. What the Belgrade represented was also novel. The Festival Hall had been conceived as a replacement for the war-damaged Queen's Hall, but its position at the heart of a celebration of British life and the occupation of its designers as architects in the service of the London County Council both hinted at a new place for the arts in the post-war world.[5] As was discussed earlier in this book, wartime governmental support for the practice of the arts was continued from 1946 by the newly founded Arts Council of Great Britain; two years later, local authorities were permitted to use a portion of their rate income to support artistic endeavours. Few authorities embraced this opportunity quite as firmly as Coventry, and by 1965 the Arts Council was itself involved in making financial contributions to building projects, partly to make up the shortfall. For Coventry, however, the opportunity to innovate by not only being the first city since 1939 to have an all-new theatre, but a civic theatre at that, seems to have been only too tempting. Described by one exasperated civil servant in the 1960s as being 'willing to consider any new ideas provided that they have not been tried out by any other local authority',[6] the council's paternalistic attitude and belief that the rapidly expanding city lacked cultural amenities spurred on moves to build a new theatre, much to the dismay of some right-wing members.[7]

The earliest surviving plans, dating from 1953-1954 and now in the City Archives, are remarkably similar to what was built (fig. 5.2). The principal change made during the design process was the omission of a building proposed for the adjacent site, allowing the creation of a substantial public square towards which the theatre presented an expansive glazed elevation. This move cemented the Belgrade's status as an important public building, highlighting the place of the arts in the rebuilt city. Internally, the spacious foyers, common to all patrons (in contrast to the price-segregated entrances and facilities of older venues) plus the auditorium's good sightlines and acoustics all demonstrated the Belgrade's conception as a 'democratic' theatre. The theatre's ambitions were summed up in a dynamic 'Three Year Plan', which promised a varied diet of culture with an emphasis on new writing and international works, as befitted the global links which the bombing raids of 1940 had allowed Coventry to develop and which inspired the gift of timber from Yugoslavia that prompted the theatre's name. Thus the early years saw the premieres of plays by the likes of Arnold Wesker and Shelagh Delaney, produced and performed by a resident Repertory company, with some of the actors living in small bed-sits provided on site. Repertory, which enjoyed a revival in the 1950s and 1960s as a result of the arrival of subsidy, functioned across the country as a valuable training ground for actors and directors, and a number of later-famous names passed through the Belgrade, including Sir Trevor Nunn.

The success of the new theatre was such that, in 1965, Laurence Olivier laid the foundation stone for an extension.[8] We might surmise that there were two motivations behind the wish for more space; the extension was to provide an additional, flexible auditorium plus a rehearsal room and staff offices.[9] On the one hand, the cramped backstage accommodation offered by the original theatre had been noted by visitors even upon its opening in 1958.[10] Second, discussion of alternatives

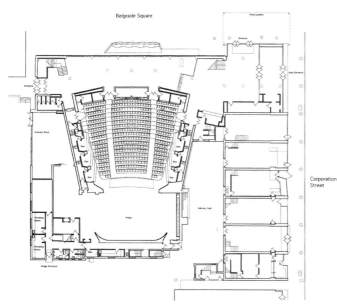

Fig. 5.2 The Belgrade Theatre, plan as built in 1958

to the proscenium-arch stage had gathered pace in the 1950s, and a number of books had been published on the subject by 1965. As a result of these debates, many new theatres of the 1960s were equipped with small 'studio' auditoria which offered flexible seating and staging, and it seems that the Belgrade management did not want to miss out. However, the extension was not to be. An 'experimental theatre' was instead brought into being in an adjacent workshop,[11] while a rehearsal room was found elsewhere. The idea periodically resurfaced, notably in 1983-1985 when extension plans were again drawn up with the aim of substantially expanding the backstage facilities and remodelling the theatre foyers.[12] Once again, however, the vicissitudes of funding meant that the works were essentially limited to a largely cosmetic refurbishment of the Belgrade's public areas, which saw large areas of Martin Froy's foyer wall mosaics (a key element of the original decorative scheme) hidden behind boarding plus the addition of vaguely 'Art Deco' mouldings and cornicing. Through all this, Olivier's foundation stone remained on the

premises, but was reportedly left languishing in a cupboard, upside down.[13]

FORMULATING A CAPITAL PROJECT, 1993-1999

In the mid-1990s, the advent of Lottery funding and the promise of substantial support for building works prompted the Belgrade to revisit its ambitions once again. However, the theatre's circumstances meant that it was unable to profit from the initial flow of money. David Beidas, who took up the position of General Manager in the late 1980s and later became the theatre's Capital Projects Director, recalled:

> The theatre had been through a fairly rough time in the mid 1990s but had emerged from that around 1997 or 1998. As a consequence of the difficulties that it had been through, it had been unable to take advantage of the advent of Lottery funding in 1994. West Midlands Arts felt the organization simply wasn't in a state where it would be prepared to support a bid. So, for the first three or four years, whilst Lottery money was flowing like water, Belgrade was having to deal with its own internal problems.[14]

A particular ambition for the theatre remained the addition of a second auditorium to replace the former workshop that had been converted to function as an *ad hoc* fifty-seat studio. As Beidas put it:

> [The studio] functioned fine within its capabilities. It was possible to create some good and exciting theatre in there, but it was uneconomic. It wasn't designed as a theatre; it was a large room, to all intents and purposes.[15]

Not only, therefore, would a purpose-built studio be more satisfactorily equipped for theatre, but it would also provide a better return by housing a larger audience than was possible in the existing space. In addition, there was an artistic need for a performance space larger than the existing studio. At the time, the Belgrade's programme included an increasing number of shows produced in conjunction with local independent theatre groups which, it was felt, would be better suited to a 200-300 seat space than the 850-seat main house.[16] With a proper studio, the original auditorium could be dedicated to larger shows, avoiding the problem of *'trying to produce small show[s] in a very large space'*.[17] More generally, the new studio would allow the Belgrade to expand the range of work that it presented, the result of which, it was hoped, would *'raise the profile and standing of the theatre'*.[18]

At least as important in driving the need for a capital project as the wish to develop the Belgrade's offerings was the condition of its existing building and the need for significant investment to bring it up to scratch. The refurbishment of 1984-1985 had been followed by further cosmetic work in the mid-1990s, leaving the foyers with new carpet and a somewhat oppressive red/blue colour scheme. Alan Stanton of Stanton Williams, architect of the eventual Belgrade II building, recalled his first visit in 2002 and the contrast between the crisp lightness of the 1958 Belgrade that had been captured in historic photographs and what the theatre had since become (fig. 5.3):

> *When we first saw the Belgrade, the whole*
> *building had become quite domesticated:*
> *patterned carpet, pictures all over the walls.*[19]

Indeed, the theatre's appearance was described as 'dowdy' in the initial design feasibility study that was undertaken in 2001 (fig. 5.4).[20] But while the Belgrade's own market research suggested that the cozy unpretentiousness of the theatre was appreciated by at least some of the audience,[21] there were clear issues with the size and inconvenient arrangement of the front-of-house accommodation. It was also becoming apparent that considerable interventions would soon be necessary behind the scenes. In 2000, the theatre was visited

Fig. 5.3 The foyers in 2005

Fig. 5.4 The Belgrade Square elevation before refurbishment

by Gerry Robinson, then chairman of the Arts Council, who was reportedly not only shocked by its 'downtrodden' appearance, but also described conditions as 'grim and cramped'.[22]

By the date of Robinson's visit, the theatre had in fact already taken steps to address the challenge of its building and to consider its future expansion:

In 1997, we submitted our first Lottery submission, and part of that was for a feasibility study for a large-scale £15 million refurbishment scheme. We also included a range of other things that needed to be done: upgrade of [the] sound and lighting installation, upgrade of the [offsite] Red Lane workshop, and ... minor building projects, tidying up the property.[23]

The results of this application were mixed. The Arts Council responded positively to much of the proposal, but the timing of the Belgrade's submission coincided with a reduction in the available support for capital projects. While money for various small improvements was forthcoming, funding for the feasibility study was rejected.[24] The theatre was, however, determined to press on in order to develop its ambitions in readiness for a future wave of Arts Council funding, and so it began to explore other avenues of funding. It is to these sources of support, and the implications of this development on the theatre's emerging brief, that we now turn.

FUNDERS AND A DEVELOPING 'VISION', 1999-2002

The news that the Lottery was unwilling to fund the Belgrade's feasibility work was accompanied by a resolve on the part of the theatre to maintain momentum:

We were somewhat upset ... , of course. [We] went away, and then, in the following year, felt [that] we still had to address the question of capital development. And so we drafted a new capital development strategy for the organization, which was focussed largely on the need for a second auditorium.[25]

Following the rejection of the initial funding application, this new strategy was more closely focussed in its aspirations. As David Beidas recalled:

We drafted the strategy in the knowledge that at some time capital funding from the Arts Council would resume, although we understood [that] it was never going to be on the scale that it had been in the mid-nineties.[26]

The likely scale of future grants also prompted the Belgrade to cast the funding net more widely:

And so we also started to talk to the City Council about [the project].[27]

Coventry City Council had, in fact, already shown itself to be willing to accommodate the theatre's ambitions. Several years previously, it had identified an area to the west of the theatre as land that would be made available to the Belgrade for an extension. With the City's support, a small feasibility study was undertaken in 2000-2001 by Levitt Bernstein Architects, examining options including 'do nothing', 'build on a new site', and a number of ways to expand the existing building, including to the west – the site of the eventual extension (figs. 5.5 and 5.6). This study broadly endorsed the Belgrade's ambitions, and was reinforced by a survey that confirmed the financial sustainability of the proposed project.

The City Council's willingness to become involved in the Belgrade's ambitions can be explained in several ways. Most obviously, the City remained the freeholder of the theatre site, which was leased to the Belgrade Theatre Trust. It was, in effect, investing in its own asset.[28] More prosaically, however, the City was at this time also exploring options for an adjacent site, next to the land that it proposed to give to the Belgrade. This area, an open-air car park, was to have been the location of the Coventry Arts and Media Centre, proposed in the mid 1990s. When that scheme fell through, a mixed-use development was considered. However, the site faced the

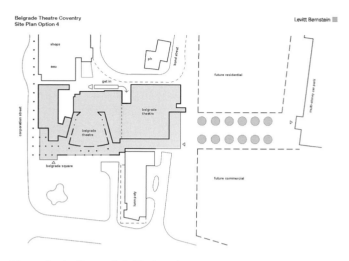

Fig. 5.5 Levitt Bernstein's 'Option 4'

Fig. 5.7 West elevation of the theatre in 2005

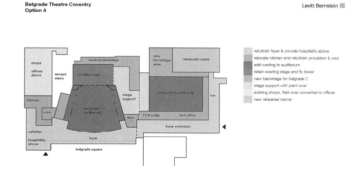

Fig. 5.6 Internal layout of Levitt Bernstein's 'Option 4'

rear side of the theatre, an uninspired, workaday elevation punctuated by metal windows and goods entrances (fig. 5.7). By offering support to the Belgrade's proposals for expansion, the council was able to guarantee that the appearance of this area would be improved. As David Beidas saw it, the City

> intended to market the large surface car park site [across] Bond Street for redevelopment, and they felt that they would get a better price for that site if the theatre were smartened up a bit.[29]

Of course, the theatre's project was always intended to do more than simply 'smarten up' the rear of the building; a second auditorium would require a structure of some substance. However, the City's ambitions were to play an increasingly important role:

> The mixed-use redevelopment ... was to [lead] the whole regeneration of that quarter of Coventry.[30]

The landmark nature of the proposed development rubbed off on thinking about the Belgrade. As Stanton Williams' project architect, Rawden Pettitt, later put it, the location of the Belgrade's proposed extension meant that the new building would 'act as a catalyst' for change, not only on the adjacent site, but also in the theatre itself as well as Coventry more generally.[31] Though separate from the mixed-use scheme, it could act as a symbol of the new quarter (as one of the first developments in the area), and thus of the new city, in much the same way as the original Belgrade had made an important contribution to perceptions of the rebuilt post-war Coventry (fig. 5.8).

Fig. 5.8 Sketch by Alan Stanton, showing the potential for the theatre extension to act as a landmark in views from the elevated ring road

The idea of a 'catalyst' certainly appealed within the theatre. Hamish Glen, the theatre's Artistic Director, later recalled that *'the Board and the City want[ed] a landmark building, state of the art, beautiful'*.[32] For Glen, there was seemingly some tension between the wish for a landmark building and the theatre's artistic aims. Indeed, at first reading, Glen's comment suggests that the aspirational aspects of the project conflicted with artistic needs, and this is a theme to which we shall return when we consider the 'Value Engineering' exercises undertaken by the theatre. However, as Alan Stanton understood it, the architectural and artistic were enmeshed to at least some extent:

[When] the Belgrade started [in 1958], it had an ambitious vision with an international dramatic repertoire. Over the years this had been replaced with limited productions and a lot of touring shows coming through. Then very bravely, the Belgrade said, "we can build ourselves a new theatre, a factory for producing new drama. ... We want ... rehearsal rooms, ... we want to attract younger audiences, we want to attract a wider audience."[33]

Hamish Glen's appointment was directly linked with this new 'vision'. Glen had established a strong reputation at the Dundee Rep, successfully reviving the idea of a resident theatre company which presented a series of shows each season.[34] He joined the Belgrade in the autumn of 2002, formally taking up his post in early 2003.

In 2001, the Arts Council announced its new capital programme, and, as had been anticipated, grants were limited – to a maximum of £5 million. The result was that the Belgrade

[had] to scale down our ambitions from the sort of £15-20 million redevelopment of the theatre that would have given us everything which we had looked at with the feasibility study. The feasibility study had reckoned we could probably achieve an £8-9 million funding package.[35]

By late 2002, the theatre was confident that it was going to be able to achieve the necessary £8 million. A £3 million application was approved by the Arts Council, while the City Council committed £2 million to the project.[36] As with some of the other examples considered in this book, funding was also sought from two bodies more usually associated with economic development, Advantage West Midlands (AWM) and the European Regional Development Fund (ERDF). Kim Kerton later recalled the changing uses to which this kind of funding was then being increasingly put:

Regional development money historically goes to the development of light industrial estates and factories, because they generate employment. This was one of the first times that the funding has moved away from that sort of area and into the leisure sector. ... So the key criteria there ... are about end employment figures. They're not overly concerned about the aesthetics and so forth of the building.[37]

Actually securing these grants was a lengthy process:

*Initially the indications were that we might get
£2 million ERDF. ... In late 2001, we submitted the
expression of interest. We were asked to submit
a full application for March 2002, which we duly
did, and by that time the sum they were prepared
to consider had come down to £1.2 million.*[38]

In all this, the Arts Council was in effect the leader; the others *'piggybacked off them'*, having been convinced of the scheme's value.[39] Nonetheless, the City Council played a particular role in persuading AWM and ERDF to commit.[40] The Belgrade also established a Development Trust to fundraise locally:

*They're a body of members, local businessmen who
know their people. The [Development Trust] has
been passionate ... networking and so forth.*[41]

In doing so, a sense of local ownership for the project was established, and more than £1 million was eventually raised by this route.

Thus far, we have traced the emergence of the Belgrade's capital project to the end of 2002, and considered the development of its funding package. In short, after an initial lack of Lottery success, the theatre was able to successfully secure funds from a varied group of organizations. In doing so, however, the terms in which their 'vision' was presented inevitably began to shift. As Kim Kerton saw it:

*Th[ere's] almost a problem in that [the funders]
are all separate and they are all asking for different
things. Some of the funders are business-case related
in terms of employment provision. The Arts Council
is much more design-related, in terms of ... the
seating in the auditorium [and] performances.*[42]

Certainly the needs of the various funders affected decision-making during the capital project, as we shall see. But first, it is necessary to look at the appointment of the design team, and then the consultation which the team undertook in order to develop the design itself.

ASSEMBLING A DESIGN TEAM

In September 2002, the Belgrade felt that its funding package was sufficiently assured to allow the appointment of a Project Manager, Kim Kerton of Buro Four, whose initial tasks included assisting with the selection of an architect and a Quantity Surveyor.[43] The scale of the project as envisaged in the theatre's feasibility studies meant that OJEC/OJEU procedures had to be followed, with the architects selected by competitive interview. As at Leicester, and as has been the case in many arts capital projects, it was by no means certain that Levitt Bernstein would be re-appointed to continue the work that they had begun in the feasibility study. Indeed, David Beidas later recalled of the process that

the architects of the feasibility study are
often at a disadvantage when it comes to the
selection process for the main commission,
as none of their ideas seem as fresh.[44]

From a shortlist of six, London-based practice Stanton Williams was appointed. In the early stages, the job was handled by the practice partners, Alan Stanton and Paul Williams. Later, Rawden Pettitt took the lead within Stanton Williams as Project Architect. The team also included Stanton Williams' choice of theatre consultant, Theatreplan, plus Arup Acoustics.[45] Davis Langdon, a major international practice, was appointed to the Quantity Surveyor role.

Though Hamish Glen did not take up his position at the Belgrade until 2003, he attended the interviews, and later recalled one of the reasons for Stanton Williams' success:

*It's partly about how well they interviewed ... They
were impressive ... I instinctively got on with them,*

and I do [still] get on all right with them. The work they had done on the National Theatre foyers I liked, Compton Verney [art gallery] I liked, ... and they felt hungry. They loved this building. Those were the sorts of things that weighed in as part of the consideration.[46]

Kim Kerton was also impressed by Stanton Williams' dedication to the project:

[By the time of] the interview, ... they'd done some vis[uals] and ... modelling, and had some ideas about the theatre and what might be ... an initial design. Which gave them the edge over other design teams when they were being interviewed.[47]

The importance attached to affinity between the client and architect – both personally and in terms of their previous work – parallels events in Leicester, where, as we shall see in the next chapter of this book, Rafael Viñoly's emotive descriptions of his 'vision' for a new theatre were an important factor in his appointment there. The choice of Stanton Williams can perhaps also be explained on at least one level by the increasing profile of the Belgrade's proposed scheme, the result of the City's ambitions for the adjacent site and the theatre Board's wish for a piece of 'catalyst' architecture that might put the Belgrade back onto the map. This was certainly Kim Kerton's understanding of the appointment:

[The client] employed Stanton Williams on their previous experience in terms of buildings. They hadn't done a new theatre, but they'd worked at the National Theatre on [remodelling and extending] the foyers. [The Belgrade] had seen Stanton Williams buildings that they liked, that were crisp, very ... monolithic. They are bold buildings, ... making a bold statement.[48]

In this respect, Stanton Williams' track record and expertise connected not only emotively with the client, but also demonstrated the architects' familiarity with award-winning, high-profile projects and thus their ability to deliver a 'bold' design that might make the desired statement in Coventry (fig. 5.9).

Fig. 5.9 'Crisp', 'bold', and 'monolithic': Stanton Williams' extension to the Belgrade

As well as assembling an external design and project team, the theatre took steps to create an efficient internal structure. David Beidas was assigned the position of lead client representative, initially in his role as Executive Director of the theatre and later in a freelance capacity. As Hamish Glen put it:

We tried to create a structure [with] David as our project manager, a full-time employee, to manage the detail of it and report back to me, and I line managed him. Then there's a capital development subcommittee, and the project manager, Quantity Surveyor, and David all bring more detailed reports to that.[49]

Thus with a full team established, both internally and externally, it was now possible to begin to give form to the Belgrade's ideas. The process by which these aspirations were explored is the subject of the next part of the chapter.

REFINING THE 'VISION': RIBA STAGE C

RIBA Stage C is the workstage at which initial ideas are developed and an outline design is refined. In the case of the Belgrade, this process was not simply a matter of aesthetic preference but was largely bound up with the necessity of achieving a financially viable scheme. Although the feasibility study had assigned a likely price-tag to the theatre's aspirations, and it had already become clear that some scaling back of ambitions would be necessary, we shall see in this section of the chapter that the detailing of those aspirations and their translation into built form were not always straightforward processes.[50]

We have already noted that it is not uncommon in the case of arts capital projects for clients to make a new design team appointment at the beginning of Stage C. Doing so can have its advantages in bringing fresh thinking to a project, and was certainly considered beneficial at the Belgrade. As David Beidas later put it in a talk at CABE:

> Don't feel constrained by the feasibility study. Use the selection process to open up other ideas.[51]

But a new appointment can also be problematic. Kim Kerton highlighted a particular challenge for arts projects which resonates with the examples discussed in the other chapters of this book:

> You do a feasibility study ... and then that becomes the basis of your design, and the figures that are in that feasibility study [are ones] which no-one on the appointed design team has actually had any responsibility [for].[52]

In this respect, David Beidas later characterized Stage C as 'a prolonged period of trying to get a workable scheme that gave us the accommodation we needed, in a layout that suited, at a price we could afford'.[53] Covering the period between January and June 2003, it was distinguished by three key themes: consultation, by means of which the brief was refined; discussion of outline designs to hone their practicality; and 'Value Engineering', as the scheme was pared down to a financially viable level. To some extent, these three themes were interconnected; a design team meeting would deal with all three simultaneously. However, in what follows, they are separated as far as is possible for ease of consideration.

Soon after their appointment, Stanton Williams began a careful process of consultation in order to refine their initial thoughts, and to elucidate more fully those of the theatre:

> We started workshops at the end of 2002 ... The theatre was going through their own transitions with Hamish Glen being brought on board as the new Artistic Director ... RIBA Stage C commenced in earnest in January [2003].[54]

Much of the task at this stage was to test and refine the requirements that the theatre has set out in their initial briefing documents. In codifying requirements, a number of successful workshops were held with the Belgrade's staff:

> Architects always need a client to bounce ideas off. For us, this was the Head of Design, Patrick Connellan, [together] with Hamish ... One of the first things that occurred was a workshop in which we took the competition [brief] and now that we had all the theatre there with Hamish, we asked them, "please go through this again and tell us what it's really all about".[55]

> We had some pretty extensive workshops with everybody. [...] We had actors, directors, ... the [cleaners].[56]

Hamish Glen felt that this aspect of the process worked well:

> The discussion within the building is good, strong and robust and that's all been fed back into the design.

There was a process whereby plans that formally affected departments were presented to them.[57]

Indeed, the theatre consultants felt that the process at times became almost too inclusive, though not without beneficial results:

We tended to have ten representatives, or eight, six representatives for the technical team, rather than them having done their homework away from us. And I'm not sure that made the process any simpler, but ... certainly in terms of them understanding and being included in part of the process, I think David made the process very inclusive ... Everyone shared in what we did or didn't do. It wasn't a "them and us" situation.[58]

Stemming perhaps from the inclusive way in which theatre productions are themselves generated, rehearsed and performed, the staff consultation allowed the architects to explore the ways in which the theatre's technicians preferred to work:

The theatre themselves were helpful in talking about the day-to-day things. "This what we need here, this is the way a Coventry theatre works."[59]

The consultation also usefully allowed the architects to test their ideas. One design issue was that of the way in which the new building would respond to the emerging urban context provided by the adjacent mixed-use development.[60] In a more conceptual sense, the architects probed the staff to discover more about the kind of theatre that they wanted.[61] Paul Williams later recalled asking whether windows might be provided to give views into the auditorium, and being slightly surprised that the staff were not willing to countenance the idea.[62] In complete contrast to the wishes of the management of what became Curve, Leicester, where views from the street into the auditorium and onto the stage were explicitly sought, the Belgrade's management was seemingly much more concerned with the notion of theatre as a distinct, special space, separated (at least in terms of the auditorium) from the world beyond.

Perhaps in accordance with this view of theatre as a 'space apart' from the world, there was less willingness to involve the Belgrade's audiences in the design process than had been the case for the staff. Glen later looked back and commented that:

I'm not that much of a democrat, if I'm absolutely honest with you. I'd rather not pretend that I'm going to listen.[63]

Glen's views are contextualized by the theatre consultants:

I'm not sure that the best theatres would ever be built to an audience, [and] what they perceive they want, because I think an audience survey inevitably talks about seat comfort.[64]

The 'vision' for the auditorium was primarily formulated in artistic terms, as befitted its intended role in developing the theatre's programme. Early designs for the Belgrade, as we shall see shortly, explored the idea of a courtyard theatre, with narrow seating galleries around three sides of the auditorium and a straight rake of stalls facing the stage at the lowest level (fig. 5.10). This form, found in key historic examples such as the Georgian Theatre, Richmond, has enjoyed something of a revival since the mid-1970s, being reinterpreted in a number of successful theatres including the Cottesloe within the National Theatre (1977), the Tricycle at Kilburn (1980), and the Swan Theatre, Stratford-upon-Avon (1986). In Coventry, the theatre consultants and Hamish Glen both recalled that the form was primarily advocated by the Belgrade's then-resident designer, Patrick Connellan:

It came from a strong brief from Patrick that whilst he wanted [the auditorium] to be adaptable, he didn't want it to be infinitely adaptable. They [sic] wanted something with a strong personality that [worked] primarily in two formats.[65]

Patrick Connellan was very much in favour of a courtyard space, a proper courtyard space.[66]

The theatre consultant welcomed Connellan's lead:

The strongest and best theatres in the country have come about where there's a strong ... artistic position.[67]

He also empathized with the aim:

If I had felt he was wrong with the horseshoe we wouldn't have done it.[68]

The idea of a performance space that responds closely to the particular ideas of an individual can be linked with the rise in prominence of the theatre director as a significant shaping force in the twentieth century, a development which is arguably responsible for the plurality of approaches to

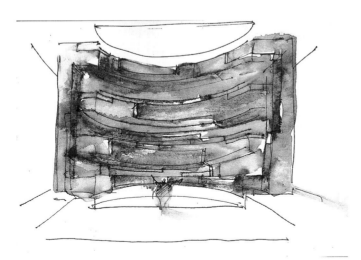

Fig. 5.10 Early sketch by Stanton Williams for a horseshoe-shaped auditorium seating structure

auditorium design that characterize the period. Giving built form to these varied aspirations has in turn been facilitated by the arrival of subsidy, both for building and for operation, in that subsidy has allowed theatre groups the luxury of creating their own performance space and a degree of artistic and (perhaps more limited) commercial licence as to what to present in it.[69] In a number of significant cases, designers have worked closely with directors in realizing these spaces: one thinks of John Bury's collaboration with Peter Hall, which was instrumental in the design of the Barbican Theatre's stage, or Tanya Moiseiwitsch's work with Colin George at the Crucible, Sheffield.[70] These examples were intended for resident groups, able to develop a response to the specificity of their own theatre. As the Belgrade's theatre consultant put it:

It's nice to have a client with passion who wanted something. That's what's nice about working for a producing theatre.[71]

There is an echo here of David Staples of Theatre Projects, who regretted the absence of a user-client in the case of The Lowry.

While they welcomed Connellan's strong lead, both theatre consultants and architects felt uneasy about the extent to which it was shared by Hamish Glen:

What we were nervous about was [that] the lead wasn't coming from Hamish, the brief was coming from the others.[72]

As Glen himself later put it,

I ran with [the courtyard]. I mean, I'm new in the job, I don't know the city.[73]

The theatre consultants similarly ascribed this position to Glen's recent arrival in Coventry and the extent to which he was balancing the capital project with changing the theatre's organizational structure whilst at the same time choosing and directing plays.[74] As we shall see shortly, this development was to have fundamental consequences.

The results of the exploratory discussions were formally set down in a document that more fully captured the theatre's aspirations and requirements than had been possible or indeed necessary prior to the appointment of the design team. As David Beidas recorded:

> By the time that we got to February [2003], we had effectively created a master design brief in some detail.[75]

For the architects, this document was highly important:

> We had to create a briefing document, [defining] the [relationships] between rooms, and what each room actually needed in detail. ... The brief we were given at the beginning was not adequate enough really to express all of that.[76]

Representing an evolutionary approach to briefing in which ideas are explored in increasingly greater detail, the true value of this exercise, however, lay less in that it codified the theatre's emerging 'vision' (indeed, Pettitt later noted that the master document that resulted was not intended to be strictly followed)[77] than the fact that the process of consultation which generated this document and the initial design ideas which resulted from it also quantified the cost implications of the Belgrade's aspirations:

> It was great to understand, but there was a feeling that it became a free-for-all, and suddenly ... there was this huge list.[78]

As a result:

> It was acknowledged that the brief was to some extent in excess of what may be affordable.[79]

This fear was confirmed upon the involvement of the cost consultants. The resulting ways in which the 'vision' was cut to size are considered in the next part of the chapter.

FIRST DESIGNS AND INITIAL VALUE ENGINEERING

David Beidas recalled the early stages of design:

> The design team went away, produced their first bash at it ... It came back about £12 million, when we had six.[80]

The result was 'what felt like two months of them going away and designing options with less and less floor space'.[81] This section of the chapter discusses the early designs, and the ways in which the theatre's various aspirations were reconciled with the reality of the budget.

In reducing the projected cost of the scheme, the main strategy in these early stages was a reduction in the scale of the brief:

> The first main step was ... not to cut down on the quality or the luxury ... of their ambitions, but actually to cut out significant portions of the project.[82]

Thus:

> We looked at ... what it is that we [could] take out of the project that would still give the theatre something that they could still use. ... I suppose it was like taking the icing off the cake. The cake is still there, and you can still eat the cake, but you can't have ... the niceties that surround it.[83]

> Two rehearsal rooms went fairly swiftly, the idea of any major revamp of the existing catering areas

went very swiftly, the idea of any major alterations to existing staging installations went very swiftly.[84]

This strategy was, the acoustician noted, entirely typical of her experience of arts projects in that the 'bottom line' of what is needed imposes a certain limit on possible reductions, at least in the initial stages of design development:

It's usually done by cutting out part of the scope, rather than trying to trim a little bit off everything.[85]

Alan Stanton deployed a more graphic metaphor to highlight the particularities of 'Value Engineering' in the arts:

On many projects, [Value Engineering is] about saving money, but it's ... 10%, 15%. At the Belgrade, [the greater scale of the client's vision and expectations relative to their budget meant that] it was about saving 40%. It's not been minor surgery, it's been limb amputation.[86]

In deciding what could be included, essential features were sized and costed according to the likely specification that Stanton Williams would employ, with the architects instructed to fit whatever they could within the remaining space:

We got to a point at one session where we ... said "well, look, at £2,500 a square metre we can afford, whatever it is, 2200 square metres. The auditorium is that, circulation will be 20%, 30%. We can therefore have a green room, these dressing rooms, and this, this and this. Go away and put that into some semblance of shape.[87]

An all-inclusive 'master' brief was retained as a statement of the 'ultimate' theatre, in case it were later possible to return some of the elements which had been omitted.[88]

For some participants in the design process, this period was one in which functional and symbolic concerns were brought into conflict. According to the theatre consultant,

the Belgrade needs more than one rehearsal room. It's only getting one.[89]

In his view, 'there's no question that [the Belgrade] could have gone for a less expensive exterior, and a different approach', perhaps along the lines of the Poole Arts Centre. In this respect, Neil Morton attributed some of the high costs of the scheme to the choice of site, suggesting that a more low-key addition within the small service yard on the other side of the original auditorium, perhaps also reconfiguring the street-facing block which had been built as actors' flats and now accommodates the theatre administration, might have been more cost-effective. However, the sheer volume of space to be added (auditorium, backstage technical facilities, rehearsal room, expanded foyers) arguably precluded such an approach; it would certainly not have necessarily been more straightforward. In fact, Levitt Bernstein had explored options for construction in this area, and their attempts had still included some new construction on the site of the eventual theatre extension. In addition, as we shall see shortly, Stanton Williams deployed materials and finishes intended to reduce the cost of the new building without compromising its power and presence.

By March 2003, Stanton Williams was able to present the theatre with a series of outline 'options' illustrating different ways of accommodating the emerging brief. Echoing what had been proposed by Levitt Bernstein in their 2001 feasibility study as well as the land-use policies of the City Council, the consistent assumption was that the new auditorium and associated facilities would be located to the west of the original theatre building. Stanton Williams' options were connected in their presumption that the extension would comprise a five or six storey building, stacking technical, performance and rehearsal facilities in an essentially cubic volume (fig. 5.11). Its greater height relative to the low-slung block of the original

1958 theatre not only made maximum use of the site, allowing all the required facilities to be fitted within a small area, but was also one way in which to achieve a piece of 'landmark' architecture that would signal the theatre's presence from the city centre and the ring road (as Alan Stanton's sketch, fig. 5.8, had explored). A variety of internal arrangements were considered. Option G (fig. 5.12), for example, placed the new auditorium at ground-floor level with the rehearsal room above. Option H (fig. 5.13) moved it to the first floor, with technical areas below and again the double-height rehearsal room at the top of the building.

The auditorium was envisaged as a relatively simple rectangular space in both Option G and Option H, with a 'chair store' at one end. It was in essence a purpose-built re-creation, albeit a significantly enhanced one, of the converted depot that the Belgrade was already using as a studio theatre.

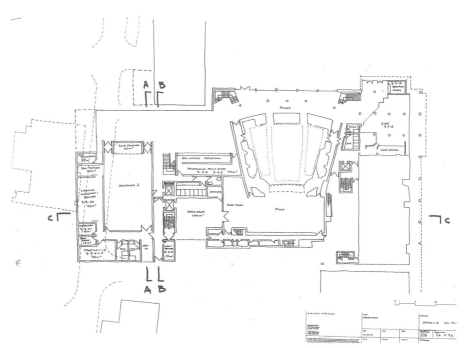

Fig. 5.12 Option G, 7 March 2003

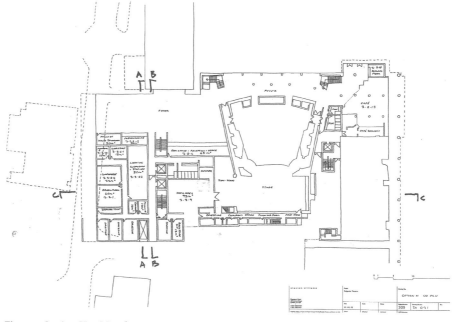

Fig. 5.13 Option H, 7 March 2003

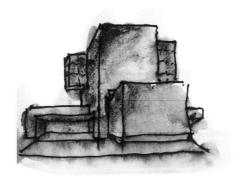

Fig. 5.11 Early concept sketch by Stanton Williams

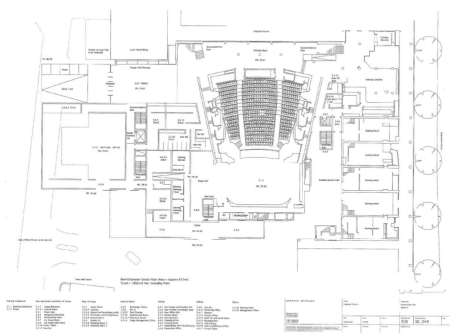

Fig. 5.14 Option K, 20 March 2003

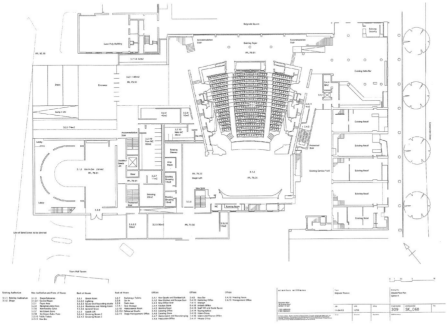

Fig. 5.15 Option N, 11 April 2003

Options K, L, and N, dated March and April 2003 (figs. 5.14 and 5.15), reflected the wish for a more formal courtyard-style auditorium. A tall space was proposed, reflecting Alan Stanton's experience of other theatres and his belief that height would *'pull in'* the walls to give a greater sense of intimacy.[90] The auditorium in these schemes has seating on three levels with a lighting grid on the fourth level and a double-height rehearsal room above that. From the rectilinear geometry of Option K, a curved form was proposed in Options L and N, though still within a rectilinear envelope.

The concept was fully developed in the eventual Stage C scheme, produced in May 2003 (fig. 5.16), in which the seating structure was joined by a striking spiral 'escape stair' in the angle of the building. As the addition of this stair shows, the concept productively allowed some circulation to take place within the performance space, that is, behind the seating structure, thus reducing the need to which the foyers need wrap around the auditorium (as they had in Levitt Bernstein's Option 4). This idea was likened by the architects to a 'piece of furniture within a room' in the way that the galleried seating structure was to be 'placed' as a semi-independent unit within the auditorium volume (fig. 5.17).[91] In this respect, there are echoes of the Renaissance theatres of Palladio and Scamozzi, which deployed tiers of wooden seating in a similar

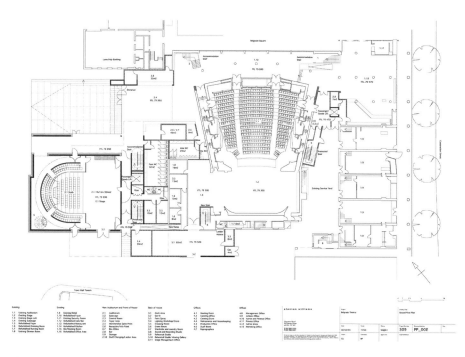

Fig. 5.16 Stage C design, 25 April 2003

Fig. 5.17 Visualization of the courtyard auditorium

way. More recent precedents include the Cottesloe (where consultant Iain Mackintosh designed the auditorium structure within the volume left for the purpose by architect Denys Lasdun), the Tricycle, whose courtyard comprises scaffolding placed within a 1920s dance hall (from which it is entirely independent in structural terms), and the Swan, where wooden galleries were inserted in 1986 within the burnt-out shell of the nineteenth-century Shakespeare Memorial Theatre.

Whilst illustrating the emerging auditorium design, the design work also reveals something of the theatre's appearance. Sketches (fig. 5.18) show the elevations ordered by rectangular panels of different colours, a de Stijl-like approach likened by Stanton Williams to a sculpture by Ben Nicholson. In the Stage C scheme, a 'lightbox' is labelled, created through the use of some semi-transparent panels that would glow by night (perhaps an echo of Herzog and de Meuron's Laban centre at Deptford?). To one side, a lower block accommodates the foyers, with an at least partially-glazed section providing the improved western entrance that the theatre sought for those patrons arriving by car or from the adjacent leisure development.

As well as allowing the design team to explore costs further, an important concern was that of practicality. Stanton Williams' designs were thus not only discussed and refined from the point

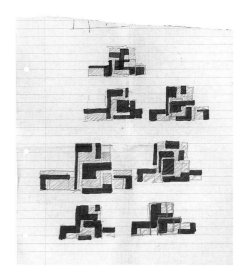

Fig. 5.18 Sketch by Stanton Williams developing possible elevation treatments

of view of their likely cost, but also the extent to which they would deliver a workable theatre:

[The discussions] would be a combination of "this doesn't work in this space, and this has got to be moved, and we can't afford this anyway."[92]

[The staff] could go, "no, we can't have the wardrobe entrance through there, it's got to be here ... "[93]

[The architects] hadn't designed a theatre before, so [they] didn't [immediately] understand the criticality of some [things]. ... Why ... you want a dressing stage near the stage instead of two

miles away. *I exaggerate, but, you know, those sorts of things.*[94]

The involvement of the theatre consultants was felt to be especially helpful in resolving these issues at an early stage:

Theatreplan was instrumental in helping us analyse the relationships between spaces. What makes a good dressing room? How do people start to move through these spaces?[95]

At the beginning of our discussion of Stage C, we noted that there is often a temptation for a new design to emerge, partly in response to the 'fresh' ideas of a new design team, or as a client's aspirations are more fully explored and their implications become clear. This process can sometimes be problematic, given that funding is often initially secured on the basis of the projected cost of the feasibility study. In the case of the Belgrade, however, Stanton Williams' initial schemes followed closely the layout proposed by Levitt Bernstein in their 'Option 2 – have everything', placing the new auditorium parallel with the old. The eventual Stage C design has definite echoes of the earlier 'Option 4 – new spaces with minimal refurbishment' proposal in turning the auditorium through ninety degrees. The principal issue seems to have been that of reconciling the indicative volume of space and

layout proposed in the feasibility study with the actual costs of developing the building in the way that was emerging.

Stage C was eventually completed by the end of June 2003. The theatre made its planning application and submitted a full report to the Arts Council in order to be granted the funding that would be necessary to continue and complete the project.[96]

It took three months. Their decision was then made. September 2003 we had planning permission, we had Arts Council confirmation of £3 million funding. We had a scheme that was costed at a construction cost of £7.5 million, which gave us a new 300-seat auditorium.[97]

COMMUNICATING AND REFINING THE DESIGN

Even as the Arts Council considered its response to the Belgrade's proposals, design work continued, and RIBA Stage D (detailed design) was reached by September 2003. A sense of urgency was imposed in part by the theatre's wish for construction work to begin in April 2004,[98] although this strategy inevitably presented a risk in that the funding application might have been refused, thus rendering the continuing work redundant. In developing and presenting their ideas, the architects used a variety of approaches; the project manager believed that the architects' success in communicating their design stemmed from the fact that *'they knew how to talk to an artistic client'*.[99] Initial work at Stage C had included bubble diagrams, drawings showing movement, abstracted layouts, as well as sketches and computer representations, with the theatre consultants playing a pivotal interpretative role for the client. As the design developed, physical models and digital visualizations were also used to good effect (fig. 5.19):

> *Models [were] by far the best way everyone could understand [the design]. Many people have trouble reading plans. Which is ... one of the reasons why we work so much in models. They become a very important element in communicating ideas.*[100]

Echoing the experience of other project teams in this book and the arts generally, the particular value of models

Fig. 5.19 Architects' models of the new building

perhaps lies in their widespread use in the theatre more generally, not least for production design purposes. In this respect, we might note the historical parallel of the Barbican Theatre, where director Peter Hall and designer John Bury 'mocked' up performances on a model of the theatre's proposed stage.[101]

Stage D in the story of the Belgrade is notable for several reasons: more Value Engineering; decisions concerning the way that the project was to proceed; and, not least, a funding crisis. The three were related. As the designs were developed, their costs became clearer, but, at the same time, even the money which the theatre already had was not secure. In September 2003, Advantage West Midlands (AWM) announced that they would no longer be able to make a contribution to the scheme, which, as David Beidas drily put it, *'was a problem, because our budget relied on £2 million from them'*.[102]

The delay had two important consequences. On the one hand, the estimated cost of the project rose. Kim Kerton believed rising costs to be inherent in arts projects, noting that the sometimes protracted amount of time necessary to secure approval from funding bodies can compound the routine issue of inflation.[103] As Pettit confirmed, whenever the project slowed for issues to be resolved, costs rose, and so the scope of works was

of necessity truncated as a result.[104] Thus at Stage D, to save money, it was decided to omit the proposed improvements to the original 1958 auditorium, not least the installation of a new ventilation system. Although over-heating had become a significant problem noted by the Belgrade's audiences, the theatre at this stage prioritized the new building over finding a remedy for the issue. The decision was described by Beidas as *'agonizing'*, but in the event the ventilation system was returned to the scope of the project at a later stage. Beidas later confirmed the strategic nature of the decision:

> *I think everyone knew in the end that it was going to have to go back in. Cutting it was merely a way of meeting a budget requirement at a particular point.*[105]

Otherwise, however, the design remained little changed in its fundamentals.

The funding-related delay at Stage D had a second consequence, over and above rising costs. It now became clear that it would not be possible to begin work on site in April 2004. This delay had particular implications for the Belgrade as a theatre organization in view of the way that it wished to structure the capital project:

We did not want to shut for a panto, and we'd always predicted the way in which the construction strategy would be developed would actually allow us just to close ... between pantos.[106]

Pantomime formed an important source of revenue for the Belgrade, and so, as Kim Kerton put it, *'it was more economic to delay construction for a year than it was to lose [the] panto'*.[107] In the event, partly to maintain momentum and minimize the risks of inflation, the construction project was split into two. Phase A, undertaken in the summer of 2004, created a new 'get in' (loading bay) and backstage area to the rear of the main auditorium, replacing facilities at the side of the theatre that were to be demolished as part of the Belgrade II project and thus allowing the theatre to continue to function for at least some of the time when the main project was underway. The intention was then to proceed with the rest of the project between April 2005 and summer 2006, with a break in December 2005 for the pantomime (which could then use the new facilities created as part of Phase A).

A further, more minor split in the project concerned the refurbishment of the theatre's offices. Located within the former actors' flats on the Corporation Street side of the theatre, the result was a somewhat *ad hoc* administrative space, but one usefully close to the main body of the theatre. The refurbishment was undertaken by a local practice on the advice of Stanton Williams.

Thus far, we have seen that inflation and business planning both impacted upon the progress of the project during the second half of 2003. As if dealing with these issues was not enough, however, the theatre was also forced to undertake some building work during this period. There was a requirement attached to the Belgrade's ERDF money that it be spent by a certain date, namely December 2003.[108] As a result, certain health-and-safety works were carried out within the technical areas of the original building. Though necessary components of the scheme, they were scheduled for implementation at this point simply in order to retain

the ERDF grant – echoing something similar at The Lowry, and, as we shall see shortly (with negative consequences), Leicester. This system no doubt has its advantages for the funding body by providing a guarantee that money will be spent, but the Belgrade's hand was, in effect, forced, and a project which might more economically have been carried out under the main contract was rushed through.

By early 2004, therefore, the capital project had begun to take shape, in terms of both design and programme. Ever-more detailed designs revealed rising costs, an issue compounded by delays that owed much to ongoing uncertainties surrounding the theatre's funding package. At the same time, the need to fit the theatre's 'vision' to the realities of its daily operation shaped the proposed timescale to an increasing degree. In what follows, we examine the construction of Phase A, before discussing the main capital project in more detail.

PHASE A AND STAGE E

Pettit later recalled of Phase A:

It was done [in] such a short time, ... the design team had to work around that. It caused a lot of problems ... it cost us a lot of extra money to do specifications again, ... to find other people in the office able to take up this package and to push it through very fast.[109]

There were positive outcomes to the work. It exposed some of the construction of the original building, thus usefully highlighting possible issues that might arise during the main part of the project whilst also giving the client body a relatively gentle introduction to the world of major building projects. However, Phase A included complex servicing work, and there were also problems when a culvert was discovered below the site (the Radford Brook, covered when the original theatre was constructed, whose exact location had been unknown). More significant, in view of the way that the project was unfolding, was, once again, the issue of money. Not only did breaking apart the contract have cost implications in itself, but the tenders that were submitted for Phase A were typically around £40,000 above budget.[110] The matter was addressed on this occasion without major consequence, but cost concerns were forcing more radical changes where the main part of the building project was concerned. In parallel with progress on Phase A, development continued on the main project, reaching RIBA Stage E in March 2004. Although the overall budget for the project had increased at Stage D, the additional money that had been given by the City Council was largely for road and service diversions. Thus there was a problem when the initial tenders that were received in February 2005 for the main project came in significantly above budget, the lowest by more than £1 million. Discussions with the funders saw some additional money agreed, but as part of a fresh round of cost savings, the theatre also took the radical step of suspending work on the design of the new auditorium:

> It was at that point that we decided to suspend the design or any further development of the Belgrade Two fit-out. We would go to contract, continue to try and raise some more money, and, if we had the funds available, we would build the whole fit-out, … as designed. If we didn't, we would do a simpler auditorium on a single tier, on a much cheaper scale.[111]

As was discussed above, the auditorium had been conceived as 'furniture within a room', a seating and staging structure within a defined volume. Thus omitting it or indeed opting for a simpler arrangement did not automatically compromise the execution of the rest of the scheme. The Belgrade would gain the envelope of the new performance space plus the rest of the building without further delay, and could then assess its options.

How should we interpret this decision? In many ways, the decision to halt work on the auditorium – the functional heart of the new theatre and the *raison d'etre* for the capital project – might seem astounding. It can certainly be understood in terms of the desire for a landmark building which had characterized earlier stages of the project. As the theatre consultant put it:

> The image of the exterior of the building was actually [given] a higher priority than the second auditorium. Which is unusual.[112]

In retrospect, however, it is also possible to understand the decision to stop work on the auditorium in terms of Hamish Glen's evolving views on the design. As has already been noted, Glen had 'run with' the courtyard-format auditorium, conceived prior to his arrival in Coventry: he was new in the city and was also occupied with restructuring the Belgrade's operation more generally. But, by the autumn of 2005, as he later recalled:

> We pulled the funders together and attracted more money. At this point the horseshoe came back on the agenda, and then I was a lot clearer about what I wanted to do in terms of artistic policy.[113]

What Glen now sought was more on the lines of the simpler auditorium design that had previously been proposed for cost-saving reasons: 'an industrial space for theatremakers to transform', far removed from the Swan-like courtyard of the original design. Once again, the potential tension between landmark building and working performance space (and the difficulty in expressing the nature of a performance space compared to a 'catalyst' building) reared its head:

> The architects have been caught between my aspirations for this space as a theatremaker and a clear brief to try to make something extraordinary for Coventry.[114]

And yet, by having conceived the space in terms of 'furniture in a room', it was entirely possible to remove the intended furniture and to substitute something else, with the decision on the form of this 'something else' being made some time after construction had begun in summer 2005. In this respect, even allowing for the additional expenditure in working up a revised version of the auditorium, both the original design concept and the decision to put the fit-out on ice proved to be remarkably canny moves. Stanton Williams responded well to the change in direction, delivering a design study in spring 2006 (fig. 5.20). As built, the auditorium has shallow galleries stacked around the space and retractable stalls seating, with fully flexible flying and lighting facilities above set within a tough aesthetic (fig. 5.21). The original courtyard scheme's parallels with the Cottesloe and Tricycle have already been noted. The realized scheme has yet stronger resonances with those examples in the

Fig. 5.20 *The auditorium re-imagined in response to Hamish Glen's ideas*

Fig. 5.21 *'An industrial space for theatre-makers to transform'*

Fig. 5.22 *A found space: the seating and staging structure was inserted within the volume of the auditorium*

way that the envelope of the 'room' and the design of the auditorium were entirely separately conceived, the audience and staging structure having to respond to the constraints of an already-existing built space (fig. 5.22).

BUILDING THE THEATRE

By the time at which a decision was reached on the auditorium arrangement, construction work was in fact underway. This section of the chapter summarizes the history of the project from the point at which it began on site in the summer of 2005 to its completion in the summer of 2007. Once again, certain themes are to the fore: rising costs, team relationships, and the specificities of programming construction work in the arts sector. Coupled to these themes are the related general issues of joining new buildings to old, and the unpredictability of construction, both of which had significant impacts on the programme and on the way in which the eventual scheme was delivered.

The second half of 2005 was characterized by detailed design work, not least where the revised auditorium was concerned, accompanied by further and repeated Value Engineering exercises as the Belgrade sought to counter constantly rising costs with savings. The process affected all aspects of the design detail, though the overall concept was fiercely guarded. As Pettitt put it:

We as a company have had to re-address the way that we design, to make it appropriate but still give it the strength and power and coherence that's wanted, but perhaps not with [the] materials and detailing we would first envisage.[115]

In contrast to the earlier stages of the project, where Value Engineering was focussed on removing parts of the scope of works, in these later stages cost savings were largely made by changes to materials and finishes. Externally, render and polycarbonate were deployed for their low cost, and the glazing of the new theatre entrance (one of the more expensive elements of the external design) was achieved more cheaply through the ingenious use of a standard system (fig. 5.23). Glen became concerned that the

Fig. 5.23 Render, polycarbonate and glass: finishes were chosen for power and economy

reductions were increasingly affecting the quality of the project: *'the punters ... don't see the M&E [mechanical and electrical] work, they see the finish!'*[116] But reductions were necessary if the power of the original concept was to be retained, while at this late stage it would have been difficult to remove further spaces or much in the way of technical equipment from the brief without damaging the viability of the completed scheme. The ultimate scope was developed through negotiation with the architects and the contractors, evaluating which elements might be reduced or altered, and which were sacrosanct.

All the shortlisted contractors had experience of arts projects. One strength of the selected contractor, ISG, stemmed directly from their experience, for they proposed a way of scheduling the works which *'turned the timetable on its head and reduced a lot of costs by breaking into the building at the beginning of the project'*, according to Glen.[117] The contract form was essentially traditional, partly prompted by Arts Council guidance. The choice of contract form was intended to minimize risk in that, in theory, a fixed price would be agreed for the scope of work. As Kerton put it, *'the concern was that, if they went [for a] Design and Build [contract], they would then be fighting against the contractor'* as far as matters of detail were concerned, something that results from theatres as complex,

bespoke buildings, rather than, say, offices with repetitive floorplates.[118]

'Nothing's gone smoothly', was Glen's later recollection of the construction experience.[119] Most significantly, there were problems with constructing the piled foundation, which culminated in a breach of the city's sewer system and the site being closed until a repair could be effected. But a delay had in fact been introduced at an early stage, with work starting three weeks late. The construction of the new building's concrete core then took longer than anticipated, and there were issues when attention turned to the original building, as it was discovered that more work was in fact necessary than had been thought.[120] While the theatre was still operating, there were occasional concerns about audible construction noise in the auditorium during matinee performances and rehearsals, despite the programme having allowed for a certain number of daytime events. And, as problems arose and costs changed, claims for variations were made by architect and contractor, complicating the relationships between client and design team. The result of the delays was that, in early summer 2006, the contractor advised the Belgrade that completion was not expected before November, just two weeks before the pantomime was scheduled to open in the original 1958 theatre. It was clear that this period would not be sufficient to commission the building and then

to open a major production, and so it was therefore decided to postpone re-opening into 2007.

The decision to delay re-opening was made in the light of several developments. A feasibility study for the second auditorium, revised in the light of Glen's desire for an 'industrial' space, had been completed in the first months of 2006 by Stanton Williams and Theatreplan. It costed the fit-out at £1.5 million, some £300,000 above budget, but the theatre was in fact able to raise the additional money. However, by April, the detailed design came with a price tag of £1.7 million attached, and so, with the shell of the new building well under way, work on the auditorium was again suspended. A Design and Build contract for the auditorium fit-out was advertised in June 2006, with construction taking place in 2007. This decision, which took the execution of the auditorium away from Stanton Williams, was intended to reduce the risk of further cost increases. Of course, it also generated another, discrete capital project for the theatre to manage, following Phase A and the main contract. However, the decision was later judged by Beidas to have been a good one: 'the outcome was a good auditorium at an affordable price' (fig. 5.24).[121] The contract produced some innovative solutions, such as travelling bridges instead of a fixed catwalk (fig. 5.25). Where problems were experienced, these were concerned with areas where

Fig. 5.24 The completed auditorium

Fig. 5.25 Bridges above the auditorium allow flexible mounting of lights and props

the brief was not specific; there was also an assumption that there would be more opportunity to develop the design, which turned out not to be the case and led to some difficulties over seating layouts and sightlines. From a cost point of view, although minor changes added costs, most of the remaining overrun related to issues with the base build. There were one or two items which fell between both contracts and had to be added in, some roof leaks which caused delay, and remedial works to an uneven floor. However, the variation on this contract was much reduced compared to the theatre's earlier works.

In addition, it had been decided by 2005 to seek additional funding for

works to the original building of 1958 from the Heritage Lottery Fund. A Conservation Management Plan was prepared by Short and Associates during the winter of 2005-2006 in support of the application, which requested a further £1 million. This work was let as a further contract (making it, in effect, the theatre's fourth), and was carried out in the summer of 2007. Most obviously, a comprehensive refurbishment of the foyers and the external envelope of the theatre swept away later accretions to reveal something of the crispness of its original design (fig. 5.26). Within the main auditorium, however, visible works were more limited, with the principal improvement comprising the long-desired new ventilation system. It is possible to understand the restricted scope of these works in similar terms to the main Belgrade II project, focussing on spaces other than those used for performance – an odd approach for a theatre, but one which was perhaps necessary to transform perceptions of the place.

Fig. 5.26 The refurbished front-of-house areas

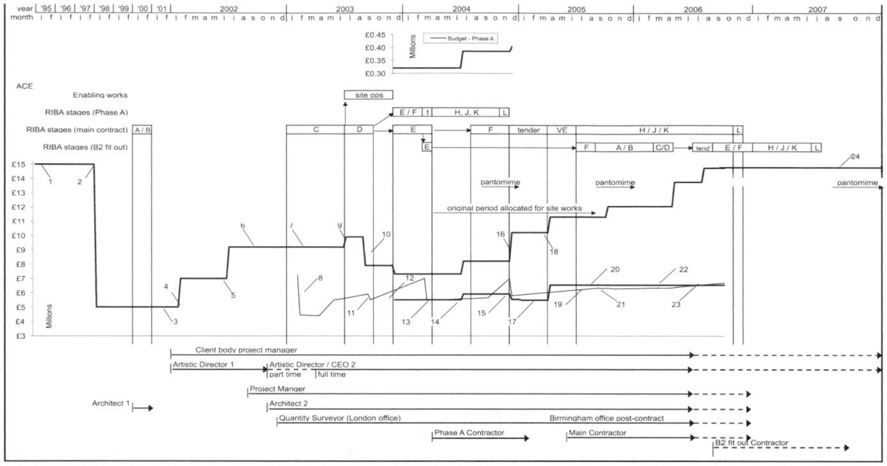

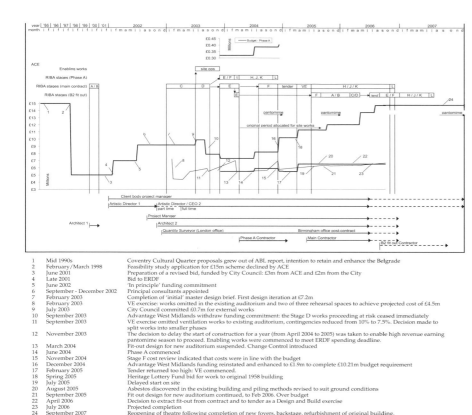

1	Mid 1990s	Coventry Cultural Quarter proposals grew out of ABL report, intention to retain and enhance the Belgrade
2	February/March 1998	Feasibility study application for £15m scheme declined by ACE
3	June 2001	Preparation of a revised bid, funded by City Council: £3m from ACE and £2m from the City
4	Late 2001	Bid to ERDF
5	June 2002	'In principle' funding commitment
6	September - December 2002	Principal consultants appointed
7	February 2003	Completion of 'initial' master design brief. First design iteration at £7.2m
8	February 2003	VE exercise: works omitted in the existing auditorium and two of three rehearsal spaces to achieve projected cost of £4.5m
9	July 2003	City Council committed £0.7m for external works
10	September 2003	Advantage West Midlands withdraw funding commitment: the Stage D works proceeding at risk ceased immediately
11	September 2003	VE exercise omitted ventilation works to existing auditorium, contingencies reduced from 10% to 7.5%. Decision made to split works into smaller phases
12	November 2003	The decision to delay the start of construction for a year (from April 2004 to 2005) was taken to enable high revenue earning pantomime season to proceed. Enabling works were commenced to meet ERDF spending deadline.
13	March 2004	Fit-out design for new auditorium suspended. Change Control introduced
14	June 2004	Phase A commenced
15	November 2004	Stage F cost review indicated that costs were in line with the budget
16	December 2004	Advantage West Midlands funding reinstated and enhanced to £1.9m to complete £10.21m budget requirement
17	February 2005	Tender returned too high: VE commenced.
18	Spring 2005	Heritage Lottery Fund bid for work to original 1958 building
19	July 2005	Delayed start on site
20	August 2005	Asbestos discovered in the existing building and piling methods revised to suit ground conditions
21	September 2005	Fit out design for new auditorium continued, to Feb 2006. Over budget
22	April 2006	Decision to extract fit-out from contract and to tender as a Design and Build exercise
23	July 2006	Projected completion
24	September 2007	Reopening of theatre following completion of new foyers, backstage, refurbishment of original building. Second auditorium fit out continued to early 2008

Timeline constructed from: project reports; QS reports; design team and project meeting minutes; client internal reports; and interview transcripts

Fig. 5.27 Belgrade Theatre: budget history timeline

CONCLUSIONS

The financial history of the project is summarized in the budget history timeline (fig. 5.27). In some respects, the story of Belgrade II is one of evolution, with the original 'vision' modified by various factors including cost (leading, for example to the omission of rehearsal rooms), artistic ambition (the auditorium design) and changing circumstances (the works to the original theatre building). For the acoustician, these developments meant that *'over the course of the project, the brief changed considerably'*.[122] But when considered as a whole, the project is also notable for its essential constancy. David Beidas reported that the scheme as set out in September 2003 was *'with the exception of the layout of the [second] auditorium, ... broadly the scheme that has been delivered'*.[123] Similarly, Kim Kerton believed that the *'strategy and vision that the Belgrade had for the front[-of-house] space ... has been very much the same all the way through and very much fixed'*.[124] Indeed, what was achieved in September 2007 (figs. 5.28 and 5.29) was in essence the scheme that had been conceived five years before, that is, an extended Belgrade with new backstage facilities plus a second auditorium and significantly enlarged foyers (figs. 5.30 and 5.31).[125] In addition, improvements had been made to the original building, not least the ventilation of the auditorium (news of which at the Gala Opening was greeted by a resounding cheer from the Belgrade's regular patrons), while, in the front-of-house areas, restoration and redecoration had swept away any lingering sense of the *'domesticated'* interior noted by the architects on their first visits.

For the client, the experience of design and construction was one of protecting their 'vision' whilst cutting it to size. When asked whether there had been any formal 'Value Engineering' sessions, Glen replied that they had taken place

> *Endlessly. Nothing but.*
> *That seems to be almost*
> *entirely all we've done.*[126]

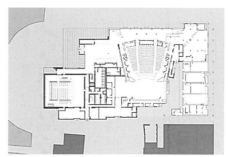

Fig. 5.28 The completed scheme: plan

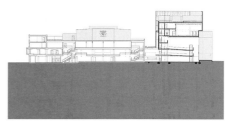

Fig. 5.29 Section through the auditorium, with the rehearsal room above

Fig. 5.30 Galleries link the levels of the new foyer with the auditorium

Fig. 5.31 The new foyer includes a bar, expanded box office, and space for display

Money has certainly been a running theme in this story, one which emerges strongly in the project team interviews. Alan Stanton, for example, noted that:

Like most theatre projects, there
have been money problems ...
We're trying to produce something
impossible, really. I suppose
each theatre project, apart from
the really big ones, struggles
with similar problems.[127]

The 'money problems' at the Belgrade came in several forms: the discovery of the likely true cost of the project as a detailed design was developed; rising costs during periods when the design was suspended for reasons of fundraising; the technical complexity of theatre design and particularly of joining a new building to a fifty-year old structure. For the client, the constantly rising cost was the source of some incomprehension. As Beidas later put it, *'at every turn, things have turned out to be more expensive than we were originally told'.*[128]

The money issue had several roots. On the one hand, the setting of grants at an early stage in capital projects provided little scope when costs rise, for whatever reason:

The budget doesn't go up, [so] the
available money decreases.[129]

However, cost inflation is a character-istic of all building projects, to some extent. How might we therefore explain the particular experience of clients in the arts, and their reaction to it? Kim Kerton thought that, in his experience, arts clients differed from those in other sectors less in that their lack of much construction experience hampered their ability to appreciate the nature of the process and more in that *'management of expectation ... is the challenge in every project'.*[130] For organizations used to surviving on a relatively limited funding stream, the sudden receipt of a multi-million pound building budget can seem rather liberating. As Kerton reflected:

What is ... hard is managing their
aspirations. You've been given
a big bag of gold. You want to
go and spend it. What is hard is
actually being able to quantify
to the client that the volume or
value of money is ... limited.[131]

Alignment (or misalignment) between budget and aspiration became especially critical in the case of the Belgrade, where the brief was not simply to add a new auditorium and additional facilities within a workaday, utilitarian structure, but to create a quality public building that might act as a landmark. In this respect, Hamish Glen thought that:

> The whole journey was hampered by the initial mission for the amount of money that they wanted to do this for. It might have been that they were given a steer by the Arts Council, but everything in my professional life tells me to completely ignore such steers. ... You run the risk of them saying "no" but the flipside of that is that at least you get a decent sum of money for what you want to do.[132]

It is tempting to speculate: would there have been a better outcome had the Belgrade 'rocked the boat'? Neil Morton certainly noted at the end of the project that, compared with others in his experience, 'the jobs that get the money have the people who break the rules'.[133]

Just as the Belgrade's ambitions were perhaps typical of arts organizations, so too might we see their attitude similarly. Neil Morton recalled 'a slight optimism on the part of the client on this project always that there will be some sort of magic thing, uniquely Belgrade, that will deliver it cheaper for them'.[134] Here, perhaps, is the adage, 'it'll be alright on the night' writ large. Certainly the theatrical metaphor is not entirely misplaced. Beidas ruefully compared the nature of theatre productions, in which all parties usually work closely together to reach opening night whatever the odds, with the construction industry, which to him seemed to be characterized by argument. Glen, trained as a lawyer before entering the theatre, described the experience as 'war from day one', with the theatre being caught in the middle of disputes between, in particular, the architect and contractor, and there being also disputes between the client and design team at various points relating to fees.[135]

For Kim Kerton, one of the hallmarks of the project was the way in which the ambition for a quality, landmark structure remained constant: 'in respect of the aesthetics ... of the building

and their expectations, they've got what they wanted'.[136] Partly this result stemmed from the strength of the original 'vision' for the building, and from the way in which the theatre safeguarded that 'vision' through a combination of strong direction and consensus. Neither reductions to the scope of the project nor the adoption of more economical finishes and materials damaged the essential integrity of the overall design concept. But in addition, the choice of architect was well made and contributed to the end result. Stanton Williams was felt by both Beidas and Glen to have fully understood and embraced the 'vision'. There was a strong connection between the ambitions of the design team and those of the client,[137] with Alan Stanton being keen to deliver a building whose aspiration was at least equal to the original building of 1958 and describing the project as 'at times the best job in the office, great fun'.[138] (For Glen, this shared understanding was expressed not simply in the design, but also more literally, in the sheer effort invested in the scheme by the architects.) The nature of the design was also critical to the outcome. The way in which the performance space was conceived allowed considerations of external appearance and foyer layout to proceed essentially independently of the auditorium arrangement, which, throughout the process, comprised a structure inserted within an independent spatial and structural volume. That the structure might be changed within this volume before it was built was not the architects' intention in proposing their design. However, the outcome proved advantageous, if unorthodox, allowing the theatre to disconnect the design (and funding) of the space whilst work on the rest of the building continued.

This account has highlighted something of an apparent tension between the nature of buildings for the performing arts as working spaces and landmarks. The two concepts are not mutually exclusive, but at times, the Belgrade project has veered clearly towards the latter, with work on the second auditorium being periodically halted to allow work to continue on the external faces of the extension, and only limited changes being made to the original 1958 auditorium. The appearance of the main house contrasts with the refurbished foyers as a result while the stage remains, in some respects, problematic, with limited space at one side. Certainly more might have been done to the existing building, had priorities been different. But the way in which the building has been received confirms Kerton's view that the theatre ended up realizing its 'vision'. The city's goal – that a revitalized theatre building might add new value to the area – was realized; the adjacent Plaza site was ultimately sold for a figure far above early estimates. And, reviewing the new building and the theatre's artistic programme, the *Guardian* asked, 'is Coventry's newly-reopened Belgrade about to become Britain's most daring theatre?'[139]

Notes

1   I am grateful to David Beidas and Alan Stanton, who read drafts of this chapter and provided useful feedback, and all those who allowed me to quote from their interviews. I would also like to thank Stanton Williams and The Theatres Trust for permission to reproduce images. Alan Stanton's quotations have been edited slightly for clarity; the original sense is preserved.

2   David Beidas, 'Back to the beginning: the Belgrade in 2007', *Theatres Magazine* 14 (Winter 2007), pp.5-7.

3   A detailed history of the Belgrade is provided in Alistair Fair, '"A new image of the living theatre": the genesis and design of the Belgrade Theatre, Coventry, 1948-58', *Architectural History* 54 (2011), pp.347-382.

4   *Observer*, 30 March 1958.

5   Rhodri Winsor Liscombe, 'Refabricating the imperial image on the Isle of Dogs: Modernist design, British state exhibitions and colonial policy, 1924-1951', *Architectural History* 49 (2006), pp.317-348. See especially p.321. For the Festival Hall, see e.g. Miles Glendinning, *Modern architect: the life and times of Robert Matthew* (London, 2008), pp.88-109.

6   National Archives, Kew, HLG 118/203, record of a deputation from Coventry at the Ministry of Housing and Local Government, 1963.

7   See e.g. *Forward*, 21 March 1958.

8   *Guardian*, 1 April 1998.

9   Coventry Archives, CCA/TC/5/4/2/5: Belgrade Theatre Annual Report, 1963-1964.

10 'Theatre in Corporation Street, Coventry', *Architects' Journal* 128 (1958), pp.199-214

11 Coventry Archives, CCA/TC/5/4/2/6, Belgrade Theatre Annual Report, 1967-1968.

12 Coventry Archives, Belgrade Theatre drawings, sequence 7315.

13 *Guardian*, 1 April 1998.

14 David Beidas to Anne Dye, 13 June 2006.

15 David Beidas to Anne Dye, 13 June 2006.

16 David Beidas, e-mail to author, 21 April 2009.

17 Kim Kerton to Anne Dye, 20 June 2006.

18 David Beidas to Anne Dye, 13 June 2006.

19 Alan Stanton and Rawden Pettit to Anne Dye, 15 June 2006.

20 Levitt Bernstein design feasibility study, August 2001, copy supplied by the Belgrade Theatre.

21 Cited in Short and Associates, 'Belgrade Theatre: Conservation Management Plan' (2005), p.35.

22 *Stage*, 22 June 2000.

23 David Beidas to Anne Dye, 13 June 2006; *Stage*, 22 June 2000.

24 David Beidas to Anne Dye, 13 June 2006.

25 David Beidas to Anne Dye, 13 June 2006.

26 David Beidas to Anne Dye, 13 June 2006.

27 David Beidas to Anne Dye, 13 June 2006.

28 Kim Kerton to Monty Sutrisna, 20 June 2006

29 David Beidas to Anne Dye, 13 June 2006.

30 Kim Kerton to Monty Sutrisna, 20 June 2006.

31 Rawden Pettitt to Anne Dye, 15 June 2006.

32 Hamish Glen to Anne Dye, 6 June 2006.

33 Rawden Pettitt and Alan Stanton to Anne Dye, 15 June 2006.

34 *Guardian*, 6 July 2002, accessed on 10 May 2009 at <http://www.guardian.co.uk/stage/2002/jul/06/whoswhoinbritishtheatre.features16>.

35 David Beidas to Anne Dye, 13 June 2006.

36 David Beidas to Anne Dye, 13 June 2006; see also *Stage*, 15 January 2004 and 1 April 2004.

37 Kim Kerton to Monty Sutrisna, 20 June 2006.

38 David Beidas to Anne Dye, 13 June 2006.

39 Kim Kerton to Monty Sutrisna, 20 June 2006.

40 David Beidas, e-mail of 21 April 2009.

41 Kim Kerton to Monty Sutrisna, 20 June 2006.

42 Kim Kerton to Monty Sutrisna, 20 June 2006.

43 David Beidas to Anne Dye, 13 June 2006.

44 David Beidas, talk to CABE Enablers, c.2004, quoted in CABE, 'Building excellence in the Arts: a guide for clients', p.34.

45 Neil Morton and Charles Wass to Anne Dye, 11 July 2006.

46 Hamish Glen to Anne Dye, 6 June 2006.

47 Kim Kerton to Monty Sutrisna, 20 June 2006.

48 Kim Kerton to Monty Sutrisna, 20 June 2006.

49 Hamish Glen to Anne Dye, 6 June 2006.

50 A short summary of the design intent, written by the present author following interviews with Alan Stanton and Paul Williams, appears in S. Bayley et al., *Volume: Stanton Williams* (London, 2009), pp.194-195.

51 David Beidas, talk to CABE Enablers, c.2004, quoted in CABE, 'Building excellence in the Arts: a guide for clients', p.34.

52 Kim Kerton to Monty Sutrisna, 20 June 2006.

53 David Beidas to Anne Dye, 13 June 2006.

54 Rawden Pettitt and Alan Stanton to Anne Dye, 15 June 2006.

55 Rawden Pettitt and Alan Stanton to Anne Dye, 15 June 2006.

56 Alan Stanton and Rawden Pettitt to Anne Dye, 15 June 2006.

57 Hamish Glen to Anne Dye, 6 June 2006.

58 Neil Morton and Charles Wass to Anne Dye, 11 July 2006.

59 Rawden Pettitt and Alan Stanton to Anne Dye, 15 June 2006.

60 Rawden Pettitt and Alan Stanton to Anne Dye, 15 June 2006.

61 Rawden Pettitt and Alan Stanton to Anne Dye, 15 June 2006.

62 Paul Williams, pers. comm., January 2009.

63 Hamish Glen to Anne Dye, 6 June 2006.

64 Neil Morton and Charles Wass to Anne Dye, 11 July 2006.

65 Neil Morton and Charles Wass to Anne Dye, 11 July 2006.

66 Hamish Glen to Anne Dye, 6 June 2006.

67 Neil Morton and Charles Wass to Anne Dye, 11 July 2006.

68 Neil Morton and Charles Wass to Anne Dye, 11 July 2006.

69 See Chapter 8.

70 Ian Mackintosh, *The Guthrie Thrust Stage: a Living Legacy* (London, 2011), p.15.

71 Neil Morton and Charles Wass to Anne Dye, 11 July 2006.

72 Neil Morton and Charles Wass to Anne Dye, 15 June 2006.

73 Hamish Glen to Anne Dye, 6 June 2006.

74 Neil Morton and Charles Wass to Anne Dye, 11 July 2006.

75 David Beidas to Anne Dye, 13 June 2006.

76 Rawden Pettitt and Alan Stanton to Anne Dye, 20 June 2006.

77 Rawden Pettitt and Alan Stanton to Anne Dye, 20 June 2006.

78 Rawden Pettitt and Alan Stanton to Anne Dye, 20 June 2006.

79 Kim Kerton to Monty Sutrisna, 20 June 2006.

80 David Beidas to Anne Dye, 13 June 2006.

81 David Beidas to Anne Dye, 13 June 2006.

82 Helen Butcher to Anne Dye, 19 June 2006.

83 Kim Kerton to Monty Sutrisna, 20 June 2006.

84 David Beidas to Anne Dye, 6 June 2006.

85 Helen Butcher to Anne Dye, 19 June 2006.

86 Rawden Pettitt and Alan Stanton to Anne Dye, 20 June 2006.

87 David Beidas to Anne Dye, 13 June 2006.

88 Kim Kerton to Monty Sutrisna, 20 June 2006.

89 Neil Morton and Charles Wass to Anne Dye, 11 July 2006.

90 Alan Stanton, e-mail to author of 2 June 2009.

91 Alan Stanton to Alistair Fair, 26 April 2005.

92 David Beidas to Anne Dye, 13 June 2006.

93 Hamish Glen to Anne Dye, 6 June 2006.

94 David Beidas to Anne Dye, 13 June 2006.

95 Alan Stanton and Rawden Pettitt to Anne Dye, 15 June 2006.

96 David Beidas to Anne Dye, 13 June 2006.

97 David Beidas to Anne Dye, 13 June 2006.

98 David Beidas to Anne Dye, 13 June 2006.

99 Kim Kerton to Monty Sutrisna, 20 June 2006.

100 Alan Stanton and Rawden Pettit to Anne Dye, 15 June 2006.

101 Photo in V&A Theatre Museum Collections, Barbican file.

102 David Beidas to Anne Dye, 13 June 2006.

103 Kim Kerton to Monty Sutrisna, 20 June 2006.

104 Alan Stanton and Rawden Pettit to Anne Dye, 15 June 2006.

105 David Beidas to Anne Dye, 13 June 2006.

106 David Beidas to Anne Dye, 13 June 2006.

107 Kim Kerton to Monty Sutrisna, 20 June 2006.

108 Kim Kerton to Monty Sutrisna, 20 June 2006.

109 Alan Stanton and Rawden Pettit to Anne Dye, 15 June 2006.

110 David Beidas to Anne Dye, 13 June 2006.

111 David Beidas to Anne Dye, 13 June 2006.

112 Neil Morton and Charles Wass to Anne Dye, 11 July 2006.

113 Hamish Glen to Anne Dye, 6 June 2006.

114 Hamish Glen to Anne Dye, 6 June 2006.

115 Alan Stanton and Rawden Pettit to Anne Dye, 15 June 2006.

116 Hamish Glen to Anne Dye, 6 June 2006.

117 Hamish Glen to Anne Dye, 6 June 2006.

118 Kim Kerton to Monty Sutrisna, 20 June 2006.

119 Hamish Glen to Anne Dye, 6 June 2006.

120 David Beidas, e-mail to author of 6 February 2009; Kim Kerton to Monty Sutrisna, 20 June 2006.

121 David Beidas, e-mail to author of 20 May 2009.

122 Helen Butcher to Anne Dye, 19 June 2006.

123 David Beidas to Anne Dye, 13 June 2006.

124 Kim Kerton to Monty Sutrisna, 20 June 2006.

125 David Beidas to Anne Dye, 13 June 2006; Kim Kerton to Monty Sutrisna, 20 June 2006.

126 Hamish Glen to Anne Dye, 6 June 2006.

127 Alan Stanton and Rawden Pettit to Anne Dye, 15 June 2006.

128 David Beidas to Anne Dye, 13 June 2006.

129 Kim Kerton to Monty Sutrisna, 20 June 2006.

130 Kim Kerton to Monty Sutrisna, 20 June 2006.

131 Kim Kerton to Monty Sutrisna, 20 June 2006.

132 Hamish Glen to Anne Dye, 6 June 2006.

133 Neil Morton and Charles Wass to Anne Dye, 11 July 2006.

134 Neil Morton and Charles Wass to Anne Dye, 11 July 2006.

135 Hamish Glen to Anne Dye, 6 June 2006.

136 Kim Kerton to Monty Sutrisna, 20 June 2006.

137 David Beidas to Anne Dye, 13 June 2006.

138 Alan Stanton and Rawden Pettit to Anne Dye, 15 June 2006.

139 *Guardian*, 18 September 2007.

6.   'Turn the theatre inside out': Curve, Leicester

Alan Short

In 1973, the Leicester Haymarket Theatre opened. Thirty-five years later, in the autumn of 2008, the Leicester Theatre Trust moved into a new venue, designed by the New York-based Uruguayan architect Rafael Viñoly and named 'Curve' (fig. 6.1; table 6.1). The new theatre was conceived as an innovative, accessible venue, this aim being reflected in the design's attempts to break down the usual separation between front-of-house and backstage functions. This chapter sets out how this strong 'vision', formulated early in the project, was translated – not without controversy – into a new building. It starts with an overview of the context, then continues with discussion of the 'vision', the key players, and the evolving design.

Fig. 6.1 Curve, located within Leicester's emerging Cultural Quarter

Table 6.1 Curve, Leicester, case study characteristics

Curve, Leicester, characteristics	
Receiving/Producing	Producing, 2 auditoria of 750 seats & 350 seats respectively
Project driver(s)	Existing building threatened by redevelopment. New building desired for new vision Opportunity for planning gain from commercial development
Vision	New Cultural Quarter. 'Theatre inside out' to attract new audiences. Regeneration of depressed inner city ward
Refurbishment/new build	New build
Feasibility study - in house or external consultant?	i) external: 'Capital Options' study by Arts Business Ltd, Levitt Bernstein and others ii) external: re-visioned study at stage C by Architect, Theatre Consultant & others
Part of bigger arts initiative?	Yes: new Cultural Quarter
Business plan - scope	i) external: 'Capital Options' study contained business plan, construction budgets of £19 million
Construction budget set?	ii) Viñoly phase: budget in constant flux until late in design
Final account/current estimated out-turn	£63 million
Funding source(s)	Leicester City Council, Arts Council of England, East Midlands Development Agency, ERDF, Leicestershire Economic Partnership & Fundraising
Lead consultant	Architect until construction, then Project Manager
Design innovation	Opening up foyer to stage and auditorium to auditorium, challenging acoustic and fire/smoke issues
Specialist inputs	Theatre consultant, technical theatre systems consultant, acoustician, fire engineer, access, catering, traffic engineers, specialist lighting, IT, party wall surveyors
Value Engineering employed? - which stage?	Substantial VE savings on first proposal of order of £20 million, theatre technical systems services edited, and production workshops on neighbouring site omitted Further VE exercise post ACE submission, continuing VE process during stages E, F, G, H to stabilise cost; all VE savings post ACE submission lost
Vision creep?	No
Political climate	Volatile, resulted in iteration at stages C/D
Contract type - contractor involvement in design? - quality/time/money priority?	Amended JCT '98 without quantities Yes, 2 stage process Quality/time/money
Organisational change?	Company restructured mid stage D

CONTEXT: THE HAYMARKET THEATRE[1]

The Haymarket Theatre of 1973 was realized as part of the boom in theatre-building that took place in Britain between the late 1950s and the late 1970s. Commencing with Coventry's Belgrade Theatre, this period saw the construction of new theatres in many regional centres, often intended for Arts Council-subsidized Repertory companies. There had seemingly been talk of a new theatre in Leicester for many years. A piece in the *Leicester Mercury* in 1958 noted that the city's old Theatre Royal would make an excellent civic theatre, 'with plenty of atmosphere',[2] and that a new building would not only cost more but would also end up 'looking like a cross between a cinema and a bus station.'

In fact, the theatre which was built looked little like either a cinema or a bus station, if for a moment we accept that there might be a 'usual' mode of expression for those building types. The new Haymarket in fact formed part of a shopping centre designed by the Building Design Partnership (BDP); the theatre itself was realized with input from members of the City Architect's Department, including Kenneth King, who had played an integral part in the design of the Belgrade Theatre whilst a member of the Coventry City Architect's office during the 1950s.[3] Leicester was not alone in combining its new theatre and shopping centre. Nearby Derby, for example, located its new Playhouse of 1975 within the Eagle Centre. The Royalty Theatre on the Kingsway in London, meanwhile, was located below an office block of 1960. There were more historic precedents, too. Seventy years before, Frank Matcham's Leeds Empire Palace Theatre had been coupled with the same architect's County Arcade, a exuberant, glass-roofed space that incidentally was one of the few non-theatre buildings ever designed by Matcham. Such a strategy had its advantages (for example, the construction and operating costs of the theatre could potentially be offset by those of the commercial premises), but also presented several challenges. Not least amongst these was the question of the public face that the theatre would present. Could it develop its own identity as part of the bigger complex? Would it inevitably have to assume a subservient position? How would it expand or change in the future? In the case of the Haymarket, the theatre was located at first-floor level within the complex, with entrances from the shopping malls and car parks plus a wide flight of external steps connecting the main foyer level to the street. Not all welcomed this solution. Colin Amery, writing in the *Architects' Journal*, thought the result 'so much part of the shopping centre that it lacks any real presence of its own'.[4] He went on to comment that the use of the same red brick as the shopping mall for the theatre's elevations, foyer walls and internal paving was 'dull', concluding that any idea of the two being knitted together was nothing more than intellectual posturing.[5]

The theatre's interior was received more positively. The *Architects' Journal*'s editorial thought it 'brilliant',[6] while Amery was much more warmly disposed to the auditorium than he had been to the exterior. Its wedge-shaped stage, thrusting into the auditorium, generated a 'hexagonal' geometry which controlled the stalls and was echoed in the cantilevered seating galleries, with a total capacity of around 700. The theatre developed an impressive reputation as a leading regional theatre. Notably, in the late 1970s it formed the launch-pad for the career of Cameron Mackintosh, who took the Haymarket's productions of *My Fair Lady* and *Oklahoma!* on tour to great critical and commercial success.

A NEW THEATRE: PROJECT DRIVERS, FEASIBILITY, ARTS CULTURAL STRATEGY, THE 'VISION'

Successful as the Haymarket was, by the late 1990s its management had begun to consider what the venue's future might be. Part of this thinking, as we shall see, crystallized around a wish to explore new relationships between street and building, actor and audience. But there were also several rather more prosaic drivers for change. The theatre lacked sufficient education, workshop, and rehearsal spaces, and had poor wheelchair access. Being at first floor level, it did not interact well with the public realm. It also had some technical problems relating to the concealment of stage machinery as a result of the 'non-existent' proscenium opening.[7] One option was simply to refurbish the theatre within its existing shell. A more ambitious scheme had already been refused funding; ironically it might have cost less than the building that was eventually completed.

The theatre's close integration with the shopping centre not only served to hinder expansion or the development of an improved relationship with the street, but also, and rather more urgently, notional expansion plans on the part of the shopping centre seemed to endanger the continued existence of the theatre. Mandy Stewart, Chief Executive of the Haymarket between 2001 and 2006, recalled this stressful acceleration of commercial pressure:

The Shires Development, which is the [main] shopping centre, was ... moving forward and the Haymarket shopping centre, of which the old Haymarket theatre is part, was behind. There was a new set of owners for the shopping centre. They wanted to get hold of the old theatre in order to make it an appropriate shopping offer ... There was a sense [that] they might put some money down towards a new theatre, but ... certain people, who never thought Leicester would build anything new, [had] huge amounts of fear. And so [it was said], "We will not move from the Haymarket, regardless of the pressure from the developer, until we see a brand new theatre." I suppose that was the right decision to take but there was an awful lot of controversy going on and no harmony at all.[8]

For the Artistic Director it was a truly awful period:

For many years before, [there was] a "will it, won't it" atmosphere ... will they just kick us out of the old theatre?[9]

In addition, at the city-wide scale Leicester was, like the East Midlands region generally, falling behind in terms of Lottery success. Coventry had already commissioned and agreed a Masterplan that included a crescent-shaped 'Cultural Quarter' (or 'Cultural Banana', as the vigorous Director of City Development John McGuigan described it).[10] It had secured a Millennium Fund Award, and Sir Richard McCormac was working up a major city centre transformation. McGuigan even talked of burying the city's elevated ring road, to deliver a Midlands version of the Vienna Ringstrasse. By late 1999, Arts Council England (ACE) was pro-actively surveying the regions to assess the likely call on Lottery funds. The city officer charged with oversight of Leicester's cultural infrastructure, Mike Candler, recalls a critical discussion with the ACE Director of Capital Services Moss Cooper:

[Moves at the] back end of 1999 [were] stimulated by a discussion that the city council had had with the Arts Council, with Moss Cooper in particular. At that point ... the Arts Council were looking at what was likely to be the call on capital funding for the arts through the National Lottery programme. ... They held a number of seminar sessions in the region, with the local authorities and key players, to talk about the [Millennium] and what that might mean. So, [the] City Council along with representatives from the Phoenix Arts Centre [and the] Haymarket Theatre met with [Cooper] to talk about what was happening in Leicester. At that time we had a kind of standalone scheme for the Haymarket theatre, a greatly reduced scheme on their original aspiration because that [had been] turned down and refused funding, so that [project now] was likely to move forward as a redevelopment on the current site working [within] the existing mass of the building. Within the Phoenix Arts Centre, we had a standalone development and they

were part way through a design competition to appoint the architect. The City Council was looking at a Phase 2 development of De Montfort Hall, the city's concert hall, and longer-term gallery development for the visual arts.[11]

In 2000, ABL Cultural Consulting was commissioned to conduct citywide consultation involving constituencies which had not hitherto been brought together. The results of this work were submitted to the City Council as 'Performing arts, film, new media and visual arts in Leicester: City Centre Capital Options Summary Report', to be politically transfigured into the council policy document 'Diverse City: A Vision for Cultural life in Leicester.' This document promised a 'commitment to celebrating diversity through the design of buildings and public spaces.'[12] This 'vision' stemmed from a critical 'after-meeting' at the Arts Council, a precisely identifiable moment at which Leicester's cultural planning changed gear, with significant architectural results:

We had a number of competing priorities at various stages of progression. Our partners left the meeting and the City Council and myself and our [then] Director stayed on and had a further discussion with Moss Cooper about a number of factors, not least that while the propositions that were around were good in themselves, they didn't start to address a ... strategic approach. Certainly they would meet [immediate] needs but [not] the needs of a much wider constituency – for example, there was no joined up approach to considerations of [the changing] demography of the City and the fact that Leicester was predicted to become the first Asian[-majority] city in the UK, and I believe also in Europe, over the next ten years. So we started to talk to Moss about this notion of a Cultural Quarter, which wasn't a new concept for Leicester: there [had] been discussion with De Montfort University who are a partner organisation in the Phoenix ... about developing the Cultural Quarter. We put the proposition that

this kind of approach could address some of the wider issues of demography change, gaps within the existing cultural infrastructure, and so on. And on the back of that conversation the Arts Council through their Capital Completion One programme ring-fenced ten million pounds to the City Council for the design of the Cultural Quarter. It was at that point that we commissioned ABL to undertake the Capital Options study to look at what was needed in the city and to benchmark that against other Local Authority areas and comparative cities. That study was completed in June 2000 and they put forward a number of proposals, and the proposals are essentially what were taken forward to date. And so it would be the new Performing Arts Centre, to bring together the produced work from the Haymarket Theatre, and the live work provided through the Phoenix, in one newbuild.'[13]

The ABL strategy recommended a Creative Business Incubator, which became the Leicester Creative Business Depot, part of Phase 1 of the Cultural programme which followed, a film and media centre, which became a 'Digital Media Centre', and plus for a Visual Arts Gallery and a new music venue, both of which are yet (2010) to be progressed.

Arts Council England endorsed the strategy, including the physical development proposals, and pledged £10 million.[14] Participants remember the consequences of the Option Study being *'painful'* for many of the existing organizations, in the Haymarket's Capital Projects Director's words.[15] Mandy Stewart could take a more detached view:

Yes, [the Options Study] seemed to be very critical in the way that it conducted itself. It expos[ed] lots of organisations and current practice in a somewhat divisive way. And when I got here in 2001, that study was still stinging. And I think, there was a sense that, "Well, because that study has exposed how inadequate so many of the cultural facilities are in Leicester, and how they are not physically positioned to engage with our wider communities. Leicester needs to look at a Cultural Quarter, where it can rebuild its cultural provision in a more twenty-first century way." But that was it. [The idea was that] "This is going to be a rebuild, a replacement and reiteration of what clearly has gone well beyond its sell-by date."[16]

The study had identified fundamental issues, not least the huge shift in the city's demographic composition (in 1991, minority ethnic groups made up 28.5% of Leicester's population; the national average was 5.5%).[17] The report reassessed the city's cultural needs and expectations and proposed new infrastructure at a prodigious scale. It still begged the question: what should take place in all this new accommodation? How would it engage with this unprecedented cultural mix? Nonetheless, the City Council's Cabinet took the Arts, Leisure and Environment Committee's Cultural Strategy and formally approved its implementation in November 2001, primarily delivering the Performing Arts Centre (the new Haymarket), the Creative Industries Depot, public realm improvement to the environment of the new St Georges Cultural Quarter, and feasibility work for components of subsequent phases. A consultant quantity surveyor was commissioned to report on the likely cost of the theatre, suggesting that a total cost of £26.5 million would be typical for this sort of project.[18] Funders were courted and a package of money assembled (Table 6.2). As was the case in Coventry, the sources of money included the regional development agency and the European Union, drawn in by the potential of the theatre for regeneration and indications that it would create 125 new jobs whilst assisting forty small-medium sized enterprises.[19]

Table 6.2 Curve: funding sources at the beginning of the project

Funding source	Contribution
Arts Council	£10.0 million
Leicester City Council	£4.4 million
Lease sales	£5.0 million
ERDF	£2.0 million
East Midlands Development Agency	£2.0 million
Sponsorship	£0.5 million
Total sourced funding	£24.0 million
Identified funding gap	£2.6 million minimum
Projected costs	£26.5 million

The 'vision' presented an almost unprecedented challenge in the UK at that time. The city's promises for the new Cultural Quarter were unambiguous, 'based on the assumption that the city's theatre, film, media and visual arts institutions need to change radically to meet the evolving cultural needs of our changing population'. Leicester could be 'a nationally significant force to foster the celebration and dissemination of South Asian and other cultures.'[20] The Haymarket's home team interpreted this challenge as a clear critique of the customary physical infrastructure of western theatre, the impenetrable solidity of the auditorium and stage, the concealment of all of the back-of-house, the mysteriousness and 'Englishness' of the foyers with their various bars and hat checks. These elements of theatre were, it seemed, inducing the same 'fear of the threshold' that Jennie Lee had identified in the 1960s in the context of social class but now translated into a multi-cultural city:

...[the theatre] was still pulling in audiences. [But] it wasn't pulling in the right sort ... to reflect [Leicester's] demographic.[21]

The team's solution to this problem combined radical theatrical intent with an evocative physical design consequence. Their strategy was borne of a moment of frustration during the concluding stages of the city wide Options Study. The then Chief Executive & Artistic Director were contributing to the consultation:

> *Paul [Kerryson] and I were sitting in the foyer of the old Haymarket, high up above everything, and we were with an architect. This architect was trying, … really trying to understand, trying to tell us what he thought we wanted with a new theatre. And it was very frustrating, because there was no sense of him understanding the reason for a new theatre, which was the vital thing of democratic engagement, underpinning it. We do say equality and diversity are the absolute cornerstones. And he just didn't. We didn't have Kully [Thiarai, later Joint Artistic Director] with us at the time, because she joined a couple of months later, so we were probably not as eloquent as I am sure she would have been. And I had to say, really out of frustration, "No. We want to turn the whole thing inside out." Which came out as this dreaded phrase, and he said, "Oh, you really, really want to turn the theatre inside out?" It was the first time that expression was said. We are not into replicating what has been. We really want to find a way where theatre can be … much more transparent, much more open, visible, part of the flow of the community. [There's a] tradition of theatre being very departmentalized into backstage and front of house … We really want to demystify that through the work, through the activity and the participation of the people, but, of course, somehow that had to be articulated through the design.[22]*

This very simple and immediately appealing idea was both a metaphor for an inverted relationship between the city and its performing arts community, and a literal image containing the germ of several very demanding technical challenges.

How could these perceived boundaries be broken down, by whom, and when?

THE PLAYERS AND THEIR FIELDS OF INFLUENCE

The critical role of the Arts Council in nudging the City Council to reorganize and address the dynamic situation of their city has been discussed. De Montfort University's interests were manifest. It had grown rapidly during the Vice Chancellorship of Ken Barker, when, as a stimulant to the city's economy (which had been damaged by the rapid loss of textile manufacturing and its supporting industries), the university had particularly developed its Faculties of Arts and Design and Humanities and Social Sciences. All these subjects were complementary to the more traditional academic offering of the older Leicester University. It had performing arts departments on both its Leicester and Bedford campuses. The Vice Chancellor was trying to plan a rationalization of this activity, but where to build a fully functioning theatre? De Montfort had a particular interest in the Phoenix.[23] In the end it kept a watching brief, pleased to see a performing arts venue arriving at others' expense and risk. The involvement of ABL ceased on publication of its report. Its co-author, Cara McMahon (who had also worked on the Coventry Arts and Media study), became a lecturer at De Montfort.

The Architect

The Labour Party habitually controlled Leicester City Council and had done for some twenty-five years by the time of its defeat in spring 2003. As has been noted, it was the City Council who acted as the client for the new theatre, delivering it for the creative team. This *modus operandi* had both advantages and drawbacks. Ruth Eastwood, who, after leading the Lighthouse, Poole, succeeded Mandy Stewart as Chief Executive in 2006, thought it beneficial on the one hand, because it took some of the worry of the project away from the theatre, but later reflected that perhaps some of that worry (and responsibility) might have been beneficial.[24]

In 2001, the Chief Executive of the council launched the search for an Architect for the new theatre, appointing MACE to manage the process under the full European Union procurement protocol. He ensured the Haymarket was well represented on the interview panel. The Chief Executive of the Haymarket later recalled the simple pleasure of seeing the advertisement and being included in the selection process:

The original brief that was put out to EU tender literally says: "Leicester Theatre and Performing Arts Centre. The ambition [is] to turn the theatre inside out". ... There were two people from the theatre at that interview panel. That was pretty huge for a city council-driven thing. Kully [Thiarai] and I went through this two-day interview process. It was absolutely fascinating. We got told time and time again about what we wanted and what had been built elsewhere and how that would suit Leicester. And there was no sense of listening. Then Rafael [Viñoly] walked into the room and the entire dynamic changed. It's all on video, and none of us will ever forget it. Because, of course, he's remarkable looking. He wears all his glasses [multiple pairs, on strings around his neck]. He was with a very beautiful woman, ... the only woman we'd seen in two days. And she was very blonde, very tall and brilliant.[25]

Very importantly this was a selection process that followed the RIBA's recommendations, and not a competition. The Project Managers tried to focus the panel's minds on process. But in that respect, they may have missed the point, because the 'vision' required an architectural idea. The Project Managers did not survive to the next stage and were replaced by Focus in August 2002.[26] Rafael Viñoly's colleague, architect Christina Seilern, later recalled:

We were told at the briefing during the competition that "all the architects here have been selected on architectural merit, we all know that you can design beautiful things and [so] we want to understand how you would run the project." And the interesting thing [was that] we were very much an odd duck, because we had just set up in the UK, we hadn't built anything in the UK, and so I just thought, "It's the same thing." I mean, here is Foster and I can't [remember] who else was there but ... all these large architectural firms that all have proven that they can put together buildings ... How do you really differentiate? They were telling us, "Do not talk about design, talk about ... the management of the design." ... Well, we talked about management of design to a certain extent but then we really talked about the [idea] of "theatre inside out" and the interesting idea of that. I think that's what got us the project but it was an interesting thing, because there was such a strong notion from the client, it was such an interesting idea, and the Project Managers hadn't quite picked up on that.[27]

This misconception, set off by current project management good practice, seems in fact to have favoured the participants who ignored the instruction from the then Project Manager and instead identified the real interest of the panel's user representatives. Viñoly seems to have struck intuitively at these preoccupations and anxieties as exposed by the Arts Council and then reinforced by ABL's study. Indeed, he later recalled as a 'wonderful coincidence' the fact that the Haymarket team's wish to subvert the traditional actor/audience relationship paralleled his own interest not only in 'diluting the filter' of the proscenium arch but also establishing new connections between performers, technicians and audiences during, before and after performances.[28]

The Haymarket's Chief Executive had vivid recollections of the interview:

It was a brilliant political performance ... fantastic. He said, "I'm here to listen". He said, "the city, it's amazing." He spoke very clearly about the city. He called it "the city of cloth." And "a maze." He kept saying that there was no iconic building in Leicester. "What you'll know of Leicester is this fantastic maze of little streets, and this city of cloth." He wasn't talking about the traditional textiles, though he might have been; it was much more about what he saw of the different people from different nations and different cultures and different experiences and they all wear different cloth or clothes. And I guess that's very true. From the headdresses and the long skirts and colour and swish of material running around these mazes. He was [saying], "I mean it's mad, it's amazing." And at the end of that day, the Leader said, "there is no discussion." We went, "no." I remember Kully and I kept walking down the road. I said, "I don't think we quite believe what we've just met!" Because we thought finally we might now have a project.'[29]

Here, then, was an interview to match those architectural coups now embedded in the discipline's mythology; Denys Lasdun's win at the National Theatre, for example.

The Theatre Consultant

Rafael Viñoly was anxious to work with a French theatre consultant, Ducks Scéno. They were formally appointed following a study tour of their work at Lyon and Nîmes as the only consultants directly employed by the Architect and not the City Council, a self-induced exposure. The Quantity Surveyor saw the theatre consultant's role as rather prosaic:

I think it would be fair to say that the architect has the bigger vision of the building, how he sees that working and looking aesthetically and visually... whereas the theatre technician is looking purely at how functional the theatre will be in the terms of putting a performance on.[30]

But for Haymarket's Production Manager and Project Director, Ducks Scéno possessed a very particular and very important set of skills:

[Ducks Sceno] were scenographers, interested in volume and space.[31]

The French were caught unawares by the precision required of designers in the UK, the need to specify every tiny item under a traditional contract form to avoid contractual action under incomplete information, and to feed information to the independent cost estimators, the Quantity Surveyors, a UK invention. European theatrical theatre practice emerged as a different phenomenon. Eventually Graham Lister, the theatre's Capital Project director, encouraged the appointment of an additional UK theatre consultant, Charcoalblue, '... who are much more job-like working theatre consultants ...'. Charcoalblue's Project Director speculated on the background to their appointment:

[Lister] felt... he was given a European solution... [Ducks Scéno], to their credit...for all the best reasons, [were] trying to say, "Well, there is this other way of working and you should consider it because the rest of Europe does it like this and you should be taking modern practice on board."... Graham [Lister] was saying, "... if the theatre works only for Belgian people, then I'm going to have trouble hiring casuals," so he suggested Ducks Scéno might consider teaming up with an English practice.[32]

The Acoustician

The Architect believed in the fundamental importance of an acoustician's design guidance to the project, and, very interestingly, how crucial it would be in the earliest stages:

'[The acoustician's] role is very important at the beginning, and then very important in the detailing.'[33]

Viñoly encouraged the selection of the Belgian acousticians Eckhard Kahle and Thomas Wulfrank of Kahle Acoustics. Kahle was very clear about the challenge of theatre design to everyone, not least the clients:

I think it should be clear that any performing arts building is a complicated building. There are real life quotations like the one which goes around in my head which is from somebody who used to design nuclear power plants who, after designing his first performing arts space, said "this is the most complicated and intricate type of building to be designed, and that is even including power plants." What we find very often is that clients are not really aware of the complexity of such a building, and especially that some clients are not aware of the information that is required from them during the design and construction process. If there is a design team, there is an architect, there is hopefully a theatre planner, an acoustician, a set of engineers and probably a cost consultant, but that doesn't actually mean that as a client, especially as a client with an existing theatre infrastructure, you can step back and just say "we've asked for a new theatre; tell us when you're finished."[34]

Kahle was bemused that the user group was not the formal client:

With this project, certainly one of the key ... complications is [that] there is a user group, but they are not our formal client. Yes, you sometimes say user groups struggle due to the excess strain that construction puts on them and that's certainly an important finding, but basically the user group should be aware ... that what we are building now is what they will live with for the next ten, twenty or thirty years, and therefore it's quite clear that they need to put some extra resources, possibly even hire somebody specifically, to either replace somebody who then becomes free to

follow the construction or to hire somebody dedicated to the construction. In Leicester it's quite clear that the Haymarket has a much clearer idea of what they want in a building and how they want it than the Client.[35]

By 'client', Kahle means Leicester City Council, by whom he had been appointed. This means of engagement, which he compared unfavourably to that by which Jean Nouvel's Convention Centre in Lucerne was achieved, seemed to generate conflict and engender cost issues.

Kahle was shrewd enough to discern that the radical intent was generated by the theatre's senior management and that the workforce was ambivalent at least:

It was quite clear that the original statement was not 100% of the Haymarket Theatre, i.e. not all of their personnel subscribed to it. It was the majority opinion, or call it the management opinion. It is quite clear that if you go to the more technical [and] day-to-day people, [that] the technician in the theatre wants to work the way he has always worked. There is a certain conservatism ... there. So while all of the Haymarket can agree on the vision, it is quite clear that some people want them to make a very bold statement and accept at least some compromise, if not possibly even severe compromise, in some of the details of the operation. It is clear that the people that are affected by the compromise want a little bit of compromise, but not too much of a compromise, not a very radical change in the way they will work. The "inside-out" concept has mainly been maintained; we had to do some amendments to it, to make some of the concept more practical and pragmatic, but we have tried to maintain the vision.[36]

And that 'vision', or Viñoly's physical manifestation of it, was a given for the competing acousticians. As Kahle observed:

The architect had created, before hiring an acoustician, ... the concept of an acoustic curtain that would be

*miraculously everything. Luckily I know him a bit, so
... the first thing I did [was] to make some calculations
to check whether it is technically feasible to do it, and
actually it turns out that it is complicated but feasible.*

The concept changed on account of fire considerations into something rather more solid, giving more acoustic isolation and meeting the operational requirement always to close the shutters in performance. The Acoustician rued its deformation to fit a two-stage procurement process and a time/budget driven process.

The Fire Engineer

Arup were appointed as Mechanical and Electrical Engineers. Not long thereafter it became manifestly clear that skilled fire engineering design was required to save the openness of the envisioned scheme from the prescriptive content of Part B of the Building Regulations and the Code of Practice for Fire in Public Buildings, BS5588. Theatres are traditionally considered high-risk environments and so the principle driving the regulations and guidance is to wholly compartment auditoria and foyers from each other and from escape routes. At Leicester, to facilitate the desired open space, there is a 'deemed to satisfy' bespoke fire-engineered alternative path. Arup modelled the journeys from auditorium fixed set positions to the exterior. Escape scenarios were modelled to the UK underground station code NFPA130, incorporating statistically derived working and queuing times. Meanwhile mechanical ventilation is designed to exhaust smoke through the roof of the concourse as it accumulates to lift the smoke layer above escapees. The model shows that everyone can exit within four minutes. However, the auditoria remain rigidly compartmented in performance and on the operation of the smoke alarms; steel shutters descend to form the compartments. In a sense this could be claimed to be the principal injury to the 'vision', but, as Kahle remarked, it considerably lifts the acoustic performance of the various

adjacent spaces. As the fire engineer observed with real chivalry:

> *Our job is to facilitate the architecture ...
> which is why we departed from traditional
> Code guidance to be able to do that.*[37]

The 'End-users'

In the face of such a radically different proposition, the Haymarket management team realized the urgent need to temper the design with the reality of staging shows in the middle of England:

> *... we totally understand the iconic nature of it ...
> However, what we must have, and the Arts Council
> will insist, is that this works magnificently.*[38]

The first Chief Executive, Mandy Stewart, stressed that the 'vision' positioned the new theatre as a

> *kind of arts social enterprise, working seven days
> a week, 100 hours a week... there for all sectors
> and all members of the community to use.*[39]

Stewart also explained that there was no point in abandoning community groups by, for example, imposing a huge hire bill for a set of lights. The business plan would fail. The user group therefore took the initiative and empowered itself by appointing a technical advisory committee to vet proposals and reinforce their position. It was not entirely well received by the designers. Graham Lister described the composition of the group:

> *My background is as a freelance production manager,
> so I tend to work with the same people. So [the group
> includes] production electricians, and there's sound
> engineers and operators and stage engineering*

people, etc. We've been very fortunate [to have had the input of these people and the benefit of their experience on the project]. [...] They were involved in many of the design team meetings that we had with [the architects]. While we were going through Stage C and Stage D, ... looking at how we can make ... this building work and still provide its 'inside-outness' and maintain the vision, they were the people that worked with us to actually come up with solutions. I think [the architects] may [have], and certainly the theatre planners have, found it quite challenging at times, because sometimes it's not been made easy for them.[40]

Lister later expanded on his point, commenting that 'everyone was aware that we were attempting to re-imagine some of the thinking and conventions that have informed our industry for many years.'[41]

For the end users, particularly Lister, the burden has been taxing, on top of everyday responsibilities.

It was no longer possible to do two jobs, to run the productions and to also work on the capital project. I seemed to be having to fight many battles, with the architects, the theatre planners and of course with Leicester City Council. In the end I managed to get the design team and the City Council to appoint Charcoalblue to bring on board a level of UK-based theatre planning expertise. This made things a little easier and they have given me a level of support that is invaluable.[42]

Stress and workload on the user client are an important theme throughout this study; in the preceding chapter we noted how the Belgrade Theatre handled consultation with its staff, and the way in which a senior member of staff was allocated time to manage the capital project. Lister complained of unscheduled demands on his time, but accepted that the designers were also working continuously against the clock and the budget:

I think that there are times when we've got very cross, because sometimes you do feel that you are just a kind of ... pawn, pushed into meetings, poorly briefed.[43]

He later expanded on this point:

Sometimes, there was a lack of understanding (sometimes not just from the design team) of other priorities (i.e., that we also were running a large-scale producing theatre).[44]

The Haymarket's Own Constituency, its Staff and Supporters

As in Coventry, the staff were subject to an exhaustive consultation as the architects rehearsed and ultimately rewrote the original brief. Lister recalled:

To [the architects'] credit I remember that they did try to immerse themselves in our work. They came up for three or four days. I remember getting Christina [Seilern] to spend time backstage during the shows ... [There was a full] consultation process [with the entire workforce, including performers, stage staff and cleaners]. They met every department [...] to try and get some understanding of what that department did.[45]

But the staff had misgivings, being fearful of the future. There was speculation on the likelihood of a new theatre, and some bafflement about the emerging 'vision', with, as it turned out, good reason. The City Officer directing the project recalls the anxieties clearly:

It was coming through the Board [that] there were tensions about. Change is always difficult, and depending where you sit in the equation ... If you're leading it, then it's exciting and it's challenging and it's rewarding. But if you're in a situation where you're not leading it but [your work is] complicated by it, then it can often feel like it's something that's being done to you. And I think there was a bit of "this is something that is being done to us" and there was uncertainty about whether or not the theatre would be a producing theatre and that's not an uncertainty that was being driven by the Council. We set out to build a producing theatre, but there's always been this ongoing debate in Leicester, and it's still around today: "Why have we got a theatre with only 750 seats? We should have a large lyric theatre than can receive touring shows." And that debate [continues], no matter how clearly we've articulated that this is a producing theatre, making productions in Leicester and growing the city's reputation as a producing City. That was the genesis of the capital strategy. [...] We wanted to become renowned. ... It's always been questioned, ... through the local press. The history of the Haymarket Theatre; there's a legacy there. A legacy there that it's more than the programme that earns a reputation... it's about the bricks and mortar, and people feel quite passionate.[46]

The Politicians

The timeline records the oscillating power structure of the City Council, Labour's unsuspected defeat in 2003 enabling the Opposition to close down the Haymarket. As Mandy Stewart later recalled:

[Something] which was very specific to this project was political. [There had been] twenty-five years of Labour rule and five years of Labour leadership by one particular person, who was a businessman and very global[ly-focussed]. I remember the first time I met him, he had just flown in from New York. That was the calibre of the Leader. He saw Leicester as a global city in an international context. And in May 2003 he lost. Labour lost [power], and he lost the leadership.[47]

Paul Kerryson remembered the time as a 'terrible coincidence', the defeat coming at a time when the Haymarket staff were occupied on other projects. The new Liberal Democrat/Conservative coalition set about dismantling the performance content of the project, requiring a redesign to allow conference use. Ironically this move simply added more cost and introduced further delay through a year of ultimately fruitless Value Engineering, with inflation gathering pace at the same time as the economy strengthened.

The Regenerators

Stimulating economic activity through the considered placing of new arts infrastructure was a relatively new concept, met by some scepticism. In the UK, The Lowry had been one of the earliest Capital Arts investments specifically engineered to trigger the regeneration of Salford Quay, while we have noted the perceived value of Belgrade II in contributing to the revitalization of central Coventry. However, in Walsall, a new gallery was less effective, while the National Centre for Popular Music in Sheffield simply failed.[48] But for Leicester's Quantity Surveyor, the literal connection that was made between a potentially iconic new theatre and the possibility of privately funded redevelopment in the St George's area of Leicester seemed self-evidently symptomatic of an upsurge in optimism:

They wanted a statement building to drive the regeneration of the St George's Cultural Quarter in Leicester. They saw it as the cornerstone for the regeneration ... – which is happening already. There's a lot of building activity going on in the surrounding region. There are residential developments in there now, redeveloping fantastic old buildings which have stood quiet for many years and it's going to give that region a real kick start. So, in that respect, it's been a success for the City Council. That was I think the driving force behind them appointing a

experience and approach, methodology [were important]. They were felt to be the right people for the job.[54]

Stewart observed simply that *'they brought some kind of sanity to the project.'*[55]

THE DESIGN

A decision was made in 2002 to adopt a two-stage contract. Under the first section, the design would be developed to such a stage that a firm price could be ascertained and agreed. Under the second part of the contract, the theatre would be delivered according to a fixed price.

Early Design, Workstages C & D

The Viñoly team inherited the ABL feasibility study, and, significantly, its budget projection, expressed as a very technical project brief giving spatial accommodation requirements, programme requirements, all adding up to 9000 square metres. The eventual project comprised some 13,000 square metres. The project manager maintained that, in the final building, little was materially altered from the brief inherited from this study, and that (as in the case of Belgrade II), it is in its architectural implementation that the emerging scheme departed from the original, rather dry, intent:

> *A very, very different building. I think the end users have married their vision of "theatre inside out" to Rafael [Viñoly]'s vision of "theatre inside out". I think what's happened here is that the traditional lines of briefing of a project, of a client brief, and an architect responding to that brief, have been blurred. [The] architects have really, in many ways, driven the brief with the end user. And dragged the City Council along with them.*[56]

Once again, therefore, we see that the feasibility study for the project provided an important indication of requirements, but that the eventual project developed in quite unexpected ways. As was true of the Belgrade, the penalty for this development was financial. The Architect's Project Director later reflected on receiving and analysing the original feasibility work:

> *The Council had a feasibility study done, which set out a brief. I think they even did a quick mock-up scheme and also set out a budget. Early on – prior to or at the time of starting the project – we immediately realized that the brief and the budget were not in line. So the first thing that needed to happen was [to align] brief and budget, in terms of ... do [they] want a 350 seat theatre and a 750 seat theatre? The first thing we had to do was to show them what they could get for £19 million. And then to allow them to make the decision as to whether the budget was more important or whether the brief was more important for the Council and for ... the city of Leicester.'*[57]

Given the city council's direct involvement as client (in contrast to the Belgrade), the answer to this question was pre-ordained politically: expenditure was to be tightly capped. In addition, Seilern was clear that when pressed *'what does the theatre inside out mean, the answer was "I don't know"... While the concept originated with them, ... the execution of it was completely unclear.'*[58]

For Viñoly's practice, however, the 'inside-out' concept was loaded with meaning and possibilities. It resonated with an approach to buildings for the arts that had been developed by Viñoly over the course of several projects in which the relationship between performers, audience and context had been explored:

> *[A] notion which I had been already researching on my own [was] the idea that performing arts have evolved over the last century and a half enormously, at a*

*greater speed the closer you get
to our time. But [they are] still
dominated, at least architecturally
and in terms of theatre planning,
by the notion that ... there is a
differentiation between the act of
production and the performance
itself, which is represented by
the transition between mystery
and reality that the proscenium
represents for people in the
theatre. I was curious of how you
work at diluting that filter...*

He continued:

*I think that one of the greatest
things about a mystery is that if you
know what is behind it, you enjoy it
a lot more.*[59]

The Kimmel Center for the Performing
Arts, Philadelphia (2001), for example,
features auditoria positioned as
freestanding objects within a barrel-
vaulted glasshouse; the foyer is treated
as an extension of the city street.
The design as a whole was intended
to provide contact between actors
and audiences, and to break down
established barriers. Viñoly's 'Jazz at
Lincoln Center' project (2004) has
a glazed wall at the rear of the stage
offering spectacular views of the New
York skyline. A competition entry for
the Oslo Opera House (2000 – not
built) conceived the auditoria as solid
masses within a space that was to be

enveloped by a glazed wall, dubbed
'a protective transparent skin' and made
of slender glass tubes placed side by
side. Similarly, Viñoly's unbuilt design
for a music venue in Gateshead (1997 –
a competition won by Norman Foster)
proposed cubic structures with highly
glazed envelopes intended to connect
local people with the activities and
performances housed within the centre.

Early sketches of c.2002-2003
by Viñoly reveal the application
and development of these ideas in
Leicester. One (fig. 6.2) shows the
entire site conceived as an extension
of the pavement – the 'public datum'
– invoking ideas of the theatre as an
integral part of the surrounding city,
and the city itself as a theatre. The
permeable nature of the building is
confirmed by a second drawing (fig. 6.3),
entitled 'Site Occupation Strategy',
which depicts the building as the focus
of a series of routes. In addition, the
'public datum' drawing implies that
the whole building was to be 'public',

*Fig. 6.3 Sketch by Rafael Viñoly with the
theatre site as a permeable extension of its
surroundings*

according with Viñoly's interest in
breaking down distinctions between
the various parts of theatre. Indeed, as
a further drawing confirms (fig. 6.4),
the whole site was considered as a
potential performance space, covered
in its entirety by a technical grid which
would allow the theatre management
to present work in any part of the
building. Viñoly proposed curtains as
a way to define performances when
necessary (figs. 6.5 and 6.6). Other
drawings explored the possibility of
more definite performance structures.
One shows auditoria inserted as freestanding 'people platforms', carved into
the datum and rising above it (fig. 6.7).

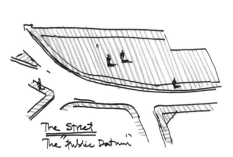

*Fig. 6.2 Initial concept sketch by Rafael Viñoly
showing the site as a 'public datum' extending
from the pavement across the theatre*

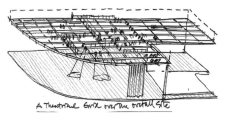

*Fig. 6.4 The entire building as potential
performance space, with a full technical
grid: concept sketch by Rafael Viñoly*

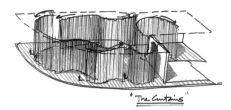

Fig. 6.5 *The boundaries between the performace spaces conceived by Viñoly as curtains*

Fig. 6.6 *Viñoly's curtains were partly inspired by the colours and textures of the fabric garments he observed being worn by the people of Leicester on the day of the interview*

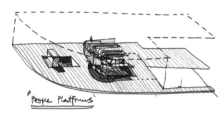

Fig. 6.7 *'People platforms', carved into and rising above the datum*

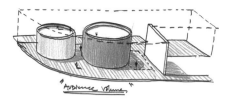

Fig. 6.8 *Defined 'volumes' house the auditoria within the universal space of the theatre*

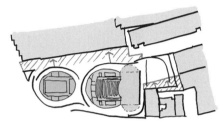

Fig. 6.9 *This drawing shows the stage of the larger performance space not yet into its eventual position between the two auditoria*

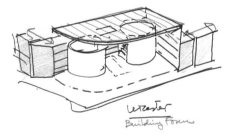

Fig. 6.10 *The two auditoria with the stage located between them*

Fig. 6.11 *The stage, like the foyers, was conceived as 'public' space as opposed to the 'private' world of the auditoria*

openly and so there is much more "given" to the street life, and acts as a frontage to the street, which is currently pretty dead.[60]

Thus the foyer *'would become an extension of the sidewalk ... if the stage could become the sidewalk so much the better.*[61] Within this shared space, roles would become blurred: indeed, Viñoly hoped that the audience would become 'actors', in a sense. So too would the stage technicians, whose work could take place in full view of the gathering audience.

The exterior of the building was treated almost like a giant proscenium arch, curving around the corner of the site and framing views of the theatre's interior (fig. 6.12). One sketch of 2002 reveals a ship-like prow at the corner of the building and full-height glass panels (fig. 6.13). Inside, ramps can be seen wrapped around the exterior of the auditorium volume: the inverse of Frank Lloyd Wright's Guggenheim Museum, where the ramped display space is placed around the inside of the

Another (fig. 6.8) has solid volumes, not far removed in concept from those in the Oslo scheme. Further drawings explored the arrangement of the auditoria, with the stage of the larger theatre being rotated from the end (fig. 6.9) to the centre of the building, allowing it to be shared between the two performance spaces (fig. 6.10).

One sketch (fig. 6.11) is especially important in that it denotes the stage as 'public' space, contrasting with the adjacent 'private' solid auditoria. Viñoly elaborated on this idea:

When [the technicans] are setting up the stage, they are doing it in natural light and visibly and

Fig. 6.12 The building envelope functions as a giant proscenium arch, twisting around the corner and framing views of the interior

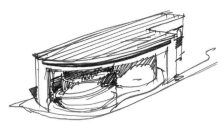

Fig. 6.14 Sketch of the building seen from above, revealing its full scale

Fig. 6.13 A ship-like prow defines the corner of the building in this 2002 sketch. Full-height glazing is visible on the elevations, while the auditorium volume within is ringed by a ramp

Fig. 6.15 The foyers ring the auditoria, bounded by a sheer wall of glass

museum's main curved volume. Here the idea was translated from a place for the display of art to the creation of a promenade on which audiences (and staff) would have been able to see and be seen in best theatre tradition. A second sketch shows the same strategy from above (fig. 6.14), while a third reveals the sheer scale of the proposed foyers (fig. 6.15).

Although clearly typical of Viñoly's work, these ideas can also be related to broader currents in architecture. The expression of auditoria as distinct, solid (often fan-shaped) volumes positioned in space was something of a trope in

twentieth-century Modernist design; a seminal example was Konstantin Melnikov's Rusakov Worker's Club (1927-1928), in which three auditoria were cantilevered out from a central core to create a building of distinct form, their masses being easily recognized by the onlooker.[62] Transparency, too, was an oft-repeated Modern theme. Gropius' *Totaltheater* proposal (1927, not built), for example, featured glazed curtain walls with stairs behind, the movement along which of people (especially when illuminated at night) would have animated the building's exterior.[63] The two ideas came together

increasingly frequently in the creation of arts buildings, not least in the influential design of the Royal Festival Hall, London, of 1951.[64] The Hall's architects positioned the auditorium as a solid volume seemingly suspended within the building envelope, the foyers flowing around and below it, with expansive glazing allowing its mass to be readily perceived from the Hall's surroundings. Mies van der Rohe's 1950s scheme for a theatre at Mannheim (1953) went yet further in exploring these relationships, comprising a glazed cubic structure whose auditoria seemingly would have had no side walls, thus allowing audiences and actors to look beyond to the theatre's setting.[65] A second echo of the Mies design is found at Leicester in the way that the stages of the two auditoria are located back-to-back at the centre of the building; this form of planning is also seen in Elisabeth Scott's first designs of 1927 for the Shakespeare Memorial Theatre at Stratford-upon-Avon.[66] And there are resonances at Leicester, too, of Manchester's Royal Exchange Theatre, where the auditorium exists as a 'pod' structure of 1976 inserted within a late Victorian hall, with the space around the 'pod' serving as both foyer and the route between auditorium and dressing rooms.

Viñoly's concept was not only intended to demystify the theatre by exposing its workings to public view, but the way in which it was hoped that the building would animate the street (as a constant 'public datum') also played a particular role in realising the aim for regeneration, according to Viñoly:

If you connect the ambition [for an inside-out theatre] with the notion that the project had the secondary role of being an urban renewal project, then the possibility of making it alive 24/7 was a lot more powerful than if you were in the West End or in a Theatre District or on Broadway here in New York where the place is already active or hyperactive without necessarily having to show everything that happens.[67]

The result was a remarkable if serendipitous meeting of minds: a client with a clear idea who had chanced upon an architect whose work had already explored some of the same themes and who was keen to give them a strong architectural form. A sense that the building could be revolutionary inspired the design team:

It wasn't just a theatre; it was a theatre with a strong idea, although nobody knew what it meant. But it was incredibly attractive to us, because it wasn't just about making a pretty space, it was about redefining the idea of a theatre.[68]

The concept was not without controversy; a lively correspondence was maintained in the pages of such publications as *The Stage*, as experienced practitioners, designers and consultants questioned the design.[69]

The enthusiasm, the 'vision', the eminence of the consultants, the political will, all augured well to achieve a remarkable project, and Viñoly had a reputation for being quick.[70] But the project's progress had been set up to falter as soon as preliminary costs were assembled:

We've struggled against budget all the way through. There have been elements of Value Engineering which looked at operational issues, but the

operational concept has been fixed since Stage C... What's driven the costs up.... [are] the complex engineering solutions that are required to deliver the architectural vision... that's where the problems arise, because it's an innovative design solution... non-load bearing façade... 20 odd metres high ...[71]

Inevitably, in retrospect:

When we were at Stage C, we knew we were £3-4 million light of funding to do everything we wanted to do.[72]

It was becoming clear that theatre equipment was falling out of the project budget.

The business plan, constantly evolving, was simply not generating enough forecast revenue to fund the pressure of equipment outside the main contract.[73]

The case study timeline (fig. 6.16) records that the first phase of Viñoly's scheme was projected to cost £45.8 million as against the anticipated £19 million construction cost inherited from the Feasibility study. The design team became deeply sceptical. Ferocious Value Engineering ensured. Viñoly's office proposed a tactic they had witnessed elsewhere, to put the shell up first:

Those were the very initial periods, brief and budget and trying to get them in line. There was also [a certain amount of] trying to understand what the user wanted in terms of operation of the theatre. Again, because there was a gap in the funding [and] the budget, [we suggested] building the waterproofing envelope as large as [possible] and then [phasing the installation of] all of the theatre equipment. [It's] one approach [to] theatre buildings, which was based on a museum in Brooklyn.[74]

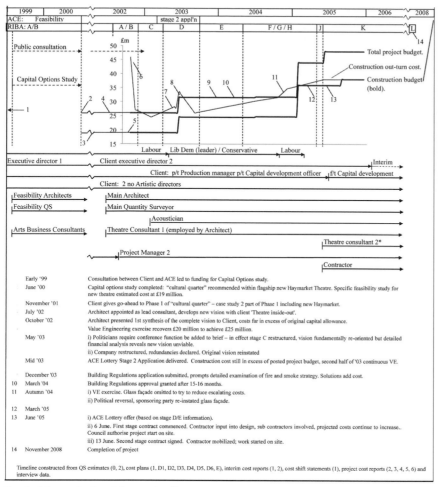

Fig. 6.16 Curve, budget history timeline

lighting fixture, and then they find something better and they want it. It's constantly [a case that] they are aiming for the Ferrari engine and we are trying to give them something great but maybe not a Ferrari.'[75]

The brief remained fluid in part as a consequence.

£20 million was edited out of the scheme notionally through autumn 2002 to reach £27.1 million. By early 2003 the timeline records the lowest projected set term construction cost achieved of £24.5 million. Backstage accommodation was removed, set construction removed to the city edge. Less site was procured. The appearance of the theatre was gradually crystallized (figs. 6.17 and 6.18). Stage C was completed with a projected out turn cost of £24.5 million. But costs rose steadily through Stage D as the technical implications latent in the 'vision' were explored. The Acoustician recorded that stage D was interminable: 'We did a Stage D, a stage we call D+, and then a stage D++.'[76]

The timeline shows costs steadily rising through Stage D and E which in reality became D+ and D++. As has already been noted, the idea of 'curtains' gave way to solid acoustic screens which allowed for the breaking down of boundaries between internal spaces whilst being more easily conceived and delivered. Political volatility shifted the emphasis in the

This suggestion, which, as we saw in the preceding chapter, would not have been unlike the approach of the Belgrade Theatre, induced huge stress in the user group although there is evidence that the client (the city council) sympathized. The theatre consultant was caught between them. The struggle to afford everything continued:

Value Engineering? Constantly. I think that's a source of conflict between the theatre consultant and the user group. Because the theatre consultant['s] role is also to serve the client, the Council. You are given a budget and you have to deliver that budget. And it's a problem, because you make certain decisions: you are only going to go for this

Fig. 6.17 The design in May 2003: the ramps around the auditorium have gone but the space above remains open to the foyers

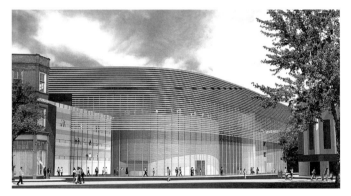

Fig. 6.18 September 2003, and the elevations have acquired 'brises-soleils' to shade the glass

brief, as Labour gave way to eighteen months of Liberal Democrat/Conservative power. The notion of adapting the project to include conference use paralleled a rise in the projected cost to £33.5 million. The volatile Stage C/D scheme was used to launch the first stage of the two stage tender process, a stage due to extend over almost twelve months. Bovis's first task was to conduct a cost health check. The timeline identifies the approved budget in mid 2003 as £31.5 million, but Bovis identified £6–7 million of additional costs. The project manager rued the failure to involve a contractor earlier, but where to find the Stage 1 fee? Fletcher commented that, with the change of state of contracting into wholesale subcontracting, cost consultants find it more

and more difficult to predict out-turn costs, particularly on highly complex one-off projects.[77] All of the savings achieved by September 2003 were lost by 2004, a recurrent theme in this study. Nonetheless, in May 2004 the city committed to a project costed at £31.5 million.[78]

The Acoustician was sceptical about the application of Value Engineering to arts buildings, and the whole management process of time and cost structures:

From experience, Value Engineering actually does not work in a performing arts building ... The time it takes to do the Value Engineering work and the possible deterioration in relationships [means that] you will not get the best out of it. In normal buildings there are enough standard solutions that have different price tags ... and you can just say, "scale this one down and we'll find a new price..." In a performing arts building, you don't always know the consequences of the ripple effect.[79]

Design Progress Stage E to Construction

The context of Stage D, in which all editing seemed to lead to project over-spend, culminated in a redesign of the façade in January 2005, the all-glass cliff of the first design (fig. 6.19) transformed into a zinc façade above a shop window-like glass strip. Viñoly threw himself into the redesign:

The façade went opaque for Value Engineering reasons; [transparent glass] came back in for political and architectural reasons. You can either say that's a very intelligent architect or you can say that's one of the mysteries of a project. We used to have a vertical facade that had seventeen metres of glazing at the bottom and five metres of metal at the top. In order to do a cost saving, under strong pressure by the client, this face was changed to seventeen metres of metal on the top and five metres of glass façade at the bottom. At which

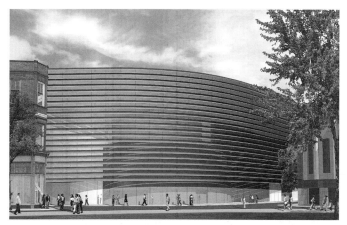

Fig. 6.19 December 2004, and the horizontal banding has become an important feature adding definition to the elevation

point we were probably in budget. But nobody really liked the façade then, [so it] changed to an angled/inclined façade … It was probably feasible. Then came the political change, another mayor and a meeting with Viñoly at which the mayor said, "I now want my glass façade back." By which time it was an angled glass façade rather than a straight glass façade. And actually, it no longer is a seventeen-metre glass façade with five metres of metal; it actually is five metres of glass façade at the bottom and seventeen metres of angled glass façade at the top.[80]

The effect of this act of political largesse was to demoralise the specialist consultants, who had laboured for months to make savings across the scheme. The Acoustician observed that the design 'sacrifice' – the change to zinc –calmed the budget, as is clear from the depiction of Stage D on the timeline. However, a council report of early 2005 costed the zinc design at £40 million, with a variant on the original glazed proposal coming in at £44 million. This latter option was selected by the council, although the cost remained a projection, as detailed design work had not yet been undertaken. The possibility of abandoning the project was dismissed for fear of what such a decision would say about the city.[81] The timeline maps the relentless rise in expected out-turn cost. Ironically

it was a Liberal Democrat leader who restored the now more elaborate glass façade, changing the agreed budget to £48 million, just in time to seal the second Stage. Bovis held 85% certainty price for six days to enable the vote to proceed on 13 June 2005 (fig. 6.20).

The two stage process was subverted by the volatility in the design, and the constant Value Engineering. The design (and, with considerations of conference use, even the purpose of the building) remained fluid in part even after work began on site – a decision informed by the fact that the ERDF grant would be lost if construction had not begun by June 2005.[82] Progression through Stage E & F detail was constantly disrupted. Whereas American and Continental European consultants may generally design through construction, working up packages of design information with tendering subcontractors, within the UK's traditional contract form late information simply fuels claims for additional payments on the basis of apparent 'variations' to the design. The Audit Commission later quoted a council Cabinet report of March 2006 which stated baldly that, partly due to the early start on site, 'the design information has proven to be not entirely complete and co-ordinated. This has resulted in numerous

Fig. 6.20 July 2005, with the glazing restored to the design after consideration of a more solid façade

changes.'[83] The project Manager was philosophical in May 2006:

Everyone went into this with their eyes open. We knew there were areas of the design that needed completing. We knew there were a number of areas which were probably not Stage F designed, because of a number of changes that came up late in the process with regard to the façade and everything else. We knew that there were issues that needed to be resolved. It's probably fair to say that we probably didn't expect the resolution of those issues to cost as much as it's looking like [they are] going to cost at the moment but that's a battle we're fighting.[84]

The Arts Council monitors started to take a keen interest, having hitherto been fairly 'hands off' in their approach. The project manager summarized the change in approach:

[At the beginning] they were only interested about receiving information at the end of a stage. Now you're in a different ballgame, really, because, if you're looking at changing something now, it has a real impact on the end product. Everything is so much more fixed, so they are much more actively involved now, with regards to monitoring the change process or any Value Engineering, because we've now got a much tighter business plan. It's much more rigid now than it was previously.[85]

There was concern amongst certain sectors of the council, too: a Scrutiny Committee report of 4 August 2005 expressed concern about the lack of a clear business plan for the operation of the venue.[86]

Costs continued to rise as the detailed implications of the design were developed and costed, and as the operational needs of the theatre were fully worked out. Further Value Engineering was undertaken, with the quality of finishes being reduced, though Ruth Eastwood recalled that some of the cheaper finishes and fittings (in the toilets, for example) simply did not last and had to be replaced within months.[87] Other changes had operational implications. The omission of transparent screens to the staff areas prompted some consideration of how employees would hold private conversations, especially on the telephone, and special portable handsets had to be acquired so that staff could *'run to a cupboard'* when necessary, as Eastwood put it.[88] To protect the operational capability of the theatre, the Arts Council ring-fenced part of their grant for technical equipment, a move which Eastwood later thought beneficial in that it meant that this provision was safeguarded from Value Engineering.[89]

In June 2006 a council-commissioned report noted that 'currently the true cost of the total project remains unclear.'[90] The scheduled completion date of September 2007 passed, and the theatre was only finally opened in November 2008. The opening had been preceded by several months of 'soft' use. Eastwood commented that the unique nature of the building had made it imperative that staff learn how to make it work.[91] Test performances were staged, allowing crews to experience the 'get-in' across the foyers (fig. 6.21). Tickets were given out for free on the basis that audiences would participate in practice evacuations.

By the time of the theatre's opening, costs had risen once more. The final out-turn cost was over £61 million, more than twice the initial estimate, with the council's contribution rising from a projected £4.4 million in 2001 to at least £35.8 million, and additional ERDF funding taking their total to £7.7 million.[92] Perhaps inevitably, the building received a mixed reaction. It won an RIBA Award and was called 'a beautiful piece of urban design' by *The Stage*,[93] though, as had been the case during the design period, performers and audiences gave the building a more mixed reception. Paul Kerryson offered a robust response to the criticism:

People have complained about the ambience and the theatre being too cold but we are a different kind of theatre. We've spent a lot on creating different

Fig. 6.21 With the safety shutters lifted, the stage is fully open to the foyer

atmospheres for different performances but if people expect to see carpeted floors and a chandelier then they'll be disappointed because that will never happen at Curve. Some of the performances have been criticized because they are different. But we get grants from the Arts Council and suchlike to produce productions that are challenging.[94]

Nationally, there was concern about the perceived value for money of the scheme. The Audit Commission was deeply critical of the process by which the theatre had been realized,[95] and there were concerns that the unusual nature of the design could lead to unforeseen future running costs (for example, relating to security) without any indication of the source of this money. Amidst the debates, Eastwood left the theatre for a freelance career.

And yet, once again, the essence of the initial 'vision' was delivered. The stage is visible from the street, the sheer height of the foyers shown in Viñoly's original sketch is there, and they offer the technical capability to accommodate theatrical lighting and props (fig. 6.22). The two auditoria, of differing size, are arranged back-to-back so that they can be opened onto a single stage if required (figs. 6.23 and 6.24). The glass

façade offers views in and out (fig. 6.25). Interviewed by the local press in February 2010, Paul Kerryson confirmed that the design was delivering the original intent:

Nobody knew the Haymarket made its own sets and the beauty about Curve is that we're very much open. You can see our sets when the side panel is lifted and we've had a great response from people about this. We've had

Fig. 6.22 Lighting and props can be mounted within the foyers, generating a mood appropriate to the performances being staged in the auditoria at their centre, or in support of foyer performances

Fig. 6.23 The main auditorium, viewed from the stage: an essentially conventional theatre space in its spatial configuration

Fig. 6.24 The second, flexible auditorium

Fig. 6.25 Glass dissolves the boundary between foyer and street

a lot of young people wanting to talk to technicians and you can see actors wondering around during rehearsals. It's an open theatre as much as it can possibly be.[96]

Postscript I: Value Engineering a Theatre

The perspective of the Belgian acoustician, Kahle, fundamentally questions the classic project management gambit of tighter and fiercer strictures on budget and programme:

So to give what they consider the clear direction, we want an opening date and want a budget. I'm sorry, this is not a good direction.

One understands that consultants do not like to be bullied and threatened, but he extends his arguments:

They need to state more clearly in which direction they want us to achieve this. And, of course, it doesn't help later on if, with political change, suddenly there are a few elements in the design that become political priorities and it's not a problem to spend a couple of extra million on basically political items, when two weeks

earlier, on practical and engineering questions, we wanted to spend half a million extra work but we know we can't spend any more money. So that has been one of the must frustrating [aspects of] the project, the insufficient will and clear direction of the client. That's actually winding up the discussion on other projects, that's been one of my findings through all projects. One of the most important people to sit in a project, and many people don't think about it that much, is the client. And if you have a strong access to a good client, you still have problems, you still have fights, possibly, you have lots of things, but it makes for a much better building and it makes a much smoother process. Actually the way the Leicester clients or the political clients behave, going to another process like a design and build may actually have been better for them. Not that we as the design team like these solutions because it puts more pressure on elements like quality control. But at least for a few moments that was basically the message that we initially got from the client, we care about budget and we care about opening dates, which basically means we don't care about quality. Then you make this one clear and say, "okay, we go with the design and build and throw you all together in a pot and you can figure it out." Then you have another project structure, which at least is a clear structure. But if sometimes the Haymarket then pushes for what is really important to them and has to take the back [seat] because they don't have any direct power it just makes everything a bit more complicated. What I find internationally now is, to go back to the Leicester client, what would have been much better is to set up a specific client body. I must say I often like projects when the actual client is not the political body. Lucerne was a very good example for that one: they basically set up a foundation which then actually became a commercial enterprise that now runs the building; the city is the main stakeholder and the state is a stakeholder, but there are private people as well. And you then have an operational board, I mean you have an operational manager for the client body who then is no longer responsible just to politicians, it's somebody who has the mission to do this project correctly and you (the manager) represent us (the stake holders). And that is a much clearer client structure.[97]

Kahle's comment implies that Value Engineering a theatre project is like taking pieces out of an expensive bespoke watch. It has to be constructed very carefully and cautiously, so time-consuming is it to do it 'safely' without affecting the integrity of another piece of the mechanism, that inflation will likely consume any financial advantage, as may additional fees and spent time. He illustrated this with a brief account of the effect of a Value Engineering drive modification of the concrete structure:

The dressing room is not a very complicated room, but you have certain requirements. So we put an acoustic ceiling into the dressing room. Then the structure was redesigned for the building which enlarged the depth of the beams, which was basically Value Engineering on the structural side. Everybody was happy with that, a new set of plans was drawn, until I looked at it and suddenly said, "Hey, I have a ceiling height of 2.3m in the dressing room. That's not really great for an artist, especially if next door in the bathroom you have 3.3m. So can't we change something?" Finally we've taken the acoustic ceiling out there, exposed the beam, which means redesign, because you have to place the absorption somewhere else, which we are doing now as a variation in the contract. This may well be that somebody comes back to us and says, "this is too expensive," and you have to re-redesign it. But the other thing you suddenly find out then in the middle of the plans is above the ceiling were lots of other things that were hidden, all the services ... So suddenly some of the services are exposed. Most of it is normal: the ventilation system is exposed, that was the same in other rooms, as there's a standard we could use, but suddenly you find some foul water pipes that come from the upper level have suddenly become exposed. So there are a lot of these little ripple effects. And to a certain degree this is another one for me which shows how dangerous Value Engineering is. If you do a Stage D, a Stage D+ and a Stage D ++, you don't really want to design in too much detail because everything can still change. As an architect, I might say, but in a way as an acoustician it's the same. You want to be able to change two lines rather than having to change 20 lines.[98]

6. Curve, Leicester

163

Postscript II: Designing and Building a Theatre in the UK

For the architects, the experience of designing and building a theatre in the UK offered a significant lens through which to reflect on the nature of design practice. And while they saw certain challenges in building for the arts (according with the views expressed in other case studies in this book, notably the consultants working on the Belgrade), they offer a damning critique of the design and procurement process more generally:

The system is very contorted. It has a lot of advantages as a result of that, and a lot of incredible disadvantages. It's extremely colloquial. It's very difficult to imagine where the real responsibility lies. ... I think it has a high degree of concern for quality, and this is not a problem of the UK alone. There has been ... a gigantic gap between what people consider to be the expectation for quality and the budgets put to satisfy that quality. This is the fault of the profession, I think, my profession much more than anyone else.

When people don't know what to ask...it's because they are uninstructed, and people need to tell them those things. So there are so many layers: the project managers, the design managers, I mean you guys have the largest collection of consultants in the world! Not the least of which [are] the theatre consultants. I'm critical of that, because I am also critical of what we [architects] do. If we knew collectively what it is that is being asked by us, or from us, we would be knowing more than we do know. So when the profession doesn't know enough, what happens is that these places get filled by people who discover that they may actually find a source of business in it. All this confusion as to who is responsible and how much you need to know about ... sightlines, or mechanical theatrical ... equipment. It becomes a natural myriad,

a collection of inputs as opposed to somebody who can actually compensate and make them make more sense.

So [a study of] the arts is in reality incredibly interesting, because it may give you a little bit of light as to how ridiculously dysfunctional the industry is, not only at the construction industry level but certainly much more [so] at the design level. And so it isn't simply because a cultural building is of a particular nature in which people [have] a lot more expectation than usual, but it is [because of] how inefficient everything is.[99]

CONCLUSIONS: CASE STUDY FINDINGS

One might conclude that project management systems and processes evolved in the UK since the huge changes in the continuation industry of the late 1980s are very taxed when confronted by genuine innovation, in this case in design.

- The Leicester design attempted to give form to a clearly articulated vision of inclusivity. But the architectural strategy, devised quickly in response to an advertisement for design services, contained within it profound challenges.
- One could argue that, preoccupied by process, the managers of the project missed this huge clue, that time was needed to unravel and explore the design.
- Fortunately a full team of specialists arrived with the architect, not just the acoustician and fire engineer, but the rigid workstage templates simply stamped down onto a highly iterative process. The level of fixity at all stages, most significantly the two tender stages, was illusory.
- Throughout, the memory of the original feasibility study budget hung in the air, punishing all concerned, not just the politicians and others who paid with their careers.

Ironically, by breaking the rules, or by simply not understanding them the architect has pretty much driven the project to realisation. The role of client and users in safeguarding the 'vision' has also been critical (fig. 6.26):

I think it's remarkable how consistency has been maintained. I'm very stubborn, but no stubbornness on the part of an architect can supplant dedication on the part of the client.[100]

Notes

1   Contextual research by Alistair Fair.

2   *Leicester Mercury*, 10 February 1958.

3   For more on the Haymarket, see Alistair Fair, 'The end of "optimism and expansiveness"? Designing for drama in the 1970s', *Twentieth-century architecture 10, The 1970s* (2011, forthcoming).

4   *Architects' Journal*, vol. 159, p.611.

5   See also Frederick Bentham, 'A tale of two cities', *TABS*, 31/4, December 1973, pp.139-143, for similar views.

6   *Architects' Journal*, vol. 159, p.607.

7   Richard Leacroft and Helen Leacroft, *Theatre and Playhouse: an illustrated survey of theatre building from ancient Greece to the present day* (London, 1984), pp.216-217.

Fig. 6.26 Quick-change rail on stage, with the foyer behind and the city beyond

8   Mandy Stewart to Alan Short and Anne Dye, 11 January 2006.

9   Paul Kerryson to Alan Short and Anne Dye, 11 January 2006.

10   John McGuigan, in conversation with Alan Short & Brian Ford, architects for the Coventry Arts & Media Centre (Lottery funded to workstage E).

11   Mike Candler to Anne Dye, 10 February 2006.

12   Leicester City Council, 'Diverse city: a vision for cultural life in Leicester', published 2001, accessed on 20 April 2010 at < http://www.leicester.gov.uk/your-council-services/lc/cultural-strategy/cspdocument/#document>.

13   Mike Candler to Anne Dye, 10 February 2006.

14   Audit Commission report 2008/09, 'The Curve Project', June 2009.

15   Graham Lister to Anne Dye and Alan Short, 12 January 2006.

16   Mandy Stewart to Anne Dye and Alan Short, 12 January 2006.

17   Leicester, 'Diverse City', section 2.

18   Audit Commission report 2008/09, 'The Curve Project', June 2009, para. 20.

19   Audit Commission report 2008/09, 'The Curve Project', June 2009, para. 29.

20   Leicester, 'Diverse city', section 2.

21   Paul Kerryson to Alan Short and Anne Dye, 12 January 2006.

22   Mandy Stewart to Alan Short and Anne Dye, 11 January 2006.

23   Alan Short, Dean of De Montfort University 1997-2001, to Pat Sterry, 24 March 2006.

24   Ruth Eastwood, in the film 'Geometry and Atmosphere: the conundrum of building for the arts' (2006), accessed on 17 June 2011 at <http://sms.cam.ac.uk/media/1090457>.

25   Mandy Stewart to Alan Short and Anne Dye, 12 January 2006.

26   Mike Candler to Anne Dye, pers. comm., 16 March 2006.

27   Christina Seilern to Anne Dye, Pat Sterry and Alistair Fair, 21 November 2005.

28   Rafael Viñoly to Alan Short and Claudia Eckert, 9 April 2008.

29   Mandy Stewart to Alan Short and Anne Dye, 11 January 2006.

30   Graham Handy to Monty Sutrisna 13 March 2006.

31   Graham Lister to Alan Short & Anne Dye, 12 January 2006.

32   Andy Hayles to Anne Dye, 17 January 2006.

33   Christina Seilern to Anne Dye, Pat Sterry and Alistair Fair, 21 November 2005.

34   Eckhard Kahle to Anne Dye, 16 May 2006.

35   Eckhard Kahle to Anne Dye, 16 May 2006.

36   Eckhard Kahle to Anne Dye, 16 May 2006.

37   Andy Passingham to Monty Sutrisna, 16 June 2006

38   Mandy Stewart to Alan Short and Anne Dye, 11 January 2006.

39   Mandy Stewart to Alan Short and Anne Dye, 11 January 2006.

40   Graham Lister to Alan Short & Anne Dye, 11 January 2006.

41   Graham Lister, e-mail to Alistair Fair, 20 January 2010.

42   Graham Lister to Alan Short & Anne Dye, 11 January 2006.

43   Graham Lister to Alan Short & Anne Dye, 11 January 2006.

44 Graham Lister, e-mail to Alistair Fair, 21 January 2010.

45 Graham Lister to Alan Short & Anne Dye, 11 January 2006.

46 Mike Candler to Anne Dye, 10 February 2006.

47 Mandy Stewart to Alan Short and Anne Dye, 11 January 2006.

48 'Lottery millions spent on struggling projects', *Times*, 13 February 2004.

49 Graham Hendy to Monty Sutrisna, 13 March 2006.

50 Steven Fletcher to Monty Sutrisna 2 March 2006.

51 Mandy Stewart to Alan Short and Anne Dye, 11 January 2006.

52 Mandy Stewart to Alan Short and Anne Dye, 11 January 2006.

53 Mandy Stewart to Alan Short and Anne Dye, 11 January 2006.

54 Steven Fletcher to Monty Sutrisna, 2 March 2006.

55 Mandy Stewart to Alan Short and Anne Dye, 11 January 2006.

56 Steven Fletcher to Monty Sutrisna, 2 March 2006.

57 Christina Seilern to Anne Dye, Pat Sterry and Alistair Fair, 21 November 2005.

58 Christina Seilern to Anne Dye, Pat Sterry and Alistair Fair, 21 November 2005.

59 Rafael Viñoly to Alan Short and Claudia Eckert, 9 April 2008.

60 Christina Seilern to Anne Dye, Pat Sterry and Alistair Fair, 21 November 2005.

61 Rafael Viñoly to Alan Short and Claudia Eckert, 9 April 2008.

62 William J.R. Curtis, *Modern architecture since 1900* (London, 2nd ed., 1996), p.209.

63 Walter Gropius and Oskar Schlemmer, *The theater of the Bauhaus* (Middletown, 1961).

64 John McKean, *Royal Festival Hall: London County Council, Leslie Martin, Peter Moro* (London, 2000).

65 Thilo Hilpert, *Mies van der Rohe im Nachkriegsdeutschland: das Theaterprojekt* (Leipzig, 2001).

66 See the plans in C.A Short, 'Factors for success', in R. Brett (ed.), *Theatre engineering and architecture, v.6 – General Management* (London, 2007).

67 Rafael Viñoly to Alan Short and Claudia Eckert, 9 April 2008.

68 Christina Seilern to Anne Dye, Pat Sterry and Alistair Fair, 21 November 2005.

69 E.g. 'Pilbrow - £48m Leicester centre impractical', *The Stage*, 14 June 2006, accessed on 11 June 2010 at <http://www.thestage.co.uk/news/newsstory.php/12918>.

70 Eckhard Kahle to Anne Dye, 16 May 2006.

71 Steven Fletcher to Monty Sutrisna, 2 March 2006.

72 Steven Fletcher to Monty Sutrisna 2 March 2006.

73 Steven Fletcher to Monty Sutrisna, 2 March 2006.

74 Christina Seilern to Anne Dye, Pat Sterry and Alistair Fair, 21 November 2005.

75 Christina Seilern to Anne Dye, Pat Sterry and Alistair Fair, 21 November 2005.

76 Eckhard Kahle to Anne Dye, 16 May 2006.

77 Steven Fletcher to Monty Sutrisna, 2 March 2006.

78 Audit Commission report 2008/09, 'The Curve Project', June 2009, paras. 38-40.

79 Eckhard Kahle to Anne Dye, 16 May 2006.

80 Eckhard Kahle to Anne Dye, 16 May 2006.

81 Audit Commission report 2008/09, 'The Curve Project', June 2009, report 2009.

82 Audit Commission report 2008/09, 'The Curve Project', June 2009, report 2009.

83 Quoted in Audit Commission report 2008/09, 'The Curve Project', June 2009, para. 49.

84 Steven Fletcher to Monty Sutrisna, 6 March 2006.

85 Steven Fletcher to Monty Sutrisna, 6 March 2006.

86 Audit Commission report 2008/09, 'The Curve Project', June 2009, para. 52.

87 Ruth Eastwood to Alistair Fair, 28 April 2010.

88 Ruth Eastwood to Alistair Fair, 28 April 2010.

89 Ruth Eastwood to Alistair Fair, 28 April 2010.

90 Audit Commission report 2008/09, 'The Curve Project', June 2009, para. 57.

91 Ruth Eastwood to Alistair Fair, 28 April 2010.

92 Audit Commission report 2008/09, 'The Curve Project', June 2009, para.11 and 63.

93 *The Stage* website, accessed on 18 December 2009 at <http://www.thestage.co.uk/features/feature.php/22639/open-house-leicesters-curve-theatre>.

94 *Harborough Mail*, 5 February 2010, accessed on 11 June 2010 at <http://www.harboroughmail.co.uk/leisure/INTERVIEW-with-the-Leicester-Theatre.6047251.jp>

95 Audit Commission report 2008/09, 'The Curve Project', June 2009.

96 *Harborough Mail*, 5 February 2010, accessed on 11 June 2010 at <http://www.harboroughmail.co.uk/leisure/INTERVIEW-with-the-Leicester-Theatre.6047251.jp>

97 Eckhard Kahle to Anne Dye, 16 May 2006.

98 Eckhard Kahle to Anne Dye, 16 May 2006.

99 Rafael Viñoly to Alan Short and Claudia Eckert, 9 April 2008.

100 Rafael Viñoly to Alan Short and Claudia Eckert, 9 April 2008.

7.   'So fabulously theatrical you can almost chew on it': Hackney Empire

Alan Short and Alistair Fair

The 1970s and 1980s saw a revival of interest in Victorian and Edwardian theatre buildings, reflecting growing appreciation for buildings of that period more generally. The first late-Victorian theatres were added to the statutory lists of buildings of historic interest in 1972; The Theatres Trust was founded by Act of Parliament in 1976 as a campaigning voice for the sector and a statutory consultee in the planning process. From the mid-1970s onwards, the refurbishment of theatres from the years around 1900 formed an important strand in practice; in some cases, the buildings were significantly remodelled and substantially expanded, with new backstage accommodation and improved foyer areas. This chapter considers the restoration and expansion in 2001-2004 of the Hackney Empire, originally opened in 1901 (fig. 7.1). Funded by the Arts Council, the Heritage Lottery Fund, Sir Alan (now Lord) Sugar, and an extensive money-raising effort, the total cost of the project was £19.8 million. Sensitivities surrounding the project mean that we cannot publish a full account here, and so, compared with the preceding chapters, the following narrative is somewhat brief, comprising a slightly extended version of what was first published by the research team in 2007 and the accompanying budget history timeline (table 7.1, fig. 7.2).[1]

Fig. 7.1 Hackney Empire, main front to Mare Street

Table 7.1 Hackney Empire, case study characteristics

Hackney Empire, characteristics	
Receiving/Producing	Both
Project driver(s)	To save historic Matcham theatre and later drive for adaptations for contemporary programme
Vision	Provocative, contemporary 'variety' in historic setting
Refurbishment/new build	Refurbishment plus new annex housing a new studio performance space and hospitality facilities (Hackney Empire, 2006)
Feasibility study - in house or external consultant	Yes, first rejected by ACE External consultants
Part of bigger arts initiative?	No
Business plan - scope	Yes Comprehensive
Construction budget set?	Original bid £33 million, 2nd bid £15 million
Final account	£19.85 million (2006)
Funding source(s)	Arts Council of England Lottery Fund, Heritage Lottery Fund, private benefactors, fundraising
Lead consultant	Architect and project manager in parallel
Design innovation	Not in concept but in details
Specialist inputs	Theatre consultants, acoustician, access consultants, conservation consultants, product designer, lighting designer
Value Engineering employed? - which stage?	On rejection of stage A/B bid, considerable editing of scheme to achieve successful second bid
Vision creep?	No
Political climate	Stable but unsupportive
Contract type - contractor involvement in design? - quality/time/money priority	Traditional, JCT 80 with Quantities No Quality/time/money
Organizational change?	High level management constant, some redundancies in the rest of the company as a result of decreased revenue during construction phase

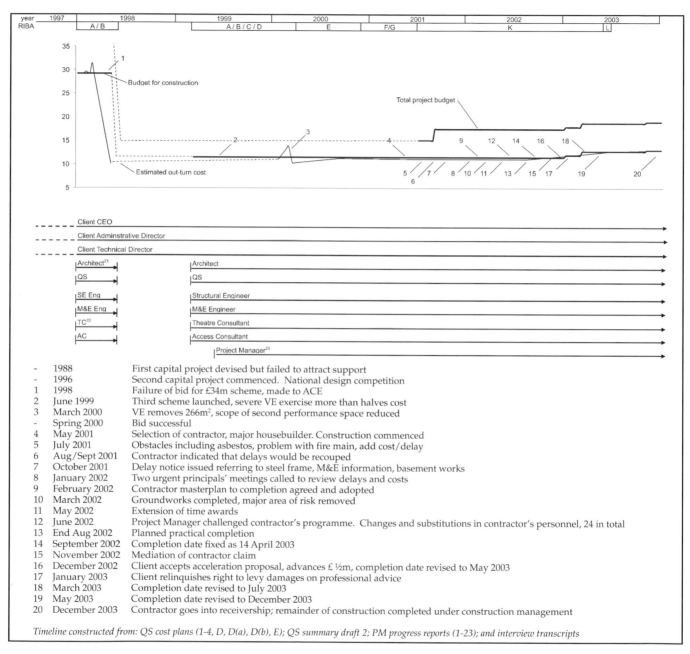

year	1997	1998	1999	2000	2001	2002	2003
RIBA		A / B	A / B / C / D	E	F/G	K	L

Budget for construction — 1

Total project budget

2 · 3 · 4 · 9 · 12 · 14 · 16 · 18

Estimated out-turn cost

5 · 7 · 8 · 10 · 11 · 13 · 15 · 17 · 19 · 20
6

Client CEO
Client Adminstrative Director
Client Technical Director
Architect[21] → Architect
QS → QS
SE Eng → Structural Engineer
M&E Eng → M&E Engineer
TC[22] → Theatre Consultant
AC → Access Consultant
Project Manager[23]

-	1988	First capital project devised but failed to attract support
-	1996	Second capital project commenced. National design competition
1	1998	Failure of bid for £34m scheme, made to ACE
2	June 1999	Third scheme launched, severe VE exercise more than halves cost
3	March 2000	VE removes 266m^2, scope of second performance space reduced
-	Spring 2000	Bid successful
4	May 2001	Selection of contractor, major housebuilder. Construction commenced
5	July 2001	Obstacles including asbestos, problem with fire main, add cost/delay
6	Aug/Sept 2001	Contractor indicated that delays would be recouped
7	October 2001	Delay notice issued referring to steel frame, M&E information, basement works
8	January 2002	Two urgent principals' meetings called to review delays and costs
9	February 2002	Contractor masterplan to completion agreed and adopted
10	March 2002	Groundworks completed, major area of risk removed
11	May 2002	Extension of time awards
12	June 2002	Project Manager challenged contractor's programme. Changes and substitutions in contractor's personnel, 24 in total
13	End Aug 2002	Planned practical completion
14	September 2002	Completion date fixed as 14 April 2003
15	November 2002	Mediation of contractor claim
16	December 2002	Client accepts acceleration proposal, advances £ ½m, completion date revised to May 2003
17	January 2003	Client relinquishes right to levy damages on professional advice
18	March 2003	Completion date revised to July 2003
19	May 2003	Completion date revised to December 2003
20	December 2003	Contractor goes into receivership; remainder of construction completed under construction management

Timeline constructed from: QS cost plans (1-4, D, D(a), D(b), E); QS summary draft 2; PM progress reports (1-23); and interview transcripts

Fig. 7.2 Hackney Empire, budget history diagram

Frank Matcham was the most prolific theatre architect of the late Victorian and Edwardian period. The Hackney Empire was one of a series of 'Empires' designed by Matcham for the impresario Oswald Stoll.[2] Like others on the circuit, the building reflected Stoll's wish to make music hall more respectable in the hope of winning middle-class family audiences.[3] The fundraising brochure produced by its original management thus described the Empire as a 'high-class theatre of Varieties',[4] and shows were presented in a seated theatre environment rather than something akin to a public house, as had previously been typical in music hall. Many well-known stars appeared over the next forty years, but declining attendances led to its closure in 1956.[5] After some years as a television studio and bingo hall, the theatre was occupied by Roland Muldoon's Cartoon Archetypal Slogan Theatre (CAST) group in 1986. CAST had begun life as a touring group presenting work with a clear political message, but later turned to what they termed 'New Variety'.[6] Buoyed by success, they began to look for a venue larger than the arts centres, clubs and pubs in which they had previously played.[7] Muldoon was drawn by the Empire's architecture. He noted that his ideal theatre was not, despite his political and social convictions, a 'democratic', modern building, but one with 'proscenium arches, a circle with good sightlines, ornate Victorian fixtures'.[8] Muldoon may also have seen his work in terms of the Empire's original *raison d'être*. The original stage door, its steps worn by the passage of famous variety stars, was retained in a niche adjacent to the new stage door.[9]

From the late 1980s onwards, CAST began moves to rehabilitate and improve the Empire. Several attempts were made to develop refurbishment projects before, in 1997, the theatre submitted a Lottery bid of £35 million to implement a scheme developed by the architects Tim Ronalds, Homa Farjadi and Sima Farjadi. However, ACE policy changed at the time of submission, with projects of national significance being favoured for higher levels of support. Despite Hackney's claim to be of sufficient national significance to warrant enhanced funding, the bid was rejected and the project was restarted. An implied funding cap of £15 million saw severe 'Value Engineering' as the design was stripped back to the essentials needed to deliver the 'vision'. The client later recorded that the scope of works had been calculated from the maximum expected matching funding. A new scheme was developed accordingly by Tim Ronalds' practice alone.

Central to the 'vision' was a concern to maintain and enhance the essentials of Matcham's architecture, as well as what the architecture revealed of the building's history. John Earl has characterized Matcham's style as 'an architecture of entertainment',[10] and performers and reviewers alike have thought the Hackney Empire's architecture to be an integral part of the theatregoing and acting experiences. Griff Rhys Jones, who championed the restoration and extension of the theatre, has likened performing there to relaxing in a 'warm bath',[11] the *Telegraph* dubbed it 'one of the most atmospheric venues in London',[12] while comedienne Jenny Eclair suggested that its atmosphere was the product of its physical geometry and its decaying appearance:

It's got an atmosphere that's so fabulously theatrical you can almost chew on it. And I quite like theatres that are a bit rough around the edges [...]. Also the way the stage is, the audience is in your lap.[13]

Tim Ronalds' approach to the auditorium was intended to suggest that it had been left largely 'as found'. The decorative scheme introduced by Mecca Bingo in the 1970s was retained and indeed embellished. Its rich reds, golds and greens were thought integral in their 'seediness' to the theatre's atmosphere by actors and management alike and so there was no attempt to recreate Matcham's original paler colours.[14] In fact, further layers of polychromatic glazes were added, and some colours were substituted for others. In this and other respects, the intention was to avoid any rigid distinction between old and new, but rather to create a certain sense of ambiguity. Ronalds' scheme was also distinctive for its retention of the original separate entrances and front-of-house facilities, contrasting with the way in which the foyers and circulation routes in many restored theatres of this period have since been combined as a common space, used by all. Ronalds noted that the 'stratification' of the building was an important aspect of the experience of its use, and that the absence of expansive foyers meant that audiences tended to stay in the auditorium at the interval, thus generating a particular atmosphere and energy.

Fig. 7.3 Hackney Empire, rear of the theatre

Although Ronalds' proposals sought, therefore, to maintain the essence of Matcham's theatre, major changes were nonetheless made to the Grade II*-listed building. Virtually everything behind the proscenium arch was entirely demolished and reconstructed, with new dressing rooms and technical facilities alongside an enlarged stage (fig. 7.3). On the 'public' side of the building, too, significant alterations were instigated. The theatre occupied an L-shaped site, wrapping around two sides of a small public house which had been rebuilt in the 1950s after bomb damage. The theatre acquired this corner site, and the original and the subsequent reduced schemes both provided new facilities here (fig. 7.4). The executed design places a public bar at street level with an education/function room above. The extension

is uncompromisingly contemporary, though in its materials – terracotta and brick – it builds on the palette of Matcham's work (the original scheme proposed translucent glass) while the design sought to abstract the three-dimensional quality of the original elevations. Large, 'Hollywood-style' letters declaim the presence of the theatre within the Hackney streetscape, nodding in their exuberance to the exotic eclecticism of Matcham's design. Just as the Contact Theatre uses a silhouette of its ventilation towers as part of its 'brand identity', these letters have been taken up by the Empire on posters and programmes.

Fig. 7.4 The side of Matcham's original building

Value Engineering sessions were led by the project manager during Stages D and E-G. The architect was adamant that certain aspects of the design should be maintained. The large letters, for example, were realized in terracotta. As Ronalds reported in an account of the completed building, 'to work as architecture, the letters had to be made of the same material as the old building, terracotta, not plastic or metal – to be and look heavy, and to float in space'.[15] As the budget history timeline shows, funding remained dynamic, complicating the Value Engineering exercise. The construction phase was not straightforward, with changing contractor personnel; the contractor ultimately went into liquidation.[16] The Project Manager recalled that *'decisions weren't much of a problem, it was making them happen that was most difficult'.*[17] There was some lack of accord about roles; the Project Manager noted that *'[the architect's idea of a project manager was that I was there to manage the client only and not the team, compounded by the fact that [the architect] was the contract administrator'.*[18] ACE policy insisted on external project management, but the architect considered that the client was, to an extent, being over-policed by the funder. The client, meanwhile, felt excluded from the project on site, both in terms of decision-making and physical access. For an organization which had developed a particularly strong affinity with their building, this sense of exclusion was difficult to stomach.

Notes

1   C.A. Short, P.S. Barrett, M. Sutrisna and A. Dye, 'Impacts of value engineering on five capital arts projects', *Building Research and Information* 35/3, pp.287-315. See p.306 for the budget history timeline. The account also draws on Alistair Fair, 'British theatres, 1926-1991: an architectural history', Ph.D. thesis, University of Cambridge, 2008, pp.217-221.

2   For a useful history of the Empire, see Judith Strong, *Encore: strategies for theatre renewal* (London, 1998), pp.76-81.

3   John Earl, 'The London theatres', pp.36-61 in B.M. Walker (ed.), *Frank Matcham: theatre architect* (Belfast, 1980), especially p.50.

4   Earl, 'The London theatres', p.51.

5   *Times*, 19 February 1956; Strong, *Encore*, pp.76-77.

6   *Independent*, 18 January 1990.

7   Strong, *Encore*, p.78.

8   *Independent*, 18 January 1990.

9   John Tuomey and Tim Ronalds, 'Curtain call: when Ronalds met Matcham', *Architecture Today* 153 (November 2004), pp.44-56. See p.52.

10 *Times*, 8 April 1972.

11 Tuomey and Ronalds, 'Curtain call', p.51.

12 *Telegraph*, 8 December 1990.

13 Quoted in *Evening Standard*, 6 March 2001.

14 Tuomey and Ronalds, 'Curtain call', p.51.

15 Tuomey and Ronalds, 'Curtain call', p. 55.

16 Short et al., 'Impacts of value engineering', pp.305-306 for an account of the process at Hackney, on which the following draws.

17 Neil Barbour, interviewed by Zeynep Toker and Monty Sutrisna, May 2005.

18 Neil Barbour, interviewed by Zeynep Toker and Monty Sutrisna, May 2005.

8. 'Many a theatrical scheme has come to grief because it put bricks and mortar before drama': Some Familiar Issues, 1926-1996

Alistair Fair

One afternoon in March 1926, the Shakespeare Memorial Theatre at Stratford-on-Avon burned down.[1] Almost instantly, debates began to rage in the local and national press about the building which was to replace it,[2] a matter which, given Shakespeare's status, took on particular significance at a time before the advent of a 'true' National Theatre.[3] There was much discussion of architectural style and auditorium layout. *The Times*, however, sounded a cautionary warning, stating in November 1927 that 'many a theatrical scheme has come to grief because it put bricks and mortar before drama'.[4]

The sometimes difficult relationship between architecture and performance is demonstrated well by a diary entry of some sixty years later. In 1988, Richard Eyre, then Director of the National Theatre, pondered potential improvements to the building, which had been designed by Denys Lasdun and opened twelve years earlier:

Fig. 8.1 National Theatre, London: the Olivier auditorium

Denys was upset about a bad review of *Bartholomew Fair* because it said the Olivier Theatre was the culprit as much as the production. Quite unconcerned about whether the review would have hurt me, he wanted me to write and complain about the insult to the architect. Bill [Dudley] and John [Gunter] and I have been talking about how to improve the Olivier and the Lyttelton, or, as Bill says, 'how to turn it into a theatre'. John's made a model ... but we don't show it to Lasdun. He tells us that we are 'custodians of the building'; we can change the 'fittings' but not the 'room'.[5]

Although reviews of *Bartholomew Fair* were in fact largely positive,[6] and others, such as the author Alan Bennett, have felt the Olivier to be a relatively good space,[7] the critic to whom Eyre referred felt the production a failure on account of the environment in which it was presented (fig. 8.1). The reviewer in question may have been Alex Renton in the *Illustrated London News*, who suggested that 'Jonson's masterpiece is chilled by its National setting', 'the Olivier's fair is without fun', while the Olivier auditorium was 'a disaster' which was 'crying out for change'.[8] For Renton, there was no doubting the (negative, on this occasion) contribution of architecture to performance.

As these examples highlight, the sometimes stormy relationship between architecture and the theatre profession that has emerged from the previous chapters of this study is nothing new. This chapter – a brief 'entr'acte' between the case studies which make up the first part of this book and the analysis with which it concludes – considers the broader context of twentieth-century theatre design. Rather than focus in detail on particular examples, it instead develops a selection of themes. It begins by discussing the evolving roles of client, architect, and theatre consultant, before continuing with three particular issues that have been especially contentious: what form the auditorium should take; how 'artistic' and 'functional' concerns might be balanced in design; and whether to build for theatre at all.

COMMUNICATION, ARCHITECTS, AND CONSULTANTS

In January 1928, the Governors of the Shakespeare Memorial Theatre announced that the commission to design their new building had been won by Elisabeth Scott, a recent graduate of the Architectural Association. Inevitably, given the profile of the project, Scott's proposals were widely publicized and were subject to particular public scrutiny. Much of the initial discussion centred around the theatre's stark brick elevations, which revealed the influence on Scott of contemporary Dutch architecture and especially the work of W.M. Dudok, the designer of many buildings at Hilversum during the 1920s and 1930s.[9] The interior, by contrast, seems at first to have attracted less critical attention.[10] Before long, however, performers and patrons alike began to highlight numerous perceived problems with its planning. Several campaigns of modification were instigated, but the results were still thought problematic in some quarters, and in 2007 the theatre was almost entirely gutted in order for a new thrust-stage auditorium to be created within its shell.

In part, changing attitudes to Scott's design can be linked with changes in fashion. Its forward-facing, straight-rake, proscenium-arch auditorium without side boxes or slips was typical of the inter-war period, finding application in both theatres and cinemas. The aim was to provide good sightlines and acoustics for all, in the spirit of technical advance that formed one of the pillars of Modernist orthodoxy. In contrast, recent decades have seen a greater interest in more 'theatre'-like spaces whose walls are 'papered with people', whose audiences are located close to the stage, and which on occasion even dispense with the proscenium altogether. Emphasis has been placed on the 'live' nature of performance, and the way in which theatre offers its audiences the possibility to experience performances from different angles and locations within the auditorium in contrast to the single focus of the camera lens. Considered in this light, Scott's design can easily look problematic.

Nonetheless, the issue was not simply one of subsequent perception. Early critics of Scott's design, indeed, noted the cramped dressing rooms and the absence of a green room in which actors might relax.[11] The primary requirement of Stratford's Governors seems to have been a grand building that would allow the annual Festival to occupy a significant position within the European theatrical landscape and which could also draw attention to Stratford through its architecture. While practicality and grandeur are not polar opposites, in this particular case detailed matters of stage functionality or auditorium design were certainly low on the initial list of priorities,[12] and it was in fact (though not entirely unreasonably) stated that such details could be worked out by the winning architect after the design competition.[13] In this respect, the real issue surely lay with the nature of the initial brief and the way in which it was developed. Thus for the historian and theatre consultant Iain Mackintosh, the completed building's faults represented something of a 'breakdown in communication' during the design process.[14] In saying this, it must be noted that several contemporary accounts note Scott's willingness to listen to theatre people in developing the design,[15] while the theatre's director, William Bridges-Adams, professed to being satisfied with at least the stage.[16] But there does seem to have been little discussion of such things in the crucial early stages, prompting the actor, critic and writer Harley Granville Barker to comment in 1926 that the views of practitioners were being overlooked when it came to the design of the building.[17] And the absence of such discussions during the project's early stages clearly had a lasting legacy. As I have shown elsewhere,[18] many aspects of the design which have since been deemed problematic were in fact either direct responses to the brief or were anticipated by it.

Mackintosh has not been the only person to note the value of communication to good theatre design, and indeed Stratford is not the only example that might be used. For Victor Glasstone, a theatre architect and historian, the difficulty was fairly obvious. Writing in 1968, Glasstone thought that the theatre profession itself was partly to blame for the problems of its buildings:

There is our old friend, 'failure of communication'. People in the theatre are, despite their protestations, unaware of their buildings, and therefore inarticulate when briefing their architects. They do not understand just where and how their buildings can assist their own work.[19]

Coming from someone who was a designer of buildings rather than a practitioner of theatre, such views were perhaps inevitable in their attribution of blame, but Glasstone was not alone in this opinion. Peter Jay, a prominent theatre technician writing in 1963, thought similarly. 'Theatre people', he noted, 'are not very good at describing their requirements in terms that are likely to be useful to architects'.[20] Of course, one might make this somewhat critical observation of clients in other sectors, but, according to Jay, there was also a particular issue in theatre design. Jay noted that few had much experience of theatre-building, because the inter-war boom in cinema and then the rise of television had both considerably reduced the number of new theatres being built, compared with the Victorian heyday of the type.[21] As a result, the theatre-building process had become distinctive for the extent to which clients and architects could be subject to something of a learning curve.

Who are the clients in theatre-building projects? In the nineteenth and early twentieth centuries, some theatres were commissioned by independent proprietors whilst others were built by such circuits as Moss Empires, a trend which continued into the 1930s. Following the Local Government Act of 1948, a number of theatres, such as the Belgrade in Coventry, were directly promoted by local authorities (fig. 8.2). In such cases, it was sometimes necessary to develop a design without knowing who the eventual user of the building would be. In other cases, new buildings replaced existing venues or were commissioned by existing theatre companies, and so capital projects were led by their managements, with local and national authorities offering financial support at a greater distance. But whichever case prevailed, clients tended not to have much experience of building at this scale: they were not the theatre magnates of the pre-1914 boom.

Fig. 8.2 Coventry's Belgrade Theatre: principal elevation in 2010, after restoration

Fig. 8.3 The Nottingham Playhouse (1963), photograph of 2006

When it comes to architects, some have become known as theatre specialists. Peter Moro and Roderick Ham, for example, chaired the Association of British Theatre Technicians (ABTT) Theatre Planning Committee in the 1960s and 1970s. Moro's commission for the Nottingham Playhouse (1963; fig. 8.3) stemmed in part from his experience as a member of the Royal Festival Hall design team in the late 1940s; in turn, Nottingham led to a number of subsequent commissions, notably the Gulbenkian Centre, Hull (1969) and the Theatre Royal, Plymouth (1982). Ham's theatres included the Thorndike, Leatherhead (1969), the Derby Playhouse (1975), and the Wolsey, Ipswich (1979), as well as several notable unexecuted designs.[22] Kenneth King worked on the Belgrade, Coventry in the late 1950s under Coventry City Architects Donald Gibson and Arthur Ling before contributing to the design of the Haymarket Theatre, Leicester (1973), in that city's Architect's Office.[23] In more recent decades, practices such as the ArtsTeam at Renton Howard Wood Levin, Tim Foster (now Foster Wilson) Architects, Tim Ronalds, and Burrell Foley Fischer have all specialized in buildings for performance. However, theatres have never formed the totality of their output, in contrast to such late-Victorian practitioners as C.J. Phipps, Frank Matcham, and W.G.R. Sprague, who built little but theatres and who were effectively ostracized from the profession at large as a result.[24] In recent decades, in fact, architects have on occasion been appointed to design theatres on account of being relatively new to the type. As was the case with Rafael Viñoly at Leicester, Alan Stanton at Coventry, and Alan Short in Manchester, it was hoped in 1964 that Denys Lasdun would bring fresh thinking to the National Theatre commission, for example. In some ways, this development has had positive consequences, avoiding the introversion of the Victorian theatre specialist by creating a more reciprocal relationship between theatres and other currents in architecture, but it also poses challenges for all involved.

The creation of the ABTT Theatre Planning Committee in the early 1960s was partly motivated by the perceived technical shortcomings of the first new post-war theatres, such as the Belgrade, Coventry, whose cramped backstage accommodation was criticized by the *Architects' Journal*.[25] The committee's existence recognized not only the lack of specialist theatre experience on the part of many architects but also the increasing technical complexity of the type. In such circumstances, theatre design became something of a collaborative effort in which specialist input was increasingly required, not least from the emerging profession of the theatre consultant. Theatre consultancy developed in post-war West Germany in response to the complexity of contemporary theatre systems and the significant extent to which these were often deployed in civic theatres there.[26]

The first British practice of this kind, Theatre Projects, was founded by Richard Pilbrow in 1957 and specialized initially in hiring out and specifying technical equipment.[27] In a growing number of cases, the consultant also provided conceptual advice to non-specialist architects. Thus Chamberlin Powell and Bon wrote in 1959 of their emerging Barbican Arts Centre proposals that:

> Dr Richard Southern, Theatre Consultant, has advised us on the type of technical equipment which should be catered for in the theatre and concert hall [...], and has collaborated with us in the design of these buildings.[28]

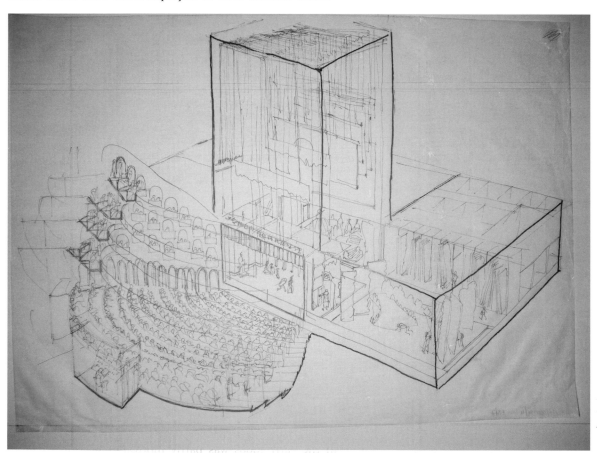

Fig. 8.4 Richard Southern, proposal for the Barbican Theatre, 1958

In the same period, Southern also worked on the Nottingham Playhouse, one of the earliest examples in which the consultant's role was explicitly acknowledged.[29] At the Barbican, Southern's appointment was apparently at the instigation of the architects, who had never previously designed a theatre and so felt that an expert opinion might be beneficial.[30] He was a well-known figure in the theatre world, a writer and an academic. Southern developed a theatre auditorium for the Barbican with somewhat Georgian overtones (fig. 8.4), reflecting his own research interest in such theatres and anticipating his efforts, with Richard Leacroft, to reopen the Georgian Theatre at Richmond, Yorkshire. The drawings, dated 1958, were then developed by Chamberlin Powell and Bon into the scheme that was submitted to the Corporation of London in 1959. Certain elements of the concept, such as the shallow galleries stepping forward from the rear auditorium wall, found their way into the executed theatre, designed in the late 1960s and completed in 1982.[31]

Thus far, it has been suggested that the relative decline in the specialist theatre architect plus the increasing technical complexity of the type both necessitate communication of a kind which has perhaps not always been forthcoming. But underlying this debate is one yet more fundamental in its implications. Iain Mackintosh has argued that one of the greatest challenges in twentieth-century theatre design has been the absence of any consensus concerning the optimum relationship between auditorium and stage, with good communication taking on a still-greater significance in such circumstances. It is to this diversity of approaches that we now turn.

THE DIVERSITY OF APPROACHES TO AUDITORIUM DESIGN

Chamberlin Powell and Bon's proposals of 1959 for the Barbican Arts Centre not only included the theatre auditorium that they had developed with Richard Southern's advice, but also a concert hall. Slightly reminiscent of Hans Scharoun's contemporaneous Berlin *Philharmonie* in its polygonal plan, it replaced the rectangular hall that had been proposed in an earlier scheme. The design was conceived with Southern to also accommodate theatre use. Curtains and screens would have allowed the concert hall to become either a thrust-stage theatre (with the stage projecting into the centre of the space) or an 'in-the-round' venue, with a central stage encircled by the audience (figs 8.5 and 8.6).[32] The proposal thus not only further reveals the assistance which a theatre consultant might provide to an architect new to theatre, but also, by allowing the Barbican to offer different relationships between performer and audience, the sometimes considerable debates in twentieth-century theatre as to the optimum arrangement of stage and auditorium. According to Michael Elliott, one of the first co-directors of the Royal Exchange Theatre (opened in Manchester in 1976), these debates about theatre layout were as important in complicating design as the inexperience in theatre-building of many of the protagonists. 'It is in every way a confusing time', he wrote.[33]

From where did this 'confusion' stem? The rise in the early part of the twentieth century of the director as a significant shaping force in theatre provided figureheads for companies who in some cases, such as Peter Hall at the Royal Shakespeare Company, became well-known amongst the theatregoing public.[34] As was especially evident in the case of Curve, considered in the first part of this book, the construction of a new theatre was thus an opportunity to promote particular artistic ideas, though, as at the Contact Theatre, in some cases, such as the Barbican, the National, or the Nottingham Playhouse, the theatre was ultimately opened and used by a different creative team from that which had 'created' the building. At the same time, some began to question the value of the proscenium-arch stage and galleried auditorium. An early critic was William Poel, who revived Elizabethan stage forms in the late nineteenth century for his productions of

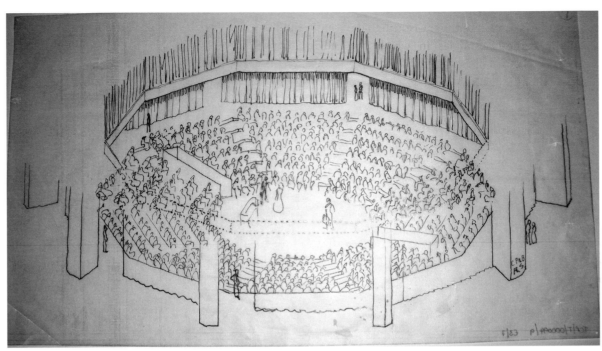

Fig. 8.5 The polygonal hall devised by Richard Southern and the architects for the Barbican in 1958 as an in-the-round theatre

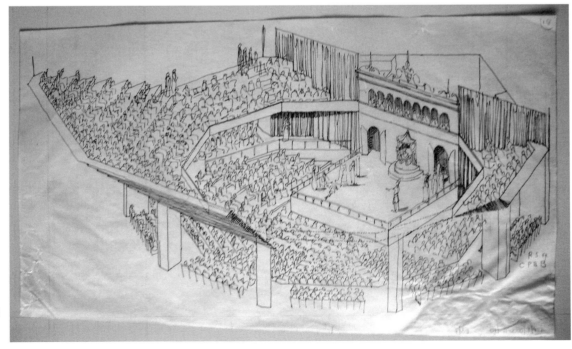

Fig. 8.6 The polygonal hall arranged as thrust-stage theatre

Shakespeare,[35] but others believed non-proscenium layouts to have wider value. Terence Gray was one such figure, in 1926 removing the arch from a small Regency playhouse in Cambridge to create the Festival Theatre, an innovative, short-lived venue with a large open stage on which abstract, geometric settings were placed.[36]

In the 1950s and 1960s, the debates intensified. *The Times*'s description in 1961 of the proscenium-arch stage as an 'operatic anachronism which no longer meets the needs of performance' is typical of the arguments put forward.[37] The critique took several forms. First, the arrangement's origins in illusionistic settings could be thought problematic at a time of scenic innovation, with the likes of John Bury and Jocelyn Herbert seeking to move completely away from any sense of a 'realistic' backdrop, not least because film and television could inevitably portray locations in a more realistic fashion.[38] New approaches could be (and were) presented on proscenium-arch stages, but developments in set design also suggested the possibility of alternative stage arrangements.[39] For others in theatre, the problem revolved around the idea that the arch distanced actors from audiences, both psychologically and physically, by creating spaces of two distinct halves. It was argued that live drama offered an opportunity for contact between performers and their public that could not be emulated by cinema or television and which should therefore be emphasized. Another line of thought suggested that the typical proscenium-arch auditorium with its multiple galleries, some of which might be far from the stage, was problematic in an age when audiences were increasingly used to the close focus of film and television and when segregated facilities were deemed 'undemocratic'.[40] A further possible argument made, for example, by those proposing the thrust-stage Crucible Theatre, Sheffield (1971), was that a non-proscenium layout would enable theatre to fashion a more 'modern' image, revitalizing it in the face of competition.[41]

Moves to give architectural form to these ideas were led by directors including Stephen Joseph (who advocated 'in-the-round' staging) and Tyrone Guthrie, whose preference for 'thrust' stages with stepped sides seemingly owed something to a period working at Gray's Cambridge theatre.[42] Joseph, who went on to work at Manchester University's Drama Department,[43] created in-the-round theatres at Scarborough and Stoke-on-Trent, while the Chichester Festival Theatre (1962) was informed in concept by a number of theatres built by Guthrie in North America during the 1950s.[44] In Edinburgh, the Traverse Theatre (1964) was named for its 'transverse' stage, with two parallel banks of audience seating facing a central stage.[45] Other notable non-proscenium theatres included Manchester's Royal Exchange (1976), which featured a central 'arena' stage, the Olivier in the National Theatre (1976), and the thrust stages of the Young Vic on London's South Bank (1970) and the Crucible, Sheffield (1971). The move away from the proscenium arch, as noted earlier in this book, was often facilitated in Britain by the advent of subsidy. Organizations could secure grants to allow them to translate their ideas into built form; subsidy also gave them the operational security to develop their ideas.

In some cases, venues were planned for total flexibility. The Derngate, Northampton (1983), is the most prominent British example, using air-cushion technology to move so-called 'towers' in order to accommodate functions including theatre, music and banqueting.[46] However, fully adaptable, multi-functional venues of this kind and at this large scale have found little favour in Britain, because subsidy has made it possible to design and operate a venue which is first and foremost a theatre, whereas in North America, the absence of such financial support sometimes necessitates other, non-theatre uses as a means of revenue-raising.

Although multi-functional venues are, therefore, fairly unusual in Britain, some theatres have nonetheless been planned to allow various actor/audience arrangements. The idea owes something, at least in the architectural world, to the German architect Walter Gropius's unbuilt *Totaltheater* proposal of 1927, whose auditorium was to offer the possibility of rearrangement by mechanical means in order to provide conventional and 'in-the-round' arrangements. Among the more prominent examples are the 380-seat Bolton Octagon (1967) and the Gulbenkian Centre at Hull University (1969, now known as the Donald Roy Theatre).[47] In the case of the Crescent, Birmingham (1963), intended for amateur use, the front part of the stalls could be rotated in a similar fashion to that proposed by Gropius.[48] The same approach was later adopted on a slightly larger scale in the New London Theatre (1972). However, most flexible theatres are small, being either the purpose-built studios that were added to many theatres and academic institutions from the 1960s onwards, or converted 'found spaces'. At this scale, it is possible for enthusiastic amateurs, crew, or students to move blocks of staging and seating around. Any greater scale necessitates the higher set-up costs of a mechanical solution, as at the New London, whilst also complicating the architectural issue, with it potentially being harder to achieve a satisfying envelope for all the various forms possible.[49] The difficulties have been recognized by architects,[50] consultants,[51] and practitioners alike.[52] It has usually been suggested that it would be better to do one arrangement well rather than provide for several badly. Larger theatres have therefore typically retained relatively fixed configurations of seating and staging. Where flexibility has been provided, it is usually within limits. Thus in the case of the Nottingham Playhouse, for example, the front rows of stalls seating could be removed to create a forestage, projecting into the auditorium.[53] In other cases, fixed elements have been combined with flexible areas, and here we might note the very successful school theatre at Christ's Hospital, Horsham (1974, fig. 8.7), in which 'boy power' was used to rearrange the stalls level for either conventional or thrust-stage use but which also provided fixed galleries around three sides of the auditorium. Designed by Howell Killick Partridge

and Amis, the concept developed that of their earlier Young Vic (1970). The idea was picked up by Iain Mackintosh in the Cottesloe auditorium within Lasdun's National Theatre, which similarly could be arranged in various ways at stalls level.[54] Gropius's vision of the entirely flexible theatre, much reproduced in architectural books,[55] has thus proved rather limited in impact.

Fig. 8.7 Christ's Hospital Theatre, Horsham

More generally, we should also exercise caution when considering the extent to which non-proscenium forms were actually taken up in practice, at least where major venues were concerned. As Peter Longman has succinctly put it, the 'brave new world' of alternatives never quite supplanted the status quo.[56] The Georgian overtones and conventional staging of Southern's Barbican Theatre proposal usefully remind us that continuity and the nuanced reinterpretation of established ideas have often remained important. There were frequently good artistic and practical reasons favouring the proscenium-arch stage, including the need for touring venues to offer consistent arrangements. On a different note, Hazel Vincent Wallace, director of what became the

Thorndike Theatre, Leatherhead, professed in the 1960s to having little time for 'high falutin' conceptual discussions when faced with the already considerable challenges of running a busy Repertory operation.[57] Yet established ideas have not been repeated unquestioningly. The Barbican designs filtered precedent through the Modernist lens of the architects, Chamberlin Powell and Bon, and the executed scheme of 1969-1982 thus transforms the ideas of Southern's earlier concept. As built, forward-stepping rear galleries and uninterrupted rows of 'continental' seating, each with its own door, were coupled with forward-facing side slips in place of the arched boxes of the 1959 scheme, while the appearance of the space, with unornamented wood finishes, polished metal, and pick-hammered concrete, was unequivocally contemporary. The stage, too, was up to the minute in its conception and equipment, responding to the needs of Royal Shakespeare Company and its directors, first Peter Hall and later Trevor Nunn. Similarly, the Thorndike Theatre offered an innovatory slant on convention, with the auditorium side walls and ceiling coming to the line of the proscenium arch, essentially hiding it, and the design reinterpreting the Greek amphitheatre in its single tier of 'continental' seating.

The case study theatres considered in the first part of this book demonstrate similar continuities. The narrow tiers of seating that 'paper the walls' of the Quays Theatre at The Lowry, for example, reinterpret the galleried courtyard type, whose roots are found in the Elizabethan and the Georgian periods. Belgrade II is essentially a semi-flexible version of the same idea. Curve, for all its radical intent, has a conventional forward-facing main auditorium whose essential concept is, in spirit, not far removed from the original Belgrade Theatre of 1958. And in addition, the expansive glazing of Rafael Viñoly's elevations also recalls earlier examples in concept and actuality. The large windows of the Yvonne Arnaud Theatre, Guildford, for instance, were intended to allow the theatre to function as its own advertisement, presenting the venue as an open, accessible, inviting place suitable for the

democratic age whilst also breaking down the boundary between building and setting in a way that anticipated Viñoly's intentions (fig. 8.8).[58] The idea of transparency has a still-longer pedigree, being related to the advent of glass curtain walling; Gropius's *Totaltheater* design represents an early application of the idea to theatre. Ludwig Mies van der Rohe's Mannheim civic theatre proposal of 1953 also anticipated Curve in its glass walls, offering views into and from the theatre's two auditoria, which, like those at Curve, were placed at the centre of the building envelope with their stages backing on to each other.[59]

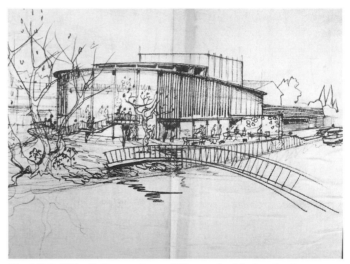

Fig. 8.8 Guildford's Yvonne Arnaud Theatre (1965), drawing by architects Scott Brownrigg Turner

Ultimately, in spite of their similarities and continuities, the key point in all this is that theatres are essentially bespoke buildings, not least where they are provided for an existing group of performers. A theatre company might want a fully flexible performance space, or they might have a particular set of precise geometric and spatial requirements, but, whether flexible or fixed in its configuration, the resulting building comprises a direct response to a specific brief, with designers drawing upon precedent, challenging and reinterpreting it. We may be able to discern similarities in basic form and 'type' but in many ways theatres counter the theory of 'mechanical selection' put forward by the architect Le Corbusier in the 1920s, namely that the perfection and ultimate standardization of each building type could be achieved through logical experiment and the refinement of detail.[60] Such an approach can be applied to other buildings, such as houses or hospitals, where an archetype can be established and then only varied as much as is necessary to suit the particularities of any chosen site. However, although Roderick Ham's brief in the case of the Derby Playhouse (1975) was for 'another Leatherhead',[61] and there was a close relationship between Norman Downie's theatres at Colchester and Salisbury, this kind of replicability is almost unknown in theatre. In fact, the similarities between Derby and Leatherhead are largely limited to the basic shape and planning of the auditoria, and the two buildings are otherwise quite different, reflecting their particular locations, funding, and patterns of use.[62]

Thus far, we have explored the subject of communication and the nature of some of the roles involved in theatre design, and have also noted that, while proclamations of the death of the proscenium-arch theatre have been premature, the existence of the debates about layout means that there is no fixed form that a theatre might take. Considerations of how a theatre is to be used, and by whom, will play an important part in shaping the design concept. But even once a spatial arrangement has been determined, the treatment of the auditorium is also open to debate, as the following section considers.

QUANTIFIABLE VS. SUBJECTIVE FUNCTION

Ernst Neufert's classic *Architects' Data* introduces the subject of theatre design by stating that the 'architect's main task is to achieve a balance between maximum seating capacity, good viewing and acoustic conditions, and easy circulation in accordance with "means of escape" and other safety regulations'.[63] Neufert offers calculations and other information by which this goal might be logically achieved. However, would the result be a successful theatre? On a purely practical level, in terms of acoustics, sightlines and escape routes, the answer is probably 'yes'. But consider the opinion of architect Michael Forsyth, writing in 1987:

> More than any other building type, theatres must as a matter of functional necessity embody a range of intangible and relatively indefinable architectural qualities such as mood, intimacy, magic and memory. It was these qualities that the new theatres of the 1960s did least to encourage.[64]

Forsyth's ideas can be related to the architectural climate of the 1980s, in which Modernism was increasingly challenged, its buildings caricatured in some quarters as being designed purely on the basis of function to the exclusion of all else.[65] However, others had made similar comments much earlier, suggesting that these 'indefinable architectural qualities' have long been thought missing in some new theatres. The historian and theatre critic Richard Leacroft, for example, wrote in 1949 that 'too often, the modern theatre auditorium, designed on scientific lines, has the atmosphere of a sterilized lecture hall rather than a theatre'.[66] For Leacroft, like Forsyth, successful theatres were not simply 'scientific' spaces. But were they ever thus? In reality, the best Modern architecture was never concerned with questions of function and science alone. The following section of this chapter explores the issue further.

Neufert's views on theatre design were very similar to those put forward by the American engineer George Izenour. Introducing his influential *Theater Design*, first published in the 1970s, Izenour defined drama as 'a performer-audience shared art entirely dependent on the sensations of seeing and hearing'.[67] By implication, the space in which that 'shared art' took place should facilitate those 'sensations'. What might be thought to diminish them? The story of the Belgrade Theatre, Coventry, offers a clue.

An artist, Martin Froy, was commissioned to collaborate with the City Architect – Donald Gibson in the first instance, and later Arthur Ling. Froy's initial proposals for a decorated auditorium were rejected. As he recorded in his notes at the time, he was told that either 'the "machine" interior [could] be left to speak for itself' or 'sacrifices [could] be made in the comfort, audibility and vision ... for the sake of what might, inadequately, be called "atmosphere"'.[68] One detects a possible echo of Gibson in these comments, which imply that 'atmosphere' and 'meaning' had no place in the functional auditorium. Such views would not have been atypical for architects in the 1950s. The fundamental premise of Modern architecture was that it rejected the reuse of the past architectural styles, calling instead for a new architecture that reflected the possibilities and needs of the twentieth century. Value was to be added to architecture not by means of symbolic decoration, but by new concepts of form and space, and by functional efficiency.[69] The styles were considered an 'assumed costume' which had been applied indiscriminately to buildings.[70] For their critics, they were redolent of outdated social hierarchy, and were at times seen as dirty ('stolid and unhygienic plush and stucco work' in one description of a theatre,[71] for example) or even vice-ridden.[72] Thus the elaborate ornament of Victorian architecture was often considered distasteful and indeed ridiculous by many architects in the middle years of the twentieth century. For this reason, and also to prevent distracting reflections during performances caused by the use of stage lighting located within the auditorium (a post-Victorian development), some nineteenth-century theatres, such as York Theatre Royal and the Aldwych, London, had their gilded auditoria painted out in muted colours.[73] And as fashion changed from the 1920s onwards, the auditoria of new theatres, too, were often relatively plain compared with their pre-1914 predecessors – the development which had prompted Leacroft's complaint about sterility in theatre architecture as early as the 1940s.

In reality, however, theatre design (like other building types) has rarely been a matter of mechanical function to the exclusion of everything else. As J.M. Richards, editor of the *Architectural Review*, observed in 1940, the best Modern buildings were 'the honest product of science and art'.[74] In other words, science alone was not enough. These ideas were expressed even in the 1960s by some theatre architects. Writing of the Yvonne Arnaud Theatre, Guildford, J.A. Brownrigg commented that:

A theatre, more than any other building except perhaps a church, is a physical enclosure for an almost entirely non-physical experience. For this reason the creation of atmosphere is even more important than the solution of a series of functional problems.[75]

Peter Moro, designer of the Nottingham Playhouse (1963), reflected that:

In the less utilitarian buildings it is essential to evoke deliberately an emotional response from those who use and see them. A relevant example of this is the design of theatres, which, although they may have the latest technology, are failures when they have no magic.[76]

Meanwhile, the critic Richard Findlater called for buildings which 'without sacrificing a shred of atmosphere, put function before pomp'.[77] Similarly, the technical specialist Frederick Bentham thought that theatres ought to be 'inspiring yet retiring'.[78]

Although Roderick Ham suggested in 1971 that some designers had over-reacted against gilt and plush (as was later argued by Forsyth), quantifiable functional considerations could be balanced with more intangible matters.[79] The New Victoria, London (1930), for example, was intended to be modern and functional yet also created the fantasy-like surroundings of a 'mermaid's palace' through elaborate sculptural forms and lighting effects.[80] Later, the Nottingham Playhouse and the Yvonne Arnaud Theatre both deployed a varied palette of materials and subtle lighting to achieve a rich, luxurious atmosphere. In the case of the Belgrade Theatre, it was stated that 'an effect of richness was to be achieved by the use of functional materials, for example the acoustic panelling, carefully detailed by the architect and chosen for its colour'.[81] It is important, therefore, that we recognize the changing terms of the debate. Theatres of the 1960s did not automatically eschew 'magic' and theatricality; rather, they sought to achieve these attributes in a particular way.

Theatres are not unique in having to balance objective and subjective factors in their design. Their particular complexity, however, results perhaps from the somewhat murky terms in which the intangible requirements are often put. For example, in his seminal work of 1968, *The Empty Space*, Peter Brook wrote that:

I have had many abortive discussions with architects building new theatres ... it is not a question of good buildings and bad; a beautiful place may never bring about explosion of life, while a haphazard hall may be a tremendous meeting place. [...] In other forms of architecture, there is a relationship between conscious articulation and good functioning. A well-designed hospital may well be more efficacious than a higgledy-piggledy one, but as for theatres, the problem of design cannot start logically. [...] The science of theatre building must come from studying what it is that brings about the most vivid relationship between people ...[82]

Brook's discussion represented a step in his own personal search for the 'rough', lively theatre, and a particular kind of 'found space'.[83] However, others have in recent years increasingly adopted a similar line, reflecting a more general interest amongst architectural theorists with the ways that spaces are perceived by their users. Thus the director Michael Attenborough has noted the key influence of what he described as an auditorium's 'personality' on actors and audience,[84] while fellow director Declan Donellan commented in 1995 that 'you are not going to design a great

theatre just with a computer'.[85] At times, this embrace of the intangible has reached almost mystical proportions, as is evident in the American theatre consultant Josh Dach's statement at a conference in 2002 that:

There's not even a word to describe that special quality that a theatre might have [which] makes it good to perform in, or bad to perform in. I've suggested to many groups [...] over the years that we need a word so that people take this concept seriously as an idea. I believe it probably has to have scientific connotations so that people take this concept seriously as an idea, so maybe *raumgeistology* or 'spirit of the room' is that word. But these are ineffable qualities.[86]

The extreme conclusion that might be drawn from Dach's statement is that communication – the issue with which we began this chapter – is ultimately futile, because the 'special quality' which makes for a successful theatre cannot be properly expressed. Perhaps his opinion is too pessimistic. Nonetheless, his views, like those of Brook, Attenborough and Donellan are a timely reminder of the fact that theatre design is rarely only a matter of mathematical setting out or logic, but requires an appreciation of the contribution that can be made by materials, lighting and, perhaps most crucially, the way in which a building relates to its users and its context.

TO BUILD, OR NOT TO BUILD?

This chapter has briefly highlighted a selection of key themes in twentieth-century theatre design, revealing that some of the dilemmas and solutions which appear in the preceding case study chapters are not necessarily new, and suggesting that those commissioning and designing theatres might productively learn much from (or, perhaps, be consoled by) the recent history of the type. *The Times'* warning of 1928 – that considerations of 'bricks and mortar' often overshadowed the needs of drama in theatre-building – might be productively modified: are questions of bricks and mortar actually dramas in themselves?

Yet the dramas of the design and construction process are not without their reward, for architecture can play an important role in theatre. Of course, not all would agree. Peter Brook was reputed to have concurred with Denys Lasdun's exasperated suggestion that Brook would prefer a 'bomb site in Brixton' to any National Theatre that Lasdun could design,[87] while others, such as Werner Ruhnau, architect of the Gelsenkirchen Civic Theatre in West Germany (1959), looked forward to the day when theatre might be fully liberated from buildings.[88] However, even outdoor performances must still be conceived in relation to the physical characteristics of the place in which they are presented; indeed, the act of performing outdoors is surely as representative of a particular artistic intent as a performance in a building. Similarly, as many critics and practitioners have noticed, the architectual choices that are made in designing a theatre and the terms used to describe it also can indicate a theatre's intentions. Thus, the 'black-box' studio, supposedly invisible in its dark-painted walls and movable seating, in fact makes just as distinctive a statement in its physical arrangement, nomenclature and aesthetic as, say, an exuberant Matcham 'Empire'. Partly for this reason, when Hamish Glen came to the Belgrade Theatre, he was clear that the second performance space was not going to be known as a 'studio' because of the associations of that word.[89]

The essential nature of the relationship between theatre and architecture was recognized by the Young Vic's first director, Frank Dunlop (formerly of the Nottingham Playhouse), for whom theatre was 'acting in architecture'.[90] His views surprised the Young Vic's architect, Bill Howell of Howell Killick Partridge and Amis, who had initially thought that 'a non-building in which you can do anything' would be best. Buildings can complement the style and aims of a theatre group by means of location and design (or, on occasion, a desirable contrast might be formed between

Fig. 8.9 Belgrade Theatre, Coventry: the foyer in 2010 after its restoration in the spirit of the original 1958 design

building and performance). We conclude with two examples that illustrate this idea.

In 1960s Britain the language of Modern architecture meant that new theatres were not only seen to contrast with older venues but also that this difference could represent the changing context in which theatre was made and experienced (fig. 8.9).[91] The link was made most clearly by *The Stage*, which suggested in 1965 that 'architects can

Fig. 8.10 Roderick Ham, Thorndike Theatre, Leatherhead, the foyer in 1969

bring a new image of the living theatre through the steel and glass playhouses which they are designing'.[92] Thus was Leatherhead's Thorndike Theatre (fig. 8.10) described by the *Morning Telegraph* as 'a far cry from the cramped, dismal places lacking space, attractiveness or character in which the theatre has languished in so many centres for so many years' on account of its contemporary appearance and spacious foyers, open all day for the whole community to use.[93] The strength of the image of theatre created by this architectural vocabulary is only confirmed by the hostile reception it gained in some quarters. Alan Bennett has cited the example of the director Ronald Eyre, who thought that the National Theatre might productively be used as an ice rink and dance hall for a few years until 'the corners had been rubbed off' and the architecture had acquired its own 'shabby, disreputable history', at which point the building might make an excellent theatre.[94] Similarly, Michael Elliott, prompted by the apparent solidity of the National, asked in 1973:

> shouldn't we try to attain a certain lightness and sense of improvization, and sometimes build in materials

that do not require a bomb to move them? In short, shouldn't we stop building for posterity?[95]

Elliott's ideas, developed by his designer colleague, Richard Negri, and Levitt Bernstein Architects, informed the conception of the Manchester Royal Exchange as a 'pod', theoretically demountable, which was inserted within the vast space of a former trading hall (fig. 8.11).

Fig. 8.11 Royal Exchange Theatre, Manchester: the theatre 'pod' inserted within the Victorian hall

Others have echoed Elliot in calling for a relationship between theatre and architecture that is less 'fixed' than the 'new image' of the 1960s, though one which still recognizes the potential value of their interaction. Peter Brook's preference for the use of redundant buildings relates partly to their immediacy (with no need to wait for a major building project) and also the possibility that they might be moulded according to his wishes for particular productions.[96] The results in some sense embody the impermanency that was called for by Elliott, being described by one author as 'living backgrounds' which evolve and record the history of their use as holes are knocked in walls and finishes are changed to suit each new play.[97] But the care with which Brook constructs the environments in which he works (and the way in which some of these environments, such as Glasgow's Tramway, have been subsequently retained as permanent performance venues) only confirms the important role played by architecture. The potential of the found space is highlighted by Brook's collaborator, Jean-Claude Carrière, who stated that the attraction of the Bouffes du Nord, Paris, was the way in which it was 'unimaginable for us: it *told* us what to do'.[98] Thus Brook's venues are surely not the 'empty spaces' implied by the title of his most famous book. Rather, they are places which in many ways possess a strong geometry and atmosphere, though without the architectural apparatus of conventional theatres. (While the Bouffes, in fact, had originally been a theatre, it might still be thought unlike 'conventional theatres' in the way that Brook's use of the building celebrates its decay). Their architecture makes some contribution to the 'personality' of the place and the way in which it is experienced.[99] Something similar is evident in the way that the brick auditorium walls of the Almeida, London, which had been stripped of their plaster when the theatre was created in 1980, were deemed sacrosanct when the building was refurbished and extended in the early twenty-first century (fig. 8.12). They had become much-loved for their colour and texture, and for what these attributes were thought to contribute to the atmosphere of the space.[100]

Architecture, though perhaps tangential to the ultimate goal of theatre – performance – cannot, therefore, be discounted entirely. Buildings do not function merely as empty containers. In the cases which have just been briefly discussed, buildings define the image of the venue, framing and shaping the acts of acting and watching, and productively so. Furthermore, even where a conscious image is not sought by performers and designers, the geometry (and the atmosphere) of a space will always impose some sort of constraint on performance. On the one hand, theatre buildings exist to accommodate and facilitate creativity: they are abstract locations in which anything might happen. And yet, at the same time, many successful theatres make a very definite statement of their presence, with their architecture not only contributing to the experience of performers and audiences but also reflecting the particularities of their local situation and the artistic contexts in which their creators and users wish to work.

Fig. 8.12 The Almeida Theatre, Islington

Notes

1   This chapter highlights some of the themes of my Ph.D. thesis, 'British theatres, 1926–1991: an architectural history', University of Cambridge, 2008. I would like to thank Peter Longman, former Director of The Theatres Trust and Housing the Arts Officer at the Arts Council, for providing helpful comments on the draft. As with the Ph.D., I would also like to thank my supervisor, Professor Alan Short, as well as the many people who assisted with information. Permission to reproduce images was kindly granted by Scott Brownrigg, Surrey History Centre, the National Theatre, Mark Foley, and Christ's Hospital. The Ph.D. was funded by the Arts and Humanities Research Council.

2   E.g. *Birmingham Mail*, 14 January 1927. For Stratford, see Marian Pringle, *The theatres of Stratford-upon-Avon* (Stratford, 1994).

3   Shakespeare Birthplace Trust, SR MS 71.2/1926: letter from Harley Granville Barker to Archibald Flower, 18 April 1926.

4   *Times*, 3 November 1927.

5 Richard Eyre, *National Service: diary of a decade* (London, 2003), entry for 8 November 1988, pp.52-53.

6 E.g. *Stage*, 17 November 1988; *Times*, 22 October 1988; *Evening Standard*, 21 October 1988; *Sunday Times*, 23 October 1988.

7 Alan Bennett, 'The National Theatre', pp.383-387 in his *Untold Stories* (London, 2005). For this, see p.384.

8 *Illustrated London News*, December 1988. Renton's review is on p.65.

9 There was much discussion of Dutch architecture at the time when Scott was training at the Architectural Association: particularly relevant are *AA Journal* v.37 (1921-1922), pp.222-224 for an exhibition of Dutch building; v.38 (1922-1923), pp.94-95 and v.39 (1923-1924), pp.4-11 for a Dutch excursion.

10 RIBA Drawings Collection, BAHO/1/6-8: letter from Hope Bagenal to Alison Bagenal, 23 April 1932, is perhaps biased in that the author was the theatre's acoustician, but is a useful indicator nonetheless.

11 J.C. Squire, 'The Shakespeare Memorial Theatre', *Architectural Review* 71 (1932), pp.222-224.

12 Shakespeare Birthplace Trust, P.71.2/1927 10,201-I: Competition conditions, 1927.

13 *Herald*, 6 January 1928

14 Iain Mackintosh, *Architecture, actor and audience* (London, 1993), p.104.

15 *Yorkshire Post*, 9 January 1928; R. Speight (ed.), *A Bridges-Adams letter book* (London, 1971), p.21.

16 E.g. letter from W. Bridges-Adams to Arthur Colby Sprague, 6 October 1948, reprinted p.36 in R. Speight (ed.), *A Bridges-Adams letter book* (London, 1971).

17 Shakespeare Birthplace Trust archives, SR MS 71.2/1926: letter from Granville-Barker to Flower, 16 May 1928.

18 Alistair Fair, 'A monumental turkey? Elisabeth Scott's Shakespeare Memorial Theatre', *Theatres* 9 (Autumn 2006), pp.3-5.

19 Victor Glasstone, 'Theatre architecture in Britain', *RIBA Journal* 50 (1968), pp.501-507. For this quotation, see p.505.

20 Peter Jay, 'Theatres: stage and auditorium', *Architectural Review* 113 (1963), pp.175-185.

21 Jay, 'Theatres', p.183.

22 For an unexecuted theatre by Ham at Bedford, see my '"The end of optimism and expansiveness"? Designing for drama in the 1970s', *Twentieth Century Architecture* 10, *The 1970s* (2011, forthcoming).

23 'Shopping centre with a cultural plus', *Surveyor* 141/4228 (22 June 1973), p.29.

24 'Who was Frank Matcham?', *RIBA Journal* 111 (2004), p.9; Andrew Saint, 'Frank Matcham in perspective', pp.10-29 in D. Wilmore (ed.), *Frank Matcham and Co.* (Dacre, 2008).

25 'Theatre in Corporation Street, Coventry', *Architects' Journal* 128 (1958); see also Stephen Joseph, *Theatre in the round* (London, 1967), p.166.

26 Mackintosh, *Architecture, actor and audience*, p.118.

27 Barnabas Calder, 'Committees and concrete: Denys Lasdun's National Theatre', Ph.D. thesis, University of Cambridge, 2007, p.70.

28 Guildhall Library, London, QL 55.4 BAR: 'Barbican Redevelopment, 1959', p.12.

29 Peter Moro, 'The Nottingham Playhouse', *Builder* 203 (1961), p.894 names Southern thus.

30 John Honer, formerly of Chamberlin Powell and Bon, telephone conversation with author, 7 June 2006.

31 For the 1958 scheme, see University of Bristol, Richard Southern papers, TCP/T/000094/25: drawings of proposed Barbican Arts Centre, 1958. For the 1959 scheme, see Guildhall Library, London, QL 55.4 BAR: 'Barbican Redevelopment, 1959'.

32 University of Bristol, Richard Southern papers, TCP/T/000094/5-10.

33 Michael Elliott, 'Exchange experience', *Architectural Review* 160 (1976), pp.361-362.

34 Tyrone Guthrie, *A life in the theatre* (London, 1960), p.126; Hazel Vincent Wallace to Alistair Fair, 25 October 2006.

35 Glynne Wickham, *A history of the theatre* (Oxford, 1992), pp.220-221.

36 See e.g. Richard Cave, *Terence Gray and the Cambridge Festival Theatre* (Cambridge, 1980).

37 *Times*, 3 February 1961.

38 For Bury, see e.g. *Times*, 5 April 1966 and also obituary, 15 December 2000.

9.   An Architect's Photographic View: the Design and Life of the Theatres

Giorgos Artopoulos

Plate I An articulation of geometric shapes signifies the entrance to The Lowry. These shapes, distinct from the sculptural envelope that encloses the internal spaces, contribute to a building complex/whole that is composed of volumes/parts. The joints between the parts become significant. The metal panels that cover the building recall industrial construction and reappear across the canal on the surfaces of Liebeskind's Imperial War Museum.

Plate II The Lowry's transparent sides allow unobstructed visual access to the canal and offer important views of the waterfront from the gallery, cafeteria and restaurant areas.

Plate III The arrangement of the rows of seats at The Lowry into three semicircular levels of different circumference creates interesting visual patterns that generate a curving 'landscape' of seats. The oversaturated colour blue that covers every surface of the auditorium intensifies this effect of being 'inside' a uniform landscape-environment. The linear treatment of lighting then produces another 'order' of curves that highlight the contours of the three levels of the auditorium.

Plate IV The strategy of using oversaturated colours to cover distinctively the internal surfaces of The Lowry's various parts, here the lower foyer, produces a series of atmospheres for every part of the building.

Plate V The geometry of the Contact Theatre's ventilation chimneys, which are arguably the most distinctive part of the building with their sculptural composition of cuboids, expresses an inner order of structuring that is more natural than might be suggested by their straight lines and construction material.

Plate VI The wooden panels separating the rows of seats at Contact intensify the sides of the auditorium and generate a three-dimensional flow of curves that gives a rhythm to the space, both in terms of visual impact and bodily movement as people from the audience move up and down the steps.

Plate VII Cast glass panels are used on the facade of the Lighthouse, Poole, to create naturally lit interiors: the foyer, the cafeteria, the information area, the box office, the first floor restaurant and most of the circulation spaces are all brought to life naturally with daylight. The translucency of the panels produces playful visual effects. Especially at the ground floor, the translucency of the glass transforms the exterior walls of the building which become a 'theatre of shadows', with passers-by casting shadows as they walk along the front side of the building that overlooks a busy street of Poole and those outside seeing the shadows, at night, of people within.

Plate VIII Adjacent to the stage at Contact is storage space for theatre infrastructure and a workshop. Its location facilitates the moving of material used in performances onto the stage and allows the flexible operation of the theatre which thus is not restrained by its small size.

Plate IX Though greater in scale than the original 1958 Belgrade Theatre, Stanton Williams' extension features a playful combination of straight lines that brings it into dialogue with the Grade II listed 1950s building.

Plate X The dialogue continues in the internal spaces of the Belgrade Theatre.
The design and construction of the foyer and circulation spaces repeat the clean surfaces and the dark colours of the new entrance to the theatre. The synergy of material and spatial transparencies enhances the internal continuity between the extension and the existing building.

Plate XI The 300 seat second performance space at the Belgrade Theatre is characterized by its small footprint, the result of its vertical organization. The tight but clean configuration of infrastructure and the visible structure of galleries and balconies, as well as the hard surfaces and materials used for their construction, create an industrial atmosphere that promises flexibility in configuration. Their size makes the visually obtrusive railings of the galleries and staircases a significant feature of the brightly lit space of the auditorium and intensifies this industrial character.

Plate XII The smoothly curving 'gills' of Rafael Viñoly's design for Curve, Leicester, are transformed by their scale and materials into an abstract geometric landscape behind the older part of the city that acts as the foreground.

Plate XIII The opposition between the repeated horizontal lines of Curve's facade and the architecture of the surrounding buildings attracts the attention of passers-by.

Plate XIV Although the mass of Curve follows the site boundary, its shape and size dramatically multiply its visual impact on the cityscape. The alternating rows of shading and glazing offer playful views of the city from the theatre foyers. The transparency of the facade at ground level gradually reveals the corner of the building block and transforms the character of the space in front of the theatre from a cross-road into a piazza, a meeting place for the neighbourhood.

Plate XV The insertion of Curve on the site has left the ground intact but the transparent base of the elevation allows the piazza in front of the building to extend into the theatre. This visual continuity of interior and exterior spaces gives the theatre lobby a more public character.

Plate XVI The backstage is separated from the streets of Leicester by an intermediate space, Curve's foyer. The movable walls of the backstage area can be raised to reveal all the 'stuff' used in performance and the supporting infrastructure to visitors and patrons as well as onlookers passing along the street.

10.   Emerging Themes

Peter Barrett and Monty Sutrisna

The individual cases described in the preceding chapters tell complex, even heroic, stories of the creation of specific theatres by particular people in particular contexts. However, there are some common themes running through these individual narratives. In this chapter, we tease out the key themes and the helpful lessons bound up in them, so that those involved in future projects, building or adapting theatres, can benefit from these hard-won insights. Each project will of course be different, but by taking into account the general lessons highlighted here it should be possible for those involved to at least better understand what is happening ('so, this is quite normal!') and then hopefully to find the optimum route forward.

The following sections look across the case study projects according to various categories that emerged during the analysis as being significant in understanding the observed experiences and which were used to order material from the case studies for comparison. These major themes are: external conditions/funding, 'visions', project stakeholders, briefing and delivery, project budget/cost, and distinguishing characteristics.

EXTERNAL CONDITIONS/FUNDING

Each project was initiated within general and specific contexts. Chapter 1 rehearsed the position over the years as to public subsidies for capital arts projects. From this it can be seen that the availability of funds has varied considerably from time to time, impacting on the scale of ambition that could be supported. In addition, the nature of funding has carried with it implications for the nature of the theatre and the activities to be accommodated. The impact of public monies made the process more accountable (and thus, perhaps, political) than it might otherwise have been. For the projects covered in the earlier chapters, after many years of limited funding to the sector, the funding from the Arts Council England (ACE) Lottery Fund was typically a major enabling factor. However, it brought with it complications that from the perspectives of the participants sprang from an apparent lack of transparency, confusion over the criteria being applied and the amount of funding potentially available, plus the sheer challenge of the complex Arts Capital Programme (ACP) bureaucracy (particularly in the cases of The Lowry and Poole). These complications were commonly compounded by attempts to combine funding from different funders (with different criteria and requirements). This funding was typically interlinked, with each tranche acting as matching funding and becoming in itself a criterion to secure funding from another source, often in a reciprocal fashion.

Specific concerns voiced in the studies were that the Arts Council was suspected of having held 'hidden contingencies' enabling it to provide additional funding to 'save' selected high profile ACP projects. The result was the illusion that funding was unlimited, inciting over-ambitious proposals.

Eventually, the ultimately limited funding available in the ACP scheme necessitated scoping down, triggering disappointment and anger at the perceived unequal distribution of funding. There were also concerns that the protocols of the ACP scheme did not seemingly consider the running cost and revenue issues inevitably deriving from ambitious building and rebuilding projects. Construction proved almost fatal for some clients: not only Contact, whose organization was violently restructured, but also, looking beyond the case studies, we might cite from recent years the examples of the Arts Theatre in Cambridge, the Dovecote Arts Centre in Stockton-on-Tees, the Midland Arts Centre (MAC), the Royal and Derngate in Northampton. The opportunities to reduce the various buildings' running costs presented by rebuilding were lost whilst projects carried the burden of overspend into their future lives. The ACE process was perceived to be frustratingly slow by some recipients (despite several attempts to accelerate procedures), with delays resulting from the assessment of applications inevitably and predictably leading to increased costs: inflation in construction costs: compounded consultant fees and increased internal costs.

'VISIONS'

Many intersecting 'visions' emerged from the case studies, from the epic scale of city regeneration (Lowry, Belgrade) to very specific staging ideas (Contact), sometimes in parallel (Leicester, fig. 10.1). Different stakeholders within each project understandably held differing visions and, on top of this, the overall shared vision inevitably evolved over the course of extended project periods, sometimes outpacing the design (Contact). The changing availability of funding sometimes necessitated the simplification of the vision (Poole, Hackney), sometimes its rapid elaboration (Poole) or augmentation (Contact). These changes were driven also by new leadership and key personnel, and changes in the governance regime (Contact, Leicester). 'Revisioning' by arts organizations was almost mandatory for Lottery success in response to changing perceptions of the appropriate target audience (younger at Contact and Poole) or other current politically-derived preoccupations (in many cases defined by the funders). These changes in 'vision' risked alienating existing audiences (Belgrade). Some declared 'visions' were more opportunistic, responding to funders' known priorities. The Lottery inevitably changed behaviours. 'Visions' in some cases were also complicated and impossibly extended by the wide consultation encouraged by funders, raising false hopes and leading to disappointed constituencies (Contact, Poole).

Fig. 10.1 Curve, Leicester, with the shutter between stage and foyer raised

For a project to succeed, someone authoritative had to broker one acceptable and communicable 'vision' (all cases). There was a generally felt imperative that all stakeholders should buy into and understand the 'vision', but there was conflict at times in how this could best be achieved. Construction professionals, particularly project managers, often did not want to be drawn into this debate and proceeded by trying to apply generic project management tools and techniques – all of which *assume* a clear 'vision'. Arts organizations, on the other hand, emphasized their uniqueness in their envisioning. The tension caused by this disjuncture emerged as being at the root of the serious practical and financial problems that emerged throughout most of the projects.

PROJECT STAKEHOLDERS

This section looks in turn at the roles played by various commonly recurring participants and thus emphasizes the distinctive viewpoints of: project funders, audiences/end users/communities/public, clients, architects, project managers/quantity surveyors, theatre consultants, engineers/acousticians and contractors.

Project Funders

The different sources of funding drawn upon, involving different funding agencies with their own protocols, priorities and pre-occupations, delivered various unintended consequences for applicants, not least the need to synchronize funders' criteria and requirements whilst fighting their own corner. There was often little or no evidence of the various funders communicating, instead leaving it to the applicants and their advisers to co-ordinate parallel bids, often as a game of 'double bluff' in the early stages.

The funders' behaviour could be very influential in the management of the project budget (alternately supportive and destructive in some cases). The level of monitoring and active involvement by the funders was naturally in proportion to their financial contribution (the more the contribution, the more the involvement) but relatively minor contributions with strict timeframes could dominate decision-making, for example the ERDF at The Lowry and the Belgrade. A funding requirement to start work by a particular date at Leicester complicated the production of detailed design information. Many criticisms were directed at the Arts Council Lottery Fund, their style of interaction and perceived lack of

understanding of construction projects. Perhaps, in fact, they understood the UK construction industry too well? In the earlier period of ACP, recipients baulked at an unreceptive and remote way of managing funds in which ACE simply allocated the money and then kept insisting the project stay within budget whilst ring fencing what in its view were the essential constituents.

Audience, End-users and Communities

ACE guidance was clear: wide and thorough consultation supporting capital proposals was an essential pre-requisite for funding success. All the clients and consultants involved in this study invested heavily in consultation with the 'end users', their existing audience (where there was one, which was not always the case), their immediate community and the wider public. However, in some cases there appeared to be some confusion over the constitution of the audience.[1] The involvement of (internal) clients/end users was considered as consultation, but the involvement of these end users was often on a managerial level only.

Doubts were expressed (for example by Wilford at The Lowry or Glen at the Belgrade) about the effectiveness of consultation. Would the audience be sufficiently technically expert and interested to make a meaningful contribution? This approach was carried over to consultations with the wider community and/or the public. Thus, these consultations were to some extent conducted at a superficial level, done as something of a public relations exercise to gain local support and blessing. Overall, there appeared to be confusion over the boundary between end users, audience and communities /public and the consultations were mainly done to 'tick the boxes' of the funders' requirements and gain the necessary support.

Clients

In some cases, the local authority (directly or through a trust) took the client role (Lowry, Leicester). There was an artistic and/or administrative lead from the theatre management in other cases. In general, the size of the client body and the expertise within it appeared to be critical. The larger their size, the more difficult it was to incorporate the voices of different constituencies into the project. Arts organizations, where they acted as the client, were exposed to various specific problems and difficulties, mainly due to their lack of major construction project experience. A client without construction experience was considered by some participants to be at the 'mercy' of the construction industry and funders. Clients at times felt alienated, dispirited or frustrated by situations encountered in design and construction (Hackney), value engineering exercises and regulatory requirements (Lowry, Contact, Belgrade). This situation was exacerbated where a poor relationship with the project team existed. Clients also found it frustrating when designs were over budget (Belgrade). Clients felt disenfranchised as their involvement in the project decreased during detailed design. It seems important for the consultant team to actively empower the client to remain closely involved in the later stages of the project, but this is patently difficult to achieve.

Architects

In some cases the architect was, at least temporarily, the guardian of the 'vision' (Contact, Lowry, Leicester), potentially at the expense of the trust of clients/funders (Leicester). The case studies revealed a recurrent discontinuity between the architect/consultant teams who produced the relevant feasibility studies and the teams that actually designed and delivered the buildings (Leicester, Belgrade). The result was a new architectural response to the 'vision' which emerged after the feasibility study and design competition (Leicester and Belgrade). Discontinuities were also observed during projects.

In one case, a Design and Build contract took the execution of part of the 'vision' away from the architect (Belgrade, fig. 10.2), with the 'vision' being inherited by the contractor. In addition, few of the projects enjoyed complete continuity and stability of client organization personnel.

Fig. 10.2 Belgrade II, Coventry: the technical gallery above the auditorium

The role and standing of the architectural profession in the UK has changed dramatically in the last twenty years. Whilst architects may have lost influence in general, they have in many cases intensified their commitment to, and involvement in, capital arts projects. The older generation of architects found this recast role as 'design service provider' uncomfortable (Hackney). Relationships between architects and co-consultants, clients and contractors were difficult in some cases, particularly in those involving high-profile architects. This was exacerbated by the continuing evolution of design ideas and detail throughout the fits and starts induced by funders' protocols and behaviour.

Project Managers and Quantity Surveyors

Architects traditionally led construction projects in the UK. In fact, the archaic contractual arrangement which enshrines this dominant role is known generically as the 'traditional' route to procurement. This situation has resulted in confusion about the Project Manager (PM) role and in some cases disappointment over the level of the project management service received by the clients. There was a tendency for the PM to do their job very clinically (i.e. 'hard nosed', efficient, methodical, literally navigating cost, time, and quality). Little effort seemed to be taken by the Project Managers to better understand the vision and the nature of the business of their clients, which might otherwise have led to a more sensitive and therefore more supportive approach. The position of the Quantity Surveyor (QS) was also found to be difficult as clients expected a higher degree of cost accuracy at an early stage than was or could be provided; these frustrations were driven by the funders' 'fixed funding' policy. In addition, the complexity and unfeasibly tight programmes of some projects significantly reduced the level of certainty possible in early estimates. Sadly, however, the first figure declared stuck inexorably throughout the projects.

Slightly better conditions (better relationships and less confusion over their roles) were found in the cases where the PM and/or QS were 'working for' the architects instead of 'working with' them. Here the architect took the co-ordinating role, with the PM and QS acting as 'second tier' consultants, assisting the more dominant architect, who had a closer relationship with the client. This seemed to be a positive factor in maintaining good relationships among the consultants, but may not have optimized their functions, the original intended benefit of involving the PM in these projects. However, although this scenario may work for the QS, it cannot be an ideal scenario for the PM, as the purpose of project management is to add significant and specific value to the process of delivering construction projects, achieved by separating the management of a project from the design and execution functions. Thus, in order to achieve the intended benefits, the PM either needs to be given the authority to do the job properly, or perhaps should not be involved at all. Clients in capital arts projects need to understand this choice (and be supported by funders in making it) to ensure that a decision is taken for the optimum benefit of the project.

Theatre Consultants

Theatre Consultants adopted different roles in the case studies, complicating attempts to define their role. In some cases, the theatre consultant acted as co-designer in a fundamental way (Lowry, fig. 10.3), in others as a technical stage equipment consultant and then supplier (Contact). Some clients were suspicious that the theatre consultant might impose their view (Contact), though in others cases this was welcomed by the design team and a constructive dialogue ensued (Lowry). In some cases, their role was so subtle that the authorship of the actual theatre spaces is unclear.

In five of the cases, a theatre consultant was appointed during the feasibility study, but only in one of these cases was the consultant retained following the feasibility stage (Lowry). In two of the cases this relatively short association appears to have been on account of, or reinforced by client dissatisfaction about the work undertaken. Clearly, the role of the theatre consultant, amongst all the other species of consultant, presents a delicate challenge.

Fig. 10.3 The Lowry, the Quays Theatre

Engineers

This category includes structural and Mechanical & Electrical engineers and, in some cases, fire engineers. Even though the engineers were considered to be core and primary consultants,

they may not be appointed, and therefore may not be able to influence the project, at the feasibility stage (Leicester, Contact, Lowry). However, in several cases, including ultimately Leicester, Contact and The Lowry, pre-existing working relationships between the principal consultants were seen to be beneficial to the project. The workload of the engineers was increased by the almost constant Value Engineering exercises that took place in some of the projects, a workload above that which would normally be expected and envisaged in the appointment conditions.

Acousticians

The interactions between the architect, acoustician and theatre consultant were especially important. Prior professional relationships with other members of the design team appear to have been important in establishing the membership of competition teams and, thus, selection for projects. The acoustician's role has emerged as being vital, but was envisaged, at least in some of the projects, as a supporting position. The timing of the acoustician's appointment is potentially crucial where there are ambitious groupings of performance spaces (Contact), an innovative design concept (Leicester), or pre-existing problems (Poole). In addition, the role was often weighted towards design rather than construction, with the consequent risk of acoustically non-compliant construction and extending even to the fundamental structure. The timeline analyses show that responding to late inputs from acousticians is potentially costly.

Contractors

Similar criteria were used to select each of the (main) contractors across the cases. To some extent these are established in good practice guidance. The criteria included:

- their track record of experience in previous complex or similar performing arts projects;
- an indication of the people who would be involved if they were selected, to establish the potential 'chemistry' of the future relationships;
- their financial status, resources and stability;
- their overall capability including their programming skills, and;
- price, although in none of the cases was the client obliged to accept the lowest price, there being a set price/quality weighting on the scoring of tenderers' offers.

The Belgrade introduced an additional selection criterion, the ability of the bidder to accommodate the client's ongoing productions within their construction programme. Reflecting on this range of requirements, it seems that it was important for clients to select the key people; the arts are a very personal matter. Conversely, contractors were keen to enrich their portfolios through successful completion of a complex, high-profile project. This euphoria faded as projects proceeded on site and financial tensions developed. Nonetheless, stakeholders' sense of 'ownership', generated early on in projects, later restrained conflict between the contractors and other stakeholders – though clients still rued the disputes.

Various difficulties with the (main) contractors were identified. These issues ranged from the deterioration in relationships between the contractors and their sub contractors and consultants, to the insolvency of the main contractor at the Hackney Empire, a development which had significant implications for the project.

RELATIONSHIPS AND INTERACTIONS

It is a truism to record that project success was achieved in part through continuing constructive collaboration between everyone involved in the projects. In complex projects that throw together participants in a demanding context it is not surprising that relationships are not always harmonious. Good teamwork and relationships, or at least successful suppression of conflict, is generally an important factor in delivering more successful projects. For the organizations in the case studies, who survive through robust collaborations, there was often a gulf between the sense of pride they felt over the completed buildings (and their enhanced reputations) and the difficulties they experienced during the project. These difficulties often extended after completion of the projects and primarily resulted from the financial uncertainties of the project funding and the adversarial potential of the construction industry. Cultural issues were also an underlying factor. For example, in one of the projects, Leicester, the US-based architects were not used to working with quantity surveyors, a uniquely British invention, and as a consequence, the architect appears to have kept them at arms length and did not provide the information that the quantity surveyors believed they needed to do their job as defined. Another common and influential pressure was the limited time available for the development of relationships between stakeholders, something which could be compounded by changes in the key personnel assigned to the project by different stakeholders.

The analyses show that different players become involved at different stages with different roles and scopes of action and authority. In practice, the dominant stakeholders in each project varied, usually as the result of specific contractual arrangements. This led to a 'skewing' of the projects with a range of advantages and disadvantages and outcomes. A clear example is the challenge of working with internationally prominent architects (Lowry, Leicester). What is clear for all cases is that a surprisingly large cast of people had to contribute a wide range of essential and complementary roles and that often the practical circumstances militated against this happening harmoniously or naturally, so that those fulfilling integrating leadership roles became of critical importance to the project success. This all happened within a context of shifting 'visions' and turbulent funding. The next two sections focus on the efforts made around briefing (the creation, maintenance and delivery of a shared vision) and cost control.

BRIEFING AND DELIVERY

The stakeholders driving the briefing process appeared to be the architects, sometimes balanced or supported by the theatre consultants, or the clients. Various end users were involved differently. The material contributions of users considered more external to the project, namely the audience and the greater public, appeared in retrospect, as we have noted, to have been more superficial than perhaps the theatre groups and local authorities intended or the ACE guidance prescribed. In the cases where clients subcontracted all briefing to their consultants, they were more likely to end up disappointed, compared to the more proactive clients. Investing time and energy at the early stages is shown to yield dividends (Poole). However, this commitment, perhaps still speculative at that stage, may create conflicts with clients' day jobs, given the demands deriving from the procession of short-term events that typifies the arts industry. The consultants were keen to drive the delivery (a 'clients don't understand' attitude prevailed rather than a willingness to empower clients) and to finalize the brief and design at an early stage. However, this could collide with the flexibility needed by arts clients if the completed buildings were to accommodate and support their current and future 'visions'. Time is clearly needed for designers to understand and give form to what their clients really desire and for clients to fully understand and accept what is possible in financial, technical, political and regulatory terms. These delicate situations were exacerbated by pressures arising from delays and the sheer complexity of designs. The end result was that it was very difficult for consultants to finalize a design that accommodated the client's and users' practical occupancy needs as well as their 'visions'.

The involvement of leading international architects clearly created challenges, sometimes stemming from the occasionally forceful attitude of these designers (what did everyone expect?) and the navigation of their ambitious design ideas. Added complexity compounded traditional difficulties in coordinating construction information across the various consultants. Contractors took the contractual opportunities to claim extensions to the contract periods with associated reimbursement adding further unanticipated financial pressures. Some clients felt betrayed by this response.

The different procurement routes (with various modifications) that were applied yielded a variety of results. However, it is difficult to establish from this evidence base that a particular procurement route is optimal for capital arts projects. The main difficulties in delivering the case study projects were found to be: tight timetables, construction difficulties (common and specific ones) and synchronizing delivery with clients' ongoing activities where existing venues were involved. Arts projects are considered by the industry to be technically complicated to design and construct. The project team has to deal with various issues – acoustics, sophisticated auditorium temperature and ventilation controls, specialist theatre equipment, critical sight lines and many other elements, all of which are highly interdependent. Change proliferates complexity and needs sophisticated management which tends to be underdeveloped in this industry. Furthermore, it can be in the optimistic nature of arts clients to hold onto 'nice-to-have' items, which may be subject to changes, inclusion and omission through the process. It seems that the complexity of constructing this type of project has often been underestimated. For example, the structural complexity (unique geometry) of innovative designs, in many cases requires execution in a particular sequence, whilst taking into account the temporary works involved.

Simple, sequential project management models can theoretically be applied to capital arts projects. However, this universal project management approach – designed to contain risk – is made very much less likely to succeed by the typical coming together of clients with little construction experience and ambitious but technically complex projects, in a volatile political and financial context, whilst also aspiring to meet demanding aesthetic imperatives. Although these factors all create risks to be managed, there is an essential need for the design to be able to evolve in tandem with the vision as it progressively crystallizes.

PROJECT BUDGET AND COST

Discrepancies between the initial estimated budget and actual delivery costs were evident in the studied cases. These discrepancies were sometimes very significant in their scale. The main cause in general terms was arguably the underestimation of these projects' complexity, uncertainties, and dynamics. The history of one case study implied that projects may be under-costed early on to allow the design to gain momentum and political support, so that when the true costs emerged it is unlikely that support would be withdrawn.

The solution applied to address cost over-runs was to carry out cost-cutting exercises, which in many cases were applied in a rather *ad hoc* manner in an atmosphere of crisis. In the shorter term, the application of 'Value Engineering' exercises seemed to help dampen the spiralling costs in the projects but the consequence of this approach was disappointment and at times very real financial difficulties on the client side. Essential operational features of some designs were lost, interactions with other elements became compromised (as potentially, might the integrity of the 'vision') and ultimately many of the omitted items had to be reinstated, probably at greater cost.

It appears that the funders, particularly the Arts Council, supported and even recommended 'Value Engineering', with a higher degree of involvement particularly at the later stages. This was of course in line with their 'fixed budget' policy, but did not seem to be balanced with an equivalent pressure to assess the additional costs that can result from VE exercises. Of course, projects have to be kept within budget and this is often done in the name of Value Engineering or its more constructive and pro-active sister discipline, Value Management (VM). However, this approach is not simply a fancy word for cost-cutting. VE/VM is designed to keep the priorities of the client's brief in focus when judging alternative areas for savings and at best it can represent a continuous, steering process throughout. It could be argued that a better risk management model is needed. It should be possible to draw on an extensive database of performing arts capital projects achieved, which as well as having a relatively high level of risk in general, must also have unique/particular kinds of risks where sharing experience could help. Such improvements in practice may be achieved by examining different perspectives; Chapman and Ward have suggested the inclusion of the contractor's perspective in addition to the more common client's perspective in order to improve project risk management.[2] The formalization of a body of knowledge related to capital arts projects is also very necessary as clients are unlikely to have been involved in another project of this type. Their inevitable naivety may be compounded by fluidity in the combinations of players in the construction industry. Thus despite the existence of specialist individuals or organizations with multiple experiences in managing performing arts projects, there is a risk that this body of knowledge will be scattered and then diluted and lost.

DISTINGUISHING CHARACTERISTICS

'Distinguishing characteristics' refer to the features distinct to each of the case study projects. In two cases, regeneration of a deprived area was the main (Lowry) or a major driver for the project (Leicester). Perhaps surprisingly, the regeneration imperative did not seem to overshadow the artistic vision originating from the resident theatre organization at Leicester; in the case of the Belgrade, Coventry, the wish for a landmark structure was borne in part of broader regeneration imperatives and had to be accommodated alongside the emerging artistic 'vision'. In other cases, the theatre was a receiving house (Lowry and Poole). Other significant drivers had no performing arts content whatsoever – at The Lowry, for example, creating a location for the City's collection of a local artist's works, which in turn opened avenues of funding from the Heritage Lottery Fund and the Millennium Commission.

Where regeneration informed the genesis and development of a project, it appeared to inject high expectations relating to the architectural expression and presence of the building, and the appointment of architects known for producing landmark architecture (Belgrade, Lowry, Leicester). In contrast, in another case the architect was chosen specifically because they were more *'down to earth'* (Hackney, fig. 10.4), though the client at the Belgrade *'got on well'* with the design team. Complexity of design was linked to iconic architecture as well as other innovations on sustainability features with consequentially higher demands on the consultant team. The innovative natural ventilation and passive cooling strategy evident in one case fundamentally informed the design of the building (Contact, fig. 10.5). In that example, the green aspects engendered additional interest in the project from the theatre organization, the host freeholder and the funders, but communicating the design to users not used to reading two-dimensional plans proved problematic. A large model was made. The users felt somewhat disenfranchised and concerned that a portion of the budget was being spent on natural conditioning to the detriment of the theatre's needs. This was before the era of governmental climate change anxieties.

Fig. 10.4 Hackney Empire, the Mare Street elevation

Fig. 10.5 Contact Theatre: north elevation

In one of the cases (Poole), the main distinguishing characteristic of the project was the unusually well managed and successful Value Engineering exercise. Triggered by a decrease in the funding available, this procedure sensitively balanced the needs and expectations of the various stakeholder constituencies. While VE was undertaken within other projects, it was not done in such a successful manner or managed by the client in such a controlled way so that some items omitted had to be reinstated later in the process. Although the client's relative commitments to different areas of the design were considered in other projects, it was only at Poole that this was made explicit through a formal quantified schedule. At the Lowry, in contrast, VE was continuous in response to increasing cost estimates and funding shortfalls.

RICH PICTURE EXAMPLES

All of the above elements interact over time in any project. How this interaction works out will of course vary, but to illustrate the sort of journey a client might experience, rich pictures have been created for two of the projects.[3] They stress the relationships between the issues and the links between (quite often) small decisions and later (quite often) big consequences. The following discussion relates to the two rich pictures below that show the project activities for, first, the Contact Theatre (fig. 10.6) and, second, The Lowry (fig. 10.7). Numerical notation has been provided on each picture which links with the numbers in the following text.

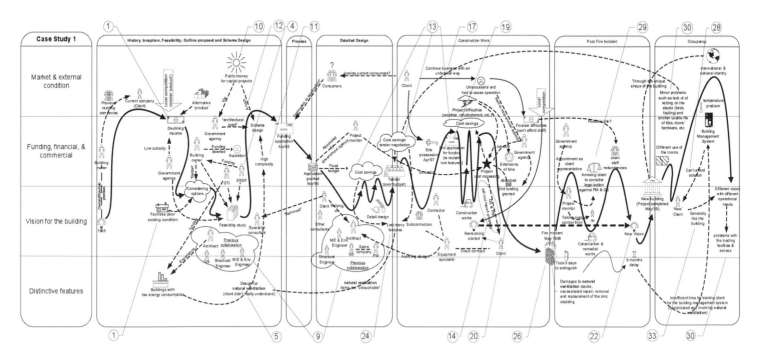

Fig. 10.6 Contact Theatre: 'rich picture diagram' illustrating the history of the project

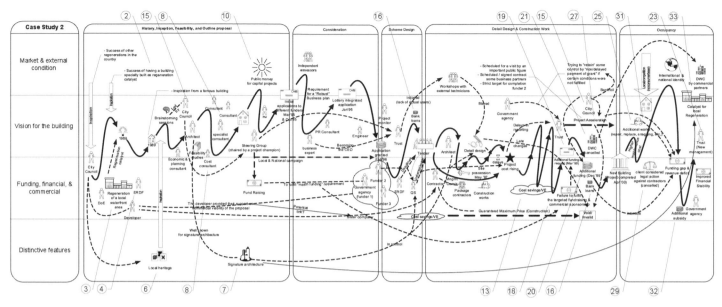

Fig. 10.7 The Lowry: 'rich picture diagram' illustrating the history of the project

At first glance it is apparent that both construction projects went through complex processes. The construction project for The Lowry (delivered using a 'management contracting' route) cost roughly ten times more than Contact (delivered using traditional procurement). As the case study chapters recorded, the drivers in the case of the Contact Theatre included the poor (existing) condition of the facilities and an implied threat from the building owner to redevelop the site in the near future **(1)**. The drivers at The Lowry derived entirely from the city council who were inspired by international examples of the apparent contribution of arts venues to catalyse dramatic, sustainable regeneration and simultaneously promote local heritage **(2)** and **(3)**. Prior to the availability of Lottery money for the arts, European funding (ERDF) seems to have been the originally intended source of funding for both projects **(4)**, which turned out to be a disappointment at Contact, but became an important funding element at The Lowry. The selection of the architects brought distinctive features to the projects. The selected architect at Contact had experience in designing for sustainability involving natural ventilation **(5)**, whilst Salford's local heritage added another dimension to The Lowry **(6)**, whose architect was internationally acclaimed for delivering iconic buildings **(7)**, which in some cases (Stirling and Wilford's Staatsgalerie in Stuttgart, for example), had been realized as part of an urban regeneration initiative.

From a comparison of the two resulting pictures, it is clear that the client at The Lowry was experienced and tried to empower themselves by recruiting various experts **(8)**, thus surrounding themselves with various consultants. At Contact, the client relied on the architect and a smaller group of consultants **(9)**. The advent of Lottery funding incited both projects to proceed and elaborate their plans **(10)**. At Contact, this development also increased the complexity of the process **(11)**, resulting from the need of engineers and physicists to prove the natural ventilation system, but within a tight timetable (with the client rushing to be among the first applicants to the Lottery in order to increase their chance of securing the funding **(12)**. The tight timetable, deadlines and complexity of both projects contributed to the delays in issuing construction details and under-estimation by the respective quantity surveyors. This eventually led to predicted out-turn costs rising and the necessity of cost-saving exercises (13), with the budget being enforced by the funders. It is also noticeable that there were delays in reporting financial problems to the clients of both projects, which may have induced a false sense of security. At Contact, the client could not even understand why the cost savings were being continuously implemented (14). The client at The Lowry was in a better bargaining position towards the funders due to the support of the city council, the original project envisioner (15), even though they needed to take on a bank loan (16).

It is evident in both case studies that the construction projects had contributed to financial difficulties for the client organizations, for different reasons. Contact failed to generate enough income from the continuation of their business in an 'unfamiliar' way, i.e., touring while their buildings were closed for construction (17). The Lowry failed to achieve planned fundraising and commercial sponsorship targets (18). Both clients had to apply for additional funding which was then absorbed by the construction process to achieve completion (19, 20). This revealed the insufficiency of the earlier construction cost estimates on both projects and ultimately the flexibility of the funders with respect to their original 'fixed budget' policies. One of The Lowry's funders even allowed the diversion of the budget originally intended for a peripheral building (21) to the construction of the main building as a part of the additional funding. At Contact, the construction project itself contributed to the transformation of the client organization into a new organization with a new vision (22). During the occupancy period, The Lowry experienced a change in governance and management arrangements as an indirect result of the funding gap and deficit in the project (23).

A combination of cost savings, VE and redesign was implemented in both projects to deal with rising costs. Contact ended up losing remarkably few of the original features but many of the backstage finishes (24), whilst The Lowry managed to put back some of the omitted items as a later phase (25). The delays at Contact, which were aggravated by the fire, late in construction (26), proved to be detrimental for the client organization's financial condition leading to redundancies, although the dismantling of the sixty-eight strong Company was later thought to have been inevitable by the first Artistic Director who inhabited the new building. At The Lowry, the client accelerated the project to achieve the targeted Millennium completion date (27), contributing to the later financial deficit of the organization. Contact's staff had to learn how to use the theatre's Building Management System (28). Both organizations considered but did not pursue legal action (29).

The transformation of Contact's organization has resulted in a different type of operation with different needs and created some problems such as unanticipated new uses for rooms, while cost savings have contributed to increased day-to-day maintenance costs (30). At The Lowry, various works had to be performed after practical completion to address the extensive snagging list, repair works, and replacement works necessary to achieve the required standards (31). These additional works eventually contributed to the client's escalating financial difficulties, which were eventually calmed by a significant additional sum from a government agency to improve their financial stability (32). However, despite the various problems encountered during the construction processes and after practical completion, both clients expressed their satisfaction with their buildings (33), which have been considered excellent tools to assist in the creation and promotion of their local, national and international identities.

SUMMARY

This chapter has looked at all of the projects and highlights the recurring volatility in funding and multiple 'visions' being pursued. Within this turbulent context, a wide range of stakeholders were involved, users were sidelined by default, unempowered actually to inform the designs whilst the designers and construction teams became immersed with the 'naïve' client. The involvement of the design and construction professionals varied in terms of the timing of their engagement, their degree of authority, pre-existing relationships and leadership influence within the project. This unsteady situation was the basis for taking forward what was likely to be an intrinsically challenging, complex project. The natural but perhaps simplistic reaction of funders to this situation is to try to fix not only the brief but also the budget early with the construction team and adhere rigidly to them. This has been revealed to be counter-productive and instead the more comfortably achieved and arguably successful projects display a value/risk management approach throughout that bolsters the vision through its practical realization whilst budgets are just about held in balance, a very considerable achievement. In the next chapter the major interactions between the categories will be examined to inform a dynamic understanding of the processes involved.

Notes

1   P. Sterry and M. Sutrisna, 'Briefing and Designing Performing Arts Buildings: assessing the role of the secondary stakeholders', *Architectural Engineering and Design Management* 3/4 (2007), pp.209-221.

2   C. Chapman and S. Ward, *Project Risk Management: Processes, Techniques and Insights* (Chichester 2002).

3   The use of rich pictures offers an alternative format to the textual storylines and provides holistic views of the construction projects. The material presented here is based on part of a paper by Sutrisna and Barrett, 'Applying rich picture diagrams to model case studies of construction projects', *Engineering, Construction and Architectural Management* 14/2 (2007), pp.164-179. The development of the pictorial approach draws from the diagrams developed in research conducted by the MIT School of Architecture and Planning's Space Planning and Organization Research Group (SPORG) known as 'process architecture' and presented by Horgan et al.

11.   The Internal Dynamics of the Projects

Peter Barrett and Monty Sutrisna

The last chapter summarized the main issues that were observed across all of the cases studied. It is apparent that many of these issues are highly dynamic and interactive. To reveal more clearly the connections, a detailed analysis of the interview transcripts was carried out, using an established social science methodology.[1] This exercise took each of the issues and allocated keywords into three associated categories, representing: 'Conditions', 'Actions/ Interactions', and 'Consequences' (CAC). 'Conditions' are a set of circumstances or situations in which the phenomena are embedded and respond to questions of 'why', 'where', 'how come', and 'when'. Actions/Interactions' (represented by the questions 'by whom' and 'how') focus on responses made by individuals or groups to issues, problems, happenings, or events that arise under those conditions. 'Consequences' are concerned with what happened as a result of those actions/ interactions, or failures to respond. The results were tabulated and then analysed to form the discussion which follows.

COGNITIVE MAPPING

Using the causal logic of the CAC categorization the keywords were mapped using a procedure known as 'Cognitive Mapping', assisted by a tool, Decision Explorer, produced by Banxia.[2] In practice, the keywords (often called 'concepts' in this sort of analysis) from the summary table were simply connected by arrows reflecting logical links from 'Conditions' to 'Actions/ Interactions', and from the latter to 'Consequences'. However, as, for example, the 'consequences' for one issue may be a 'condition' for another issue this had the effect of creating an interlinked set of causal relationships. The resulting cognitive map was very complex with more than two hundred closely related concepts (fig. 11.1). Therefore, further analyses were conducted using Decision Explorer to highlight two particular perspectives. The first perspective sought to give prominence to the most influential factors. The second was to specifically adopt the client's view of the issues.

The Top 7+ Concepts

To determine the most influential factors, the idea of the 'pervasiveness' of the concept was explored using two different analyses, namely 'domain analysis' and 'centrality analysis'.[3] A comparative analysis of the rankings from these two analyses clearly identified seven concepts as being by far the most influential in the connecting together the map of factors. The Top 7 most pervasive concepts are highlighted in fig. 11.1 and shown (with immediate connections) in fig. 11.2. It can be seen that the primary forces at play stem from the sheer *complexity* of the projects studied, which put the *reliability of project management and cost estimate models* under severe pressure, whilst at the same time creating various other *project difficulties*. The strained project and

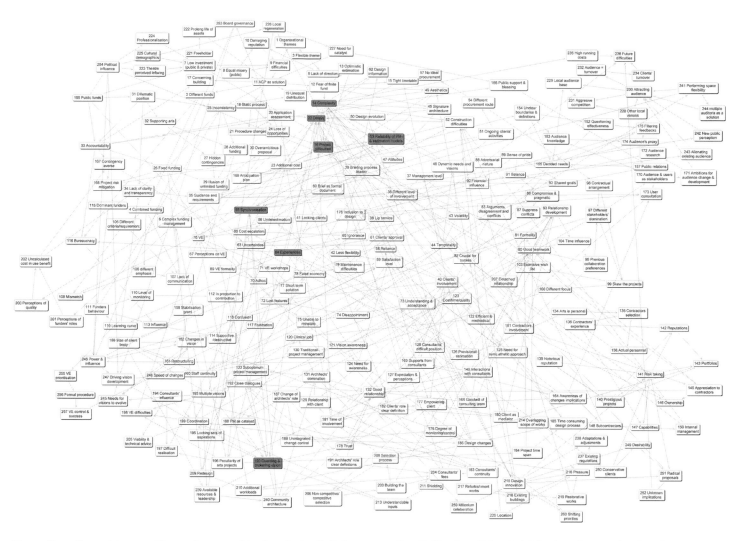

Fig. 11.1 Overall cognitive map illustrating a combined analysis of all the case studies, linking 'conditions' with 'actions/interactions', and 'consequences'

cost management, together with the efforts made in *guarding and brokering the (multiple) visions* of the project created a need for a high level of *synchronization*, which was not consistently achieved. All of these factors, in conjunction with the often low level of *experience* of the project stakeholders, led in many cases to *delays* which then further compounded the *difficulties* in these projects. This can be seen as the 'essence' of the key concepts and the forces at play between them.

The above is of course a huge simplification of much more complex relationship among these and other concepts. Therefore, in order to see a more complete picture to better understand the matter, the concepts relating immediately to each of the Top 7 concepts were added back, using a feature in the Decision Explorer software called 'Explore'. As a result, seven

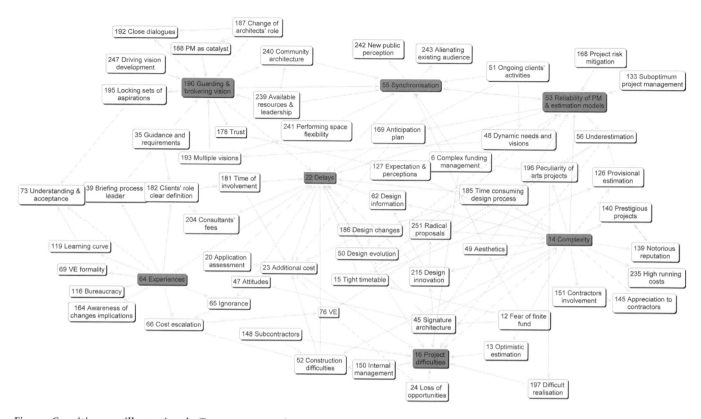

Fig. 11.2 Cognitive map illustrating the Top 7 most pervasive concepts

mini-cognitive maps were produced. These are each discussed below before being are combined (also by adding various related and/or relevant concepts) into a more comprehensive 'Top 7+ map'.

Complexity

The mini-cognitive map of the *'Complexity'* concept (fig. 11.3) presents the factors, arising across the case studies, that link around the concept of complexity. All construction projects are complex, but the specialized nature of arts buildings (and their funding processes) compounds the challenge. Despite this complexity, many of the clients exacerbated the formal aspects of projects, in some cases developing innovative concepts or employing prominent architects with radical proposals. That such decisions were made is understandable as many of these projects were prestigious and high profile, involving a considerable sums of money. As is discussed further below, high-quality, high-profile design was one way to demonstrate a level of aspiration that might appeal to funders. But this emphasis put immense pressure on the teams and made it a real challenge to avoid disappointment and/or financial problems.

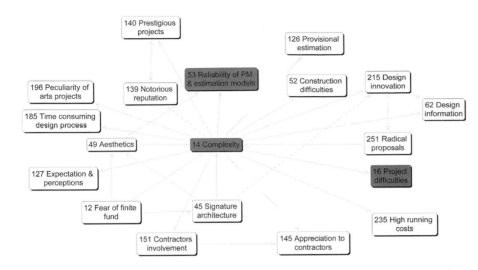

Fig. 11.3 Mini cognitive map showing the 'complexity' concept

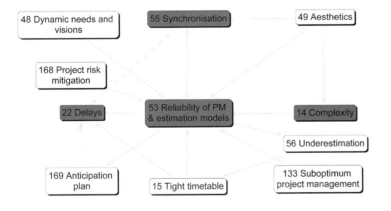

Fig. 11.4 Mini cognitive map showing the 'reliability of project management and estimate models'

The complexity of these projects is clearly manifested in the time-consuming design processes and, at times, delays in the production of design information. It also necessitated high levels of design and construction team involvement, often much appreciated by clients. The complexity and specificity of arts projects appeared to reinforce the difficulties which would normally be expected when value engineering. Sub-optimal solutions resulted, in some cases, in higher running costs upon project completion (occupancy) for the client/users.

Reliability of Project Management and Estimate Models

The mini-cognitive map of the *'Reliability of project management and estimate models'* concept (fig. 11.4) shows continuous pressures on project management and cost activities owing to the sheer complexity of the project (as above), an emphasis on formal processes, and also the dynamic needs and 'visions' (particularly of the clients and users) whilst in most cases there was also time pressure from a tight timetable. The time dimension was variously the result of unrealistic estimates, a rush to submit funding applications, pressure from inflation, and consideration of fees.

The reliability of the management models was influenced by the way the stakeholders mitigated the risks and approaches employed for the project management task. The tendency to underestimate (in financial, time, and complexity terms) stemmed from the high level of synchronization needed to combine information and knowledge from a range of sources. In many cases the outcome of these problems was progressive delay, sometimes because of a failure to anticipate the implications of complex decisions.

Project Difficulties

The mini-cognitive map of the *'Project difficulties'* concept is given in fig. 11.5. This map simply brings together the various factors that contributed to the difficulties in the case studies. These factors were: their complex funding management (involving multiple funders with different criteria, requirements and emphasis); complexity and practical problems of realizing what was planned; optimistic estimates (i.e., underestimates) that later led to delays and additional costs; and lost opportunities (for instance to add value and/or reduce the running costs). In some cases, the project difficulties were caused by 'problems' within the (internal) management of the project stakeholders' organizations and/or their collaborators such as subcontractors. These main factors highlight the pressures upon this sort

of project. They would be compounded by additional factors further out in the mapping.

Fig. 11.5 Mini cognitive map showing the 'project difficulties' concept

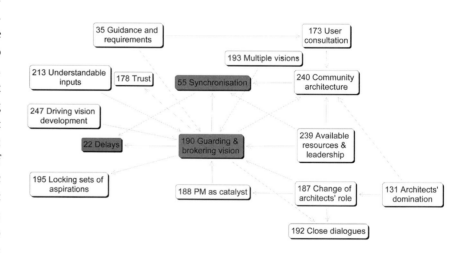

Fig. 11.6 Mini cognitive map showing the 'guarding and brokering visions' concept

Guarding and Brokering Visions

The mini-cognitive map of the 'Guarding and brokering visions' concept is given in fig. 11.6. It centres on the constant and dynamic negotiation between different stakeholders and/or issues in shaping the nature of the case studies. Attempts to guard the 'vision' sometimes reduced flexibility to accommodate other sets of aspirations. On the other hand, user consultation was expected (and often required) by funding bodies, echoing a shift in the design professions towards community architecture and the 'democratization' of design. Despite architects' traditional domination, this shift resulted in the project manager (PM) being active as a catalyst for guarding and brokering the 'vision' through many close dialogues and by translating the different 'languages' of the stakeholders into an understandable input for the construction project. A high level of synchronization is required; any failures here led to delays.

Synchronization

The mini-cognitive map for the 'Synchronization' concept is fig. 11.7. It highlights the wide range of issues that need to be brought together. These include: complex funding management; mismatches around various issues (for instance the amount of funding available versus expectations and original multiple visions); the requirement for

a participatory design process (with, at times, differing ideas about the format and nature of performing spaces being held by clients and consultants). Also important is the need to bring together available resources and leadership in the client organization, and also in the project team, both heavily impacted by staff continuity. The client's on-going activities (which will occupy staff time in parallel with the construction process) must also be synchronized with involvement in design and construction. All of these highly practical issues occur alongside attempts to guard and broker the vision, as described above.

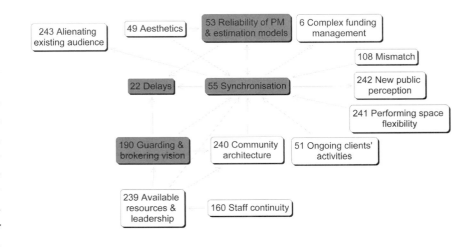

Fig. 11.7 Mini cognitive map showing the 'synchronization' concept

Any deficiencies in the always-challenging synchronization process resulted in delays. The broader outcomes of the wide-ranging efforts made to synchronize the elements of the projects were sometimes to create a new public perception of the theatre in question, but at the same time there was a potential to alienate existing (previous and regular) audiences.

Experience

The mini-cognitive map in fig. 11.8 captures the impact of stakeholders' 'pre-experience' (or lack of it) where various construction project issues are concerned. Where clients lacked experience, there were problems owing to their limited awareness of the implications of seemingly small changes, whilst in other

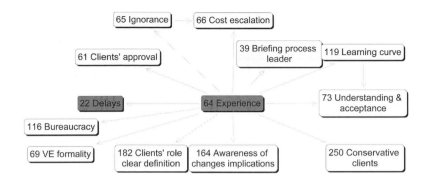

Fig. 11.8 Mini cognitive map showing the 'experience' concept

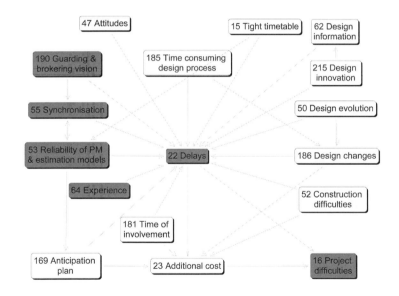

Fig. 11.9 Mini cognitive map showing the 'delays' concept

instances they were perhaps overly conservative. This influenced their effectiveness in giving key approvals in the decision-making process. The result is that it is necessary to define the client's role in such projects, although initially inexperienced clients sometimes gained understanding and acceptance in a broader role as their projects progressed.

The project stakeholders' levels of experience determined the locus of leadership in the briefing process. The more experienced the client, the more they are empowered to take an active or leading role in the briefing process. For the consultants, the greater their experience, the more formal the Value Engineering (VE) processes adopted in the project. A lack of experience on their part at times resulted in a lack of awareness of project stakeholders' needs and characteristics, which could lead to cost escalations and delays.

Delays

The mini-cognitive map of the *'Delays'* concept is shown in fig. 11.9. A wide range of factors can be identified as contributing to delays. The sheer complexity of the design process was time-consuming and was often compounded by the necessity for a design to evolve as clients' experience and confidence grew and their requirements emerged. Furthermore, the presence of technical innovations in designs themselves created delays in the production of design information. In some cases, the late stage at which specialist consultants were involved led to changes that delayed the design process further. In addition, delays resulted from efforts to guard and broker the vision, and problems of synchronization. The problems were compounded by the lack of reliability of the project management and estimate models used, all the more so where stakeholders displayed a limited capacity to anticipate problems. Of course, delays have to be judged against expectations and there were clear underestimates about the time realistically needed to develop the brief and design response, with the resulting 'delays' leading to additional costs and manifold project difficulties.

The Top 7+ Map

Taking a linear view, and focusing on the interactions between time, cost, quality and vision, a typical prospect saw:

- A rush to secure funds with ambitious proposals, resulting from a fear of 'losing out'.
- Optimistic timetables, leading to delays.
- Over-optimistic estimates formulated early in a project becoming budgets that seemed to be cast in stone.
- Issues with project management and cost estimate models.
- The need to synchronize multiple 'visions' and processes.
- Difficulties in reconciling time, cost, and quality.
- Unsubtle attempts at Value Engineering.
- Turbulent design interaction.
- Eventual resolution (usually) through heroic efforts.

The individual analyses above dissect the issues and may be thought to highlight deficiencies. However, it is important to stress that those involved in the case study projects were competent people, endeavouring to bring about successful buildings. Thus, in order to better appreciate the nature of the challenges faced and the problems described, the seven mini-cognitive maps have been merged to form a 'Top 7+ Map' (fig. 11.10). This map captures the seven most pervasive concepts (that is, the most connected, directly and indirectly) and their inter-relationships.

Despite its various criticisms, the opportunity to secure Lottery funding for capital projects was regarded as a potential saviour for the arts.[4] It is understandable that arts organizations feared that they might find themselves at the back of the queue; this belief instilled a certain degree of urgency lest the source of funding run out. Organizations which were slow off the mark might lose out to their competitors (for example, the Belgrade might have received far more money had it been able to submit a funding bid in the mid-1990s). Parkinson's Law ironically states that work always expands to fill the time available for its completion,[5] and has led to a belief in some quarters that working with a slightly tighter-than-average schedule, coupled with suitable incentive programmes, results in an efficient project.[6] In addition, consultants could only be engaged to continue projects if they actually secured the funds. So, crudely put, a pragmatic approach to project formulation does whatever is necessary to secure the grant as soon as possible, with the detail being left until a later stage. This way of working can have financial implications. Even though it is generally known that cost estimates in the early project stages tend to be highly, systematically and significantly deceptive, and consequently responsible for cost overruns in large projects,[7] some kind of estimate is needed by the funders to make decisions regarding which proposals are to be funded. Therefore, these 'underestimated' figures were forwarded to the funders as the proposed amount of project funding needed. When assessing proposals, the funders would naturally select the combination of proposals that appeared to maximize impact for a given sum of money. As a consequence, projects with higher risks may have been selected. There are similarities with the adoption of the lowest bid in a tender, only it is very difficult to draw any comparison among a body of very different competing project proposals.

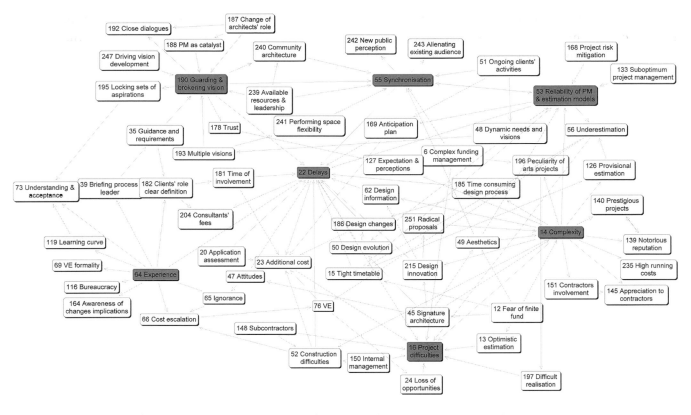

Fig. 11.10 The 'Top 7+' map, showing the most pervasive concepts (darker boxes) and their inter-relationships

There is a clear and logical connection between project complexity and the duration and cost of that project.[8] To increase their chances of securing a grant, many organizations placed particular emphasis on high-quality design; some of the designs adopted innovative approaches as a way to add value. Politically, this strategy addressed the desire to invest in high-quality buildings that would withstand the passing of time and which might, in certain cases, stand as monuments to the Millennium. There were thus significant funding criteria regarding sustainability and architectural merit, though, while innovation can increase the prestige of a project, it may also engender risk. Also important was the view that the arts should contribute to urban regeneration programmes.[9] As a result, many of the funded projects were also intended to be centrepieces of local regeneration, adding a layer of complexity to the 'purpose' of these buildings which could in certain circumstances begin to conflict with their core function as places for performance. Iain Mackintosh has highlighted the occasional but dangerous way in which the original creative purpose of a capital project may be lost or diluted by other agendas on the part of the design and consultant team;[10] funders' ideas can have an important influence, too. As the needs and 'visions' of the client may well be multiple and dynamic in themselves, particular care needs to be executed to ensure that key project objectives are guarded and realized.

The dynamics of stakeholders' roles and relationships have been characterized in terms of the experience of the stakeholders and the balance of leadership in key processes. Also significant was the continuity of staff within the stakeholders' organizations during the course of projects. The identification of clear roles and remits was important in balancing caution with an appropriate response to risk. Relationships were inevitably tested by project difficulties. It has been suggested that relationships are also influenced by the chosen procurement route.[11] In the majority of the studied projects, the required procurement approach was the 'traditional' route, owing to a belief that traditional procurement would lend itself to high quality design and auditing, yielding a notional fixed price. On the other hand, the traditional route has been criticized for its slow speed, due to its sequential nature, and the incidence of time and costs overruns, attributed in part to the lack of input by the builder during the design phase.[12] In practice, amendments and modifications can be applied to the traditional procurement approach to suit specific project conditions and to reap some of the benefits of other types of procurement (such as the involvement of a contractor during the design phase).

At times, initial financial estimates and timescales proved to be unrealistic, resulting in additional costs being incurred and unexpected delays. An observed cause of instability was the late involvement of specialist consultants. The RIBA Plan of Work implies that the fundamentals of a design should remain relatively fixed as it is developed. But, with funding for consultants usually only available at the stage of detailed design or beyond, the inherent issues in a design from, say, an acoustic point of view may not known until this point in the process, meaning that it can be necessary to revisit the initial concept at a stage when it is supposed to be fixed. Thus conventional project management and cost prediction models became unreliable in dealing with the dynamics and complexity of the case study projects. When budgetary and programming problems became evident the professionals involved resorted to redesign and Value Engineering (VE).

However, these VE exercises were mostly *ad hoc* and only conducted reactively. This resulted in VE becoming a temporary solution in many of these projects.[13] VE can be perceived as a subset of the systemic Value Management or VM approach[14] but there was no evidence of true VM practices in the studied cases. Walker and Greenwood have discussed the prejudices often held against VM,[15] centring on the notion that the entire process diminishes the quality of the architecture produced. Thus in order to achieve the full benefit of VM, this perception must be tackled to allow the project team to implement the VM procedures fully rather than simply conducting cost savings in an ad-hoc manner and dubbing the results 'VE'. Although theoretically there is no time limitation to VM, there is a well-established format of a forty-hour workshop at which the contribution of the design as it stands to the clients' aspirations can be comprehensively assessed and tuned.[16] Even if a formal workshop is not employed this multiple-perspective approach could be usefully built into the project programme at various points.

To bring this discussion together it is instructive to compare actual practice with 'best practice'. A framework derived from generic recommendations by CIRIA about managing project change in the construction industry,[17] particularly during project execution, was used as a basis for evaluation (Table 11.1). It is apparent that there are some 'familiar' issues that have been discussed in various research and good practice publications over the years. For instance, a research project conducted in the University of Salford in the late 1990s on briefing isolated the major problems associated with the briefing process and recommended the key solution or improvement areas as: empowering clients and managing the project dynamics, supported by appropriate user involvement, appropriate visualization techniques, and appropriate team building.[18] In terms of addressing segregated project information, solutions have been proposed, such as concurrent engineering techniques that offer scope for more effective co-ordination and integration;[19] however, such an approach is not uncontested and a further investigation has pointed out that generally the construction industry is not yet ready to adopt collaborative and concurrent engineering.[20] The 'gap' between theory and practice highlighted in the table reflects the general problem for construction industry practitioners (in the UK) to absorb and act directly upon the results of research.[21]

Table 11.1 Comparison between recommended best practice and the studied cases

The Process	Recommendation (CIRIA)	In the studied cases
Briefing	• Briefing as an iterative process • Briefing enables the project team to bring its combined expertise and experience to assist the client in the development of the base brief for each project stage • The key stakeholders to be involved should include the client organization (senior executive management, main users, operators and facility managers), funders, statutory authorities, adjacent landowners and operators	At least one of the clients in the studied cases recognized briefing as an iterative process. However, in the other cases, where there was no construction expertise on the part of the client organizations, the consultants' ways of operating appeared to be 'to get the job done' rather than to assist the clients in better understanding the process and empowering them to take better ownership of their projects. As a consequence many of these clients found the processes to be frustrating. There was also evidence to suggest a general failure to involve key stakeholders such as the audience, local communities (superficial consultation), and even the performers.
Value Management	• A powerful method for assisting the client in deciding what is really important and must be retained as proposed, and also where a more pragmatic approach may be acceptable • Options are reviewed to ensure that these objectives are being met in a way that matches the client's requirement for value • VM assists in resolving and agreeing the "big issues" • VM can assist in the recognition of possible elective changes and their optimization as early as possible	No evidence of authentic VM, and hence no optimization on the strategic level. There were VE exercises applied as ad-hoc solutions, but appeared to be temporary solutions (as the costs kept on rising). Those projects that had prioritized the 'elements' of their projects from the early stages (formally or informally) appeared to handle the VE process better. Here the clients had better control over the 'cutting' process compared with those reacting in the later stages, where the clients 'delegated' this control to their consultants.
Design Management	• Recognition that the modern construction industry needs to integrate many more components and more special elements • The design process must accommodate just-in-time design decisions from the client who wishes to keep options open as long as possible • 'Time compression' becomes a requirement, where activities are undertaken in the minimum time and the achievement of programme dates is critically dependent on complete and correct information • The programming of both design and construction should be undertaken with knowledge of the processes involved. The role of suppliers and contractors in developing design and design coordination should be recognized and allowed for the programming • The role of design coordinator does not inevitably lie with the architect or civil engineer	The higher level of complexity involved made it more difficult for the integration of different components and elements of the projects. In most cases the architects were the design coordinator (traditional approach and also due to the complexity of the design). Design decision-making was often presented to clients without sufficient information on financial implications (sometimes seemed to be a deliberate ploy to get clients' approval). Typically, there were delays in the progression of the design process and the production of the design information, mainly due to the level of complexity involved. This had a knock-on effect to subsequent project activities and disrupted the already tight timetable. In some cases, poor design management practises (coordination) were also identified. The contractors were involved in varying degrees from fully advising in the detailed design and construction programme to simply providing advice on constructability and health and safety matters.

The Process	Recommendation (CIRIA)	In the studied cases
Risk Management	• If undertaken comprehensively, the process should indicate where change is likely, provide valuable information on its scope and possibly its timing, identify where the project information provided is incomplete and/or where there is a known likelihood to change • As a result, risks can be evaluated and allowances made against the baseline cost, time and process plans • Subsequently, appropriate contingencies may be prepared in terms of both process and finance (considering budget, programme, and specification).	Due to the inherent complexity and peculiarity of each performing arts project, risk management (particularly risk identification) is a difficult task to perform. The lack of a database of 'typical projects' required the consultants to deal with uncertainties as they arose. However, there was no real evidence of proactive risk management in the studied cases. Even though it may not be feasible to completely handle the high level of complexity in these projects, appropriate risk management of the 'more usual/ordinary' elements of these projects could have helped reduce the level of uncertainty.
Establishing and Maintaining Communication	• Methods of information flow and communication should ensure the appropriate people/parties are receiving the information at the time and in the form they require (without being overloaded with non essential communication) • General communications should be distinguished from request for approvals, changes to budgets, the brief and the scope of services • While open communication should be encouraged, there should be a system for tracking changes that are naturally initiated both during meetings and also through more informal communications • Regular meetings should confirm that actions have been implemented. Reliance on electronic communication alone will not suffice, as different parties will have different lists of priorities for action • Open communication is assisted by co-location of the project team (including the client representatives) • The use of information technology in change management system (e.g. three dimensional modelling) to assist fast and more detailed assessment of the impact of a proposed construction changes • Forums for discussions including regular open workshops, co-location, routine debates, 'good ideas' notice board (including a IT notice board), availability to/easy access of all information (design, cost, programme, etc.), involvement of supply chain.	There was little evidence of comprehensive information management in the studied projects. The archival studies of the cases tracked the changes that occurred in these projects mainly through (paper) correspondence between the different parties. IT-based tools (such as a shared IT notice board or a system that can assist by showing the detailed impacts of construction changes) were not used in the studied cases, perhaps because the facility was not readily available at the time. Some of the interviewees described visualization problems, particularly due to the complexity of the design and mentioned how IT-based tools may have been helpful with this problem. Various meetings were identified in the studied cases. Different type of meetings typically involved a certain type of stakeholder only. Thus, instead of a fully open information policy for all stakeholders, there seems to have been 'different information for different stakeholders'. Whilst this 'segregation of information' may be necessary for some 'sensitive' information, a wide application of this may have contributed to the myopic views of different stakeholders, instead of a shared integrative view of the project. Some interviewees did mention the importance of the spread of geographical locations of different stakeholders (including for the clients) and, in some cases, some geographically distant stakeholders made an attempt to co-locate.

The peculiarities and inherent complexity of arts projects makes risks difficult to identify and hence manage. Whilst acknowledging the significant role of risk management in good project management practice, Chapman and Ward have advocated that risk management should be seen simply as an improvement to the basic project planning process.[22] The key question should be 'how much formal risk management and in what style is the best on this occasion?' rather than 'is risk management worth it?' The primary basis for identifying risks is generally accepted as historical data, experience, and insight.[23] Thus the construction industry's limited experience of this type of work makes it more difficult to identify the risks in performing arts projects. However, this study goes some way to forewarning project participants about what to expect and also heading off some of the problems early.

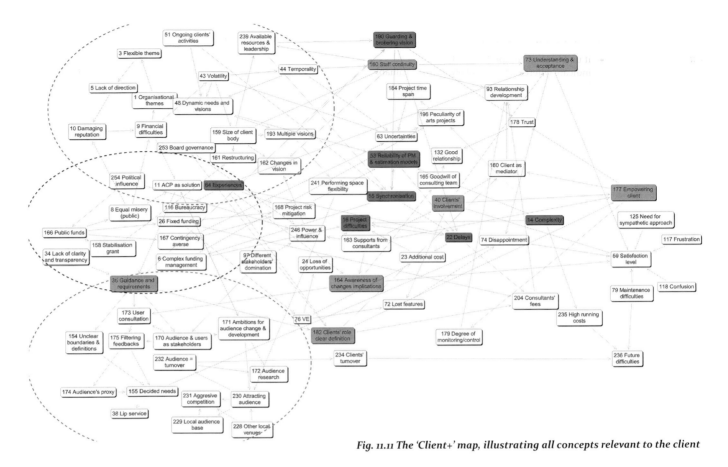

Fig. 11.11 The 'Client+' map, illustrating all concepts relevant to the client

THE CLIENT+ MAP

In parallel to the development of the Top 7+ Map, similar principles were applied to develop another map specifically from the client's perspective. This view is important as the influence of the performing arts organization itself is crucial to project success, which will ultimately be judged by the extent to which it meets their aspirations. Thus a second map was developed involving all concepts relevant to the client and known as the 'Client+ Map' (fig. 11.11). The groupings indicated by the circles are, from the top, clients' organizational issues, external factors, and, lastly, issues around audiences/users. The general issues emerging from this map can be summarized as follows:

- 'Visions' were multiple and volatile.
- Lottery funding was perceived as an opportunity.
- The political policy context impacted on projects.
- Consultation with audiences and the community was often imperfect.
- Staff continuity played an important role in safeguarding 'visions'.

- Inexperienced clients embarking on their projects had to face an often overwhelming range of challenges.
- Client satisfaction was related to their level of involvement in projects.
- Some future difficulties were identified resulting out of the general project complexity and savage VE experiences.

Discussion of Client+ Map

The above issues stem to a large degree from the characteristics of the performing arts sector in the UK at the time the projects studied were initiated (many aspects of which will still pertain). The cultural sector in the UK is characterized by an educated workforce, significantly non-standard employment patterns (with many in self-employment or temporary jobs), but higher levels of unemployment than in the labour force in general.[24] The sector is typified by small organizations with tightly run administrations and little spare resource. During the period in question, they had relatively low support from the private sector coupled with continuously decreasing number of performances, by around 11% from 1993 to 2001. As a consequence, the arts industry in the UK – then as now – was highly volatile and temporal with high organizational and staff turnover, and tight competition for survival.

Although the Arts Council distributes funding at 'arm's length' from government, its agenda and ability to support the sector is inevitably dictated to an extent by the policy context and the size of the total grant which it receives. The policy was long known as 'equal misery for all'.[25] The introduction of funding from the Lottery offered a valuable injection of resources into the sector, and was coupled with increased revenue funding. Subsidy for the arts supports the creation of 'cultural goods' which in turn will benefit the economy, 'environmental quality' and 'welfare'.[26] The Capital Programme allowed organizations to improve their accommodation (for their own benefit and for the benefit of their audiences) and potentially to expand or change

their work or their organization. There were warnings that capital funding was only a distraction from the cash crisis that affected a number of arts organizations at that time,[27] but the sector would have been foolish to turn down the opportunity to renovate, refurbish or rebuild their facilities, even as projects began to publically unravel.[28]

As well as the influence of the national political policy context on projects (in creating and operating the capital programme), the internal political dynamics of local clients (particularly in the case of local authority clients) also proved to be important, leading at times to competing multiple 'visions'. Previous research has classified the purposes of buildings into four groups, namely for consumption, for direct financial gain, for indirect financial gain, and for social purposes.[29] For performing arts buildings, indirect financial gain (using the building to accommodate performing arts events, thus generating income) and also social purposes (as public buildings) are important. With different layers of 'visions' co-existing, it can become still more difficult to 'synchronize' the direction of the projects, which move beyond the purely artistic to the social purpose of the new or refurbished building and the potential role that the projects might play in regeneration. Whilst valid justifications were found for these different layers of purpose, compromises were needed to reconcile them. In making this reconciliation, the creative purpose of the building – to house and support performance – should be central.[30]

The official guidance for applying for Lottery grants required evidence of support from the main user groups and other funders, plus evidence of the involvement of artists, and also consultation with others such as public arts agencies.[31] The RIBA Plan of Work advises the designer to elicit all necessary information, including user studies, during its Stage B (feasibility study), while CABE recommended that clients conduct consultation during the pre-design phase with stakeholders,[32] including staff, board members, artists, the existing or potential audiences, the local community, and funders. Many of those listed above could be termed 'secondary project stakeholders'.[33] Even though the above guidance and much other literature advises the involvement of these so-called the 'secondary users', particularly in the earlier phases of the project, it occurred to varying degrees in each of the projects studied. A failure to specify who constituted the stakeholders caused confusion. There are varying degrees of participation in decision-making according to the amount of power that is transferred from the responsible authority to the public.[34] The projects indicate the difficulties faced by client and design teams in engaging with the secondary stakeholders (i.e., audiences, artists, and or public/local communities). One fear was the risk of the exercise generating an extensive wish-list, raising expectations. Consultation in some cases was in essence largely a public relations exercise to acquire support, with the results being filtered further to protect the guiding project 'vision'.[35]

Arts clients are normally inexperienced in major construction and sometimes needed or expected a particular approach from their consultants, something more sympathetic and less efficient / 'clinical'. Green has argued that construction professionals need to build up good relationships with clients to be able to understand their needs, preferences, and requirements.[36] A survey of UK construction clients has also confirmed the ways in which many small, one-off clients rely on the guidance of advisors.[37] Support from consultants thus plays an important role in empowering clients.

In addition to the rather unpleasant experience of project delivery, the experience of the building in use has sometimes been problematic, relating to items cut during the VE exercises. The 'new' building may impose or necessitate structural change within the arts organization.

SUMMARY

The chapter has considered and mapped the interacting issues running across the studied cases. Rigid funding models; ambitious, creative projects; multiple, turbulent and often inexperienced stakeholders – a toxic mix that seemingly inevitably led to huge stresses, problems and missed opportunities. The concluding chapter of this book aims to make positive suggestions for improving conditions, and the probability of success.

Notes

1   For this analysis, the approach suggested by Strauss and Corbin in their *Basics of Qualitative Research: techniques and procedures for developing grounded theory* (Thousand Oaks, 1998), and further developed in P.S. Barrett and L. Barrett, 'The management of academic workloads', report, Leadership Foundation for Higher Education, 2008, accessed on 21 May 2010 at <http://www.research.salford.ac.uk/maw/cms/resources/uploads/File/Barrettlongreportlinksfinal.pdf>, was employed.

2   F. Ackermann, C. Eden, and S. Cropper, 'Cognitive Mapping: Getting Started with Cognitive Mapping', accessed on 28 July 2006 at <http://www.banxia.com/depaper.html>.

3   The 'Domain analysis' ranked each concept based on the direct arrows connected to that concept. The 'Centrality analysis' ranked the concepts not only based on the direct connections, but also taking into account indirect connections through other concepts. These indirect connections, however, were weighted according to their 'distances' to the particular concept. The further away a connection from a concept, the lower the score of that connection loading to the particular concept.

4   'Arts: Lottery with violence', *Independent*, 3 February 1999, p.10.

5   C.N. Parkinson, *The Pursuit of Progress* (London, 1958).

6   G.J. Ritz, *Total Construction Project Management* (Boston, 1994).

7   B. Flyvbjerg, N. Bruzelius, and W. Rothengatter, *Mega-Projects and Risks: an anatomy of ambition* (Cambridge, 2003).

8   K.I. Gidado, 'Project complexity: the focal point of construction production planning', *Construction Management and Economics* 14/3 (1996), pp.213-225.

9   M. Reeves, *Measuring the economic and social impact of the arts: a review* (London, 2002).

10 Iain Mackintosh, *Architecture, actor and audience* (London, 1993); P. Sterry, M. Sutrisna, P.S. Barrett, C.A. Short, and A. Dye, 'Designing performing arts buildings for stakeholders and users: a fresh perspective', pp.602-612 in M. Dulaimi (ed.), *Joint International Conference on Construction Culture, Innovation, and Management* (CIB/BUiD/CICE, 2006).

11 G. Winch, *Managing Construction Projects: An Information Processing Approach* (Oxford, 2002).

12 S. Rowlinson and T. Kvan, 'Procurement systems', in M. Murray and D. Langford (eds.), *Architects' Handbook of Construction Project Management* (London, 2004), pp.141-157.

13 C.A. Short, P.S. Barrett, A. Dye and M. Sutrisna, 'Impacts of value engineering on five capital arts projects', *Building Research and Information* 35/3 (2007), pp.287-315.

14 John Kelly and S. Male, 'Value Management', pp.77-99 in John Kelly, R. Morledge, and S. Wilkinson (eds.), *Best value in construction* (Oxford, 2002).

15 P. Walker and D. Greenwood, *Risk and Value Management* (London, 2002).

16 J. Kelly and R. Poynter-Brown, 'Value Management', pp.54-64 in P. Brandon (ed.), *Quantity Surveying Techniques: New Directions* (Oxford, 1992).

17 CIRIA, *Managing Project Change: a Best Practice Guide* (London, 2001).

18 P. Barrett and C. Stanley, *Better Construction Briefing* (Oxford, 1999).

19 J.M. Kamara, C.J. Anumba, and N.F.O. Evbuomwan, 'Developments in the implementation of concurrent engineering in construction', *International Journal of Computer Integrated Design and Construction* 2/1 (2000), pp.68-78.

20 M. Khalfan, C.J. Anumba, and P.M. Carrillo, 'Concurrent engineering readiness assessment tool for construction', *Architectural Engineering and Design Management* 1/3 (2005), pp.163-179.

21 D. Gann, 'Putting academic ideas into practice: technological progress and the absorptive capacity of construction organisation', *Construction Management and Economics* 19/3 (2001), pp.307-315.

22 C. Chapman and S. Ward, *Project Risk Management: Processes, Techniques and Insights* (Chichester, 1997).

23 For instance H. Al-Tabtabai and J.E. Diekmann, 'Judgmental forecasting in construction', *Construction Management and Economics* 10/1 (1992), pp.19-30.

24 B. Casey, R. Dunlop, and S. Selwood, *Culture as Commodity? the economics of the arts and built heritage in the uk* (London, 1996).

25 'Scottish Arts Council abandons policy of "equal misery for all"', *Glasgow Herald*, 16 February 1993.

26 A. Peacock, 'The design and operation of public funding of the arts: an economist's view', in A. Peacock and I. Rizzo (eds.), *Cultural Economics and Cultural Policies* (Dordrecht, 1994).

27 'The losing numbers come up again: Arts Council', *Sunday Times*, 6 November 1994, p. 19.

28 'Arts: Lottery with violence', *Independent*, 3 February 1999, p. 10.

29 S.D. Lavender, *Economics for Builders & Surveyors* (New York, 1990).

30 Sterry, Sutrisna, Barrett, Short and Dye, 'Stakeholders and users'; see also P. Sterry and M. Sutrisna, 'Briefing and designing performing arts buildings: assessing the role of the secondary stakeholders', *Architectural Engineering and Design Management* 3/4 (2007), pp.209-221.

31 [Arts Council England], *Building projects under the capital programme* (London, 1998).

32 CABE, 'Client Guide for Arts Capital Projects' (2002, formerly available from CABE).

33 R. Newcombe, 'From client to project stakeholders: a stakeholder mapping approach', *Construction Management and Economics* 21/8 (2003), pp.841-848.

34 J. Petts and B. Leach, *Evaluating Methods for Public Participation: Literature Review* (Bristol, 2000).

35 Sterry and Sutrisna, 'Secondary stakeholders'.

36 S.D. Green, 'A metaphorical analysis of client organisation and the briefing process', *Construction Management and Economics* 14/2 (1996), pp.155-164.

37 A.G.F. Gibb and F. Isack, 'Client drivers for construction projects: implications for standardisation', *Engineering, Construction and Architectural Management* 8/1 (2001), pp.46-58.

Conclusions

The Research Team

Financial audits, much publicized at the expense of recipients and funders alike, reveal relatively little – far too little, we believe – on which to recast capital funding policy, certainly for the arts. Existing published accounts of contemporary projects, meanwhile, tend to skim the surface of their subject. The particular interdisciplinary meshing of qualitative research, historical analysis, and construction management science that has been the focus of this book reveals the unique complexity of the case study projects, each a substantial narrative in its own right. Having set out their chronology and revealed how the original 'vision' was translated into architecture, and having presented a cross-case analysis of the findings, we can now propose answers to our initial questions with a little more confidence.

'HAVE CAPITAL ARTS PROJECT CLIENTS BEEN NEGLIGENT AND INCOMPETENT?'

The research findings absolve the participants in the projects investigated in this study. In more than forty hours of transcribed interviews, and the thorough exploration of very substantial project archives, we found no evidence of negligence; quite the reverse, in fact. Heart-aching quantities of time, effort and goodwill were expended, particularly to service the apparently endless and cyclic requirements of the various funders. Where costs have been contained, this has often been at the partial expense of the 'vision'. Ruthless Value Engineering may deliver on budget but strip out the 'vision' – at least as perceived by some participants in the process. The interior fit-out of Belgrade II, Coventry, was eventually procured as a separate design and build project breaking the architectural singularity of the original design. That intent could not be married with the funds made available, despite many attempts until the rope ran out. However, the completed auditorium is more flexible, and is more in line with the Artistic Director's intent.

'DOES THE LINEAR "NO GOING BACK" PROCESS STIFLE CREATIVITY?'

The post-war, industry-standard framework for managing a Capital Project, the RIBA Plan of Work, has evolved over the course of several decades from a Ministry of Education Guidance note. It was single-mindedly linear but presented tentatively. More than fifty years on, the funding regimes discussed here all conform to its unfolding logic, which is rarely questioned. But design is iterative. Much design research, by the likes of Christopher Jones, Geoffrey Broadbent, L. Bruce Archer, and Christopher Alexander, has been devoted to the revelation of the cyclical patterns within which design thinking unfolds to increase creativity. That work was intended at the time to counter the school

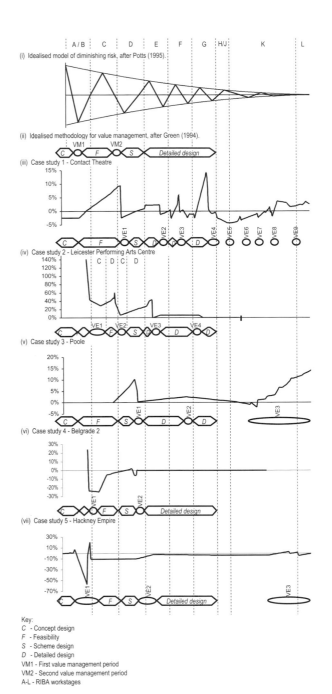

Key:
C - Concept design
F - Feasibility
S - Scheme design
D - Detailed design
VM1 - First value management period
VM2 - Second value management period
A-L - RIBA workstages

(currently resurgent) which insists that 'inspiration', the unfathomable state of poetic reverie, should not be disturbed for fear of extinguishing it. 'The most attentive study of the most homogeneous milieu, of the most closely woven concatenation of circumstances, will not serve to give us the towers of Laon,' observed the mid-century aesthetician Henri Focillon.[1] This is the stuff of nightmares for the National Audit Office, the design for a Capital Project materializing in a séance, but this notion still underpins all attempts at the iconic in Architecture.

The budget history timelines give clues to the 'discomfort' of each project within its arbitrary work stages, but our analysis of variance of cost from budget, using real data, makes all too visible the recurrent and dramatic departure from the idealized model of a smooth running project (fig. 12.1). In this mythical world, the variance, the risk of over- or under-spend, diminishes very rapidly indeed as the project progresses. All is decided in the feasibility stage, and all is concluded well before detailed design. Our case histories suggest this ideal is a fiction which suppresses the very nature of design, at least for complex one-off buildings.

'WILL GREATER STRICTURES HELP?'

We can respond to this question immediately. The budget variance analysis suggests that yet-tighter enforcement of the linear process, particularly in the early stages, may well make matters worse. We saw this in Leicester. Contact in Manchester aspired, very topically, to unprecedented innovation in the sustainable design of performance spaces. The pattern of funding denied the input of the specialists required to prove the concept until the budget left no capacity to respond to their recommendations, triggering a ferocious round of reactive Value Engineering. Even less money during

Fig. 12.1 Budget variance diagrams. From top: the idealised model of diminishing variance of cost from budget

(after Potts, Major construction works); Contact Theatre; Curve; Poole; Belgrade; Hackney

the early stages and a refusal to allow any redesign thereafter would have delivered a dysfunctional design.

'ARE ARTS BUILDINGS DIFFERENT'?

The Industry treats Arts Capital Projects as all others. Our research strongly suggests that this is a mistake. Arts buildings tend to be functionally complex in a peculiarly nuanced way, with many constituencies to satisfy who really care about the building that they will receive. There are usually very high aspirations to design quality and 'impact'. As Viñoly commented, they demand a disproportionate effort, 'with a level of fervour unjustified by the rewards', compared to other building types. Everyone involved needs to be aware of this. Nothing could be further from the culture of the contemporary construction industry, a fair part of which was recently under police investigation for fraudulent tendering.[2]

'AT WHOM SHOULD CREATIVITY BE AIMED?'

Governance was an issue raised in many of our conversations. Should a theatre company, particularly one with a radical 'vision', be given a highly specific new base? Theatre is transient by its very nature. Should the built infrastructure therefore be owned and managed by others, with the tenants required to prove their artistic vitality to remain in residence? How diluted would a 'vision' become, how unspecific would the Architecture have to be? Might this stifle or promote creativity in design and performance?

There is certainly a school of thought in theatre which equates the design of successful venues with a strong initial creative idea. We opened this book with a quotation from Vikki Heywood: *'a client that can't design its own theatre space is probably not going to be a very good client'*, while our discussion of Belgrade II cited the theatre consultant's view that *'the strongest and best theatres in the country have come*

about where there's a strong [...] artistic position'. Flexibility, it was suggested in Chapter 8, is something of a chimera which is rarely fully embraced. The issue is encapsulated by the example of the Young Vic, London (1970), whose director Frank Dunlop considered theatre 'acting in architecture' and countered the initial proposition of the architect, Bill Howell of Howell Killick Partridge and Amis, that what was needed was 'a non-building in which you can do anything'.[3] In other words, architectural specificity was desirable.

However, a degree of generality may be inevitable. The Lowry, for example, was conceived to accommodate a wide range of touring shows. Is it an unsuccessful venue as a result? There are no doubt some who that feel its architecture is better suited to certain types of production than others, but responses to the building are surely largely subjective.[4] In fact, the building does retain a degree of specificity in that its auditoria are theatres, not multi-purpose halls. In addition, even a theatre designed to a very specific idea, such as the Young Vic, the Almeida, or Manchester Royal Exchange (discussed in Chapter 8), can change. Having said that, elements of the Young Vic's architecture were felt to be so integral to the vibrancy of its company's productions that the architects of its refurbishment in 2005-2006, Haworth Tompkins, were painstaking in their retention of the configuration of Bill Howell's original auditorium. Clearly key is that theatres must be borne of a carefully defined need and intent, refined and honed by the design team with significant input from users.

'A REFORMED PROCESS?'

The research indicates that the late-twentieth century process breeds difficulties. Between 1994 and 31 October 1998, 3779 applications were made to the Arts Council Lottery for £2.39 billion of capital funding. Ultimately 2055 awards were made in this period amounting to £1 billion, 51% of which went to twenty-eight large scale projects of £5 million or more, an overall success rate of 55%, although it is not clear how many 'large scale' project applications were received.[5] This massive programme, in which just over half the projects succeeded, made a huge impact in the arts sector, but was not an unqualified success. It represented the latest in a cycle of funding famine followed by feast which seems to repeat every fifteen or so years, with the overheating caused by this cyclical experience leading to the cost, time and quality problems that were roundly criticized by the National Audit Office. At a more detailed level, the case study analyses in the earlier chapters have charted how manifold problems were faced by those involved and that heroic completion is ultimately not the same as maximizing the benefit of the investment made. Trust is a huge issue. Recipients complain of funders' wavering commitment, switching effortlessly from the role of critical friend to adversary and back again. Waiting for staged approvals generated the 'stuttering progress' described by interviewees, the breaking of continuity, whilst inflation gathered strength and finance charges accumulated.

Taking the current process as a given for a moment, a better experience, allowing creativity to prosper, would align the role of the client more closely with what emerges from the case studies and cross-case analysis as the 'ideal', which could be summarized as follows:

- Make sure that there is enough time and space in an organization to be an effective client.
- Continuity of the key people is important for all parties.
- Keeping stakeholders informed is important. Invite them to contribute to the design and witness the work once construction starts.
- Be an intelligent client, and make an explicit prioritization matrix which can act as an aide-memoire to the political weightings attached to your shopping list.

One might draw parallels with the actor's working method, as is discussed in the accompanying box, which finds resonances with Stanislavski's method.

BUILDING, STANISLAVSKI'S WAY

Drawing from the classic text for actors, *An Actor Prepares*,[6] the following table suggests parallels between Stanislavski's advice to actors engaged in the process of creating a play and the approach that should be taken by those involved in the creative act that is a capital arts project, especially the early stages.

Element of Stanislavski's system	Parallel in briefing for capital arts
Preparing by exploring the 'given circumstances' of the play and experimenting with them creatively through purposeful action (p.104) using the 'magic if' (pp.46-47; 51-52)	Building the client's experience and capacity in the pre-design phase, by allowing time to both reveal the context factors through wide stakeholder consultation and to experiment with alternatives for various aspects
Progressively building up of an 'unbroken line of circumstances' linked to a 'solid line of inner visions' to illustrate each part (pp.63-64; 68)	Begin brokering a vision in pre-design by surfacing the volatile/multiple visions of the stakeholders involved. Maintain involvement of key players and especially client personnel
Using circles of attention ('nearest', 'small', 'medium', 'large') – progressively broadening the scope included, but returning to a smaller focus if attention begins to waver, and then building again. Removing the physical tenseness that 'paralyses our actions', especially at times of great stress (pp.81-84; 96-99)	Cope with complexity by using visualization tools to help clients and other stakeholders understand the progressively widening connections between the parts. Employ staged design management that allows those involved the time and conducive environment so they can take stock calmly and objectively.
Choosing major units, each with creative objectives, that 'mark your channel' towards the main objective. Using only as many as necessary to avoid losing a sense of the whole/core of the play. Using verbs to ensure objectives are 'lively'. Linking parts by 'blocking out a line of physical actions'. Keeping to essentials – 'cut 90%' (pp.114-17; 123; 142; 162)	Provide careful project management that employs 'Value Engineering' at intervals to ensure that the functional parts of the design are optimally contributing to the overall aims of the project and that any extraneous elements are pruned. Ensure that these exercises add up around the vision into an authentic 'Value Management' process
Creating an 'unbroken line of communication' on the stage that ebbs and flows continuously and exhibits real communion/understanding between the players, who adapt to the variety of relationships that confront them. (pp.196; 201-203; 224; 254)	Maintain the synchronization of the inputs of multiple stakeholders. To do this: actively avoiding superficial consultation; and, as far as possible keep the individual players and their shared tacit understandings constant throughout the project.
Through an arduous joint search, a shared 'super-objective' and 'through line of action' should emerge. These then provide a strong, unifying focus for all of the subsidiary 'units', their objectives and associated activities. They also actively engage the individual trajectories of the actors, with the thrust of the play (pp.271-73; 301; 306-7)	Settling on a shared vision after extensive experimentation and interaction of the key stakeholders. Then guarding this vision, but also allowing it to evolve as appropriate, throughout the design and construction phases into use. Infuse the design with wide user consultation without moving away from the established vision.

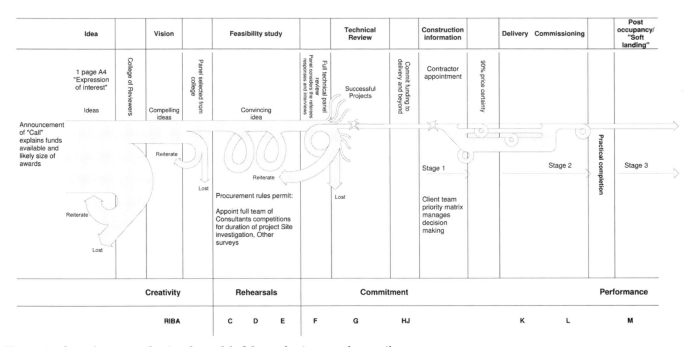

Idea		Vision		Feasibility study			Technical Review		Construction information		Delivery	Commissioning		Post occupancy/ "Soft landing"

Fig. 12.2 A reformed process, adopting the model of the academic research councils

However, we believe that the process could (and should) be reformed. It could be better for all parties, not least given the current stark realities of capital funding for the arts which will remain with us for some time. A new process might adopt some of the protocols of the world of academic research funding, regulating the flow of resources more evenly (fig. 12.2). It would announce a 'Call for Applications' twice yearly, indicating the funds available and the expected number of projects to be funded from within those funds. Applicants would write a one page 'Expression of Interest' (EoI), which would be submitted to a College of Reviewers, each member of which would be sent bundles of EoI's for assessment against agreed and transparent criteria. Policy and standards across the national College would be assured by the standard quality mechanisms familiar to the national Higher Education research councils. No central funding would be available to applicants for their EoI, though not much would be required. Nonetheless, external funding

would indicate local support for the proposition. These EoIs ultimately would be judged against a simple criterion: is there a 'compelling idea'?

A proportion of EoIs would be approved for development into a second stage bid of, say, eight pages, arguing for the 'vision' and the organization proposing to deliver it. For this effort, a reasonable package of funding would be provided to release key staff within the arts organization and to fund specialist advice. There is minimal design at this stage; this is about applicants' capabilities and needs, their positioning in the arts marketplace and the creative opportunities which the project will enable. Applicants would distil a 'priority matrix' balancing the relative values of the items on their shopping list against political funders' accommodations and drivers. The College of Reviewers will decide if the developed idea is consistent and yet more compelling.

At this gateway, if successful, the project would receive substantial funding to test whether the idea really can deliver on its full promise, and to develop what we call a 'real' Feasibility Study. Such an exercise would be a rigorous, full interrogation of the applicant's proposition, with the involvement of all the consultants and specialists who would be involved in the final delivery of the project working through its implications. The consultants would be expected to deliver fully their specialist contribution, yielding the financial implications of their area of involvement. The result will be a rigorous costing – not rough 'per square metre' estimating, but a robust elemental costing based on 'real' proposals. The award of money for the Feasibility Study would in itself underwrite the College's view that the project would be ultimately viable, providing comfort to other possible funders and galvanizing the applicant's money-raising efforts. An important gateway would loom towards the conclusion of this process, namely a Technical Review. This would be a full technical audit of the emerging design by specialists nominated by the College, in other words, genuine peer review, markedly absent from the construction world. The result would be a detailed draft report to which the applicants would respond, the final draft going back to the College of Reviewers. The applicants would be interviewed thoroughly on the basis of the report. At this point the commitment to fund the full project would be made if appropriate, enabling applicants to secure reliable funding from other sources. Funders would be held to their commitments through a bond. The result of this process might be that fewer projects would receive funding. This proposition may be politically contentious, but while the scattergun approach initially placates more constituencies, ultimately a more selective method might mean that more projects would survive and prosper.

Disappointed applicants would be encouraged to consider a revised resubmission if it is felt that a beneficial proposition can be developed through revision. Enabling help will be required for applicants who have reached this stage but continue to stall. At the commitment to fund (in its entirety) the process, a contractor is selected to assist in the production of construction information and to advise on,

and then tender, construction packages. Value Management and the skills required to deliver it will be critical in this stage. The client team will have its priority matrix prepared so that they have a methodology for editing the proposals quickly as required.

The delivery stage should follow seamlessly, with the contractor formally appointed as price certainty reaches 95%. Unexpected discoveries and events will inevitably disrupt progress and consume resource, but the priority matrix will guide the client in further editing their shopping list and reintroducing wished-for items. Commissioning is extremely important and the contract period will allow for adequate commissioning of systems, not least environmental systems and a full year's post occupancy period will pick up further latent commissioning issues to achieve a soft landing. Here we reintroduce the long-lost RIBA Workstage M.

A candid case study account would be put in the public realm to contribute to an evolving archive/database for future applicants. This not inconsiderable exercise would be funded as part of the award. Pursuing and developing the methodology employed in this book, and not simply that of the accountant, the case studies would be of interest not only to the arts community. As attention focuses on delivering the Olympics and debates the merits of building new schools, colleges, hospitals and polyclinics, the results would provide more evidence addressing the conundrum, 'what is really needed to deliver a successful Capital Project?'

Notes

1   Henri Focillon, trans. C.B. Hoghan and G. Kubler, *The life of forms in Art* (New York, 1989).

2   See e.g. the decisions of the Office of Fair Trading relating to this case: <http://www.oft.gov.uk/news-and-updates/press/2009/114-09>, accessed on 16 June 2010.

3   Bill Howell, 'The Young Vic: theatre on a budget', *RIBA Journal* 78 (1971), pp.287-289. See p.288 for this quotation.

4   For a selection of responses, see Steve Rose, 'But does it work?', *Guardian* 21 July 2007, accessed on 16 June 2010 at <http://www.guardian.co.uk/artanddesign/2007/jul/21/architecture>.

5   National Audit Office, 'Arts Council of England; monitoring major capital projects funded by the National Lottery', (report, 1999).

6   C. Stanislavski, *An Actor Prepares* (London, 1936, translated by Elizabeth Reynolds Hapgood).

Select Bibliography

BOOKS, ARTICLES, AND PUBLISHED REPORTS

Al-Tabtabai, H. and J.E. Diekmann, 'Judgmental forecasting in construction', *Construction Management and Economics*, 10/1 (1992), pp.19-30

Anon., 'Theatre in Corporation Street, Coventry', *Architects' Journal* 128 (1958), pp.199-214

Anon., 'Shopping centre with a cultural plus', *Surveyor* 141/4228 (22 June 1973), p.29

Anon., 'The losing numbers come up again: Arts Council', *Sunday Times*, 6 November 1994, p.19

Anon., 'Arts: Lottery with violence', *The Independent*, 3 February 1999, p.10

Anon., 'Who was Frank Matcham?', *RIBA Journal* 111 (2004), p.9

Appleton, I., *Buildings for the Performing Arts: a Design and Development Guide*, Oxford, Butterworth, 1996

[Arts Council England], *Building Projects under the Capital Programme*, London, Arts Council England, 1998

[Arts Council of Great Britain], *Housing the Arts in Great Britain*, London, HMSO, 2 vols, 1959-1961

Attenborough, M., 'Directing for the RSC', pp. 89-91 in Ronnie Mulryne and Margaret Shewring (eds.), *Making Space for Theatre*, Stratford, Mulryne and Shewring, 1995

Audit Commission, 'The Curve Project', report 2008/09, 2009

Barrett, P.S., C.A. Short, P. Sterry, M. Sutrisna and Z. Toker, 'Briefing for Arts Construction Projects: capturing the needs of arts clients', pp.2-15 in A.S. Kazi, (ed.), *CIB 2005 Symposium: Combining Forces – Advancing Facilities Management & Construction through Innovation Series, Volume 3: Systematic Innovation in the Management of Construction Projects and Processes*, Helsinki, CIB, 2005

Barrett, P. and C. Stanley, *Better Construction Briefing*, Oxford, Blackwell Science, 1999

Barron, M., *Auditorium Acoustics and Architectural Design*, London, E. and F.N. Spon, 1993

Bayley, S., I. Scalbert and D. Taylor, *Volume: Stanton Williams*, London, Black Dog, 2009

Beidas, D., 'Back to the beginning: the Belgrade in 2007', *Theatres* 14 (Winter 2007), pp.5-7

Bennett, A., 'The National Theatre', pp.383-387 in his *Untold stories*, London, Faber and Faber, 2005

Bentham, F., 'The Crescent Theatre, Birmingham', *TABS* 22/4 (1964), pp.6-11

Bentham, F., 'A tale of two cities', *TABS* 27/4 (1969), pp.10-21

Bentham, F., *New Theatres in Britain*, London, TABS, 1970

Binney, M. and Runciman, R., *Glyndebourne: building a vision*, London, Thames and Hudson, 1994

Blyth, A. and Worthington, J., *Managing the Brief for Better Design*, London, Spon, 2001

Bordass, B. and Leaman, A., 'Making feedback and post-occupancy evaluation routine. 1: A portfolio of techniques', *Building Research and Information* 33/4 (2005), pp.347-352

Brett, R. (ed.), *Theatre Engineering and Architecture, vol. II: architecture and planning*, London, ABTT, 2004

Brett, R. (ed.), *Theatre Engineering and Architecture, vol. VI: general management*, London, ABTT, 2007

Brook, Peter, *The Empty Space*, London, MacGibbon and Kee, 1968

Brook, Peter, *There are no secrets: thoughts on acting and theatre*, London, Methuen, 1993

CABE [Commission for Architecture and the Built Environment], 'Client Guide for Arts Capital Projects', CABE, 2002

CABE [Commission for Architecture and the Built Environment], 'Creating Excellent Buildings: a Foundation Guide for Clients', CABE, 2003

Carlson, M., *Places of Performance: the semiotics of theatre architecture*, Ithaca and London, Cornell University Press, 1998

Casey, B., R. Dunlop and S. Selwood, *Culture as Commodity? the economics of the arts and built heritage in the UK*, London, Policy Studies Institute, 1996

Cave, R., *Terence Gray and the Cambridge Festival Theatre*, Cambridge, Chadwyck-Healey, 1980

Cave, R., 'Only by failure', review of P. Cornwell, *Only by failure: the many faces of the impossible life of Terence Gray*, in *Theatres* 3 (Spring 2005), p.19

Chapman, C. and S. Ward, *Project Risk Management: processes, techniques and insights*, Chichester, John Wiley & Sons, 1997

CIRIA, *Managing Project Change: a best practice guide*, London, Construction Industry Research and Information Association, 2001

Cornwell, P., *Only by Failure: the many faces of the impossible life of Terence Gray*, Cambridge, Salt Publishing, 2004

Crickhowell, N., *Opera house lottery: Zaha Hadid and the Cardiff Bay project*, Cardiff, University of Wales Press, 1997

Crum, L.W., *Value Engineering: the organised search for value*, London, Longman, 1971

Curtis, W., 'History of the design', pp.37-227 in Eduard F. *Sekler* and William Curtis, *Le Corbusier at work: the genesis* of the Carpenter Center for the Visual Arts, Cambridge, Massachusetts, Harvard University Press, 1978

Curtis, W., *Modern Architecture since 1900*, London, Phaidon, 3rd edn, 1996

Davies, C., 'Derngate Theatre', *Architectural Review* 175/4 (1984), pp.72-78

DCMS [Department for Culture Media and Sport], *Creative industries mapping: performing arts*, London, DCMS, 2001

Donellan, D. and N. Ormerod, 'Directing, designing and theatre space', pp.104-106 in Ronnie Mulryne and Margaret Shewring (eds.), *Making Space for Theatre*, Stratford, Mulryne and Shewring, 1995

Earl, J., 'The London theatres', pp.36-61 in B.M. Walker (ed.), *Frank Matcham: theatre architect*, Belfast, Blackstaff, 1980

Earl, J. and M. Sell, *The Theatres Trust guide to British Theatres: 1750-1950*, London, The Theatres Trust, 2000

Eisner, E.W., *The Enlightened Eye: qualitative inquiry and the enhancement of educational practice*, New York, Macmillan, 1991

Elliott, M., 'On not building for posterity', *TABS* 31/2 (1973), pp.41-44

Elliott, M., 'Exchange experience', *Architectural Review* 160 (1976), pp.361-362

Evershed-Martin, L., *The impossible Theatre: the Chichester Festival Theatre adventure*, London and Chichester, Phillimore, 1971

Evershed-Martin, L., *The Miracle Theatre: the Chichester Festival Theatre comes of age*, London, David and Charles, 1987

Eyre, R., *Utopia and other places*, London, Bloomsbury, 1993

Eyre, R., 'Directing for the Royal National Theatre', pp. 92-96 in Ronnie Mulryne and Margaret Shewring (eds.), *Making Space for Theatre, Stratford, Mulryne and Shewring*, 1995

Eyre, R., *National Service: diary of a decade*, London, Bloomsbury, 2003

Eyre, R. and N. Wright, *Changing Stages: a view of British theatre in the twentieth century*, London, Bloomsbury, 2000

Fair, A.J., 'A monumental turkey? Elisabeth Scott's Shakespeare Memorial Theatre', *Theatres* 9 (Autumn 2006), pp.3-5

Fair, A.J., 'A people's theatre: the conception and design of the Belgrade Theatre, Coventry', *Theatres* 14 (Winter 2007), pp.2-4

Fair, A.J., 'Building of the Month: Nottingham Playhouse', *C20: the magazine of the Twentieth-Century Society*, Spring 2009, p.19

Fair, A.J., 'Converting spaces, creating theatres', *Theatres* 27 (Spring 2011), pp.8-12

Fair, A.J., '"A new image of the living theatre": the genesis and design of the Belgrade Theatre, Coventry, 1948-58', *Architectural History* 54 (2011), pp.347-382

Fair, A.J., '"The end of optimism and expansiveness"? Designing for drama in the 1970s', *Twentieth Century Architecture 10, The 1970s* (2011, forthcoming)

Findlater, R., *The Future of the Theatre (Fabian tract 37)*, London, Fabian Society, 1959

Flyvbjerg, B., N. Bruzelius and W. Rothengatter, *Mega-projects and Risks: An Anatomy of Ambition*, Cambridge, Cambridge University Press, 2003

Focillon, H., trans. C.B. Hogan and G. Kubler, *The Life of Forms in Art*, New York, Zone, 1989

Forsyth, M., *Auditoria: designing for the Performing Arts*, London, Mitchell, 1987

Gann, D. 'Putting academic ideas into practice: technological progress and the absorptive capacity of construction organisation', *Construction Management and Economics*, 19/3 (2001), pp.307-315

George, C., 'Suicide or salvation?', *Yorkshire Architect* 17 (1971), pp.386-390

Gibb, A.G.F. and F. Isack, 'Client drivers for construction projects: implications for standardisation', *Engineering, Construction and Architectural Management* 8/1 (2001), pp.46-58

Gidado, K.I., 'Project complexity: The focal point of construction production planning', *Construction Management and Economics*, 14/3 (1996), pp.213-225

Glasstone, V., 'Theatre architecture in Britain', *RIBA Journal* 50 (1968), pp.501-507

Glendinning, Miles, '"Teamwork or masterwork?": the design and reception of the Royal Festival Hall', *Architectural History* 46 (2003), pp.277-319

Glendinning, M., *Modern Architect: the life and times of Robert Matthew*, London, RIBA Publishing, 2008

Gorst, T., 'Civic life cycles: Short and Associates in Lichfield', *Architecture Today* 143 (November 2003), pp.34-46

Green, S.D., 'Beyond value engineering: SMART value management for building projects', *International Journal of Project Management* 12/1 (1994), pp.49-56

Green, S.D., 'A metaphorical analysis of client organisation and the briefing process', *Construction Management and Economics* 14/2 (1996), pp.155-164

Gropius, W. and Schlemmer, O., *The Theater of the Bauhaus*, Middletown, Wesleyan University Press, 1961

Guthrie, T., *A life in the theatre*, London, Hamish Hamilton, 1960

Guthrie, T., 'Theatre at Minneapolis', pp.30-49 in S. Joseph (ed.), *Actor and architect*, Manchester, Manchester University Press, 1964

Ham, R., *Theatre Planning*, London, Architectural Press, 1972

Ham, R., 'A theatre architect's view', *Architectural Review* 151 (1972), pp.91-92

Ham, R., 'Buildings update: theatre and performance spaces', *Architects' Journal* 174 (1981), pp.309-323 and 355-369

Hayes, N., *Consensus and Controversy: party politics in Nottingham, 1945-1966*, Liverpool, Liverpool University Press, 1996

Hayes, N., '"An English war?" Wartime culture and "Millions like us"', pp.1-32 in N. Hayes and J. Hill (eds.), *'Millions like us?'*

British culture in the Second World War, Liverpool, Liverpool University Press, 1999

Hayes, N., 'More than "music while you eat?" Factory and hostel concerts, good culture, and the workers', pp.209-235 in N. Hayes and J. Hill (eds.), *'Millions like us?' British culture in the Second World War*, Liverpool, Liverpool University Press, 1999

Hayman, R., *The First Thrust: the Chichester Festival Theatre*, London, Davis and Poynter, 1975

Hayman, R., *British Theatre: a reassessment*, Oxford, Oxford University Press, 1979

Hewison, R., *Culture and Consensus: England, art and politics since 1940*, London, Methuen, 1997

Higgins, J. and A. Eggleston, *Theatres of Achievement*, Great Shelford, ET Press, 2006

Hillier, J. and M. Blyth, *Poole's Pride Regained*, Poole, Poole Historical Trust, 1996

Hilpert, T., *Mies in postwar Germany: the Mannheim Theatre*, Leipzig, E.A. Seeman, 2003

Hoepfl, M.C., 'Choosing Qualitative Research: a primer for technology education researchers', *Journal of Technology Education* 9/1 (1997), pp.47-63

Horgen, T.H., M.L. Joroff, W.L. Porter and D.A. Schön, *Excellence by Design: Transforming Workplace and Work Practice*, New York, John Wiley and Sons, 1999

Izenour, G.C., 'The origins, evolution and development of theater design since World War Two in the United States of America', pp. 45-69 in James F. Arnott et al., *Theatre Space*, Munich, Prestel-Verlag, 1977

Izenour, G.C., *Theater Design*, New Haven and London, Yale University Press, 2nd edn, 1996

Jay, Peter, 'Theatres: stage and auditorium', *Architectural Review* 113 (1963), pp. 175-185

Joseph, S. (ed.), *Actor and Architect*, Manchester, Manchester University Press, 1964

Joseph, S., *Theatre in the Round*, London, Barrie and Rockliff, 1967

Joseph, S., *New Theatre Forms*, London, Isaac Pitman and Sons, 1968

Kamara, J.M., C.J. Anumba and N.F.O Evbuomwan, 'Developments in the implementation of concurrent engineering in construction', *International Journal of Computer Integrated Design and Construction* 2/1 (2000), pp.68-78

Kelly, J., 'The West Yorkshire Playhouse', pp.74-79 in Ronnie Mulryne and Margaret Shewring (eds.), *Making space for theatre*, Stratford, Mulryne and Shewring, 1995

Kelly, J. and S. Male, 'Value Management', pp. 77-99 in J. Kelly, R. Morledge and S. Wilkinson (eds.), *Best Value in Construction*, Oxford, Blackwell Science, 2002

Kelly, J. and R. Poynter-Brown, 'Value Management', pp. 54-64 in P. Brandon (ed.), *Quantity Surveying Techniques: New Directions*, Oxford, Blackwell Scientific, 1992

Kennedy, Dennis (ed.), *The Oxford Encyclopedia of Theatre and Performance*, Oxford, Oxford University Press, 2003

Keynes, J.M., 'Art and the state', pp.1-7 in C. Williams-Ellis, *Beauty and the Beast*, London, J.M. Dent, 1937

Khalfan, M., C.J. Anumba and P.M. Carrillo, 'Concurrent engineering readiness assessment tool for construction', *Architectural Engineering and Design Management*, 1/3 (2005), pp.163-179

Klotz, H., trans. R. Donnell, *The history of Postmodern Architecture*, Cambridge MA and London, MIT Press, 1988

Lavender, S.D., *Economics for Builders & Surveyors*, New York, Longman Scientific & Technical, 1990

Leacroft, R., *Civic Theatre Design*, London, Dennis Dobson, 1949

Leacroft, R. and H. Leacroft, *Theatre and Playhouse: an illustrated survey of theatre building from ancient Greece to the present day*, London, Methuen, 1984

Le Corbusier, tr. F. Etchells, *Towards a New Architecture*, Oxford, Butterworth, 1989

Lewis, E.W., 'An internationalist at home', *London Architect*, January and March 1972, pp.8-10 (January); 8-12 (March)

Liscombe, R.W., 'Refabricating the Imperial Image on the Isle of Dogs: Modernist design, British state exhibitions, and colonial policy, 1924-1951', *Architectural History* 49 (2006), pp.317-348

Longman, P., 'It's people who make theatres', *Theatres* 5 (Autumn 2005), p. 1

Longman, P., 'What goes around', *Theatres* 5 (Autumn 2005), pp. 7-10

Loos, A., 'Ornament und Verbrechen', pp.276-283 in A. Loos, *Trotzdem: 1900-1933*, Vienna, 1963

Mackintosh, I., 'Rediscovering the courtyard', *Architectural Review* 175/4 (1984), pp. 64-71

Mackintosh, I., 'Unworthy scaffold', *Sightline* 24/4 (October 1989), pp. 5-9

Mackintosh, I., *Architecture, actor and audience*, London and New York, Routledge, 1993

Mackintosh, I., *The Guthrie Thrust Stage: a living legacy*, London, ABTT, 2011

Marwick, A., *The Sixties*, Oxford, Oxford University Press, 1998

McKean, J., *Royal Festival Hall: London County Council*, Leslie Martin and Peter Moro, London, Phaidon, 2nd edn, 2001

McMillan, J., *The Traverse Theatre Story*, London, Methuen, 1988

Muthesius, S., *The Post-war University: utopianist campus and college*, New Haven and London, Yale University Press, 2000

Myerson, J., *Making The Lowry*, Salford, Lowry Press, 2000

National Audit Office, 'Arts Council of England: monitoring major capital projects funded by the National Lottery', report, 1999

National Audit Office, 'Progress on fifteen major capital projects funded by Arts Council England', report, 2003

Neufert, E., ed. and rev. by R. Herz, *Architects' Data*, London, Crosby Lockwood, 1970

Newcombe, R., 'From client to project stakeholders: a stakeholder mapping approach', *Construction Management and Economics* 21/8 (2003), pp.841-848

Parkinson, C.N., *The Pursuit of Progress*, London, John Murray, 1958

Patton, M.Q., *Qualitative Evaluation and Research Methods*, 2nd edn, Newbury Park, Sage Publications, 1990

Peacock, A., 'The design and operation of public funding of the arts: an economist's view', in A. Peacock and I. Rizzo (eds.), *Cultural Economics and Cultural Policies*, Dordrecht, Kluwer, 1994

Petts, J. and B. Leach, *Evaluating methods for public participation: literature review*, Bristol, Environment Agency, 2000

Pevsner, N., *Pioneers of the Modern Movement: from William Morris to Walter Gropius*, London, Faber and Faber, 1936

Pevsner, N., *A History of Building Types*, London, Thames and Hudson, 1976

Potts, K., *Major Construction Works: contractual and financial management*, Harlow, Longman Scientific, 1995

Pringle, M., *The theatres of Stratford-upon-Avon, 1875-1992: an architectural history*, Stratford, Stratford-upon-Avon Society, 1993

Reeves, M., *Measuring the economic and social impact of the arts: a review*, London, Arts Council England, 2002

Richards, J.M., *An Introduction to Modern Architecture*, Harmondsworth, Penguin, 1940

Ritz, G.J., *Total Construction Project Management*, McGraw-Hill, Boston, 1994

Roots, W.L., F.E. Price and A.H. London, *The Local Government Act, 1948*, London, Charles Knight and Company, 1948

Rowell, G. and A. Jackson, *The Repertory Movement: a history of regional theatre in Britain*, Cambridge, Cambridge University Press, 1984

Rowlinson, S. and T. Kvan, 'Procurement systems', pp.141-157 in M. Murray and D. Langford (eds.), *Architects' Handbook of Construction Project Management*, London, RIBA Enterprises, 2004

Royal Institute of British Architects, *RIBA Handbook of Architectural Practice and Management*, London, Royal Institute of British Architects, 1967

Ruhnau, W., 'The new theatre', *Architectural Design* 33 (1963), p.546

Saint, A., 'Frank Matcham in perspective', pp.10-29 in D. Wilmore (ed.), *Frank Matcham and Co.*, Dacre, Theatreshire Books, 2008.

Shaw, R., *The Arts and the People*, London, Jonathan Cape, 1987

Short, C.A., 'Factors for success', in R. Brett (ed.), *Theatre Engineering and Architecture*, v.6 – General Management, London, ABTT, 2007

Short, C.A., P.S. Barrett, M. Sutrisna and A.R. Dye, 'Impacts of value engineering on five capital arts projects', *Building Research and Information* 35/3 (2007), pp.287-315

Sinclair, A., *Arts and Cultures: the history of the fifty years of the Arts Council of Great Britain*, London, Sinclair Stevenson, 1995

Speight, R. (ed.), *A Bridges-Adams letter book*, London, Society for Theatre Research, 1971

Squire, J.C., 'The Shakespeare Memorial Theatre', *Architectural Review* 71 (1932), pp.222-224

Sterry, P. and M. Sutrisna, 'Briefing and Designing Performing Arts Buildings: assessing the role of the secondary stakeholders', *Architectural Engineering and Design Management* 3/4 (2007), pp.209-221

Sterry, P., M. Sutrisna, P.S. Barrett, C.A. Short and A.R. Dye, 'Designing Performing Arts Buildings for Stakeholders and Users: a fresh perspective', pp. 602-612 in M. Dulaimi, (ed.), *Joint International Conference on Construction Culture, Innovation, and Management*, CIB/BUiD/CICE, 2006

Stonehouse, R., *Colin St John Wilson: buildings and projects*, London, Black Dog, 2007

Strauss, A. and J. Corbin, *Basics of Qualitative Research: techniques and procedures for developing grounded theory*, 2nd edn, Thousand Oaks, Sage Publications, 1989

Strong, J., *Encore: strategies for theatre renewal*, London, The Theatres Trust, 1998

Strong, J. (ed.), *Theatre buildings: a design guide*, London, Routledge, 2010

Sutrisna, M. and P.S. Barrett, 'Applying rich picture diagrams to model case studies of construction projects', *Engineering, Construction and Architectural Management* 14/2 (2007), pp.164-179

Todd, A. and J-G Lecat, *The Open Circle: Peter Brook's theatre environments*, London, Faber and Faber, 2003

Walker, P. and Greenwood, D. (2002), *Risk and Value Management*, RIBA Publication, London

Watkin, D., *Morality and Architecture Revisited*, London, John Murray, 2001

Wickham, Glynne, *A History of the Theatre*, Oxford, Phaidon, 2nd edn, 1992

Wiles, David, *A Short History of Western Performance Space*, Cambridge, Cambridge University Press, 2003

Wilford, M. and R. Muirhead, *James Stirling Michael Wilford and Associates: buildings and projects 1975-1992*, London, Thames and Hudson, 1994

Winch, G., *Managing Construction Projects: An Information Processing Approach*, Oxford, Blackwell, 2002

Yin, R.K. *Case Study Research: design and methods*, Thousands Oaks, Sage Publications, 2003.

KEY ONLINE DOCUMENTS

Ackermann, F., C. Eden and S. Cropper, 'Cognitive Mapping: Getting Started with Cognitive Mapping', accessed on 28/07/2006 at <http://www.banxia.com/depaper.html>

Barrett, L. and Barrett, P., 'The management of academic workloads', report, *Leadership Foundation for Higher Education*, 2008, accessed on 21 May 2010 at <http://www.research.salford.ac.uk/maw/cms/resources/uploads/File/Barrett%20long%20report%20links%20final.pdf>

Commission for Architecture and the Built Environment, 'Building excellence in the Arts: a guide for clients', accessed on 27 December 2009 at <http://www.cabe.org.uk/publications/building-excellence-in-the-arts>

Hollis, P., 'Janet (Jennie) Lee' entry in the *Oxford New Dictionary of National Biography*, accessed on 27 October 2007 at http://www.oxforddnb.com/view/article/39853>

Leicester City Council, 'Diverse city: a vision for cultural life in Leicester', published 2001, accessed on 20 April 2010 at < http://www.leicester.gov.uk/your-council-services/lc/cultural-strategy/cspdocument/#document>

Stanton Williams Architects, accessed on 21 May 2010 at <http://www.stantonwilliams.com>,

Stephen Joseph papers at the John Rylands Library, *Manchester: biographical sketch attached to the catalogue*, accessed on 26 February 2007 at <http://archives.li.man.ac.uk/ead/search/eadSearchHandler?operation=full&recid=gb-0133-sj>

Young Vic Theatre, history, accessed on 28 May 2007 at <http://www.youngvic.org/about-young-vic/history-of-young-vic>

THESES AND UNPUBLISHED REPORTS

Calder, B., 'Committees and concrete: Denys Lasdun's National Theatre', Ph.D. thesis, University of Cambridge, 2007

Fair, A.J., 'British theatres, 1926-1991: an architectural history', Ph.D. thesis, University of Cambridge, 2008

Iles, P, 'Issues in theatrical management: Howard and Wyndham and the evolution of the British touring circuit', M.Phil. thesis, Glasgow University, 1997

Short and Associates, 'Belgrade Theatre Conservation Management Plan', report, 2005

Index

References to illustrations are in **bold**

decoration 184-5
see also under individual theatres

Bain, Laurence 27, 31
Baines, Grenfell 51
Barbican Theatre, London 126
    auditorium design **177**, 178, **179**, 182
Barker, Harley Granville 175
Barker, Ken 143
Barrett, Peter 83, 94, 102
BDP (Building Design Partnership) 51, 139
Beidas, David 110, 112, 113, 115, 116, 117, 120, 126, 131, 132, 133, 134
Belgrade Theatre, Coventry 7-8, **8**, 15, 107-35, 149, **176**, 183-4,
    200-2
    ACE input 125, 130
    auditorium 8, **122-4**, 128, **131**, 183-4
        bridges over **131**
        completed **131**
        courtyard 123, **124**
        gallery links **133**
        lighting **129**
        re-imagined **129**
        seating/staging **129**
        section through **133**
        Stanton Williams **119**, 131
        technical gallery **212**
        vertical organization **201**
    backstage accommodation, criticism of 177
    budget history timeline **132**
    capital project, 1993-9 110-12
    case study characteristics 108
    completed scheme, plan **133**
    concept sketch **122**
    construction work 129-32
    cost increases 126, 133-4
    design team 115, 120
    early history 109-10, 183-4
    elevation

Belgrade Square **107**, **111**, **176**
    treatments **125**
    west **113**
ERDF money 114, 115, 127
extension **200**
external finishes 130, **130**
foyers **111**, **133**, **186**, **201**
front-of-house area **131**
funders 112-15
internal spaces **201**, **202**
ISG contractors 130
landmark view **114**
Levitt Bernstein 121, 125
    plan 112, **113**
Lottery money 112, 131
main entrance **107**
models, use of 126, **126**
name origins 109
Options G/H/K/L/N **122**, 124
pantomime shows 127
Phase A 127-8
plan (1958) **110**
reflections 132-5
Stage C/D/E 117-20, 123, 124, **124**, 125, 126, 128
Stanton Williams 115-16, 117, 120-1
    auditorium **119**, 131
    extension **116**, **200**
Theatreplan consultants 115, 125, 131
Value Engineering 121, 129, 132
ventilation system 126, 131, 132
vision 114, 115, 134, 135
Bennett, Alan 187
Bentham, Frederick 184
best practice, case studies, comparison 233-4
Blyth, Martin 79
Bolton Octagon 181
Bonar Keenlyside 83, 85
Bordass, Bill 4